Tolley's

Tax Essentials: Value Added Tax 2003–04

by
A St John Price FCA

LexisNexis™ UK

Members of the LexisNexis Group worldwide

United Kingdom	LexisNexis UK, a Division of Reed Elsevier (UK) Ltd, Halsbury House, 35 Chancery Lane, LONDON, WC2A 1EL, and 4 Hill Street, EDINBURGH EH2 3JZ
Argentina	LexisNexis Argentina, BUENOS AIRES
Australia	LexisNexis Butterworths, CHATSWOOD, New South Wales
Austria	LexisNexis Verlag ARD Orac GmbH & Co KG, VIENNA
Canada	LexisNexis Butterworths, MARKHAM, Ontario
Chile	LexisNexis Chile Ltda, SANTIAGO DE CHILE
Czech Republic	Nakladatelství Orac sro, PRAGUE
France	Editions du Juris-Classeur SA, PARIS
Germany	LexisNexis Deutschland GmbH, FRANKFURT, MUNSTER
Hong Kong	LexisNexis Butterworths, HONG KONG
Hungary	HVG-Orac, BUDAPEST
India	LexisNexis Butterworths, NEW DELHI
Ireland	Butterworths (Ireland) Ltd, DUBLIN
Italy	Giuffré Editore, MILAN
Malaysia	Malayan Law Journal Sdn Bhd, KUALA LUMPUR
New Zealand	LexisNexis Butterworths, WELLINGTON
Poland	Wydawnictwo Prawnicze LexisNexis, WARSAW
Singapore	LexisNexis Butterworths, SINGAPORE
South Africa	LexisNexis Butterworths, DURBAN
Switzerland	Stämpfli Verlag AG, BERNE
USA	LexisNexis, DAYTON, Ohio

© Reed Elsevier (UK) Ltd 2003

A CIP Catalogue record for this book is available from the British Library.

ISBN 0 7545 21303

Typeset by Columns Design Limited, Reading, England
Printed and bound in Great Britain by Hobbs the Printers Ltd, Totton, Hampshire

Visit LexisNexis UK at www.lexisnexis.co.uk

Author Biography

John Price qualified as an accountant in 1963. He has worked extensively in professional practice and in industry, including spells in France and the Sudan. He has been a self-employed consultant, specialising in Value Added Tax for the last 25 years. His successes at VAT Tribunals include such leading cases as Direct Cosmetics Ltd and the Yoga for Health Foundation Ltd. This latter case led to a change in UK law in order to comply with the Sixth EC VAT Directive.

John Price was for ten years editor of Croner's Reference Book for VAT and for sixteen years wrote a weekly column for Accountancy Age. He is a regular contributor to 'Taxation' and lectures widely on VAT.

Contents

Introduction

This is the book for you if you need a sound grounding in Value Added Tax but without going into every detail. I offer an in-depth understanding of all the key parts of VAT and of what really matters in the practical running of a business. I have divided the subject into three sections:

1   Those parts of the system which you will meet sooner or later.
2   Other parts such as the rules on property and the export of goods and services, which are important for the many businesses they affect, though that might not be yours.
3   Specialist topics, such as the Retail Schemes, which concern only certain businesses.

If you own a business, you will find an overview of what can be a daunting subject for the layman. You will not need to read all of it; you can pick from the later more specialised chapters, those which affect you.

If you are a student, you will obtain a sound working knowledge of most if not all of what you need for your exams, together with enough understanding of the law to find the rest for yourself.

If you are a bookkeeper or accounts assistant, the book covers everything you need to know.

If you are a qualified accountant or lawyer, the thorough coverage and practical explanations of the law which I offer, will enable you to understand the nature of a problem. The legal references and numerous cases quoted will give you a sound basis for research on anything which you need to study in more detail.

There are many books on VAT. They tend to be solid textbooks rather than readable guides because of the amount of detail they try to cover. This one is different. I do not attempt to cover everything. Instead, I concentrate on what everyone needs to know and on explaining the principles in plain English using practical examples. If you understand the contents of this book, you will know more than most people do about VAT! You can then go on to study the particular complexities which affect your business or your clients.

VAT is an enormous subject because it affects every kind of business. No one person can be familiar with every aspect of it — even within Customs and Excise. When, after long years of experience, some of us think we are getting quite close to that ideal, they change the law! Even more disconcerting are the Court decisions, which, from time to time, force us all to rethink some aspect of the tax which we thought we had understood!

So, a warning: in trying to cover what matters but to keep it concise, I am bound to have over simplified here and there or I may have omitted a detail, which could be relevant to your problem.

Before taking action on the basis of what you read in this book:

- Always check whether the law, on which it is based, has changed.
- Think carefully about the facts of your case. Do they match the law and/or the situation described?
- If the sum at risk matters to you or you are in any doubt, take advice!

Dedication

I dedicate this book to the thousands of delegates whose questions have helped me to such understanding as I have of VAT in over 16 years of presenting the seminars organised by Hilary Morgan and her colleagues at Quorum Training Ltd.

I thank Alan Dolton of Butterworths Tolley for his technical assistance and help in preparing some of the material.

I gratefully acknowledge the tolerance of my family during the stress of making the deadline.

A St John Price

Preface to Fourth Edition

When I finished the third edition of this book, I fondly hoped that, at last, I had the subject under control and that the fourth would be an easier ride! Wishful thinking! There are significant changes to 29 out of the 39 chapters.

Many record the numerous changes in the law or in the interpretation of it resulting from court decisions. Others record changes in Customs' policy or guidance and some record my ever expanding understanding of this tax. After 30 years, nearly all of them as a VAT specialist, I am still learning about it and the pitfalls and planning points I offer you continue to grow. That alone justifies buying this edition if you have a previous one.

To new readers, I say that this is not just a reference book. It contains numerous planning points (straightforward ones, not those cunning plans which keep getting upset in the Courts!), highlights many pitfalls and provides much advice on practical aspects of tax, which you will not find anywhere else.

It would be great to hear what you like or do not like about the result. You can e-mail to me or write to LexisNexis UK. See page 419 at the back of the book.

A St John Price

July 2003

Abbreviations and Statutory references

Throughout this book, legal references are to the Value Added Tax Act 1994 unless otherwise stated.

The Act is divided into sections, sometimes abbreviated as 's' and schedules abbreviated as 'Sch', within which there are Groups and/or paragraphs.

'SI 19xx/xxxx' refers to a Statutory Instrument, followed by the year of issue and number. Statutory Instruments are either Treasury Orders divided into articles abbreviated as 'art' or a single SI called The VAT Regulations made by Customs. References to this are abbreviated as 'reg'.

In case references LON, MAN, EDN and BEL refer respectively to the London, Manchester, Edinburgh and Belfast Tribunal Centres.
'The 6th Directive' means the European Community 6th VAT Directive – explained in Chapter 2, *Where Do I Find the Law?*
CA = Court of Appeal
Ch D = Chancery Division of the High Court. An appeal from a tribunal decision is normally to the Ch D although a procedure used occasionally permits reference direct to the CA.
'CJEC' means the Court of Justice of the European Communities.
CMLR = Common Market Law Reports
'FA' = Finance Act
HL = House of Lords
'LVO' means Local VAT Office
NAS = National Advisory Service
STC = Simons Tax Cases
SWTI = Simon's Weekly Tax Intelligence
VATTR = Value Added Tax Tribunals Reports published by *The Stationery Office*

Contacting Customs

The days when you could ring up your local VAT office with a query are gone! Now, one normally only deals with the Local Vat Office ('LVO') on points arising out of a visit. One can contact Customs by telephone, by letter or by email and the systems are different. In addition, there is much information available from Customs' Web site, www.hmce.gov.uk.

Telephone inquiries

The National Advisory Service number is 0845 010 9000 Monday – Friday 8 am–8 pm. This is a call centre operation so a call could be routed to, for instance, Cardiff and another to Glasgow a few minutes later. Ask for a call reference both so that you can follow up the enquiry later and so that you have a record of it, if Customs subsequently dispute what you think you were told.

E-mail enquiries

You can e-mail a query to Customs at the centre nearest to you from the following list. The address is ....@hmce.gsi.gov.uk, the prefix to '@' being as follows:

Belfast	ni	London	lon
Birmingham	wm	Newcastle-upon-Tyne	yhne
Cardiff	wales	Nottingham	em
Cheadle	nw	Poole	sw
Hove	se	Reading	sec
Glasgow	sco	Southend	estn

Postal inquiries

Check at www.hmce.gov.uk/business (click *contact us*) for the current list of postal enquiries centres. Supposedly these are being centralised like the telephone enquiries.

However, as I write this, there are still about 17 offices based on post codes of the enquirers.

Registration offices

VAT registration applications are now handled in four offices in Carmarthen, Grimsby, Newry and Wolverhampton. To find the addresses on the website, click **Business and trade**. In **Quick links**, click **VAT registration**, go to foot of page and click *Where do I send completed registration forms?*.

Membership of the EU

In May 2004, membership of the EU is due to expand from 15 to 25 countries.

Existing Member States

Austria, Belgium, Denmark, Finland (*excluding the Aland Isles*), France (*including Monaco but excluding the overseas French territories such as Martinique*), Germany, Greece (*excluding Mount Athos*), Ireland, Italy, Luxembourg, Netherlands, Portugal (*including the Azores and Madeira*), Spain (*including the Balearic Isles but excluding the Canaries, Ceuta and Melilla*), Sweden, United Kingdom (*including the Isle of Man but excluding the Channel Islands and Gibraltar*).

States due to join in May 2004

Cyprus, Czech Republic, Estonia, Hungary, Latvia, Lithuania, Malta, Poland, Slovakia, Slovenia.

The above is as expected as this edition went to print so confirm at the time that the expansion has occurred. Also, there may be minor exclusions from individual countries as there are with the existing Member States.

1. How VAT Works — an Outline of the System

An explanation for beginners

This chapter outlines the subject of value added tax for those who know nothing about it whatsoever. It discusses how the tax works, and basic stuff like the difference between an input and an output and between zero-rating and exemption.

Value added tax is an indirect tax

People call VAT an 'indirect' tax and income and corporation tax the 'direct' taxes. That may sound odd since VAT is direct enough when you have to pay it. The idea is that individuals and organisations, which cannot recover VAT, are taxed out of their after-tax income; ie after paying the direct taxes. Thus, it is a tax on consumption.

In the United Kingdom, Customs & Excise handle VAT, not the Inland Revenue. This was a decision taken in 1973 because Customs had administered purchase tax and already had some experience of visiting traders whereas the Revenue normally deals on the basis of annual accounts and through professional advisers.

The European basis for VAT

Although VAT was invented in Europe and is in use by all the members of the European Union, it has spread throughout the world with countries as far apart as Mexico, Russia and New Zealand also adopting it.

The VAT system provides the basis for measuring the contributions by each member of the EU towards the Community's budget. Another important advantage of VAT has been to provide the means of harmonising the fiscal treatment of transactions throughout the EU. A common basis of indirect taxation has been essential to the process of simplifying trade and reducing distortions in competition between traders in the different States.

In theory, the rates of VAT in the Member States are supposed to be coming closer together with the objective of having the same rates throughout. In practice, this is proving to be a slow process. For example, the United Kingdom and Ireland have far more zero-rating than any other Member State. Thus most tax food, although often at a reduced rate rather than the standard one.

Inputs and outputs

Inputs are the goods or materials you buy or the expenses you incur upon which you incur input tax. Outputs are sales and other transactions upon which you have to charge output tax.

The Theory of VAT

VAT is charged by the supplier and recovered by the customer at each stage of the commercial chain until one reaches the final consumer. In the example below, a manufacturer buys in materials costing 200p and has overheads of 70p on which he incurs input tax of 12p. When he sells on to the wholesaler B Ltd at 520p, he charges output tax of 91p, deducts the input tax he has paid totalling 47p, and pays the balance of 44p to Customs on his next return.

B Ltd in turn incurs overheads, sells on to the retailer C & Co and pays 16p to Customs. Finally, C & Co sell to Mrs D, the consumer, at £10 (1,000p) on which the output tax is 175p. The net sum due to Customs is 52p.

If we draw a line after the sale by C & Co to Mrs D, the final consumer, and start again, we have the final price of £10 charged by C. Deducting the cost of the goods and the total of the three sums of overheads gives a 'value added' down the chain of 640p. 17.5% of this is 112p. This tallies with the output tax of 175p less input tax on materials of 35p and on expenses of 28p and also agrees with the total of the three payments to Customs.

Incidentally, the profit margins of the three businesses may look large in the example but remember that they are before deducting costs, which do not carry VAT like salaries and business rates.

Example

Note. The VAT is rounded to the nearest penny

	Net	17.5% VAT	Payable to Customs
Manufactured by A & Co from materials costing	200p		
+ VAT on materials		35p	
Standard rated expenses of A & Co	70p	12p	
Sold to wholesaler B Ltd	520p	91p	44p
Standard rated expenses of B Ltd	40p	7p	
Sold to retailer C & Co	650p	114p	16p
Standard rated expenses of C & Co	50p	9p	
Sold to Mrs D (final consumer)	1,000p	175p	52p
Final price charged by C	1,000p	175p	
Less:			
goods	200p	35p	
expenses	160p	28p	
Total 'Value Added'	640p		
Total payable to Customs		112p	112p

It doesn't matter what you sell

The tax works in the same way no matter whether you are a manufacturer, a wholesaler or a retailer, whether you supply goods or services or whether you are acting as an agent. VAT is charged down the chain of transactions until reaching someone who is not registered for VAT. Thus, VAT covers every single commercial transaction, although not everything is standard-rated.

VAT is suffered by the consumer

A 'consumer' for VAT purposes is not just a citizen buying in a private capacity. It also includes any organisation not registered either because it does not make any taxable supplies or because its sales are below the registration limit. It further includes the non-business side of an organisation, like a charity, whose main activity is outside the scope of VAT but which is registered because it is also in business because of, say, a charity shop.

Rates of VAT

The standard rate of VAT, at the time of writing, is 17½%. There is also a reduced rate of 5%. This is growing in importance and now covers various supplies such as fuel for domestic heating, women's sanitary protection and certain work in converting or renovating living accommodation.

Then there is zero rate. Zero-rated sales are taxable at a nil rate of tax, odd though this may sound.

The trader doesn't have to charge any output tax on zero-rated sales but can recover all the related input tax.

At the time of writing, such goods as food, books and newspapers and children's clothing are zero-rated. However, as already mentioned, the UK is the exception amongst the EU States in zero-rating so extensively. In the long term, it is likely that the UK will also tax these things at a positive rate of VAT.

The difference between exemption and zero-rating

Exemption is not a rate of tax. Thus, although the good news for the trader making exempt sales is that he charges no output tax to his customers, the bad news is that he cannot recover the input tax he incurs which is related to those exempt sales.

Examples of exempt transactions are insurance premiums, interest on loans, sales of shares on the Stock Exchange and healthcare.

In contrast to zero-rating, which is a derogation from the normal EU rules, the exemption rules are, in theory, the same throughout the EU. It is therefore much less likely that these rules will change substantially in the UK although they are amended on points of detail from time to time.

Try not to confuse zero-rating with exemption

The difference between zero-rating and exemption is important because of its impact on input tax recovery. Try to use the correct words. One hears people using exempt when they mean zero-rated. If you do that, you may confuse both yourself and others.

Outside the scope of VAT

This fifth category is transactions which, although business, do not carry VAT. There are two main kinds:

- Sales, mostly of services, for which the place of supply is treated as being outside the UK, are outside the scope of UK VAT. Input tax incurred in the UK may or may not be recoverable. The rules are complex and are explained in Chapter 22, *Exports and Imports of Services*.

- Sundry transactions which, for a variety of reasons, are not subject to VAT. Because these are business transactions, input tax related to them is nevertheless recoverable. Examples include:
  - (a) a government subsidy paid to a manufacturer towards the cost of building a factory in a high unemployment area.
  - (b) transactions between companies within the same VAT group. See Chapter 4, *VAT Groups*.

Non-business

The sixth category is non-business. If a transaction is non-business, any related input tax is not recoverable. To put it another way, if you receive some money in the course of a non-business activity, the corollary of not charging output tax is that you have no right to recover any input tax.

Once you are in business, it is unusual to receive money in the course of something which is not a business activity, as explained later. Such non-business transactions as go through your accounts are likely to be expenses rather than income, examples being:

- Local authority business rates. These are a local tax, not payment to the local authority for services which it provides.

- Wages and salaries of your staff. They do provide services to you but they do so as employees, not as independent contractors in business.

However, non-business activities can be an important part of the VAT accounting of some organisations. That is to say, they are in business for a part of what they do but they also have a non-business side. Examples are:

- charities, which raise money via business activities such as charity shops, but whose main activity is charitable without charge;

- museums to which entry is free but which charge for special exhibitions;

- churches where entry to the main body of the church is free, but which charge for access to certain parts or have shops selling books, souvenirs etc.

In such cases, the organisation has to be careful to distinguish between VAT related to its business side, which it can recover and that related to the non-business one, which it cannot.

VAT catches all manner of transactions

VAT is an all-embracing tax. It catches for instance:

- sales of goods;
- sales of services – whether manual repair work or professional charges such as of accountants and lawyers;
- charges between associated businesses, often called 'management charges';
- leasing or renting goods;
- royalties from copyright and similar rights;
- sales of land and buildings;
- sales in the canteen, of old equipment, to staff etc;
- recharging the salaries of your staff.

It is irrelevant whether the transaction is part of the sales of the business on which you earn a profit or simply something which is incidental to it, such as sales in the canteen. If you charge somebody money for it, the transaction is probably within the VAT system.

What is a 'supply'?

The word 'supply' is used in VAT as an alternative to 'output'. It covers much more than the ordinary sales of the business, as you can see from the above examples.

So what is it then which makes one liable to register?

The law on this is in *VATA 1994, s 4*. You have to register if you make:

- taxable supplies,
- as a taxable person,
- in the course or furtherance of any business you carry on.

Taxable supplies means positive rated or zero-rated ones, not exempt ones.

Taxable person includes someone who should have registered but hasn't got around to telling Customs yet.

The phrase *in the course or furtherance of any business carried on by him* is deliberately wide and vague because it is intended to be all-embracing. If you charge somebody money for something, the chances are that it is done in the course or furtherance either of your existing business or of some new one.

However, an individual can make a sale which is not a part of his business. For instance, a shopkeeper can sell a piece of his house furniture. Although furniture is standard-rated, the sale would not be made as part of the retail business — unless, perhaps, he was unwise enough to put it in the shop window.

Section 94 says that the word *business* includes any trade, profession or vocation. See Chapter 27, *Am I in Business?* for more comment on what is or is not a business.

Who then must register?

If you are a sole trader, you can only have one VAT registration for all the business activities you own.

In contrast, a partnership must register separately if the partners are different. Thus, a mother and father might be in partnership in one business, the father and their son in another and the mother and their son in a third. There could be three separate VAT registrations, each family member being a partner in two of them.

An ordinary partnership is not the same as a Limited Liability Partnership (LLP), although there is only one main difference for VAT purposes. The Limited Liability Partnerships Act 2000, which took effect from 6 April 2001, enables LLPs to register with the Registrar of Companies as corporate bodies. This means that, if the partners in an LLP control a limited company, the LLP can be grouped with it. See Chapter 4, *VAT Groups* for information about grouping.

A limited company must register for VAT on its own unless it is part of a VAT group. If companies are under common control, they can be grouped for VAT purposes with one of them acting as the representative member of the group. See Chapter 4 on *VAT Groups*.

Other kinds of organisation such as clubs, societies and charities are also potentially liable to register. It doesn't matter who you are or what you do. Even a temporary committee set up to organise an event can be caught.

No matter how worthy your objectives, you must register if you make 'taxable supplies in the course or furtherance of a business' to a value exceeding the registration limit.

See Chapter 3, *Should I or Must I Register for VAT?* for more on registration.

It is irrelevant whether you make a profit

VAT is a tax upon transactions, not on profits or losses. You do not escape liability to register merely because you are not out to make a profit. If in doubt whether you are a business for VAT purposes, take professional advice. There are penalties for failing to register promptly which could make getting it wrong very expensive!

Some input tax is not recoverable

Not all input tax can be recovered. Obviously you cannot recover tax on private expenses. VAT on these is not input tax in the first place, let alone recoverable input tax. When you incur living costs, you are a consumer even if you have a VAT registration.

Tax is also disallowed on a number of specific expenses of which the main ones are motor cars, with limited exceptions, and entertaining.

The VAT fraction

The VAT fraction calculates the amount of tax in a tax inclusive sum. For example, if the amount is £117.50 you know without thinking that the tax included at 17½% is £17.50. To calculate the tax in £3,000, is not so easy.

The calculation is not 17½% of the amount — 17½% of £117.50 is not £17.50.

It is $\dfrac{17.50}{117.50}$ or $\dfrac{\text{VAT rate}}{100 + \text{the VAT rate}}$

This can be simplified to 7/47ths

Thus, the tax included is £3,000 × 7/47ths = £446.81.

Some questions to check your understanding. Review your answers with the text.

- What is the difference between an input and an output?

- Who is a 'consumer' for VAT purposes?

- In the UK there are 6 categories of transaction. The first is standard-rated. What are the other 5? Give examples of each.

- List some of the different kinds of business transaction affected by VAT.

- What are the 4 categories of person or organisation quoted who may have to register for VAT?

- What is the VAT fraction?

- Having exempt outputs increases a trader's costs. Why?

2.   Where Do I Find the Law?

Why is the second chapter of this book about the law itself when the book is supposed to be a plain English guide to VAT? Well, it is important to know what is law and what is not, if only because Customs officers sometimes quote a VAT Notice, for example, as if it is the law when it is merely guidance. Therefore, even a layman needs to have some idea of what the law consists of in order to distinguish between a ruling from Customs for which there is direct legal authority and one which is merely based on an interpretation of the law.

Then, throughout the book, there are references to where to find the law which is being discussed. Readers who wish to refer to the law itself need to know a little about the structure of it in order to understand those references.

Also included is some comment about the VAT Notices published by Customs, VAT Notes and Court decisions, which are not law but which often play an important role in the 'system'. So, even if you seek a layman's understanding rather than a detailed knowledge of the law, there are still important points for you in this chapter.

VAT law consists of:

- Various *VAT Directives* of the European Economic Community. The 6th Directive is the main one.

- The *Value Added Tax Act 1994*.

- Certain statutory instruments.

- Certain VAT Notices published by Customs & Excise.

The 6th VAT Directive

The starting point for VAT law is the *6th VAT Directive* of the European Economic Community which took effect from 1/1/78. VAT has existed in the UK since 1973 and in other Member States for longer still. The purpose of the 6th Directive was therefore to eliminate many of the variations between the different national systems.

Much of the 6th Directive is mandatory upon the Member States because Article 189 of the Treaty of Rome, which, in 1957, established the European Economic Community, empowers the Council and the Commission to issue directives. It says that 'a directive shall be binding, as to the result to be achieved, upon each Member State to which it is addressed, but shall leave to the national authorities the choice of form and methods'.

The Court of Justice of the European Communities (CJEC) has stated that 'the freedom left to the Member States by Article 189 as to the choice of forms and methods of implementation of directives does not affect their obligation to choose the most appropriate forms and methods to ensure the effectiveness of the directives'.

Various cases before the CJEC have established that Member States must implement the 6th VAT Directive accurately. Should a State fail to embody a provision of the Directive in its national law, the Directive has direct effect. That is to say, an individual in that State can rely upon the Directive in the absence of the appropriate provision in the national legislation.

That's not just a piece of legal theory. Such a situation has occurred in the UK. In the case of *Yoga for Health Foundation ([1984] STC 630)* I argued in the tribunal that the taxpayer was entitled to exemption for its residential courses in yoga because they qualified as welfare services for which there was an exemption in the Directive. The tribunal did not accept this but, on appeal in October 1984, the Divisional Court reversed the decision in favour of the taxpayer. This case showed that there was a gap in UK law, which was only filled when the exemption for welfare services was added to what is now *VATA 1994, Sch 9 Group 7*. In the interim, indeed since 1/1/78 when the Sixth Directive came into force, one could rely upon the latter.

Not all the provisions of the Directive are mandatory. In some cases, the Directive says that Member States *may* rather than *must* do something and thus gives them discretion. They also have a certain amount of freedom in the way in which they implement the Directive, though subject to the comment of the CJEC quoted above that the form and method of implementation must be appropriate to ensure the effectiveness of the Directive.

Mostly, UK law does implement the Directive. However, if you have an argument with Customs on a particular point it could be worth checking the Directive to see whether or not UK law accords with it.

The Value Added Tax Act 1994

The main UK legislation is the *Value Added Tax Act 1994* otherwise known as *VATA 1994*.

However, the Act is by no means the end of the matter. It contains most of the main principles of VAT law but it omits many key details. Nowadays much law on many subjects is made by statutory instrument.

Statutory instruments

A statutory instrument is effectively law made by administrative decree. It does have to be laid before Parliament but it does not go through all the lengthy procedures required for an Act. SIs provide a means of simplifying and speeding up the process of government by allowing Ministers and their departments to sort out the detailed rules once the principles of a law have been decided.

In VAT there are two kinds of SI, *Treasury Orders* and *Customs Regulations*.

As the names suggest, Treasury Orders are made by the Treasury whereas Customs Regulations are made by Customs & Excise.

For example, when the registration limit alters, the change is made by Treasury Order. Alterations to the rate of VAT applicable to a supply are also often made by SI.

Treasury Orders also restrict the recovery of input tax. *Section 25(7)* gives the Treasury a general power to make an order disallowing the recovery of input tax on such kinds of expense as it may decide. Examples of disallowances under the *Input Tax Order (SI 1992/3222)* are tax on entertainment and on motor cars.

Similarly, various provisions of *VATA 1994* give the Commissioners of Customs & Excise power to make Regulations about such details of the way VAT works as the precise information required on a tax invoice.

The rules made by Customs are mainly to be found in a single SI called the *VAT Regulations (SI 1995/2518)*.

Thus, some SIs are law in their own right, such as the Input Tax Order and the VAT Regulations. Others merely amend the existing law as when the registration limit is raised.

How VAT law changes

Every Finance Act amends the VAT Act in some respect. They cannot stop messing about with the system! Thus, for the current law, you need an updated version of *VATA 1994*, consolidated for all the changes, such as that in *Butterworths' De Voil Indirect Tax Service*.

Unfortunately that's far from being the end of it. A Finance Act can contain new law in its own right as well as amendments to the existing law. For example, for 9 years, the main rules were in *VATA 1983* but those on penalties were in *FA 1985*. At the time of writing, there has been no substantial new law in a Finance Act, as opposed to amendments of the VAT Act. However the UK does not have a system of putting all changes in taxation legislation into a single Act. As a result, Consolidating Acts were needed in 1983 and again in 1994 to bring all the law together.

Meanwhile, the law also changes regularly with amending SIs. SIs do not just amend the VAT Act. They are also used to change those SIs which are law in their own right, such as the Input Tax Order.

There have been as many as 49 SIs in a single year. A more normal number is around 16 – 18 so you can see why, taking the Finance Act changes into account, it can be said that VAT law changes on average twice a month.

VAT notices published by Customs

Customs publish numerous notices and leaflets on VAT. Most of these are no more than interpretation and guidance. Take care with statements such as 'you must do so and so' or 'such and such a product is standard-rated'. Most of the time Customs are right. Nevertheless, Tribunal and High Court decisions regularly show that they have got it wrong on a particular point so never take what a Notice says for granted. Customs from time to time publish a new version of a Notice without mentioning in it that they have lost a case on a particular point it covers. Their excuse for this is that they have appealed against the decision and are maintaining their view in the meantime. See later in this chapter for more on Court decisions.

Even though most of the Notices are no more than interpretation and guidance, they can still be valuable as an explanation of that interpretation on which you can rely. If, for example, Customs say in a Notice that something is zero-rated, they will stand by this until they announce a change of mind, provided of course that your product is exactly the same. On a few occasions, Customs have been accused of reneging on something said in a Notice but the circumstances have been of limited significance. Generally, you can rely on a Notice *provided* that your version is up-to-date for any changes in the law.

The pitfall in out of date notices

When asking a Customs & Excise Advice Centre for a Notice, either do so in writing or make a note, signed and dated, of your telephone conversation. It is also advisable to ask whether the current version of the Notice is up-to-date. It can take a year or more before an up-to-date version is published following a change in the law.

In my experience, staff responsible for sending out Notices have little understanding of them. They regularly send the out of date version when the new one, with issue date quoted, has been specifically requested in writing. Or, when an update has been asked for, they send the original Notice without the update! It can take weeks and sometimes months to get the correct information. A non-specialist asking for the relevant Notice on the subject would probably not realise that the one sent to them was out of date and/or missing one or more updates to it. If asking for a new version of a Notice or an Update to one, state the issue date or Update number so that you can check that what you get is what you asked for.

This is not just nit picking! Customs officers routinely quote the Notices to traders and use the dates of them as an indication of when a trader is supposed to have been told about points contained in them. On a number of occasions, I have demonstrated that a trader, who had been assessed, could not have known about a change of policy at the date from which tax had been demanded but that is only because I have a knowledge of how the system works. Most traders and all too many Customs officers assume that the date quoted in a Notice is when it was available.

The notices which are law

As Customs have power to decide what records traders must keep, any requirement on records stated in a Notice arguably means that the Notice has the force of law to that extent.

More importantly, certain Notices are law because they are what is called tertiary legislation; ie, Customs publish them under powers given to them by SI to make further regulations. Thus, *VATA 1994* gives Customs power to make Regulations providing for the Retail Schemes. They have done so in an SI called the *VAT Regulations (SI 1995/2518)*. However, the relevant regulations say relatively little but give Customs power to make further detailed rules in the form of the *Retail Schemes Notice*.

The reason for this is that the rules concerning the calculations which a scheme user must make and the records which must be kept have to be enforceable in law but also have to be explained to every scheme user. So, for Schemes such as those for Retailers, Tour Operators, Cash Accounting, Annual Accounting and Payments on Account, the relevant Notice is law, at least to the extent that it describes the records to be kept and the calculations to be made.

Court decisions

One can appeal to a VAT Tribunal against a ruling by Customs & Excise. Either side can then appeal that decision to the High Court, Chancery Division and from thence to the Court of Appeal and to the House of Lords. In Scotland appeals go from the Tribunal to the Court of Session and thence to the House of Lords.

VAT Tribunal decisions are published in batches several times a month. Many are either unimportant or concern points of interest only to specialists. Most of the more interesting ones are reported in the professional press.

High Court decisions are far fewer but do of course tend to be much more important. Court decisions do not either make or change VAT law. The English tradition of common law developing through case law does not apply to VAT because we have a code — the VAT Act. Thus, in VAT, the Tribunals and the Courts merely interpret the law. However, those interpretations do from time to time change our understanding of what the law means.

When the trader wins, it is common for businesses in the same sector to find that they have paid too much VAT. Anyone who takes VAT seriously needs to keep an eye on the reports of cases going through the VAT Tribunals and, on appeal, through the High Court. This is an important planning point because, if one pays too much VAT, one can only reclaim it from Customs for 3 years prior to the date on which one submits the claim to them. If someone else wins a Tribunal case on a point, which affects your business, it is vital to get your claim into Customs as early as possible.

Do not wait for the appeal to go through the Courts, as the process can take several years. If a point is referred to the Court of Justice of the European Communities, it is likely to add at least another 2 years to the process. If, in the meantime, you have not protected your right to reclaim overpaid VAT by submitting a claim to Customs, they will only repay you for a maximum of 3 years. See Chapter 5, *The VAT Return* under *The three-year cap*.

VAT Notes

VAT Notes is a mini-newsletter from Customs which is issued 4 times a year with VAT returns. As quarterly returns are sent out over a 3-month period as the month end return dates come up, some businesses do not get VAT Notes for up to 2 months after others do.

It is as well to get hold of VAT Notes as soon as it is available because you could find that it gives details of changes which are important to you and of which you are expected to know as soon as your return with it attached is sent to you. As some of these changes are brought in at short notice, the sooner you know of anything, which affects you, the better. You do not have to wait for your return to arrive. VAT Notes is published on the Customs site on the internet (http://www.hmce.gov.uk).

If Customs change their minds on a point of interpretation of VAT law, the only way they can tell all traders is via VAT Notes. Suppose you had a ruling 10 years ago that one of your products was zero-rated. If Customs announce a change of policy on this in VAT Notes, the individual ruling to you is automatically cancelled. If you fail to read it, that is your problem!

You will still be able to appeal against the decision if an officer several years later assesses you for the VAT, which you have not charged. However, the sum at risk if you lose will be much greater than if you had noticed the change of policy and had started the argument at once.

A further more specialised point is that the main publicity for any changes to those Notices, which have legal effect, is also in VAT Notes. Since you would be deemed to have been notified of that change when you received your copy, the latter might effectively alter the law covered by the Notice, though of course technically it is the amendment slip to the Notice which does so from the date it is issued, never mind when you get to know about it.

That's less worrying than it may sound because it only concerns those Notices, which have legal effect. As explained above, most of them are not law, only advice and guidance.

It is not so just because Customs say it is!

Laymen tend to think that, because an officer of Her Majesty's Commissioners of Customs & Excise says something is so, it must be so. Hopefully, you know better after reading this chapter. Being human, Customs regularly make mistakes. This book has numerous references to cases which they have lost. Of course Customs get it right most of the time but, if you do not like what they tell you, check what the law says. If you can't see that the law says what they say it says, don't assume they are necessarily right!

Some questions to check your understanding. Review your answers with the text.

- What does VAT law consist of?
- On what European law is UK VAT law based?
- Although court decisions do not change the law, why is their practical effect often similar to a change?
- Although most Notices are not law, a few are. Which are they?
- Why is it important to read VAT Notes when you receive them?

3. Should I or Must I Register for VAT?

This chapter is about when and how you have to register for VAT. It highlights a number of pitfalls in the process and is primarily of interest to businesses not yet registered for VAT and those who advise them. It is only relevant to a business already VAT registered if the turnover is not much above the registration limit and the points on de-registration might therefore apply.

Who must register?

See the explanation of who must register under that heading in Chapter 1, *How VAT Works — an Outline of the System*.

The registration limit

From 10/4/03, the registration limit is £56,000 a year but it is increased from each Budget day so check the current figure. The law is in *VATA 1994, Schs 1, 2 and 3*:

You *have* to register for VAT if:

(a) Your taxable outputs, which includes zero-rated sales, have exceeded the registration limit in the previous 12 calendar months; or

(b) There are reasonable grounds for thinking that your taxable outputs in the next 30 days will exceed the limit; or

(c) You take over as a going concern a business to which (a) or (b) applies. See later under *Buying an existing business*.

Check your turnover at the end of each calendar month.

Note: The sale of a 'capital asset', such as office equipment, a van or building does not count towards the limit. But the sale of a building, which you have opted to tax, does.

The past turnover measure

In your first year, add up your sales cumulatively month by month. If after, say, 8 months, you have exceeded the registration limit, you must tell Customs forthwith and you will be registered from the end of the month following that in which you exceeded the limit.

Once you have traded for 12 months without exceeding the limit, you add a month and drop off the earliest one each time. Thus, if you have traded for the full calendar year 2002 without exceeding the limit, you must review the position at the end of January 2003, adding in that month and dropping off January 2002.

If you take over an existing business, which is not registered, see also under *Buying an existing business,* below.

The future prospects rule

The future prospects rule, under which you must register if you expect your taxable outputs in the next 30 days to exceed the limit, is designed to catch large 'one-off' transactions such as a property deal. If the transaction is standard-rated, you must tell Customs once the completion date is less than 31 days away. You will be registered from the start of the 30 day period in order to catch the transaction.

Have you identified all your taxable sales?

Sales, which count towards the limit include:

* Zero-rated sales — but not exempt ones, which are not 'taxable'.

* Subsidiary activities in the same ownership — a farmer with holiday cottages or a camp site.

* A 'hobby' carried on in such a way, on such scale etc as to constitute a business — such as, a plumber, who also performs as an entertainer in clubs.

Have you got the values right?

To get your registration date right, you must measure your turnover correctly. Could it be understated? One pitfall is income, such as royalties or holiday lettings, which comes net of commission via an agent. It is the gross values which count for VAT registration.

Under the *Second-hand Goods Scheme*, the value of the supply and thus the turnover for registration purposes, is the selling price, even though you only account for VAT on the profit margin.

In contrast, turnover under the *Tour Operators Margin Scheme* is the margin, which is subject to VAT, not the price charged to the customer. For a disaster related to this pitfall, see later under *Registering too early is also a mistake!*

Buying an existing business

If you take over an existing business under the *Transfer of a Going Concern* rules explained in Chapter 37, *Buying or Selling a Business*, you must register immediately if the vendor is a taxable person (*Para 1(2)(a), Sch 1*). '*Taxable person*' includes someone liable to register but who has not done so. In *Shu Yin Chau (LON/1343 No 1726)*, a purchaser, who had been given accounts by the vendor showing sales for the last three years above the registration limit, was held liable for VAT from the date of the takeover, not when her own sales subsequently exceeded the limit.

If you do not have to register immediately, you must count as your outputs those of the vendor when working out your liability to register from that date on the rolling twelve month basis *(s 49)*.

Registration due to acquisitions of goods or the reverse charge

An unregistered business, which buys goods from other EU States to a value above the registration limit in the *calendar year to 31 December* must register. This would be an unusual situation since buying that quantity of goods would normally mean that you were making taxable supplies in the UK and liable to register in the usual way. However, a business, which only made exempt supplies and which bought the goods to use in its business rather than for resale, might not be registered. This rule prevents such a business benefiting by buying goods in another Member State at a lower rate of VAT than that in the UK.

Unlike the normal registration limit, that for acquisitions restarts on 1 January each year and ignores sales in the preceding year.

Similarly, if an unregistered business spends more than the registration limit on services from outside the UK, which are subject to the reverse charge — explained in Chapter 22, *Exports and Imports of Services* — it must register. In that case, the normal VAT registration limit rules do apply, the value of the reverse charge merely being added to any existing taxable supplies.

Registration due to distance selling in the UK

A business in another EU State, which sells goods by mail order to private customers in the UK, must register here if the value of its sales in the UK exceeds £70,000 a year. See Chapter 19, *Exports of Goods* under *Distance selling (mail order)* for more details. As with acquisitions of goods, the registration limit is for the calendar year to 31 December and restarts on 1 January each year.

Registration due to electronic supplies via the Internet

Under the EC *VAT E-commerce Directive 2002/38/EEC* in effect from 1/7/03, a business based outside the EU, which electronically supplies services to private customers, has to register in the EU. The services in question include those relating to websites, computer software, including maintenance of it, pictures, text and information, music and distance teaching. See Chapter 22, *Exports and Imports of Services* for more details.

The business can choose the Member State in which to register. It will then charge each customer at the VAT rate applicable in the State of that customer.

It must notify electronically the Member State of its choice with its name and address, electronic addresses, including websites and its national tax number if it has one, together with a statement that it is not already registered within the EU.

It must then submit electronically a VAT return for each calendar quarter within 20 days of the end thereof showing the total of its supplies in each Member State, the VAT rate and the VAT due thereon. The return must be in euros, unless a Member State, which has not adopted the euro, requires it in its national currency — as does the UK. The exchange rate used shall be that of the last day of the reporting period, as published by the European Central Bank. Payment shall be in euros or in the currency of the State.

If the non-EU business incurs any VAT within the EU in relation to its electronic sales, it can reclaim it under the *13th VAT Directive* from the Member State in which it incurs it . See Chapter 26, *Recovery of Foreign VAT.*

Non-EU businesses can register electronically in the UK at www.hmce.gov.uk/business. Then click on *Electronic services* and, in that page, on *VAT on E-services special scheme for non-EU businesses.* That refers you to various information sheets but, for specific guidance, of which the key points are those above, click *Welcome Page* at the foot. That page includes buttons for the electronic registration form or to log in if you are ready registered.

The detailed rules are in *Schs 3A* and *3B* including on such points as the submission of returns and the correction of errors.

Registration of trusts

Many trusts do not have to register because they only have exempt investment income. However, a trust can have taxable income such as rents from commercial property, which are standard rated if opted to tax — as explained in Chapter 25, *Property* — or royalties from books written by the deceased author, who created the trust.

Customs normally register the trustees in the name of the trust because it is they who are making the supplies. Trusts can be registered under *s 46*, as an unincorporated association or under *s 45* as a partnership where there is joint ownership of land. However, in the case of a bare trust — where the trustees merely hold the assets on behalf of the beneficiary — it can be the latter who is making the supplies. Give Customs the full facts when suggesting in whose name the registration should be.

If in doubt, take advice

If you are not registered but might be liable to do so, take professional advice on the basis of all the facts. There are penalties for late registration so it could be expensive to delay!

When you have to tell Customs

You have to tell Customs:

* Within 30 days of the end of the relevant month (past sales); or

* By the end of the 30-day period (expected sales).

Date of registration

Past sales

At the end of the month after that when annual limit was exceeded.

Example:

Limit exceeded in the 12 months to 31 January.
The 30-day notification period runs to 2 March. (*28 days in Feb*)
But registration will be from 1 March.

Future prospects

At the beginning of the 30-day period during which you expect, or rather, by then, expected, to exceed the registration limit.

Be careful with your application form

Think about your answers to questions on the form. Trouble sometimes arises because of careless completion. For example, 'any old figure' is entered for, say, expected future sales. Or the date of the first expected taxable supply is unrealistic. This can cause awkward questions later.

The right date is your problem!

You have to state the date on which you are liable to register. Your application goes to a special processing centre, which does not check that date — it does not have the information to do so anyway. Customs only check the date when they visit you, which could be years later. If they then find that you failed to register early enough, they will backdate your registration, which could prove very expensive.

This catches out people who fail to check their sales properly and do not realise they have gone over the limit.

- When Customs find out, the registration is backdated to the correct date, which could be years earlier.

- It's then no good pointing out that your sales have since reduced below the registration limit again.

Consider the sad story of Mr Bruce

PS Bruce (LON/93/2930 No 12484) began trading in tyres in his spare time in April 1990. By October it was evident that, in the coming year, his sales would exceed the limit.

His registration application dated 29 October showed:

- the date of the first supply as 11/4/90;

- his sales in the 12 months from then as £25,000 — the limit then being £25,400;

- the date of 11 April as that of both compulsory and voluntary registration.

An officer, who queried this, clearly failed to explain the difference between the date of starting trading and that of liability to register. She later said that *Bruce* had agreed registration from 11 April. He thought the date of registration was 7 November, that of the large LVO rubber stamp.

The assessment for £1,516 VAT not accounted for from 11 April to 7 November was dated 15/10/93, *3 years* later.

Granted, the problem resulted from Bruce's inability to understand the basic rules or failure to read the paperwork properly but what's new? In theory, Bruce's accountant could have spotted the problem when doing the accounts, but did he or she even think to check the registration date?

Registering too early is also a mistake!

If you miscalculate your sales and register too early, you cannot subsequently demand retrospective de-registration. *N Goodrich t/a UYE Tours (LON/01/584 No 17707)* should have used the *Tour Operators Margin Scheme.* He thought he had to register because his sales exceeded the limit whereas, as noted earlier under *Have you got the values right?*, it is the profit margin which counts under that Scheme.

Although Customs repaid the VAT on the difference between his profit margin and his sales values, that left a substantial sum of VAT on the profit margin. As that margin had been below the limit, he never needed to register. However, having done so, his registration was, in effect, voluntary as explained below. It could not be cancelled retrospectively in order to get back the VAT paid unnecessarily.

The penalty for late registration

The law is in *section 67*. Late registration incurs a penalty of up to 15% of the net tax due from the date you should have registered to that on which you eventually notify Customs or they find out. See Chapter 38 on *Assessments and VAT Penalties*.

You can register voluntarily

If your sales are below the limit, or you have not yet made any, you can apply to register voluntarily, thus enabling you to reclaim the input tax you incur.

Voluntary registration is not intended to allow you to recover input tax without ever making any taxable supplies. Taxable supplies remember include zero-rated ones, so that doesn't necessarily mean that your output tax must exceed your input tax. You are entitled to registration at the start of a project, even if it may be several years before it produces taxable outputs, provided that you can show that you have genuinely started a business. See Chapter 27, *Am I in Business?*

If all your outputs are exempt, you cannot register. This is because you are not allowed to recover input tax, so of course there is no point in your registering.

Do I want to register voluntarily?

You *do not* want to register if you sell mostly to the public and charging VAT means that you either must increase your retail prices or reduce your profits.

You *do* want to register if you sell to other registered businesses, which are fully taxable. They can recover the VAT which you charge to them. Your costs are reduced by the input tax, which you can recover.

If you sell to businesses which have exempt outputs, such as finance or insurance brokers, undertakers, schools or hospitals, which cannot recover all their VAT, they may prefer you not to be registered. However, they have to pay VAT on most of their transactions with other businesses anyway and being VAT registered may give you an increased credibility, which will make it easier to sell to them.

If you are incurring VAT now, act now! The rules explained below give you only limited rights to recover input tax retrospectively so think about the date. You can only ask for a retrospective voluntary registration at the time of registration. Once you are registered, any application to backdate, so as to recover VAT incurred earlier, will be refused.

VAT which you can recover upon registration

When you register, you are entitled to recover VAT under *VAT Regulations (SI 1995/2518) Reg 111* on:

- assets used in the business and goods for resale held at the date of registration which you bought within 3 years previously and on which you incurred VAT; and

- services received for the purpose of the ongoing business within 6 months prior to the date of registration.

The services must be those used in the ongoing business, not ones consumed prior to registration. Thus, for example, you cannot recover on telephone calls prior to registration or on professional fees in preparing accounts up to that date.

You can recover on professional fees for advice concerning registration, or on forming a company or partnership through which you will trade.

You claim on your first return. Keep lists of both the goods and services together with the invoices.

The only extension of the above rules is a concession concerning VAT incurred prior to opting to tax a property. See the comments on the option to tax in Chapter 25, *Property*.

Clubs and associations — do your accounts tell the truth?

Show the gross turnover figures in the accounts of clubs and associations in an extra schedule or note if necessary. Such accounts often show net sums after charging expenses against income for specific activities. Examples are:

- bar — gross profit only shown;

- publications, seminars and exhibitions — costs netted against income.

This means that it is impossible to tell what the taxable outputs are. Possible consequences include:

- liability to register not realised;

- it is impossible to compare turnover per accounts with figures declared on VAT returns;

- gross profit shortages are concealed.

Are you a professional accountant?

VAT registration is the one aspect of VAT on which a professional accountant is likely to have an immediate duty of care towards the client. Failure to advise could commence from the initial contact with the client. So, if a new client is not VAT-registered, I suggest that you should ask what the current levels of turnover are and point out the penalty for getting it wrong, if there seems any likelihood of the registration limit being exceeded. I think that this advice should be in writing because it is all too easy for clients to forget what they are told and subsequently to claim that they were not properly advised, especially if the advice is given at the time of starting up the business.

Your letter should also say that it is then up to the client to feed you prompt information if you are to advise further on whether there is a liability to register. However, when you prepare the annual accounts, you should check the registration position. This means reviewing not just the turnover shown in the accounts but the figures on a rolling 12 month basis throughout the year.

Failure to realise that a business has become liable to register at sometime during the year, even though the annual accounts show the turnover as below the registration limit, is a pitfall which has caught out many small businesses and their professional advisers.

When you do find that a client is liable to register and advise accordingly, do you follow up the matter before you receive the next set of papers from which to prepare the accounts?

In many late registration cases, accountants have been shown up as perilously close to negligent in not confirming with clients that action has been taken to register. Perhaps you do not see it as your duty to nanny the client to this extent. However, many small businesses have had to pay substantial penalties because neither they nor their accountants have dealt efficiently with registration. Sometimes, the form is said to have been sent off but no action is taken to chase it up when Customs fail to react. Sometimes the client thinks the accountant has dealt with the registration and vice versa.

The above may seem overkill but real money is involved, in some cases sufficient to bankrupt new businesses. Chasing up need not involve partner time. Why not give your receptionist the interest and the responsibility?

De-registration — how can I escape the system?

The law is in *Sch 1 paras 3 and 4, and Sch 4 paras 8 and 9*. See also Notice 700/11 *Cancelling your registration*.

You *must* de-register if you stop making taxable supplies — or you stop intending to if you have registered voluntarily in advance of doing so. Stopping making taxable supplies means that you have no right to recover any input tax.

You can *ask* to de-register:

* If your outputs in the last 12 months have been below the registration limit.

* If you can persuade Customs that your outputs in the next 12 months will be below the de-registration limit. At the time of writing, the latter is £2,000 below the registration limit.

* If your outputs are above the registration limit but you will be due repayments because they are zero-rated. However, if the situation is clear cut, the net repayment will probably justify the cost of filling in the VAT return.

The transfer of a business as a going concern

If you sell or give away your business or you transfer it to another owner, such as a limited company, the transaction may be outside the scope of VAT as the transfer of a going concern. See Chapter 37, *Buying or Selling a Business*.

Do not delay your application

If you want to de-register, get on with it! De-registration will only be backdated if you have ceased to be entitled to registration because, for instance, you have sold your business. If you are de-registering voluntarily because your sales are below the registration limit, Customs will refuse to backdate it.

- Customs can only consider an application to de-register once it is made to them. That of course cannot be done until they are aware of your liability to register in the first place.

- So, even if you then immediately request de-registration on the grounds that your sales are below the registration limit, this will be a voluntary exit from the system, which cannot be retrospective.

Watch it if your business changes

These sad stories show the need for thought if the nature of your business alters.

Mr H Zemmel (LON/77/298 No 498) was a wholesaler, who became a taxi driver. Because he failed to request de-registration, he had to pay VAT on his taxi takings despite their being well below the registration limit.

In *WA Renton (EDN/79/12 No 870)* a coal merchant inherited a boarding house. Although the Tribunal accepted that he had handed over his coal business to his daughter, albeit without telling Customs, he remained liable for VAT on the boarding house sales because he had not de-registered.

Until your existing registration is cancelled, you owe VAT on your sales no matter how small they are.

When you de-register, you owe VAT on the assets held

You have to account for VAT on assets held at the date of de-registration if the tax exceeds £1,000 (*Sch 4 para 8*).

The assets in question include:

- stock;
- plant and machinery , office equipment and furniture;
- commercial vehicles — and on any car on which you recovered VAT because, for instance, you were using it as a taxi;
- land and property if you recovered VAT on it when you bought it, the vendor having opted to tax it.

VAT is not due on anything on which you did not recover input tax when you bought it — with the exception of goods acquired as part of a business bought as a going concern. See Chapter 37 on *Buying or Selling a Business*.

But you can reclaim certain VAT after deregistering

There are two situations in which you can recover VAT after having deregistered. Ask the *NAS* (see *Contacting Customs*, page viii) for form 427 on which to claim.

- You can claim VAT *incurred earlier* on either goods or services which you did not claim on the correct VAT return either because you did not have the purchase invoice or because of a mistake.
- But VAT *incurred after* deregistration is only recoverable on services, not on goods (*Reg 111(5)*).

The three-year time limit applies in both situations.

Dividing a business to escape registration

It is difficult to divide a business into two parts so as to avoid registration for one or both. Customs can direct under *Sch 1 para 2* that two or more businesses be combined for VAT purposes if, as a result, they catch one or more for registration.

Customs need only be 'satisfied' that the activities in question are all part of the same business. Worse still, the Tribunal can only allow an appeal against such a direction if it considers that Customs 'could not reasonably have been satisfied that there were grounds for making the direction' (*s 84(7)*). It is tricky to show that Customs could not reasonably have been satisfied about something. It has been done but the chances are that, if you have divided a business to avoid registration, it will be obvious and therefore reasonable for Customs to direct you. (For examples, see the High Court cases of *Chamberlain* (*[1989] STC 505*) and *Osman* (*[1989] STC 596*).)

A directive cannot be retrospective. Separation is therefore effective until Customs spot the situation. If none of the businesses concerned are registered and Customs therefore do not visit them, VAT may be avoided for some years even if a direction is eventually imposed.

If you try to separate two businesses in order to keep one or both out of VAT registration, do it properly with written agreements, separate records etc. Customs do not need to use their powers to direct that they be treated as a single business if they can show that they were never in fact separate. The problem is to demonstrate that as a matter of substance and reality:

- the so-called separate businesses are sufficiently at arm's length from each other; and

- they have normal commercial relationships with each other.

These criteria were approved in *Burrell* (*[1997] STC 1413*) in which the Divisional Court supported the Tribunal's decision that Mr Burrell was not in partnership with his father in an aerobics business separately from a health club.

In *RE & RL Newton (t/a RE Newton) (LON/2000/84 No 17222)*, two partnerships of a carpenter with his father, which was VAT registered and an unregistered one with his mother were held to be genuinely separate businesses, despite the latter having been formed specifically to do work for customers, who could not recover VAT. The Tribunal noted the following factors for and against:

For separation

- There was a written partnership agreement;

- The unregistered partnership was formed to do private work, which would otherwise have been lost to unregistered competitors and which was therefore not available to the registered partnership;

- Separate invoices;

- Separate records, bank accounts, annual accounts and Inland Revenue returns;

- The only vehicle used by both partnerships was Mr Newton's car which was not in the accounts of either;

- The small value of supplies by the unregistered partnership meant this was not a case where separation kept both businesses out of registration;

- The Tribunal was satisfied that the unregistered partnership was properly formed and existed independently;

- If a contract was about to be lost because of the addition of VAT, the customer was told of the unregistered partnership so its customers knew that it would do the work.

Against separation

- All advertising was done by the registered partnership — though the spend was small and most work was obtained by personal recommendation;

- Some confusion in the accounting over the allocation of suppliers' invoices — though little or no input tax incorrectly claimed;

- Most expenditure charged to the registered partnership — though the use by the unregistered one was small and it might not have been worthwhile to separate it;

- The parents on occasion worked for both partnerships — though the work by the mother for the registered partnership could equally have been done in her capacity as a mother and, as a matter of substance and reality, relationships between a son and his parents would not be expected to be wholly at arm's length or commercial.

Neutral factors

- Only the registered partnership had a public liability insurance policy; but it was not needed by the unregistered partnership, presumably because the work was done in the customers' houses;

- There was only one set of tools — but the son owned these.

As you can see from that list, decisions on whether or not businesses are separate are often based on fine points of detail and on the relative balance between the factors each way. Customs have often won in the numerous other cases on this subject over the years but by no means always. Many arguments have concerned whether catering in a public house, often run by the publican's wife, was separate from the publican's sales of alcohol. Normally, it is difficult to show that it is, if only because the two businesses go together naturally and because of the close relationship between the owners. Thus, in *AE Fraser and ME Fraser (LON/99/0453 No 16761)*, a restaurant run by the wife was found to be a part of the public house business which she and her husband ran. The restaurant made no contribution towards the premises costs and each activity supported the other. In contrast, a cafe run by a husband and wife in partnership was held to be separate from a fish and chip business run by the husband from the same premises. (*BR Parker and JG Parker (t/a Sea Breeze Cafe) (LON/98/1284 No 16350)*.

Then, in *G & M Treta (t/a The Golden Fry) (1/2 EDN/99/119 No 16690)*, a nephew, who took over a fish and chip shop for eight weeks whilst the owners, his employers, were on holiday, was held to be in business for that period on his own account. In *AC James and GC James (LON/00/29 No 16988)*, a high quality dry cleaning business run by a father was held to be separate from the normal high volume one run by his son from the same premises.

In *D Townsend and M Townsend (LON/00/349-50 No 17081)*, a husband and wife were found to be running separate businesses consisting of the wife's shop selling pottery painted by herself and local artists and the sale of handmade pieces made by her husband through the shop and elsewhere. This was despite the informality of accounting. The types of pottery were different and the couple had no involvement in each other's businesses.

On the bare facts above, some of these cases seem unlikely victories but they show the vital importance of clarifying the full facts and of producing evidence in support of them. Remember that, once Customs are aware of the situation, they can consider directing that the businesses be treated as one for VAT purposes — as they may well have done in the above cases after having lost the argument about whether they were separate — and that such a direction is much more difficult to defeat because of the limited powers of the Tribunal to overturn it.

A trap re partners: s 45(2)

A departing partner has an ongoing liability for VAT:

- on future trading if Customs are not informed of the change;
- on past trading until the VAT return is submitted and tax paid;
- on any errors subsequently discovered in past returns.

That this problem is for real was confirmed by the Divisional Court in *Jamieson ([2002] STC 1418)*. This confirmed the liability of Mrs Jamieson for VAT due on trading in a public house for periods after she had left a partnership with her husband. So, if you leave a partnership, see that the VAT returns are up-to-date before you go and make sure that Customs are informed of the change!

Some questions to check your understanding. Review your answers with the text.

- What is the current registration limit?
- What are the reasons for compulsory registration?
- What VAT is recoverable when you register?
- If you wish to de-register voluntarily, why should you apply at once?
- What do you owe VAT on when you de-register, apart from your sales up to the de-registration date?
- Is there are a de minimis limit for that extra VAT?
- If you separate a business into two or more parts to avoid registration, what are the two ways in which Customs may challenge that separation? Note: one has retrospective effect; one does not.

4.   VAT Groups

This chapter explains how two or more limited companies can form a VAT group, which has a single VAT return covering all the companies in the group. Only 'bodies corporate' can be grouped for VAT purposes. This normally means limited companies although, for instance, universities are corporate bodies and can therefore be grouped with their trading subsidiaries. Limited liability partnerships also qualify. The law is in *ss 43 and 43A–C*.

The main advantage is to avoid creating output tax on, say, management charges between associated companies, where the recipient company cannot recover input tax because it is partially exempt. Thus, associated companies in the financial and insurance sectors are usually grouped together.

Effect of grouping

One company acts as the 'representative member' of the group. All inputs and outputs are treated as being those of the representative member. Transactions between companies in the same VAT group are ignored.

Key points

- Companies and limited liability partnerships only; not ordinary partnerships. A sole trader can only have one registration anyway.

- At the option of the trader. He must apply to group — or to de-group, should he wish to alter the group. Customs can refuse or can remove a company from a group but these powers are normally only used if they think you are trying to save VAT with an artificial scheme.

- The companies must be under common control. 'Control' usually means over 50% of the votes of the share capital. Normally that means a majority of the shares.

- Control can be by another limited company, not necessarily a member of the VAT group, by an individual or by two or more individuals carrying on a business in partnership. The controlling person can be anywhere in the world.

- Alternative criteria are that a company is empowered by statute to control the other company's activities or that it is the holding company under *Companies Act 1985, s 736*: ie, it has a right to appoint a majority of the directors.

Do not confuse the concept of VAT grouping with that under different rules for corporation tax or under the *Companies Act*.

Effect on input tax recovery

Grouping does not increase the amount of input tax recoverable. It merely prevents the creation of irrecoverable output tax. Thus:

- If company A makes a management charge to company B, whose outputs are mostly exempt and they are not in a VAT group, VAT on the management charge would be largely if not entirely attributable to the exempt outputs of B.

- If they are in a VAT group, A does not have to add VAT to its charge.

- However, some of A's input tax may be disallowed because it relates to the exempt business of B, which A is supporting through the services it provides.

The extent of any disallowance of input tax to A will depend upon the precise circumstances and upon the partial exemption method adopted.

Entertainment

A minor advantage of grouping is no disallowance for entertaining when executives of companies within the VAT group visit each other. The normal disallowance does apply for visits to an associated company which is not VAT-grouped.

Disadvantages of grouping

Every company within a VAT group is responsible for the entire VAT debt of the group. This could disadvantage minority shareholders in a grouped company since, if part of the group becomes insolvent, the rest must pay its VAT liability.

An administrative disadvantage is that, to get the group VAT return to Customs on time, the other companies in the group must submit their figures to the representative member earlier than if they sent them in direct. Some groups ask for the figures as early as the middle of the month. This imposes an unnecessary demand for speed and thus an additional strain on the accounting resources of the subsidiaries. It also means that the cut off for recovery of input tax on invoices received from suppliers is at least a week earlier than it need be, with an obvious cash flow disadvantage.

Consider collecting the figures by e-mail. Then they can be collated on a spreadsheet electronically both faster and avoiding transposition and arithmetical errors. This would mean that they need only be received one day before the return is due to be despatched to Customs, plus whatever safety margin is deemed sensible to allow for any unexpected problems.

The group liability pitfall

The liability for the VAT debt of the group, mentioned above, can take time to materialise and is a potential loss for any member, past or present, of that group. See Chapter 37, *Buying or Selling a Business* for the pitfall in buying a company out of a VAT group. Notice 700/2 *Group and divisional registration* refers.

In *J & W Waste Management Ltd/J & W Plant and Tool Hire Ltd (LON/02/239 No 18069)*, VAT owed by the group's representative member, a company put into liquidation 9 months earlier, was claimed from two other group members. Customs argued that only the Liquidator had the right of appeal. The Tribunal rejected the idea that entry into a VAT group implied giving up that right, though it directed the Appellants to obtain confirmation of whether or not the Liquidator intended to appeal.

Group payment and repayment companies separately

A company claiming repayments is best not grouped with one making payments because a repayment can be claimed on a monthly return as soon after the end of the month as the return is ready. That could get you a repayment up to two months earlier than you could offset it against the payment due quarterly.

Payments on Account Scheme

A possible reason for not grouping is that, if the total payable by the VAT group exceeds £2 million a year, the *Payments on Account Scheme* will apply. See Chapter 5, *The VAT Return*.

A separate company for exports?

If you put your export sales through an export company, the latter can recover on a monthly return the tax charged to it by your other companies perhaps 2 months before they pay it. This provides a 'one off' gain in working capital.

This scheme is only suitable for very big companies. To justify the cost of running the export company, the interest saving must be substantial. Even £1m @ 10% for two months is only £16,667 a year.

The anti-avoidance rules

The law on grouping gives Customs extensive powers to refuse to allow a company to be grouped or to compulsorily de-group it. These resulted from *Thorn Materials Supply ((1998) STC 725)* which concerned an attempt to use the grouping rules legally but artificially to reclaim several £ millions of input tax. *Thorn* having won in the tribunal, the law was changed to introduce some serious potential complications. However, these will not affect you unless you too have a cunning plan. If you do, you will have expensive advisers on whom you will rely so there is no more to be said about these rules here — except to add that *Thorn* eventually lost in the House of Lords. One of the problems with artificial tax planning is that, no matter how clever it is, if the end result seems not to 'smell right', the judges can often find a way of deciding against it!

Date of leaving a VAT group

In *Barclays Bank plc ([2001] STC 1558)*, the Court of Appeal held that, when a member of the group ceases to be eligible because, for instance, ownership of the company has changed, the date of its departure from the group is that specified in a notice issued by Customs, not that of the change of control.

In theory, this could lead to serious problems over the submission of VAT returns for the group, which must include the figures for the business now sold during the period between the change of control and the date of leaving the group. The liability for any outstanding VAT could also be an issue. Whether that is so in practice remains to be seen. *Business Brief 30/02* sets out Custom's policy.

Property transactions

See Chapter 37, *Buying or Selling a Business* for the position when a tenanted property is bought into or sold out of a VAT group.

Some questions to check your understanding. Review your answers with the text.

- Can you include a partnership in a VAT group?
- What are the criteria of control which must be met in order to group companies?
- What is the main advantage of VAT grouping?

5. The VAT Return

This chapter is not just for people who have never seen a VAT return before. If you have, no doubt you'll skim the first couple of pages but do check the rest for points you may be unaware of.

Basic accounting for VAT

VAT is accounted for on a VAT return — see the example on the next page.

Box 1 – you enter the output tax, which you have charged to your customers.

Box 2 – is for any tax you owe on 'acquisitions' — goods which you have acquired from a supplier in another EU State. There being no frontier controls within the EU, VAT is not collected when the goods enter the UK. You declare it as acquisition VAT. In most cases, no VAT is actually paid because the same sum is recoverable as part of the input tax in box 4.

Acquisition VAT is only a cost if it is not recoverable because it relates to an exempt transaction. For more details, see Chapter 20, *Imports and Acquisitions of Goods*.

Box 3 – is the total of boxes 1 and 2.

Box 4 – you enter the input tax you are reclaiming on the goods or services you have bought. This includes tax on any capital expenditure, such as buildings or equipment, not just that on your running expenses — though there are some limits to what you can reclaim as explained later.

Box 5 – you put the net difference, normally the sum payable by you but which could be a repayment due to you.

Boxes 6 and 7 are for the statistics. These are your outputs for the quarter in box 6, including any which are zero-rated or exempt and your inputs in box 7. Both figures are net of VAT. The inputs figure includes most of your costs but not wages or salaries and certain other items. There are instructions on what to include or leave out on the back of the VAT return so I comment no further here.

Boxes 8 and 9 record, if applicable, your sales of goods to, and purchases of goods from, other Member States of the EU. These boxes are for sales of goods only. The wording does mention 'associated services' but this means only insurance and freight related to the goods.

How often is the return due?

Most traders have to submit quarterly returns. The quarters are staggered so that some finish at the end of March, some at the end of April and some at the end of May. However, you can ask to have the return date, which suits you. You can even have dates which coincide with your accounting periods if you work in 12- or 13-week periods, rather than in calendar quarters.

If you regularly reclaim tax from Customs, you can have a monthly return in order to get the money back quicker.

Form VAT 100

Value Added Tax Return
For the period
to

For Official Use

HM Customs
and Excise

Registration number   Period

You could be liable to a financial penalty
if your completed return and all the VAT
payable are not received by the due date.

Due date:

For official use D O R only

Fold Here

Before you fill in this form please read the notes on the back and the VAT leaflet *"Filling in your VAT return"*. Fill in all boxes clearly in ink, and write 'none' where necessary. Don't put a dash or leave any box blank. If there are no pence write "00" in the pence column. Do not enter more than one amount in any box.

£   p

For official use			
	VAT due in this period on sales and other outputs	**1**	
	VAT due in this period on acquisitions from other EC Member States	**2**	
	Total VAT due **(the sum of boxes 1 and 2)**	**3**	
	VAT reclaimed in this period on **purchases** and other inputs (including acquisitions from the EC)	**4**	
	Net VAT to be paid to Customs or reclaimed by you **(Difference between boxes 3 and 4)**	**5**	
	Total value of **sales** and all other outputs excluding any VAT. **Include your box 8 figure**	**6**	00
	Total value of **purchases** and all other inputs excluding any VAT. **Include your box 9 figure**	**7**	00
	Total value of all **supplies** of goods and related services, excluding any VAT, to other **EC Member States**	**8**	00
	Total value of all **acquisitions** of goods and related services, excluding any VAT, from other **EC Member States**	**9**	00

Retail schemes. If you have used any of the schemes in the period covered by this return, enter the relevant letter(s) in this box.

DECLARATION: You, or someone on your behalf, must sign below.

If you are enclosing a payment please tick this box.

I, ...declare that the
(Full name of signatory in BLOCK LETTERS)

information given above is true and complete.

Signature ....Date ....19...............

A false declaration can result in prosecution.

VAT 100 (Full)   PCU (June 1996)

When is the return due with Customs?

The return is due with Customs on the last day of the month following the end of the period to which it relates (*Reg 25(1)*). If Customs have agreed special return periods to coincide with, for instance, 13-week accounting periods, the return is due a month after the end of the period.

Cheque payments compared with electronic payments

Being on time with a payment means having it in Customs' hands on the due date. However, if the last day of the month is a Saturday, a Sunday or a bank holiday, Customs accept the next working day as on time. Thus, a cheque due on Saturday 31 March is on time on Monday 2 April and may be debited in your bank account on Thursday 5 April.

Customs offer you an extra 7 days if you pay electronically. Unfortunately, that offer is not necessarily what it seems! Firstly, although your bank may offer you various alternatives, you will probably find either that they are relatively expensive or that your account is debited straightaway instead of when your cheque is presented.

Secondly, if the 7-day extension ends at a weekend or on a bank holiday, payment must be in Customs' account at the Bank of England by the previous working day. Thus, in contrast to the cheque payment example above, a *Bankers Automated Clearing System (BACS)* debit to your bank account might have to be on Monday 2 April in order to meet the due date of 6 April. Thus, using BACS probably means losing 3 days, not gaining 7!

There are systems which allow one to give instructions in advance for same day payment. The increased cost of these may not matter if the VAT cheque is merely one of a batch of payments or if the convenience and certainty is worth it to you. However, be aware that the seven-day offer will often only gain you a day or two at the most.

Note also that the extension does not apply to the very big businesses, which pay under the Payments on Account Scheme.

Internet electronic VAT Return service

To use this service, you need an electronic signature. The *Chambersign* version is being redesigned at the time of writing. Try www.chambersign.com. *Equifax* costs £25 and you can register online at www.equifaxsecure.co.uk. The system may have efficiency advantages if the electronic signature can be used for other purposes too. However, the efficiency is questionable. The VAT return is a simple document, quick to fill in by hand, once one has the figures. Depending on precisely how the electronic form works, it may even be easier to make mistakes in transferring the numbers from your accounting system onto it.

Evidence of electronic payment

Think about this one; with physical posting, you can get a certificate or make a file note as pointed out below. With electronic payment, you have no such record. Often a bank's system does not allow you to print a note of the instruction and it is questionable whether any file note, even dated and signed, will have the same credibility for an electronic entry as it would for a physical posting of a letter. The only way you could create a record would be to go back online the following day and print a copy of the statement. However, this would merely duplicate that eventually received through the post. Whilst that would establish when the money was sent, it would be no help if, for some reason, the paying bank's computer system failed to implement an instruction. In any case, how many people, who key in BACS payment instructions online, go back online the following day to confirm that they have all been put through?

What if the return is late?

If your return is late, the default surcharge system applies. See Chapter 38, *Assessments and VAT Penalties*. The default surcharge is a draconian penalty to be avoided at all costs.

You get out of the surcharge if you can show a reasonable excuse for late payment. It is a reasonable excuse to have posted the cheque at a time at which you were entitled to expect its delivery on time. If you can show that you posted the cheque first-class the day before the due date, it must be reasonable to point to the current first-class delivery percentage. Supposing this is around 90%, it must be reasonable to suppose delivery on time is probable and this has been accepted by VAT Tribunals in the past.

What if Customs delay a repayment?

If Customs are slow to repay you, you may be entitled to a *Repayment Supplement*. To qualify for this, your return must be on time and accurate to within £250 or, if higher, 5% of your repayment claim. If Customs then fail to repay you:

- within thirty days of the date on which they receive it;

- or, if later, within thirty days of that on which it was due;

- as extended by any time taken by you to answer reasonable inquiries, which Customs may make or in bringing your past returns up-to-date or by Customs in correcting any errors in the return,

you are entitled to a repayment supplement of 5%, with a minimum of £50 (*Section 79 & VAT Regulations, Regs 198/199*). The supplement is free of income or corporation tax.

Do I get interest too?

No. In the *Leisure Two Partnership (LON/99/373 No 16876)*, Customs refused to repay a claim, which they subsequently accepted was correct. The Tribunal rejected their argument that, having denied the claim, they had dealt with the return so that, when their mistake was recognised, only interest was due. However, interest was not payable as well as the repayment supplement. See Chapter 38, *Assessments and VAT Penalties* for the rules on interest payable by Customs under *s 79*.

In the *Leisure Two Partnership* case, the repayment supplement was higher than the interest. This will usually be so but not necessarily. If the argument about a repayment claim went to a tribunal hearing, the delay could easily exceed a year, in which case the interest rate of 5% or more would mean that the gross sum would be higher than a repayment supplement. However, income or corporation tax is payable on interest received from Customs but not on a repayment supplement so the latter might still be a better deal.

Why might a repayment be due?

The most likely reason for receiving regular repayments is that you sell zero-rated goods or services. Because they're taxable, you can reclaim all the associated input tax. If you have few standard-rated outputs, the input tax you reclaim may be more than the output tax you owe.

A trader who normally makes payments may have an exceptional repayment if he incurs a large amount of input tax on, say, a standard-rated building or a large machine. If this happens to you, write to your local VAT office (LVO) warning them and explaining why there will be a repayment as soon as you are aware of the situation. Later, when you send the return itself to Customs at Southend, copy it with a letter referring to your earlier one to the LVO. If the Southend computer rejects your return for further enquiry because of the exceptional repayment, the LVO will probably deal with it quicker if they have already had an explanation.

Do *not* attach letters to your returns to Southend. They give the computer there indigestion.

Some traders also occasionally receive repayments because their businesses are seasonal. Thus, an ice cream vendor at the seaside will have most of his sales in the summer with perhaps not enough to cover his expenses subject to VAT during the winter. A fireworks manufacturer will have large sales each autumn out of all proportion to those during the rest of the year. Either might receive a repayment in the quarter with the lowest sales.

Who signs your return?

Look what it says above the signature. Whoever signs declares 'that the information given above is true and complete'. That means that only the owner or, in a large business, someone senior should sign because only such a person has the overview of the business needed for such a declaration.

This is particularly important because one routinely hears from the delegates who come to VAT seminars, that, having just joined their company, they have been told to take over the VAT return! No one wants that job so the latest arrival gets it — the person who knows least about the company's affairs!

Sometimes junior staff are being asked to sign the return as well. Now that suggests a wanton disregard for the accuracy of the return on the part of the person in charge of finance.

Of course, the routine compilation of the figures is not a senior responsibility. However, signing for them is!

Submitting your VAT return

It is all too easy to make mistakes when filling in a return, such as transposing the figures for input tax and output tax so that the sum in the Net Tax box becomes a repayment instead of a payment. This may sound unbelievably careless or silly but it does happen because we all make careless mistakes from time to time. The trick, of course, is to spot them before they do any harm.

If you underpay the VAT due as a result of such a mistake, you will be charged interest and may also be liable for a penalty. So, if you have sole responsibility for the return, reward yourself for its completion with a few moments relaxation with, say, a cup of coffee. Then, take another look at it. In a larger business, get someone else to do this.

Commonsense precautions include checking:

* figures correctly taken from backup schedules?

* figures in correct boxes?

* arithmetic correct?

* tax due or repayable makes sense? How does it compare with the last return or with the same period for last year?

* return signed and dated?

* retail scheme box entered if applicable?

* copy of return kept for VAT returns file?

* payment instruction correct?

If payment is by cheque,

* do the words and figures agree?

and is it

* for the right amount?

* not postdated?

* with correct signatures?

* drawn on the correct account?

* in the envelope?

All the above points are mistakes which other people have made!

Get a certificate of posting for postal delivery

If you leave posting your VAT return until the last moment – as I do — get a certificate of posting from the Post Office or have the person, who puts it into the post box — not merely your out mail tray — sign and date a written note of the location of the post box and the time of day. That should be good enough, if the return is delayed, as evidence of when you posted it.

Back-up schedules

Your return should be supported by proper back-up schedules, which show:

- The source of all the figures, such as purchase day book, cash book, petty cash book or salaries summary sheet. If the figures are taken from the VAT account in the nominal ledger, have you checked that all the routine postings have been made?

- Journal entries required, such as for scale charge on private petrol, VAT included in deductions from salaries or recovery of tax on expense claims.

- Any special checks or information routinely required.

Examples of the latter are:

- Any income or payments by standing order picked up from bank statements.

- Agents' statements of sales made, rents collected etc, which may include VAT.

- Hire-purchase agreements entered into, which may be for sums including VAT.

- Royalties statements, which can include both output VAT on income and input VAT on any commissions

Use typed schedules in standard format — set them up in your computer even if you fill them in by hand — so that any missing figures are highlighted.

Spotting the cockups

If you or your staff mess up the recording of VAT on a transaction for a significant sum, what is the chance of you spotting the mistake before the return is sent in?

Plastic Developments Ltd (MAN/00/914 No 17416) incurred VAT on imported goods, which it paid to its handling agents. The invoice from the agents asking for the VAT of £6,345 was not of course the document required to recover that sum as import VAT. The document needed for that was form C 79, which arrived in due course. Meanwhile, the bookkeeper had recorded the total payment to the agents as carriage and packaging. The VAT was therefore treated as a cost, not recoverable tax. Presumably, the C 79 was simply filed, it not occurring to anyone to check the import VAT recovery.

The mistake was only discovered after the three-year time limit, explained below, had elapsed. The Tribunal confirmed Customs' refusal of the repayment claim.

The first line of defence against such mistakes is for the person who signs the return to review the figures to see whether they make sense in the light of what has gone on during the period.

Of course, whether the omission of a sum of either input tax or output tax was obvious would depend on its amount in relation to the size of the business. However, do you ever compare the figures on your return with those for previous periods?

I suggest that a graph or a bar chart, prepared on your word processor, would be more effective than simply recording the figures on a sheet of paper. You need to compare the output tax and input tax figures not just the net payment or repayment. A graph or a chart will show their relationship more effectively and highlight any changes from the norm which need investigation.

The three-year cap

As explained in Chapter 38, *Assessments and VAT Penalties*, Customs can only assess to correct errors retrospectively for three years. Similarly, *s 80(4)* says you can only claim back for three years' VAT, which you have overpaid. That means that, as soon as you are aware of an overpayment, you should submit a claim to Customs for the past three years in order to stop time running against you. It is not enough merely to argue with Customs or even to lodge an appeal to the VAT Tribunal.

If your claim is then held up because of a case in the High Court, update it every 12 months.

What if I discover errors either way made over three years ago?

The three-year cap explained above works both ways. Although you cannot correct an overpayment made more than three years ago, you do not have to tell Customs of any underpayments over three years ago either. Thus, if a mistake continues for several years, the three-year cap limits the payment or repayment.

Note: The three-year limit for an assessment by Customs runs from the end of the VAT period in which the error occurred (*s 77(1)*). In contrast, the right to repayment of overpaid VAT under *s 80(4)* runs from the date on which the payment was made. To avoid complicating the review of claims, Customs accept that this means the date by which the return was due, even if the payment was earlier. Under *Reg 29* the same applies if there was no payment because the error was in understating a repayment claim.

However, if correcting an overpayment turns a payment return into a repayment one, the payment date time limit applies only to the sum overpaid. *Reg 35* makes the time limit for the balance, ie the repayment now due, the end of the VAT period. What a complication!

A reader contacted me about a client whose affairs he had had to bring up to date with accounts covering four years! The client's returns had understated the VAT due in the earliest year but had overstated it in the following three. Bad luck Customs; only the overpayments had to be corrected!

Warning — do not abuse the three-year time limit by not disclosing an error, once found, in the hope that Customs will not discover it in time. To do so converts an innocent error into a dishonest one and raises the time limit to 20 years, as explained in Chapter 38, *Assessments and VAT Penalties* under *Time limits and the three-year cap*.

Do you have a permanent VAT file?

Supporting notes on a permanent file should make it possible for anyone to understand the entries required and where the information comes from. Many an error has resulted from someone having to take over the VAT return because key staff are on holiday, are sick, have left etc. If the previous schedules are hand-written, probably with little or no explanation, mistakes are likely.

VAT groups

The representative member of a VAT group should receive at least some supporting information with the internal returns for each member company. Whether it should receive full schedules is a policy decision but, unless some details are obtained, the person signing the return has no way of assessing whether the figures are likely to be right. See Chapter 4 re VAT grouping.

The Payments on Account Scheme

The *Payments on Account Scheme* is a means of collecting VAT earlier from the very largest businesses.

If the VAT payable by a company or a VAT group, exceeds £2 million a year, it is required to make monthly payments of estimated amounts. It then prepares the return for each quarter in the usual way, deducts the two payments on account already made and pays or reclaims the balance.

The law is in regs. 44–48, *VAT Regulations (SI 1995/2518)*, made under the *Payments on Account Order (SI 1993/2001)*, as amended, which was itself made under *s 28*.

Customs notify you of the monthly payments on account, which they calculate by dividing the annual liability during the previous reference year by 24. The sums can be altered if your annual liability varies by more than 20%.

Both the estimated and the quarterly balancing amounts have to be paid by the last working day of the month in which they are due and no extension for electronic payment is allowed. See Notice 700/60 *Payments on account*.

Some questions to check your understanding. Review your answers with the text.

- Sometimes recoverable VAT exceeds that which you owe, resulting in a repayment claim. Some traders receive repayments regularly. Others do so occasionally. Can you remember two reasons for occasional repayment?

- Can you choose to have return dates which coincide with your financial year?

- When is the return due with Customs?

- What are some of the checks which it is sensible to make before sending the return?

6.   So What Must I Charge VAT on?

In Chapter 1, *How VAT Works*, I explained that VAT is chargeable on most sales at the standard rate but that some are reduced rated, some are zero-rated, some are exempt and some are outside the scope of VAT. Reduced rating, zero-rating and exemption are explained in more detail in their respective chapters and international 'outside the scope' sales in that on Exports of Services.

Here I discuss when VAT is due on sundry other transactions, which are not 'sales' in the sense of what the business earns its living from. The chapter covers:

- Why you usually owe output tax on sundry receipts — and some exceptions.
- Cases where you have multiple supplies at different rates of tax.
- Those where there is a single compound supply and the dominant supply decides the rate.

Money in means VAT payable

As stated in the introductory chapter *How VAT Works,* VAT is due on:

- taxable supplies,
- made by a taxable person in the course or furtherance of any business.

Once someone is in business, anything they do is likely to be either:

- in the course of that business; or
- in the course of an activity amounting to another business, which is covered by the same VAT registration.

So, if you charge someone money for doing something, you have to add VAT, unless the supply happens to be zero-rated, exempt or outside the scope. Of course, once your accounting system is set up to account for VAT, charging it on your invoices or, if you are a retailer, on your takings, is relatively simple.

However, a business of any size may have various sources of cash coming in for which a sales ledger invoice has not been issued and which are therefore treated as cash book receipts. Such income often gets omitted from VAT returns. Sometimes this is because it never occurs to people that VAT might be due.

If in doubt, try the 'what if?' question

People tend to look for excuses why VAT is not due on money in. For instance, they see canteen sales as being part of being 'staff welfare' and assume that in some way makes them outside the scope of VAT. The 'what if' routine is a useful defence mechanism against incorrect assumptions. 'What if' canteen takings were indeed outside the scope of VAT? It would create a distortion of competition between the canteen and the café in the street. The canteen is probably already subsidised; if it did not pay VAT on the prices charged, that would distort the position further. Often, stopping to ask 'what if?' suggests that one's first reason or excuse for not accounting for VAT is unlikely to be correct.

If you receive money for something, output tax is usually due. If you start from the principle that tax is payable unless you can find a good reason why not, you will be less likely to delude yourself because of the particular circumstances.

Sales ledger receipts

Obviously, VAT is not normally due when payment is received against a sales ledger balance. VAT was accounted for in the period in which the tax invoice was issued. There are two exceptions:

- If bad debt relief has already been claimed, VAT is due on any sum subsequently received from the customer. See *Bad Debt Relief*, Chapter 16.

- If you are a small business, using the *Cash Accounting Scheme*; see Chapter 33.

Money on which VAT is not due

There are a few special cases which are outside the scope of VAT.

A *dividend* is outside the scope because it is not payment for any supply by the shareholder. It is merely a share of the profit earned by the company.

A *Government grant*, such as a payment towards the cost of building a factory in a high unemployment area, is outside the scope, if nothing is done in return for it.

However, the definition of the consideration for a supply under *Art 11A(1)(a) EC 6th VAT Directive* includes a subsidy. The latter can be a part of the value of the supply if:

- the price of the goods or service is fixed at the time of the event triggering the subsidy;

- the right to receive it depends on the recipient making a supply to a third party.

In *Keeping Newcastle Warm C-353/00 ([2002] STC 943)* the CJEC held that payments of £10 by the *Energy Action Grants Agency* to an organisation, which advised householders how to improve energy efficiency, were part of the consideration received by that organisation for the work it did for the householders.

That case illustrates the difference between a global subsidy to cover general operating costs and one paid to facilitate a specific service to a third party. Public subsidies are granted to further the public interest rather than to procure goods or services for the State so any supply must be to a third party.

Compensation is usually outside the scope of VAT being compensation for a loss suffered by the recipient, not payment for a supply by that person.

Examples are:

- Your offices are damaged by fire. The money received under your insurance policy is compensation paid towards your loss in putting right the damage. The insurer pays your costs net of VAT unless that VAT is not reclaimable by you because your business is partly exempt.

- Another business infringes your copyright. A sum received in settlement of your claim for damages is not payment for any supply made by you.

Do not assume that compensation for the termination of a contract is outside the scope of VAT. Although Customs have often accepted that it is, I have long thought there was a pitfall here and *Themis FTSE Fledgling Index Trust plc (LON/2000/501 No 17039)* has now highlighted the problem. Customs argued that compensation for the right to terminate a contract early was a taxable supply of services. They lost the case because this particular contract had been repudiated first. Once the other party had accepted this, the only right surrendered by that party in return for the compensation was the right to pursue a claim in the courts. This was not a variation of the contract or a surrender of rights under it.

Although this decision does not fully clarify the position, it seems likely that, if instead of one side simply repudiating a contract, the two parties negotiated terms upon which it could be terminated, Customs would argue that there was a standard-rated surrender of rights. I believe that a Tribunal would agree.

Goods on which input tax was not recovered, such as a second-hand car are exempt when sold (*Sch 9 Group 14*).

Charges to staff for the use of cars are outside the scope of VAT assuming that input tax was not recovered on the purchase price of the car.

Fees received by a business for the services of a partner or owner

Partnerships often require that fees received by their partners for outside appointments are paid into the business. Customs are likely to argue that such fees are payment for a standard rated supply of the services of the individual if the appointment results from and involves the use of the professional expertise exercised in the business. This is inconvenient if the body in question cannot recover that VAT. See leaflet 700/34 *Staff* for Customs' views.

However, in *Birketts (LON/1999/1007 No 17515)*, a tribunal held that fees from non-executive directorships of Health Service Trusts, held by partners in a firm of solicitors, were not subject to VAT because the individuals had been appointed on the grounds of their personal merit, occupational skills and standing in the community as distinct from professional expertise. Therefore, they had not been accepted in the course or furtherance of their profession as solicitors. In contrast, a directorship of a Building Society *was* so held because the partner was expected to provide the experience of a property solicitor and to keep the Board up-to-date on conveyancing practice. Since the fees from the Building Society were paid into the partnership as compensation for the time spent on the appointment and were treated as income of the practice, they were received in the course or furtherance of the partnership business.

For a partnership, the way round this problem is to allow the individual partner to receive the income personally. That is not of course possible for a sole trader, since business income remains business even if paid into a private account.

Companies whose directors hold other directorships

If fees to a director of company *A* are paid to company *B*, rather than received by the director personally, Notice 700/34 *Staff* says that they are payment for a supply, except where *B* has a legal or contractual right to appoint the director — as to a subsidiary or a company in which it holds an investment. See also under *Management charges* in Chapter 23, *Partial Exemption*.

Part-time judicial appointments

The *Birketts* decision, mentioned above, also notes that Customs accept that part-time judicial appointments, such as a chairman of the Insolvency Practitioners Tribunal, a member of a VAT and Duties Tribunal or as a Clerk to the General Commissioners of Income Tax, are outside the scope of VAT.

Examples of sundry income

Cases where a tax invoice may not have been issued are sales:

- to staff, such as of surplus or substandard goods;

- of scrap;

- in the canteen or from vending machines;

- of assets, such as machinery or commercial vehicles;

- of management services.

Transfers in your accounting records, called in accounting jargon 'journal entries', are especially dangerous because they are outside the main VAT accounting system. It is all too easy for the person making the journal entry to ignore the VAT.

Management charges to associated businesses are often made provisionally in draft accounts. Whilst the mere inclusion of a figure in draft accounts does not create a tax point, the formal approval of the accounts by the directors does, because the sum then becomes a debt due to the maker of the charge.

Moreover, if any sums have already been received on account, either in cash or by offset against amounts owing to the associated business, tax points for those amounts may have been created earlier.

Costs recharged are standard-rated

You must standard-rate charges made to recover your costs. You do not resell your own expenses. They are part of the price of what you sell.

Thus, if a consultant charges a client for the cost of a rail ticket, it is standard-rated. The zero-rated rail travel is supplied by the rail company to the consultant. The latter in turn sells consultancy services, not rail travel. The re-charge is merely justifying a part of the fees for consultancy in relation to the cost which the consultant has incurred.

Salaries re-charged are standard-rated

Similarly, salaries recharged by an employer to another UK business are standard-rated as a supply of the services of the employee to the other business. This is so even if there is no profit element. If the other business is outside the UK, the supply is probably outside the scope under the place of supply rules. See Chapter 22, *Exports and Imports of Services* re para 6 Sch 5.

The exception is where the salary is being collected from the business with which the employee has a contract of employment. This only happens when a business administers the payroll of another, and reclaims from the other the salaries which it has paid out on its behalf.

If the secondee organisation cannot recover VAT, consider the concession in Notice 700\34\94 *Supplies of staff*. Customs say: *If the recipient of the staff pays their salary to them direct or meets the employer's obligation to make payments to third parties (eg PAYE, National Insurance or pension contributions), you need not account for VAT on these amounts. However, you must still account for VAT on any payments that the recipient makes direct to you. These rules apply whether you supply full-time or part-time staff.*

That fits in with *Central Council of Physical Recreation (LON/00/1354 No 17803)*. The Tribunal held that there was no supply of staff when *CCPR*, in its capacity as trustee of the *British Sports Trust* and out of funds held for the latter, paid for the salaries of people whose contracts of employment were with *CCPR*.

Service charges for property

Service charges made under a property lease are another example of the theme that costs change their nature when recharged. The service charge is just rent under a different name because it is an additional sum due under the lease. Its status is therefore the same as the rent and is exempt unless, under a waiver of exemption, the rent is standard-rated.

Disbursements

A disbursement for VAT purposes is a sum of money which you pay out on behalf of someone else for a supply which they receive, not you. A disbursement is outside the scope of VAT. However, what a solicitor calls a 'disbursement' is often no such thing for VAT purposes.

In Notice 700 (April 2002) *The VAT Guide*, para 25 Customs say that, to qualify as a disbursement for VAT, a payment must meet *all* the following conditions. It must be:

(a)   for goods or services received and used by the client, not by you and which are clearly additional to those supplied by you;

(b)   shown separately on your invoice as the exact sum paid out;

(c)   paid as the agent of your customer;

(d)   a sum for which your customer was responsible for paying the third party;

(e)   authorised by the customer to be paid on his or her behalf;

(f)   for a supply which your customer knew would be provided by a third party.

The above is a simplified version of muddled guidance! The key criteria are (a) and (b). Conditions (c) and (f) are automatic if (d) and (e) are met. The danger is that the agent may have no evidence of any such responsibility or authorisation.

For instance, MOT test fees paid to a test centre by a car repair workshop are a frequent pitfall. The outside the scope status of the fee can be maintained if the sum paid out is shown separately on the workshop invoice. Any further sum charged is accepted by Customs as a standard rated fee for arranging the test. However, the test centre probably has no relationship with the customer and the paperwork of small businesses is not usually designed with the care needed to establish points (d) and (e).

All too often the workshop receives a discount from the test centre but charges the full fee without VAT on its invoice. Customs then say that the payment to the test centre was not a disbursement and have won various tribunal cases on the point.

Another pitfall is the difference between a fee paid by a solicitor for a personal search of, say, the Land Registry and a fee for a postal search. Customs see the former as a supply of access used by the solicitor in order to provide advice to the client; in contrast, they say a document by post is obtained on behalf of the client and normally used by the latter for his or her own purposes, such as to obtain a loan. What a subtle complication!

If you recharge something as a disbursement:

- no VAT can be recovered on the item by you;

- no VAT invoice can be issued by you in respect of it;

- your client, if registered, can only recover VAT on the disbursement if you pass on the original invoice which must be in the client's name.

A disbursement should be shown as a separate entry on a VAT invoice. For clarity, it is best to sub-total the sum subject to VAT, add the VAT and then add the disbursement.

Example

	£
Fees for advice	1,000.00
VAT @ 17.5%	175.00
Disbursement paid out on client's behalf	100.00
Invoice total	£ 1,275.00

Treating an item as a disbursement only conveys a VAT advantage if the client is unregistered and there was no VAT on the expense in the first place. Stamp duty is an example.

It makes no difference if the cost is standard rated — say hotel accommodation. Since the agent cannot recover the VAT on the expense, because it was a supply to the client, the agent must recharge it to the client gross. Thus, if the VAT rate is 17.5%, the cost to an unregistered client is still the gross, £117.50, not £100.

Postage charged by mailing houses

When a mailing house bulk mails brochures, Customs only accept that the postage is an outside the scope disbursement on behalf of the client if the exact sum is charged. This means that, if the mailing house receives a bulk mail discount, it must pass that on to the client, if necessary by apportioning between clients any overall rebate.

In Notice 700/24 (April 2003) *Postage and Delivery Charges,* Customs also require that:

- the client receives the postal services — which of course occurs when its material is posted on its behalf and is responsible for paying;

- the mailing house is authorised to act as the agent of the client in making that payment;

- the postage disbursed is shown separately on the mailing house's invoice;

- the client either produces the mailing list or is given access to it prior to dispatch;

- the mailing house's responsibility for the mail ceases on acceptance by Royal Mail.

What if the tax invoice is in the agent's name?

If an agent incurs an expense on behalf of a principal, but the invoice is addressed to the agent, not to the principal, Customs do not object to the agent recovering the input tax provided that he in turn issues a tax invoice to his principal and accounts for the corresponding output tax. This has the same effect as if the item had been treated as a disbursement but ensures that a principal, who is registered for VAT, receives a tax invoice in his name, which supports the recovery of tax.

Giving goods away can cost you VAT

If you give goods away, which cost you more than £50, whether bought in or produced in-house, you owe output tax on that cost. In practice, Customs usually accept that you can disallow the input tax when you buy the goods, which may be more convenient than having to pay output tax when you give each one away.

Thus, gifts of goods are caught if:

- the cost of the gift to you exceeds £50 net of VAT; or

if you make more than one gift to the same person:

- *Up to 30/9/2003*, VAT was due on the cost of each gift, regardless of the value.

- *From 1/10/2003*, VAT is only due if the cost of that gift, plus those in the previous year, exceeds £50. Thus, if the total cost of your gifts to someone within any twelve-month period goes over £50, you account for VAT on that cost. A new twelve-month period then starts with the value at nil (*Sch 4 para 5*).

However, there is a relief for samples provided that, if more than one is given to the same person, they differ in a 'material respect'. The rule covers CDs sent out by a music company to retailers. Although they may be similar in physical appearance, the key factor is the music. If this is different, they differ materially.

Note that the £50 limit only applies to business gifts. If you cannot justify the gift as being for business purposes, it is taxable whatever its cost.

Examples:

- a desk diary embossed with your company logo, cost £25, is not caught;
- but a leather bound version costing £60 is — regardless that it advertises your business.

Many people find it difficult to believe the impact of the gifts rules until it is spelt out for them. Even then, they often do not at first believe that they affect such routine commercial transactions as:

- long-service awards;
- Christmas gifts;
- display equipment given by a manufacturer to a retailer;
- prizes or incentive awards for salesmen;
- equipment given by a manufacturer to a local school or university.

This is a draconian rule, which is intended to prevent avoidance. Without it, an employer might be able to buy in goods selected by staff and give them to the latter free of VAT. The price of preventing such artificial schemes is that the rule catches numerous ordinary commercial situations. However, with careful aforethought, one can sometimes avoid the rule in such cases.

Don't give it, lend it!

Display equipment given to a retailer by a manufacturer is caught by the gifts rule. You may think it absurd that a manufacturer must account for output tax on a merchandiser, such as a unit designed to display cosmetics or confectionery on the retailer's counter. The provision of such units to customers is fundamental to the business of many manufacturers and there is no element of VAT avoidance in doing this. However, Customs have said they would assess for output tax in such cases under the gifts rule.

It is common practice to avoid this pitfall by sticking a label on the back of the units stating that they are the property of the manufacturer and must be returned upon request. In this way, ownership has been retained so the item is not a gift. As explained below, there is a rule which catches the loan of a business asset for a non-business purpose. However, this is unlikely to apply in such a situation because the manufacturer could argue that the unit was lent for the purposes of its business — furthering sales of the products displayed.

Could you sell it rather than give it?

Businesses often give used equipment away to local institutions, such as schools. Such transactions are also caught under the gifts rule, although VAT will be due on the current value of the item, not on the original cost.

The most common example must be of computer equipment. In the case of an individual machine, the current market value may well be so low that the output tax is trivial. However, it would be more material if a number of machines were being given. The tax could be significant if a manufacturer gave away a piece of sophisticated production equipment. Suppose you are having to re-equip in order to remain competitive. The old machine, though no longer state-of-the-art, may be fine for training students in modern production techniques and thus very useful to the engineering department of a local college or university, which produces potential recruits for your factory. Suppose the machine originally cost £100,000 four years ago and could now be sold for £20,000; your willingness to give it away — partly out of self-interest and partly because of the benefit to the local community — will cost you £3,500 output VAT.

To avoid this pitfall:

- You could donate, say, £117.50 or £1,175 to the local institution; and
- the institution could buy the equipment for £100 or £1,000 plus VAT.

Yes, the price is artificial and, yes, there is an artificial prices rule, which I explain in Chapter 8 on *The Value of Supply Rules*. However, it only catches transactions between 'connected persons' and the local institution and the manufacturer will not be so related. However, selling the item for £1 would be asking for trouble. If you wave such a red rag at your local VAT officer, he or she is likely to argue the matter, which will give you aggravation even if you win. Give Customs a little output tax on a more substantial sum and the officer may well decide not to challenge the transaction.

Beware of 'entirely free gifts'

Beware of gifts which are not gifts. 'Entirely free gifts' are usually no such thing because something has to be done in order to get them. That means that there is 'non-monetary consideration' received in return. See Chapter 8 on *The Value of Supply Rules* for how that can increase the output tax due and sometimes makes it due on low value goods, despite the transaction not being caught under the gifts rules explained earlier.

Free supplies of your own services

The gifts rules apply only to gifts of goods. There is no VAT due if you provide your own services free. Thus, no output tax is due on the services provided free of charge when:

- an accountant prepares accounts for a local charity;
- a plumber installs a bathroom for his brother — but, if the plumber takes goods, such as piping, from stock on which he has recovered input tax, the gifts rules apply to those goods;
- a lawyer does work for a potential client at no charge.

In such situations, remember that there must be nothing done in return. If there is any non-monetary consideration in the form of services or goods received in exchange, VAT is due on the market value of the supply, as explained in Chapter 8, *The Value of Supply Rules*.

A loan of goods is a supply of services

If you lend a business asset for a non-business purpose, that is a supply of services, which is taxed on the cost of making the item available. (*Sch 4 para 5(4) and Sch 6 para 6 (7)(b)*).

Suppose your business owns a yacht for business reasons; perhaps you build yachts, you make equipment for yachts or you charter them out. However, when the yacht is not in use for business purposes, your family use it. The business is liable for output tax on the cost of making the yacht available.

The rule applies primarily to such assets as yachts and aeroplanes although, in theory, it catches such minor cases as the loan of a digger by a builder to his brother for the weekend.

Output tax is due on the basis of the total cost of running the yacht, including depreciation, divided by the number of days during the year on which it is in use. The High Court has rejected an argument that the cost was based on a 365-day year because, of course, if that were the right calculation, anyone owning their own business could reduce considerably the expense of owning something like a yacht by putting it through the business and only paying VAT for the days on which they used it.

Services bought in are taxed if put to private use

If you buy in a service for business purposes, which you then put partly to private use, you are liable for output tax under the *Supply of Services Order (SI 1993/1507) as amended.* The value for this purpose is that part of the value of the supply to you which *fairly and reasonably represents the cost to (you) of providing the services.*

Most cases caught are likely to be of non-business use of a part of a service. If none of it is used for business, there will often be no right to recover input tax on it in the first place.

In *Telecential Communications Ltd (LON/97/321 No 15361)*, the telephone and cable TV services it sold were held not to be provided for business purposes when supplied free to staff.

Obviously, there are only a limited number of cases in which a service bought in, as opposed to created from the business' own resources, is of interest to staff. In such a situation, you may be able to avoid the pitfall if you can justify the provision to others without charge on business grounds, such as requiring quality control reports.

Legal and tax advice may be a more common problem than Telecential-type situations. As explained in Chapter 13, *What Can I Recover Input Tax on?*, it is usually very difficult to justify the reclaiming of input tax on legal expenses incurred in defending the owners or senior management of a business. However, supposing that defending an employee can be justified for business reasons, as in the *P & O* case explained in that chapter, Customs might be able to demand output tax on the grounds that, despite the business justification for input tax recovery, there must be some non-business use for the private purposes of the person concerned.

The same applies if advice on tax and/or completion of the tax return for an employee is included in a tax adviser's invoice.

> ### Example from my own experience
>
> When the rule came in, Customs quoted the example of someone who enlarges their house to provide an office, something which I had just done — and told them of! In my case, what I spent enlarging my office will certainly have been justified by 12–15 years business use when I retire but the value of the building work will not have depreciated; indeed, it may have enhanced that of the house. However, I think the subsequent value of the work to a private owner is not the same as a fair and reasonable cost to the business, if the latter has used it for business over an extended period.
>
> Suppose a company pays for an extension to its owner's house but has to leave three years later because of the expansion of its business. What will be the cost to the company? Given only three years business use, there will be a written down value of the expenditure in the balance sheet.
> Arguably, there is no cost of provision of the services for private use at that stage. The extension, which represents those services, is merely having to be abandoned, its value *to the company* having been reduced to nil. However, Customs are likely to argue that the 'full cost of providing the service' is at least that reduction — the sum written off from the balance sheet.

From 10/4/03, the law was extended to catch supplies after that date of major interests in land, of buildings, of civil engineering works or of goods incorporated in either a building or a civil engineering work.

- Firstly, if, at the date of purchase, there will be an element of private or non-business use, an apportionment must be made. This amendment stops you gaining a major cash flow advantage by claiming the input tax and then accounting for output tax on ongoing supplies of the private use element.

- Secondly, if, subsequent to purchase, the use changes from fully business to partly private or non-business, that creates a supply as described above. See Chapter 13, *What Can I Recover Input Tax on?* for various cases on the apportionment of work on living accommodation used partly for business.

The CJEC judgment in a German case, *W Seeling C-269/00: [2003] STC 805),* infers that the above legislation is invalid. It repeats the principle, held in *Lennartz,* that all the input tax on goods, which are used at least in part for business purposes, is recoverable if the trader then pays output tax period by period on the value of the private use. See Chapter 13, *What Can I Recover Input Tax on?* under *Input tax on expenditure partly for private purposes.* In *Seeling,* the German government complained that the output tax thus accounted for could be far less than the input tax recovered. The CJEC said that was merely the consequence of a deliberate choice by the Community legislature.

Mobile telephones

If you allow staff to claim for calls on their mobile telephones, some of which are private, you may have to account for output tax on the latter. See Chapter 13, *What Can I Recover Input Tax on?*

Some questions to check your understanding. Review your answers with the text.

- Is compensation subject to VAT?

- Give five examples of sundry income which is subject to VAT.

- Must VAT be added if you re-charge the salary of a member of your staff, at cost, to another business?

- What is the difference between charging your expenses to a client and charging something as a disbursement?

- To what transactions do the gifts rules apply?

- When is one 'caught' for output tax on a free supply of services?

7. The Time of Supply Rules — When You Must Pay

Everyone needs to read this chapter because the time of supply or tax point rules are a fundamental part of the VAT system. They fix the VAT return on which you must account for output tax and on which you are entitled to recover input tax.

The tax point rules are not difficult but they do need to be understood properly. If you get your tax point wrong, it will not affect the total VAT you eventually pay or recover but it will cost you interest payable to Customs and, possibly, a penalty if you recover too early or pay late. Of course, if you make a mistake the other way round by, for instance, claiming input tax late, you have a cash flow disadvantage.

The law is in *Section 6*, and for continuous supplies of services, in *VAT Regulations (SI 1995/2518), Regs 90, 90A and 90B*.

The key rules

The tax point, or time of supply, is the earliest of the following dates:

- the issue of a tax invoice (to the extent of the sum invoiced); or

- a payment is received (tax value is the sum received, which is treated as including VAT); or

- the goods are supplied or the services performed (tax value is the full price of the supply).

The issue of a tax invoice creates a tax point

Issuing a tax invoice in advance of making a supply creates a liability to pay the output tax shown on it regardless of whether you are ever paid by the customer or, indeed, whether you ever supply any goods or services. The reason is that the customer can reclaim the input tax shown on the invoice.

Having issued a tax invoice, you may be able to reduce the value of it with a credit note. However, you must account for output tax in the VAT period in which you issued it. You can't just ignore it, even if the customer has returned it to you.

Bad debt relief will in due course become available if the customer doesn't pay you. See Chapters 15, *Watch Your Credit Notes* and 16, *Bad Debt Relief* for more details.

The supply of the goods or services creates a tax point

For goods, the tax point is usually created by physical delivery. However, that is not necessarily so. It can be varied by the terms of the contract.

Suppose a customer wants, say, 1,000 units of a product and the supplier needs to produce the order in a single production run and has no room to store the goods. The supplier might agree with the customer that the latter will take delivery but that ownership of the goods will only pass once they are used by the customer or according to an agreed schedule. The date ownership passes will be the tax point, not that of delivery. (*VAT Regulations (SI 1995/2518), Reg 88(1)*).

An example might be new signs for a chain of retail shops, to be installed over a period of several months. An alternative situation would be a customer wanting, say, 10,000 components for his own product, which he expects to produce at the rate of 2,000 per month. However, the supplier again needs to produce them in a single run in order to keep the price down. They agree that the customer will pay for them but that they shall remain in the supplier's warehouse until the customer calls them off. This time the tax point occurs when ownership passes upon payment, even though physical possession remains with the supplier and delivery will be over an extended period.

Services being intangible, the tax point is usually when the invoice is issued because this is done either under the terms of a prior agreement or because the customer or client agrees that the supply has been completed. However, see the comment on *Continuous supplies of services* below.

If you've had the money, you owe some VAT

Money received in advance of doing the work creates a tax point. Some businesses routinely take deposits from customers. Examples include double glazing or fitted kitchen suppliers and holiday accommodation.

Even if such a deposit is returnable, it creates a tax point when it is received because it is always intended that it shall be offset against the price of the transaction in due course. Examples are:

- A double glazing company must account for output tax on the value of a deposit received in the VAT return covering that period even though it may not supply the goods for some months.

- A seaside landlady may have to register in January because of deposits received for holidays to be taken during the summer even though they are returnable.

The only circumstances in which a deposit does not create a tax point are where it is always intended that the full amount shall be returned to the customer. There are not many such cases but one example is the deposit for a hotel safe key. The hotel charges a rate per day for use of the hotel safe. The deposit taken in addition is returned when the key is handed back. Should the key be lost, the hotel retains the deposit as compensation for the loss incurred as a result of having to cut the safe open.

The exception for continuous services

For services which qualify as 'continuous', *Reg 90* says that performance does not create a tax point. The latter occurs only when:

- a tax invoice is issued; or

- payment is received.

So, if you issue a request for payment rather than a tax invoice, you do not owe any VAT until you are paid. Then, of course, you must issue a tax invoice.

That is a very useful cash flow planning point for anyone who supplies continuous services. Note that this only applies for services, not goods.

See the example of a request for payment on the next page; note that this does not show either a VAT number or the amount of VAT. Local VAT Officers sometimes accept that a request for payment may show the VAT number provided that it does not state the amount of VAT. Alternatively, the officer may allow it to show the amount of VAT provided that there is no VAT number.

I suggest that to show either may lead an inexperienced member of the customer's staff to reclaim VAT to which the customer is not entitled at that stage. Indeed, I have often seen documents, which look so like tax invoices that they might have been designed to encourage mistakes by the customer! So, take care with your layout.

A long job is not 'continuous'

A service is not 'continuous' merely because it is provided over a long period. There must be an ongoing relationship. Examples include:

- The services of professional accountants normally count as continuous because audit or tax advice is given throughout the year.

- Those of a lawyer or a consultant mostly do not because, by definition, he or she is usually engaged for a specific one-off task. It may take a very long time to complete the job — the author's longest running case went on for 8 years — but it is still a one-off instruction.

Of course, if a one-off job continues for a long time, there is no performance tax point until it is completed. Therefore, one can use a request for payment rather than a tax invoice to ask for money on account as one goes along. The practical difference is that, when the job is completed, one must invoice for all work done.

In contrast, a supplier of continuous services does not have to invoice up-to-date if it becomes apparent that the customer has ceased paying. For what it is worth, the supplier thus receives automatic bad debt relief straightaway rather than having to wait 6 months under the usual rules.

An example of poor cash flow planning

If you maintain equipment under annual contracts payable in advance and you do not understand the VAT rules you may miss an opportunity for cash flow planning. Worse still, you could create bad debts for VAT unnecessarily!

Take a provider of computer maintenance to small businesses. When the annual renewal date approaches, how does such a supplier know that the PCs in question are still in use? On several occasions, I have received VAT invoices for my equipment in, say, June for a renewal date at 31 October. Of course, the supplier does this in the hope of a quick payment since computer problems frighten most businesses. Relatively small invoices may well therefore be processed quickly in order to make sure that the customer has cover.

However, the supplier will probably only get the cheque in November. Meanwhile, if the supplier's VAT return ended at 30 June, the output VAT will have been paid by 31 July. Yet an invitation to renew the contract in the form of a request for payment would have done just as well!

Another example of creating a liability for VAT before you need to is issuing a tax invoice for standard rated rent, rather than a rent demand.

An Example of a Request for Payment

Knock-em-Out Accounting Associates
Taxation House
53 Old Road
London

Request for Payment

Mr and Mrs Client
Greasy Joes
2021 High Road
London

Date: 21 September 2003

Request Note No: 543

Professional services up to 30 September 2003
including VAT

£1,175.00

VAT is not recoverable against this document. We will send you a VAT invoice on
receipt of your payment

The law is in *VAT Regulations (SI 1995/2518), Regs 90, 90A, 90B*. Similar continuous supply rules apply to royalties, services of barristers and advocates and to the construction industry (*Regs 91–93*).

Pro forma invoices

Pro forma invoices are similar to requests for payment but are usually used for goods. For instance, a manufacturer who does not wish to give credit to a retailer, can issue a pro forma invoice listing the goods ordered, prices, values etc, the total of which the retailer must pay before the goods are delivered.

A pro forma invoice does not create a tax point. However it should be clearly marked as such and should state that it is not a tax invoice.

Watch your tax points!

Getting your tax points right requires more than just knowing the basic rules explained above. Ask yourself how the business you are dealing with works, consider when tax points occur as a result of work being done, invoices issued or money coming in and check the procedures for accounting for the tax generated.

Beware of exceptional transactions. Exceptional outputs can cause trouble by the very fact that they are exceptional and are thus not necessarily automatically picked up by the accounting system. This can affect inputs as well as outputs. Thus, there could be a risk of not recovering input tax through overlooking its existence.

Hire-purchase

Hire-purchase transactions can cause trouble. Is there a tax invoice or does the agreement serve as one? There is output tax to account for or input tax to recover when the agreement starts.

Do not make the mistake of assuming that a tax invoice will be issued to you when you pay the initial deposit or you sign the hire-purchase documents. This can occur several weeks before the transaction is processed by the finance company — which has first itself to obtain title to the goods from the supplier so that it can sell them on under the agreement. When you eventually get the tax invoice, it may therefore be dated in a VAT period subsequent to that in which the documents were signed or the deposit paid. If you have already recovered the VAT, you have screwed up!

Tax point problems for retailers

A retailer's takings are recorded weekly and the dates do not match the calendar quarters. Agreeing special return dates to match 12 or 13 weekly periods only sorts out the takings problem up to a point. How are the weekly takings arrived at? When are the retail tills cashed up? If this is at, say, 4 pm instead of at the close of business on the Saturday night, has this been agreed with Customs? Theoretically, output tax is due in that period for the money taken between cashing up and closing time. Customs have been known to raise the point and might demand that an estimate be made.

What about the purchases? Are they accounted for to the same dates? If the goods are imported from outside the EU, what about the import VAT records? They must be on the same basis, not in calendar months.

Money received without your knowledge

Is money received at locations outside your immediate control?

If so, your accounting routine needs to be adequate to pick up this income at the end of the VAT period.

Examples:

- Takings from vending machines and telephones at a shopping mall. The tax point is when the machines are emptied and the money banked, not when the cash is credited on the bank statement, perhaps after the end of the VAT period.

- Income, such as royalties or standard-rated rents, which is received by an agent on your behalf but not forwarded immediately. Perhaps the agent even retains some of it to fund expenditure. You need to ensure that you get prompt statements of account from the agent.

Income confirmed by bank statements

Are your bank statements received only monthly? If so, is the statement made up to a date shortly after the end of your VAT period, rather than just before?

With the increasing use of direct payment into or out of bank accounts, it would be easy to miss standing orders received or paid and other items if the statement is not available for the full period covered by the return. Getting the statement early in the next month gives you the time to pick up these items.

Property transactions are an example already mentioned. If the sale or the rent is standard-rated, who has issued the tax invoice and where has it got to? It could be with your solicitors or in a file outside the accounts department.

If an agent is collecting the rent using the tax point rules correctly with a demand rather than a tax invoice, that agent will be responsible for issuing tax invoices for rent, which you have opted to tax, when it is received. How will you make sure you are notified of it in time to account for the tax on the correct VAT return?

What if I am asked to re-invoice someone else?

If the business to which you have issued a tax invoice asks you to cancel it and re-invoice another business, do not destroy the first document. A good computer system will refuse to allow you to re-invoice using the same invoice number anyway.

Issue a credit note to the first business cross-referring to the second invoice. Then invoice the other business.

However, be careful what you say on that invoice. If, as far as you are concerned, your supply was to the first business, say so together with wording such as '*goods delivered to ABC Ltd. Invoiced at their request to you*'. ABC Ltd may have good reasons for wanting the bill addressed to XYZ Ltd but it is for the latter to satisfy Customs that it is entitled to recover the VAT — for instance because the goods were passed on to it. However, people sometimes think that VAT, which is not recoverable by one company because it is related to exempt outputs, will be recoverable if the invoice is addressed to another company, which is fully taxable. Do not aid and abet a possible fiscal fraud by issuing a document purporting to show a supply to XYZ Ltd simply because you are asked to invoice that company.

Some questions to check your understanding. Review your answers with the text.

● What are the three events, any of which creates a tax point?

● How does that change in the case of a continuous supply of services?

● Does the receipt of a deposit create a tax point?

● What are the differences between a request for payment, a pro forma invoice and a tax invoice?

8.   The Value of Supply Rules —
How Much You Must Pay

The value of supply rules are another fundamental part of VAT law. Whilst most of the time you simply charge VAT on the value of your sale, there are a few exceptions to this. It could be very expensive to get the rules wrong.

This chapter deals with such topics as discounts, barter transactions (when part or all of the payment you receive is in goods or services rather than cash) and when a 'gift' is not a gift because the recipient has to do something in return; ie provides 'non-monetary consideration' for it.

Then the last part of the chapter covers some of the more sophisticated cases, which concern, for example, discounts given in the form of vouchers.

For additional guidance on some marketing methods, see Notice 700/7 *Business promotion schemes*. For details of the *Linked Supplies Concession* concerning minor items at different rates of VAT, see Chapter 12, *Have I Got One Supply or Two?*

Special offers

Normally, VAT is due on the price you charge if that is all you get. However, see later re barter transactions and non-monetary consideration.

You can offer *Buy 1 get 1 free, 13 for the price of 12* or *buy a sofa and get a free foot stool* and Customs accept the deal as for an all in price. The only complication is if it has to be apportioned because the goods are at different rates of VAT.

A retailer, who offers to 'pay the VAT' on a sale is offering a discount. To calculate the tax due, apply the VAT fraction to the sum that the customer pays.

Prompt payment discounts (Sch 6 para 4)

If you offer your customer a discount for paying promptly, you charge VAT on the optional lower price; ie, the price net of the discount. It is irrelevant whether or not the customer takes that discount.

For example, you offer 2.5% cash discount for payment within 30 days:

On an invoice for:	£100
The calculation of VAT is 17.5% of £97.50	£ 17.06
Invoice total	£117.06

This rule is mandatory, not optional and is a point sometimes overlooked by computer programmers when setting up new systems. Whilst it makes no difference to fully taxable businesses, it offers small savings to those which cannot recover the VAT.

People sometimes wonder whether it offers an opportunity for some cunning VAT planning. Suppose you offer a discount of 99% to a customer, who cannot recover VAT, on the understanding that it will not be taken? That would reduce the customer's non-recoverable VAT nicely whilst still giving you the same price.

Well, if it sounds too good to be true, it probably is. One of Price's rules of commonsense in VAT is *Customs Are Not That Stupid.*

If this principle were applied more often by those, who think they have found a clever dodge in VAT, many people would avoid foolish mistakes. I use the word 'foolish' because it is not sensible to suppose that a bright idea you've had is likely to be a way around the system before you've carefully considered what anti-avoidance rules there may be.

On the whole, the VAT system is both logical and well designed. It is not easy to obtain an artificial advantage with a clever dodge. Planning opportunities do exist. There are some artificialities but they are not numerous. Take advice and think carefully before assuming that you have found one. To put it another way, most bright ideas of this kind have already been thought of by someone else and Customs usually got there before either of you!

Admittedly, *Sch 6 para 4* merely refers to *terms allowing a discount for prompt payment* and does not impose any limit on the amount. However, in a case I argued many years ago, the Tribunal refused to accept that a 20% discount was for prompt payment and that was in a situation in which the customers took it.

If you offer a high discount you will have to show that the offer is genuine, which will normally mean that it is part of your standard terms or, at the very least, that it is set out in a letter to the customer. You will then have to explain firstly to Customs and secondly to the Tribunal, since Customs will certainly challenge it, why the customer failed to take up such a marvellous offer!

Turnover discounts and volume rebates

Do not confuse prompt payment discounts with turnover discounts or volume rebates. These are only earned after the event, being based on the value of purchases by the customer over a stated period of time. The price to the customer is then reduced by a credit note. It is up to the supplier and the customer to agree whether VAT should be added to the value of the credit. Naturally, a customer, who was unable to recover the original VAT, will want it to be included on the credit note.

See also later in this chapter under *More on discounts, rebates and commissions.*

The artificial prices rule

The artificial prices rule in *Sch 6 para 1* stops you reducing your non-recoverable input tax by, for instance, forming a management services company, which incurs all costs and re-charges them to the main business at a lower price. Customs can catch you retrospectively for 3 years by directing the substitution of market value for the price charged if a supply is:

* at an artifical price; and

* between connected persons; and

* the purchaser cannot recover his input VAT — being unregistered or partially exempt.

In *Oughtred & Harrison Ltd (MAN/87/160 No 3174)*, the Tribunal confirmed the direction in a case where charges for use of a computer by an insurance broker had been at below cost.

The party plan rules

Businesses, which sell under the party plan system, often do so through unregistered representatives or demonstrators. If the latter buy and re-sell the goods, rather than take a commission as agents, the profit margin escapes VAT.

Sch 6 para 2 gives the Commissioners power to prevent this by issuing a direction to the business to pay tax on market value rather than on the price, which it invoices to the representatives. In theory, this stops them competing unfairly with retail shops. The effect is that, to earn the same profit margin, they have to charge the same price as the shop.

That's the theory. In practice, prices of goods sold direct under the party plan system are not necessarily lower than those in ordinary shops. The system involves substantial selling costs and there may be little difference. Moreover, party plan directions catch businesses selling surplus stocks of, for instance, cosmetics to women in factories and offices who re-sell to their workmates. They also catch school photographers who sell to the schools, who re-sell to the parents.

Neither of these businesses compete directly with ordinary retailers since the surplus stocks have already failed to sell through normal outlets whilst the school photographers provide a different service to that of the high street photographer.

Any party plan direction, which Customs issues to you, cannot be retrospective. However, that will be little consolation. There is unlikely to be anything which you can do about it, because the subject has been well aired in the courts. In *Direct Cosmetics Ltd ([1985] STC 479; [1988] STC 540)*, my client's case was referred twice to the CJEC. The story is well-known amongst VAT specialists because this was the first case from a UK VAT Tribunal to the CJEC. My client did win the first time but not on the second occasion which established that, having obtained the derogation, which they had initially failed to get, Customs had the right to issue directions. More recently, *H Tempest Ltd ([1993] VATTR 482 No 11210)* has thoroughly ventilated the subject in relation to school photographs, also without success. If you need to know more, study these cases together with *Traidcraft plc (MAN/02/230 No 18189)*.

Barter transactions — the gross values count!

If you trade goods or services in part payment for purchases, you must account for VAT on the gross values. VAT is a tax on transactions, not on the net money paid as reduced by something taken in part exchange.

If two businesses regularly buy and sell from each other, VAT is due on each transaction, not the net sum payable at the end of the month. This is important because either business may not be able to recover the VAT it incurs. If one could net off transactions against each other for VAT purposes, it would be easy to subvert the system!

The law is in *s 19*. Its effect is that, if the consideration for a transaction is wholly or partly not in money, tax is due on the full value of the transaction. This is because the money paid is not the full measure of the deal.

Example

If you buy a new car for £10,000 and sell a commercial vehicle in part exchange, such as a van, you pay VAT on the £10,000, not on the net £6,000. The correct arithmetic is as follows:

	£	£
New motor car		10,000
Add VAT @ 17.5%		1,750
		£11,750
Less trade allowance on used van	4,000	
Add VAT	700	
		4,700
Net payment		£ 7,050

The net payment of £7,050 is the same as would have been arrived at by charging VAT on the value of the car less the trade-in allowance. However, the consequences of doing it the correct way are different.

Firstly, input tax on the new car of £1,750 is probably not recoverable. Secondly, you must account for output tax of £700 on the van. The motor dealer accounts for £1,050 being his output tax less the input tax charged to him on the van. He recovers this input tax because he is buying a used commercial vehicle on which he will charge output tax when he sells it.

Thus, VAT is charged on the gross value of the deal, not the net cash paid.

Note: The sale of a second-hand *car* is exempt if you did not recover VAT when you bought it for use in your business.

Consideration means VAT catch

If the terms of a deal require your customer to do something in addition to paying money, there is 'non-monetary consideration'. In that case, VAT is due on the full value of the deal, not just on the money element.

This affects a variety of situations such as:

- part exchange deals like the vehicle one explained above;
- discount offers — special prices in certain situations;
- 'gifts' which are not gifts because something has to be done in return.

The jargon of the law

The rule on non-monetary consideration is in *s 19(3)*. It states:

'If the supply is for a consideration not consisting or not wholly consisting of money, its value shall be taken to be such amount in money as, with the addition of the VAT chargeable, is equivalent to the consideration.'

If you find that obscure, join the club! It means that, if part of the price paid is not in money, VAT is due on the full value of the transaction. Thus, if you swap goods or services for other goods or services, you have to pay VAT on that full value.

How does one value non-monetary consideration?

Usually, the value applicable is market value and, since that is a term readily understood in comparison with cost, it is used in this book. However, it is not necessarily the correct figure which could be some other value which the two parties have attributed to the transaction.

For instance, in *Empire Stores Ltd (LON/89/887 No 8859)* gifts were offered to new mail-order customers, which were not included in the catalogue and for which there was therefore no retail price. The Tribunal noted that the CJEC had stated in *Naturally Yours Cosmetics ([1988] STC 879)*, a case quoted later, that a supply for non-monetary consideration is only taxable on its open market value if the parties have not themselves attributed a value to it. The taxable amount is thus to be ascertained subjectively. Since the recipient could only guess at the value whereas *Empire* knew the cost, the latter was the value of the supply.

That view was confirmed in *Ping (Europe) Ltd (MAN/99/74 No 17001: 2001 STC 1144: [2002] EWCA Civ 1115, [2002] STC 1186)* — explained later under other trade-in situations. An exchanged golf club was held to be worth the subjective value to the supplier, not the objective difference between the sum paid and the normal retail price. Moreover, that objective difference was based on a hypothetical market, which could have existed had some customers preferred to sell their clubs together with the right to exchange rather than exercise it. The case concerned the actual exchanges by *Ping*, not hypothetical transactions.

The cases which are commented on below show that the subjective value depends upon the facts of each case. However, the judge in *Ping* referred to the *sound taxation principle that no one should be accountable to tax on more than the value to him (that is the subjective value), of what he had received.*

In *Bertelsmann AG ([2001] STC 1153)*, the CJEC ruled that the value of goods given in return for introducing customers included the cost of delivery to the recipient.

Consideration is sometimes difficult to spot. It can seem to the layman a tenuous concept — in English law it can be a peppercorn. The European view of consideration is somewhat different, as demonstrated in the *Boots* case explained below.

Money-off coupons

Boots The Chemists ([1990] STC 387) sold certain products with which purchasers got a 'money-off' coupon giving them a reduction in price if they then bought another product. The UK courts decided that there was non-monetary consideration in the form of the coupon. The customer only got the reduced price from the second product as a result of having bought the first one.

However, the CJEC ruled that the coupons were merely acknowledgement of the commitment to give the consumer a reduction on the second purchase. They had no value in themselves so the value for VAT purposes of the second transaction was merely the money received.

See later in this chapter for more on this subject in the comment on the cases concerning vouchers.

Some examples of non-monetary consideration

In *Naturally Yours Cosmetics ([1988] STC 879)*, a company selling at private parties, allowed the independent dealers, through whom it sold, to buy items of cosmetics at below the normal price. The dealers gave the cosmetics to party hostesses as rewards for recruiting hostesses for future parties. The CJEC held that, in addition to the money paid, there was further non-monetary consideration provided — the finding of more hostesses — so VAT was due on the full retail price.

Pippa Dee Parties Ltd ([1981] STC 495) sold clothes using the party plan system. A hostess could have a commission in cash of £4.57 per £100 of clothes sold at the party in her house; alternatively, she could choose £11.67 worth of clothes at catalogue value. Pippa Dee argued that it was only liable for output tax on the cash commission earned. Naturally, Customs demanded it on the catalogue value.

The Divisional Court held that market value applied, as the hostess only obtained the right to the clothes by holding the party, which was non-monetary consideration. Output tax was therefore due on the catalogue value, not on the cash commission foregone.

Another case concerning this point is *Rosgill Group Ltd ([1997] STC 811)*.

The promotional gifts problem

As explained in Chapter 6, *So What Must I Charge VAT on?*, you have to pay output VAT on the cost of goods, which you give away, if the cost exceeds £50. If you receive non-monetary consideration in return so they do not qualify as gifts, the result is:

- output tax is due whatever the value;
- and it is calculated on the market value of the gifts, not on their cost.

Thus, the non-monetary consideration rule catches some transactions which would not be caught under the gift rules, being below the £50 limit.

In *GUS Merchandise Corpn Ltd ([1981] STC 569)*, a set of baking tins was held to be a reward to prospective mail order agents who:

- Applied to become an agent with a view to obtaining future orders (consideration does not have to be instantaneous: give me the baking set now and I'll try and get you more orders); and
- Obtained an initial £10 order.

Both these actions were held to constitute consideration and *GUS* were thus caught for output tax on the baking set. Had the gifts rules applied, they would have escaped, the cost being under the limit.

Awards and rewards

In Notice 700/7 (March 2002) *Business promotion schemes*, para 3.3, Customs accept that a prize to a salesman for reaching a sales target or to your champion salesman is not for non-monetary consideration and is therefore a gift. This reasoning seems odd since the goods are in return for achieving the sales target or for selling more than anyone else. However, the point will usually not matter since the goods will have been bought in at market value anyway.

Customs also accept that a reward to a customer for buying more than a stated quantity is a gift.

Some more complicated points

So far this chapter has dealt with the main points, which everyone needs to understand. From here on it deals with some of the more sophisticated arguments, which have occurred concerning the value of supply of transactions, many of which are complicated and concern special situations.

Interest free credit

'Interest-free credit' is often offered by retailers. Granted the customer only pays the normal price despite doing so in instalments but credit is not interest-free from a finance house. The finance company charges the retailer interest.

So, supposing that the retail value of the goods is   £1,000
and the finance house charges interest of   £ 100
so the retailer receives net   £ 900

Is the value of the sale by the retailer for VAT purposes £900 or £1,000?

The leading case on this is *Primback Ltd (LON/92/1142 No 10460: CA [1996] STC 757: CJEC C-34/99: [2001] STC 803)*. The Tribunal held that the value of the goods was that invoiced to the customer. The deduction by the finance house was for interest. The Divisional Court agreed but the Court of Appeal said the VAT was only due on the sum actually received by *Primback* via the finance house. The House of Lords then referred the matter to the CJEC, which held that the value of the sale was that agreed between *Primback* and its customer. The Court found it important that that price did not vary whether the customer paid up front or by instalments through the finance house and that the customer was unaware of the charge made by the finance house to Primback. Although *Primback* might allow a discount for immediate payment, it did not offer this; the customer had to ask for and negotiate it and it would therefore not necessarily be the same amount as the commission charged by the finance house. The Court saw that commission as an expense of *Primback* incurred in order to increase its sales and to avoid having to accept payment by instalments.

The planning point there seems to be to sell the goods to the finance house at a reduced price and for it to then sell them on to the customer at the retail value. Thus, in *A & D Stevenson (Trading) Ltd (LON/97/696 No 17979)*, Customs' arguments based on *Primback* were rejected and a conditional sale agreement was held to involve a sale by the dealer to the finance company, the value of the supply being the sum the dealer got; ie, it was net of the interest charged, not the full sale price agreed with the customer.

Cars returned or repossessed under hire-purchase agreements

In *General Motors Acceptance Corpn (UK) plc (LON/01/242 No 17990)*, it was held that the original value of supply under a hire-purchase agreement was reduced if the hirer exercised a right to return a car instead of making the outstanding payments. The reduced value was the sum paid plus the outstanding payments. It did not include the proceeds of the car, when sold by the hire-purchase company. That sale was outside the scope of VAT just as was the sale of a car repossessed because of a customer default (*Art 4(1)(a) The Cars Order (SI 1992/3122)*).

The three year limit did not apply to the reduction in value where the supply was over three years ago. *Article 11(C)(1)* of the *EC 6th VAT Directive*, in allowing a Member State to impose conditions, did not permit it to limit that right.

This is a complicated case and that is just a summary. See *VAT Information Sheet 06/2003*, in which Customs announced an appeal against various aspects of it, for more details.

Trade-in values offered by motor dealers

People, who part exchange cars, like to feel that they are getting a good trade-in price for their existing vehicle. Motor dealers exploit this as part of their sales techniques but often they either do not understand the VAT consequences or they try to adjust the values subsequently. Consider the following example.

	£
Price of new car including VAT	15,000
Trade-in allowance for part exchange car	5,000
Net payment due	£10,000

If the dealer can only sell the part exchange car for £4,000, there will be a loss of £1,000 under the *Second-hand Goods Scheme*, which, under the rules explained in Chapter 30, cannot be offset against profits on other vehicles. Output tax will of course be due on the £15,000 paid for the new car.

If the dealer had reduced the price of the new car by a discount of £1,000 and shown the trade-in allowance as only £4,000, output tax on the new car would have been due on £14,000, not £15,000 and there would still be no output tax due under the *Second-hand Goods Scheme*. Many Tribunal cases have concerned attempts by dealers to alter the values in their records. The problem is of course that this is subsequent to the deal and the customer is unaware of the change.

It is clear from the CJEC's decision in *Primback* discussed above that it saw the key to the answer as being the subjective value advertised and invoiced to the customer. In other words, if you tell the customer that the price is £x, you cannot argue that the VAT owed to Customs should be based on £y. This supports the decisions in *North Anderson Cars Ltd (EDN/97/93 No 15415)* as confirmed by the Court of Session on 13/8/99 and *Lex Service plc (LON/98/287 No 16097; [2001] STC 697; [2001] EWCA Civ 1542; [2001] STC 1568)*, as confirmed by the Divisional Court and the Court of Appeal. In the *North Anderson* case, cars were sold under hire-purchase agreements to finance companies with trade-in values inflated so as to create the necessary deposit required by the company. The Tribunal regarded these manual invoices as correctly stating the value of the supply, not the sales order forms and internal computer-generated sales invoices, which showed the realistic trade-in values as agreed with the customers.

In the *Lex* case, the value of supply of part-exchange cars was again held to be that agreed with the customers and shown in the documents even in cases not financed under hire-purchase, rather than the lower sum repayable under a 30-day guarantee of satisfaction if the customer returned the car bought and the trade-in car had already been sold.

Hartwell plc (LON/00/101 No 17065; [2002] STC 22; [2003] STC 396) solved the problem with *Purchase Plus Discount Notes* given to customers on top of the sum given for the trade-in vehicle. Those vouchers then formed part of the deposit required under the hire-purchase transaction for the replacement vehicle. This avoided inflating the price of the trade-in vehicle whilst assisting with the deposit required by the finance company. The Court of Appeal confirmed that the vouchers were not issued in return for any consideration and were not part of the consideration for either vehicle. Thus, VAT was only due on the sum received from the finance company.

Other trade-in situations

Now, here's a teaser for you! *Alfred Bugeja (LON/96/341 No 15586; on appeal [2000] STC 1)* sold videos at £20 each, which could then be exchanged for others for a further £10 a time. Customs argued that the value of the later deals was £20 being the £10 cash plus the value at £10 of the video returned. The Tribunal rejected that saying that, since *Bugeja* was obliged to accept the returned video, if it was in good condition, the value was £10 only. Do you think that was correct?

On appeal by Customs, the Divisional Court held that the consideration consisted partly of the £10 in cash, and partly of the second-hand video, since that could be resold. However, its value was the price at which *Bugeja* could buy in videos for stock. Finally, the Court of Appeal said that the second-hand video was worth £10 because that was the difference between the first time sale of £20 and the sum payable when a video was part-exchanged for another. Mr Bugeja would resell the part-exchange video for £10 — or £20 on a first time sale.

In such a situation, the additional £1.49 payable on the part-exchange value would be a serious drain on profit. The solution appears to be to use *Global Accounting* under the *Second-hand Goods Scheme*. See Chapter 30.

Now think about trade-ins! If a retailer offers a trade-in allowance for, say, an old television set, which then has to be scrapped, Customs normally accept that the allowance is in reality a discount off the price of the new set and the VAT is only due on cash received.

The case of *Ping (Europe) Ltd (MAN/99/74 No 17001: [2001] STC 1144): [2002] STC 1186)* concerned *Ping Eye 2* irons declared not to conform to the rules of golf and which players would therefore have to cease using. *Ping* offered to exchange them for a new conforming version at a special price of £22, which was just above cost. The normal wholesale price was £49.99 and the recommended retail price £72. Customs of course argued that there was non-monetary consideration — the old club and that the value of this was the price reduction from wholesale.

Ping received nothing for the surrendered clubs from the manufacturer, to which it returned them. If you'd like to try working out that teaser, think for a moment before you read on.

The Tribunal noted that each surrendered club represented a burden on *Ping*, not an advantage to it. It would be surprising and unfair if *Ping* had to pay VAT on £49.99 for each new club supplied when it had only received £22. The difference between the latter and the wholesale price was likely to be a secret kept from a retail customer. If that reduction was unknown to the latter, it could not form the subjective value of the old club. The subjective value of it to *Ping* was nil so VAT was due on the £22. This was confirmed on appeal. The value in question of the returned club was that to *Ping,* not that to the owner returning it.

More on discounts, rebates and commissions

A retrospective discount, such as a volume rebate, reduces the taxable value of your sales, as noted earlier in this chapter. Sometimes, a commission can count as a discount too.

Article 11(A)(3) of the EC 6th VAT Directive says;

The taxable amount shall not include:

(a)   price reductions by way of discount for early payment;

(b)   price discounts and rebates allowed to the customer and accounted for at the time of the supply.

Thus, if, as part of your marketing, you offer price reductions, the question is whether they are:

- Discounts or rebates, which reduce your taxable sales; or

- Rewards to the recipient for doing something in return, which do not reduce the value of your taxable supplies.

An example of a rebate situation is *Co-operative Retail Services Ltd (MAN/89/843 No 7527)*. Customers, who deposited at least £50, became members of the Co-op. They were entitled to a shareholder Visa card and to a 'dividend' of 5% on all non-food purchases, which was credited annually into the share account. Customs argued that this was a distribution of profit. The Tribunal found that it was a contractual obligation to the members rather than a share of net profit and that it could therefore be treated as a rebate on taxable sales. The use of the word 'dividend' was irrelevant because this had a double meaning in the co-operative movement.

It did not matter that you had to be a member in order to qualify and to have a minimum balance in your share account. Many companies offered benefits to shareholders. Once you had purchased goods, you were entitled to the 5%, subject only to retaining that balance. It was in that sense accounted for at the time of supply and it did not matter that it was only credited annually. The Tribunal held that a discount must mean something different to a rebate and that the latter was the relevant word here.

Littlewoods Organisation plc (MAN/98/99 No 16318; [2000] STC 588; [2001] EWCA Civ 1542; [2001] STC 1568) offered discounts to mail order agents. The agent earned a commission of 10% when she paid for goods bought either for herself or for a customer and an additional 2.5% if she used the commission to buy additional goods rather than offset it against the outstanding balance on her account or take it in cash. Customs accepted that the commission was a reduction in the price of goods if it was taken in cash. They also accepted that 10% was a discount if additional goods were bought — so that the transactions were treated the same. However, they argued that the extra 2.5% was payment for the service of generating sales to customers.

The Tribunal found the 2.5% to be an extra discount. The Divisional Court disagreed, saying that it was a further payment for finding the customers but the

Court of Appeal overruled that. There was no direct link between the 2.5% and the sales to customers. It was only credited to the agent as the payments were received and was indeed an extra discount on the price of the further goods.

The time of supply of a discount

In *Freemans plc (Case C-86/99:* [*2001*] *STC 960)*, the CJEC held on *29 May 2001* that a discount could only be deducted from the value of a supply at the time at which it was used by the recipient. *Freemans* credited a sum to the account of an agent each time a payment was received. The agent could then either draw it in cash or use it to buy other goods. The time of supply of the original sale was when the products were adopted by the agent, and at that time the amount payable by the agents was the full catalogue price. The 10% credits only occurred later as and when instalments of purchase price were paid and the value of supply of *Freeman's* sales was only reduced when the agent used those credits.

Book tokens, gift vouchers and telephone cards

Face value vouchers, such as book tokens, gift vouchers and telephone cards, issued on or before 8/4/03 were only taxable at the time of issue to the extent that the price paid exceeded the face value — ie on any commission or service charge *(Sch 5, para 6)*. VAT was due on the goods or services supplied when the voucher was redeemed.

That is often still the case for vouchers issued since but, to prevent certain avoidance schemes, the rules have been changed to repeal *para 6* and substitute *Sch 10A* as explained below.

Retailer and credit vouchers

A *retailer voucher* is one issued by a trader, who will either redeem it for goods or services or will reimburse another trader who does so. A gift voucher is an example.

A *credit voucher* is one issued by an organisation, such as a trade association, which will not redeem it but will reimburse the trader, who does.

In both cases, the initial issue price of the voucher is outside the scope of VAT — *unless* the trader redeeming it fails to account for the VAT due on the goods or services supplied against it. Any subsequent sales of *retailer vouchers* by other traders are subject to VAT as explained below under *Sales to and by intermediaries*. That does not apply to *credit vouchers*.

Electronic and top up vouchers

Electronic vouchers are treated in the same way as paper ones. That covers, for instance, top up cards, which do not bear a face value, the sums being recorded electronically.

Postage stamps

Postage stamps remain outside the scope of VAT as before. The eventual supply of postal services by the Post Office is of course exempt.

Other kinds of face value voucher

Other kinds of face value voucher not covered above are taxed when sold at the rate applicable to the goods or services against which they will be redeemed. If different rates are involved, an apportionment must be made on *a just and reasonable basis*.

Sales to and by intermediaries

A retailer can still reduce its own output tax by selling *retailer vouchers* at a discount to an associated company. The rules are as follows:

- The retailer does not account for the VAT included in that discounted price until it redeems the vouchers.

- However, the intermediary can recover that tax as input VAT but needs a tax invoice.

- To sort this situation, Customs suggest in *VAT Information Sheet 03/2003* that the retailer issues a VAT invoice and states on it, as justification for not immediately paying the VAT shown on it, *The issuer of the voucher will account for output tax under the face value voucher provisions introduced in Schedule 10A VAT Act 1994*. The invoice should also show the percentage split at different rates of VAT if applicable and if known at the time of sale; see below.

- When the intermediary then sells the vouchers on, it must charge VAT. If it can show that the vouchers will be redeemed against non-standard rated supplies, the intermediary can use a percentage split to calculate the VAT due, based on information from the redeemer. The split can be on an average basis such as retail scheme percentages. If the information is not available at the time of the sale, the adjustment can be retrospective.

These rules stop avoidance schemes based on *Argos Distributors Ltd (MAN/94/307 No 13025: CJEC C–288/94: [1996] STC 1359)*. *Argos* sold vouchers at a discount from face value to other organisations which typically used them as incentives for staff or customers. The CJEC said that, when the voucher was redeemed by *Argos*, it only had to account for VAT on the sum it had received.

This meant that a voucher could be sold at a discount to an associated company, which could resell it outside the scope at a profit. The profit thus escaped VAT. Taxing the sales by intermediaries prevents that.

Vouchers supplied with other goods or services

If you include a voucher with goods or services at a price which is the same or not significantly different to the normal one, the voucher is treated as supplied for no consideration. This prevents one reducing a taxable supply by the value of a voucher in circumstances such as:

- A hotel issues vouchers to customers when they pay their bills — knowing that few will return and redeem them.

- A retailer offers a voucher with sales above a certain value but with restrictions which limit the number of customers able to redeem it.

- A mobile phone includes a telephone card but the customer cannot reduce the price by rejecting the card.

In *Hartwell plc (LON/00/101 No 17065;* [2002] *STC 22;* [2003] *STC 396),* the Court of Appeal held that no part of the sale value of a car could be attributed to MOT vouchers included with it, the sale price not having been split on the invoice.

In *Tesco plc* [2002] *EWHC 2131 (Ch);* [2002] *STC 1332,* the Divisional Court held that *clubcard* points were the offer of a discount on future purchases so the reduction in the sales value was of the redemption goods, not that of the sale against which they were issued.

Discount vouchers

A voucher, which offers a discount, is not a face value voucher and is taxable when sold, as was held in *F & I Services Ltd (LON/98/869 No15958:* [2000] *STC 364).* The books of vouchers, which offered discounts on various goods and services, did not give the right to them, merely to a reduction from the normal price.

Cashback coupons

A manufacturer, who offers consumers refunds against cash-back coupons printed on the packaging of its products, can deduct their value from its taxable sales .

In *Elida Gibbs Ltd v C & E Comrs (CJEC C-317/94:* [1996] *STC 1387),* the goods had of course first been sold to the wholesaler or retailer at the normal price. Customs objected to the reduction because the repayment was to a third party, the retail customer. The CJEC said a basic VAT principle was to tax only the final consumer on the price paid by that consumer. *Gibbs* should be taxed on the sum received net of the repayment. Otherwise, Customs would collect tax on more than the consumer paid.

The value of a voucher when redeemed

Following *Elida Gibbs, Yorkshire Co-operatives Ltd (MAN/97/207 No 15821: C-398/99:* [2003] *STC 234)* argued that the value of a sale for which it accepted a price reduction voucher was just the cash element and that the subsequent refund of the value of the voucher by the manufacturer was a rebate or discount. The CJEC rejected that, holding that the value of the supply to the consumer included sums paid by the third party, the manufacturer.

Your taxable supply is not reduced by a discount given by someone else

The CJEC ruled on 19/6/03, in *First Choice Holidays plc (C-149/01:* [2003] *STC 934),* that a tour operator must account for VAT on the full price paid to it by travel agents. It could not reduce the value of its supply by discounts allowed to customers and funded by the travel agents out of their commissions.

Goods given in return for accumulated stamps or points

If you give your customers stamps or points, which they can redeem in due course against 'free gifts', output tax is due on those gifts if their cost exceeds the limit explained in the comment on the gifts rules earlier in this chapter.

Kuwait Petroleum (GB) Ltd (LON/95/2338 Nos 14,668 & 16,582: CJEC C-48/97: [1999] *STC 488)* failed with an argument that the gifts were included in the price charged for its fuel and that therefore no further output tax was due. The petrol station sold the fuel to the motorist on the basis that he would receive 'sails' in relation to the volume of fuel bought. The sails were tokens with a minute cash value. Under the rules of the promotion, *Kuwait* promised to redeem the sails against redemption goods as chosen. Only when the motorist handed in sails at the garage did *Kuwait* become liable to do that. The Tribunal found that the sails were in this sense obtained 'free of charge'. In buying the petrol the motorist was not making a part payment towards possibly acquiring the redemption goods. On referral to the CJEC, the latter supported the Tribunal's view that:

- There was no agreement between the customer and the petrol station that part of the price paid for the fuel was for the sails or for the redemption goods.

- The latter were supplied *otherwise than for a consideration* and were therefore taxable under the gifts rules.

Deductions by credit providers from payments to retailers

When a retailer submits credit card slips to a credit card company, the latter deducts a discount from its payment to the retailer. However, this is not a reduction in the latter's taxable sales. *Diners Club Ltd (CA [1989] STC 407)* established that it is payment for the financial service of extending credit to and collecting payment from the card-holder.

Similarly, in *Kingfisher plc (LON/09/990 No 16332 affd [2000] STC 992)*, discounts deducted from the value of *Provident* vouchers paid to retailers were payment for the exempt service of dealing in money, not a reduction in the taxable supply made by *Kingfisher*.

Some questions to check your understanding. Review your answers with the text.

- If you offer a 5% prompt payment discount to a customer, on what figure do you calculate the VAT?

- If a car dealer accepts a cheque for £10,000 plus a trade-in vehicle valued at £5,000 in payment for a new vehicle, what is the value for the new vehicle upon which he must charge VAT?

- If someone has to do something in order to obtain a 'gift' from you, what are the consequences for VAT?

- When *Rank Hovis McDougall* was assessed under the gifts rules for gold watches given to employees who had served for 25 years, the company argued that the watches were an unwritten term of the contracts of employment. Everyone knew that, if you stayed for 25 years, you got a gold watch so it was outside the scope of VAT just like the salary. Why did that argument not only get the company nowhere but risk increasing the value of the supply from cost to market value, had it been accepted?

9. So What is Reduced Rated?

The reduced rate rules used to be in *Sch A1*. From 1 November 2001, they were moved to a new *Sch 7A*. They have been expanded in recent years although the coverage is still limited. If any of the more important zero ratings, such as for food, books or children's clothing, were to be abandoned, it would probably be the reduced rate which would then apply rather than the standard rate.

The contents of Schedule 7A

Group 1	Domestic fuel and power
Group 2	Installation of energy-saving materials
Group 3	Grant funded installation of heating equipment or security goods or connection of gas supply
Group 4	Women's sanitary products
Group 5	Children's car seats
Group 6	Residential conversions
Group 7	Residential renovations and alterations

At the time of writing, the reduced rate is 5%.

Several of the above Groups are of limited general interest. For comment on *Groups 6 and 7* concerning the conversion, renovation or alterations of certain buildings, see Chapter 25, *Property*. Below are some brief comments on the rest.

Domestic fuel and power — Sch 7A Group 1

Group 1 covers coal, gas, fuel oil, electricity etc when sold for:

- domestic use; or
- use by a charity for non-business purposes.

Domestic use means in a dwelling, for a relevant residential purpose, for self-catering holiday accommodation, for a caravan or for a houseboat.

Relevant residential purpose is defined in *Note 7(1)*, which is the same as *Note (4)* to *Sch 8, Group 5*. See Chapter 25 on *Property*.

There are various de minimis quantities such as, for fuel oil, up to 2,300 litres, for which the supply is always deemed to be for domestic use. Alternatively, if at least 60% of the supply qualifies, the entire sum can be reduced rated. Otherwise, it must be apportioned.

Installation of energy-saving materials — Sch 7A Group 2

Group 2 covers both supplying the materials and installing them in:

- residential accommodation;
- a building intended for use solely for a relevant charitable purpose.

Energy-saving materials does not just mean insulation and draught stripping. It includes central heating and hot water system controls, solar panels and wind and water turbines. Do not confuse the coverage of this group with that of *Group 3* under which, for instance, a central heating system must be grant funded.

Residential accommodation means dwellings, including caravans permanently lived in and houseboats, together with buildings used for a relevant residential purpose. The latter is as defined in *Group 1*. Ie, it is the same definition as in *Sch 8, Group 5* re constructing buildings — as is also the definition of *relevant charitable purpose*. See Chapter 25 on *Property*.

Certain grant funded work — Sch 7A Group 3

Group 3 covers a range of supplies such as supplying and installing heating appliances, mains gas supplies, central heating systems and security goods but only when they are grant funded and to people aged 60 or over or who are in receipt of certain benefits.

If you think that a supply might be covered, read the rules carefully.

Women's sanitary products — Sch 7A Group 4

Group 4 covers tampons, panty liners and sanitary belts but not incontinence products, protective briefs or any other form of clothing.

Children's car seats — Sch 7A Group 5

Group 5 includes seats designed for use also with a framework as a pushchair together with booster seats and cushions.

Residential conversions — Sch 7A Group 6

See below.

Residential renovations and alterations — Sch 7A Group 7

Groups 6 and 7 deal with conversions of buildings into living accommodation of various kinds and with the renovation or alteration of living accommodation which has been empty for at least three years. For full coverage of the rules, see Chapter 25 on *Property*.

Some questions to check your understanding. Review your answers with the text.

- What does the reduced rate for domestic fuel cover?

- There are 6 other groups in *Schedule 7A*. How many of the headings can you remember?

10. So What is Zero-rated?

The law

The law on zero-rating is mostly in *Sch 8*, although that for commodity transactions is in *s 34* and the *Terminal Markets Order*.

The Terminal Markets Order

The Terminal Markets Order (*SI 1973/173*) zero rates transactions on a large number of terminal markets, such as those for metals, rubber, oil, bullion, foods such as cocoa, coffee and sugar, futures markets, such as those for meat, grain and potatoes together with the London Securities and Derivatives Exchange. Notice 701/9/02 *Derivatives and Terminal Markets* refers.

The zero rating is limited to transactions involving a member of the market involved and is subject to various rules such as that, if one of the parties is not a member of the market, it must not lead to delivery of the goods.

If you come across commodity transactions on one of the markets, do not take the zero rating for granted. I have seen several situations in which it did not apply so check the detailed rules.

The zero rating in Schedule 8

This chapter is obviously of most interest to readers who are involved with businesses selling zero-rated goods or services. Of course, each would like a detailed explanation of the particular rules of interest to him or her. Unfortunately, if this book was to cover everything, it would have to be expanded significantly. At the time of writing, there are:

- 16 groups (not counting the deleted *Group 14*), ie main headings, in the zero-rate rules; and

- 15 groups in the exemption rules.

Some of these groups contain numerous items qualified by extensive notes so detailed comment would require many pages. Moreover, much of that detailed comment would soon become out of date due to cases going through the Courts or to changes in the law.

So, if you want to be sure of what the precise position is currently on either zero-rating or exemption, you must check firstly with the law and commentary in a looseleaf reference book such as *De Voil Indirect Tax Service (Butterworths)* or *Tolley's Practical VAT Service* and then with the update section of the book in case there has been a change in the law not yet reflected in the law pages or a recent decision not yet reflected in the commentary. That may be tiresome but, if getting the answer wrong could cost you money, it is never safe to rely upon a bound book.

However, if your interest in the zero-rating or exemption rules is general rather than specific, you need an overview of them and an understanding of the purpose of each rather than full coverage of every detail. That understanding is what this chapter and the next on exemption try to provide. Then, if you do have to understand the precise law applicable to a transaction, you'll have a head start when consulting a reference book.

This chapter and the next one on exemption are best read in conjunction with a copy of the law because, when trying to understand the latter, there is no substitute for looking at it. If you do not have one of the loose-leaf reference books available, try Notice 701/39 *VAT liability law*. Unfortunately, this may not be up-to-date. However, it is free and most of the law in it has probably not changed!

The contents of Schedule 8

Group 1	Food
Group 2	Sewerage services and water
Group 3	Books
Group 4	Talking books for the blind and handicapped etc
Group 5	Construction of buildings etc
Group 6	Protected buildings
Group 7	International services
Group 8	Transport
Group 9	Caravans and houseboats
Group 10	Gold
Group 11	Bank notes
Group 12	Drugs, medicines, aids for the handicapped etc
Group 13	Imports, exports, etc.
Group 14	*This has been deleted*
Group 15	Charities
Group 16	Clothing and footwear

The following Groups are not covered in this chapter

Sch 8 Group 5 — Construction of buildings etc

See Chapter 25 on *Property* for coverage of this Group.

Sch 8 Group 6 — Protected buildings

See Chapter 25 on *Property* for coverage of this Group.

Sch 8 Group 7 — International services

See Chapter 22 on *Exports and Imports of Services* for coverage of this Group.

Don't ask if it's standard-rated!

The question 'Is it standard-rated?' is a natural one to ask but it should be banned! The law does not contain any list of transactions which are standard-rated. There is a list of what is zero-rated and another of what is exempt in the respective schedules of the VAT Act. Everything else is standard-rated — assuming that the place of supply is in the UK: ie, the supply is not covered by the rules for exports of goods or services.

What about outside the scope?

There is one other possibility — that a sum of money you receive is outside the scope of VAT because it is not payment for any supply. There is no list of such transactions in the law but, for most traders, they are unimportant. They tend to be expenses such as wages and local authority rates. See Chapter 6, *So What Must I Charge VAT on?* for comment on dividends, government grants and compensation.

'Outside the scope' is a term also used to describe transactions where the place of supply is not the UK under the rules for exports of goods or services. See those chapters for more details.

Once you understand that a sale, which is not reduced rated, zero-rated, exempt, or outside the scope of VAT, must be standard-rated, it follows that the questions are:

- Is it reduced rated under *Sch 7A*?
- Is it zero-rated under *Sch 8*?
- Is it exempt under *Sch 9*?
- Is it perhaps outside the scope?

No? Then it must be standard-rated!

This is of course assuming that the sale is one made in the course or furtherance of your business. If you have any doubts about whether the transaction could be treated as non-business, see Chapters 6, *So What Must I Charge VAT on?* and 27, *Am I in Business?*

Before you start, think what it is you are supplying

The question 'what am I supplying?' is often a valuable aid to clear thinking. Usually, the rate of VAT depends on what's supplied:

- not who supplies it;
- nor who the customer is;
- nor what the customer thinks he's getting;
- nor the nature of the supplier's costs.

There are exceptions but, if a customer says you ought to zero-rate your supply, ask which part of *Sch 8* the customer thinks applies. All too often, customers haven't a clue what the law says and many such claims are based on fantasy.

There are some zero-ratings which depend on who the customer is but they are limited to specific circumstances. The most likely ones are the rules on Aids for the Handicapped in *Sch 8 Group 12* and on Charities in *Sch 8 Group 15*. In both cases, the customer is required to provide a certificate. Obviously, demanding from one's customers certificates of who they are or what they intend to do with the supply is not practical for the majority of commercial situations.

Check what the law says

Popular perceptions about what the law covers are often inaccurate. It is vital to look up the law to check precisely what it says in relation to the transactions you are considering. Numerous tribunal decisions over the years have contained stories of people getting into trouble because they have failed to do that.

Food — Sch 8 Group 1

It is a popular fallacy that food is zero-rated. Of course, most food is, but *Sch 8 Group 1* contains numerous exceptions. Some of these are well known, such as ice cream and potato crisps. Others are not at all what one would expect, such as orange juice and mineral water.

If you have a book containing the law available, you will find the following explanation easier to understand if you have the law open in front of you as you read. Incidentally, *Group 1* is one of the most complicated. Most of the rest are more simple!

The zero-rating for food is set out in four parts:

1 The *general items*, which are zero-rated.

2 *Some exceptions*, which are standard-rated, for instance, catering and beverages.

3 *Exceptions to the exceptions* which put back into zero-rating, for instance, such drinks as milk, tea and coffee.

4 *Notes*. When reading the law, always check the notes. Often, when you think you have found a zero-rating or an exemption in the items, you will find underneath a note, which either removes the relief or qualifies it.

The law begins by saying that the following are zero-rated:

● human food;

● animal feed;

● seeds or the means of propagating plants which produce either of these;

● live animals of a kind generally used as, yielding or producing human food.

Catering

The exception for catering is right at the start of *Group 1*. It includes (*note (3)*):

● food sold for consumption on the premises on which it is supplied;

● 'hot' takeaway food. In other words, 'cold' takeaway food is zero-rated.

Unfortunately, it is not that simple because, to qualify as 'takeaway', the food must be removed from the premises on which it is sold. That doesn't just mean the café or snack bar; 'premises' includes any area to which access is restricted, such as a racecourse or an amusement park, even though not owned by the food outlet trading from it.

However, in *J Bishop and P Elcocks (LON/01/690 No 17620)*, the premises were held to be the portakabin from which the food was sold, not the entire Royal Naval Air Station, Culdrose in which it was sited under a licence from the Secretary of State for Defence. See that case for a review of many of the earlier ones.

There have also been many cases on what is or is not 'catering' when food is supplied ready for consumption. If a sandwich bar makes up platters containing a finger buffet complete with napkins and paper plates, so that all the host or hostess has to do is to remove the cling film, the supply is likely to be a supply of standard-rated catering even though the food is cold.

However, the point is a fine one and in *Safeway Stores plc (LON/94/2963 No 14067: [1997] STC 163)*, 'party trays' packed on disposable foil trays in a display box for 12–20 people were held not to be catering. Similarly, in *Remo Bardetti and Anna Bardetti (t/a Obertelli Quality Sandwiches) (LON/99/0561 No 16758)*, sandwiches on platters delivered to offices were held to be not catering. There was little difference between them and bags of sandwiches. There was no accompanying service, the supply was not for any party or event and it included no crockery, cutlery or other items.

In *Happy Place Ltd (t/a The Munch Box) (LON/00/1218 No 17654)*, the platters did include paper plates and napkins but, on the basis of the *Safeway* case, the factors pointing towards catering were outweighed by those against it, including the impression that the food tended to be bought for office meetings over lunch.

In *A Leach (t/a Carlton Catering) (LON/01/46 No 17767)*, food delivered to a school hot, as required by the *Food and Hygiene Regulations*, was held not to be a supply of catering. The school reheated and plated the food.

That the standard-rating for catering *includes* food sold for consumption on the premises and hot takeaway food means that those two inclusions are merely examples of what is standard-rated. They do not limit the definition; thus if a supply qualifies as catering by its nature, it is standard-rated even if the customer collects the food. Whilst much catering is in relation to events, such as a party, an individual meal cooked for a single person could also be caught.

There have also been cases on what is or is not *hot food*; ie food heated for consumption whilst hot. A pie may be hot when sold because it has just been cooked. The sale is not necessarily standard-rated just because the cooking was deliberately timed for a meal time. Thus, in *John Pimblett & Sons Ltd ([1988] STC 358, CA)*, hot pies, baked on the premises in time to be sold at lunchtime, were held to be zero-rated. The baking created a pleasant smell and atmosphere and the objective was to provide freshly baked pies. Pimblett neither kept them hot nor reheated them. Some customers bought pies to eat at once; others did not.

In *Lewis's Group Ltd (MAN/89/389 No 4931)*, chickens cooked on the premises and then kept warm for food safety reasons were also held to be zero-rated. Lewis's did not heat the chickens so their customers could eat them hot, or warm, or at any particular temperature. If the customer wanted hot chicken and timed the purchase accordingly, that was a consequence, not the purpose of the cooking.

Again, in *Great American Bagel Factory Ltd (LON/00/659 No17018)*, toasted bagels were held not to be standard rated hot food because they were heated to give a crisp inner texture, not for consumption when warm. They cooled rapidly, yet were often taken back to customers' offices and they remained crisp when cool.

See Notice 709/2 *Catering and takeaway food* for Customs' views.

Human food

There are numerous exceptions to the zero-rating for human food, as you can see if you have the law in front of you. Some are obvious, such as ice cream; others less so. For instance, a yoghurt is zero-rated but a frozen one is caught by *Excepted Item 1*.

Did you think that orange juice was zero-rated? After all, everything else in a typical English breakfast is! However, *Excepted Item 4* covers beverages including fruit juices and bottled waters. Bet you never thought water was standard-rated!

The distinction between chocolate cake and chocolate biscuits can be seen in *Excepted Item 2* for confectionery. It goes like this:

- food is zero-rated,

- but not confectionery,

- except cakes or biscuits, which are therefore zero-rated,

- other than biscuits wholly or partly covered with chocolate, which are therefore standard-rated!

One of the best known tribunal cases is that on Jaffa cakes (*United Biscuits (UK) Ltd (LON/91/160 No 6344)*). Customs argued that Jaffa cakes were biscuits. Since they are partly covered in chocolate, that would make them standard-rated. The Tribunal noted that, when a cake goes stale, it goes hard whereas a biscuit goes soft. Apparently, Jaffa cakes go rock hard and it decided that they were zero-rated!

Peanuts are covered in *Excepted Item 5*, which standard-rates various snack products when packaged for human consumption without further preparation including:

- salted or roasted nuts;

- other than nuts in shell.

Excepted Item 5 also standard rates various products made from the potato, such as potato crisps and *savoury food products obtained by the swelling of cereals or cereal products*. This produces the curious result that *Hula Hoops*, corn hoops made from maize, are zero rated whereas an otherwise identical one made of potato is standard rated *(United Biscuits (UK) Ltd (MAN/01/60 No 17391))*! The phrase *obtained by the swelling* was interpreted as meaning on purpose as part of the manufacturing process. Though *Hula Hoops* swelled by about $1/3$, this was incidental, not a part of the process.

Over the years, there have been a number of cases on the difference between dietary products which count as food and those which do not. For instance, Customs accept that meal replacement products for slimmers are zero-rated, unless caught as confectionery. However, appetite suppressants in pill or powder form are not.

In *SIS (Science in Sport) Ltd (MAN/98/844 No 16555)*, a powder, which was mixed with water in order to take it, was argued by Customs to be a drink and thus caught by *Excepted Item 4*. The Tribunal held that the product taken in liquid form was zero-rated as a 'dietary integrator' which happened to be made up as a drink for sports persons. It was not a sports drink, which would be caught as a beverage. The Tribunal considered that Customs' policy was flawed in failing to distinguish between 'sports drinks' that were in reality drinks, and 'dietary integrators' made as drinks.

In *Rivella (UK) Ltd (LON/99/562 No 16382)*, Rivella, a drink comprising 35% lactoserum, an extract of milk was held to be covered by *Overriding Item 6* (overriding the exceptions) as milk. Its ingredients and the manufacturing process were decisive factors, supported by the marketing process, which linked in the minds of consumers the principal source of the product as extracts of milk. This was despite it being a clear fizzy liquid, herb flavoured and with no resemblance to milk.

For Customs' Views, See Notice 701/14 *Food*.

Animal feed

Zero-rating for animal feed is restricted by *Excepted Item 6*, which standard-rates *pet foods, canned, packaged or prepared; packaged foods (not being pet foods) for birds other than poultry or game; and biscuits and meal for cats and dogs*. This then creates the interesting distinction between food for dogs kept as pets and that for working dogs such as sheepdogs and greyhounds.

See Notice 701/15 *Food for animals* for Customs' views. For instance, they accept zero-rating for food specifically packaged for working dogs provided that it is not sold as equally suitable for all breeds, sizes and ages of dogs.

In *Bambers Frozen Meats Ltd (MAN//01/0629 No 17626)*, a product, described on the packaging as a biscuit and which was produced in rough bone shaped lumps, was held not to be a biscuit. The description was a mistake, which should be corrected! The texture was rougher and flakier than that of biscuits. It also contained the nutrients normally absent from dog biscuits and it swelled in the digestive system rather than merely disintegrate in contact with gastric juices, as did biscuits. The product was a cereal, not meal, because it was 73.5 % wheat. It therefore qualified for zero rating, being sold for working dogs.

Seeds and plants

The coverage of this is obvious much of the time but be careful. Shrubs and trees are generally standard-rated but a walnut tree producing edible nuts is zero-rated, as are fruit trees generally. Notice 701/38 *Seeds and plants* provides extensive guidance.

Live animals

The fourth category of zero-rating for *Live Animals of a kind generally used as yielding or producing human food* covers farm animals generally. It also includes rabbits and ostriches!

It does not include a horse, even a carthorse, because the latter does not yield as a cow yields milk or produce like a hen produces eggs. Although it may assist in the production of a crop by tilling the land, that is too far removed from the sense in which the word 'producing' is used.

Even if it were possible to show that horsemeat was occasionally eaten in the UK, that would not enable zero-rating because such consumption would not meet the *generally used as* test. If you see such words in the law, they mean you must be able to show that the event in question happens regularly and all over the UK. That is not the same as saying that it happens everywhere and all the time but it must be common.

Sewerage services and water — Sch 8 Group 2

This group is largely self-explanatory but it does not cover:

- water supplied to organisations carrying on a 'relevant industrial activity'. That means one of those described in divisions 1–5 of the Standard Industrial Classification;

- distilled water, de-ionised water and water of similar purity;

- the bottled water excepted from the zero-rating in *Group 1* for food;

- hot water — this stops avoidance schemes based on outsourcing the heating of water and then claiming zero-rating for it.

Notice 701/16 *Sewerage and water* refers.

Books — Sch 8 Group 3

The law on the zero-rating for books, newspapers etc is as delightfully brief as that for food is lengthy. Unfortunately, this brevity has not provided the simplicity necessary to avoid disputes and there have been just as many tribunal cases concerning *Group 3* as there have on *Group1*.

Arguments have mostly concerned the nature of:

- a book;

- a booklet, brochure, pamphlet or leaflet;

- a newspaper, journal or periodical.

The key test

The key test is often whether the item in question qualifies as reading matter designed to be held in the hand. Thus, a poster does not qualify, even though it may contain a substantial amount of text, because it is not a brochure, pamphlet or leaflet and it is designed to be displayed on a wall. Nor does something like a score card qualify because, essentially, it is designed to be filled in.

Brochures and application forms

To cope with the case of something like a brochure with an application form, Customs have a rule that it can be zero-rated provided that the space occupied by the application form is no more than 25% of the total. The entire page is counted if there is nothing else on the page, not just the spaces to be completed. That is not law, merely an administrative ruling, but it might be difficult to persuade a tribunal that any item with less than 75% text qualified as a brochure, pamphlet or leaflet.

The 25% ruling assumes that the form for completion is intended to be detached. If the entire item is intended to be returned, Customs say it is standard-rated.

Other items

Notice 701/10 *Printed and similar matter* lists Customs' views on numerous other items. Again, these rulings are not law, merely interpretation, but they are mostly common sense.

So ...

If something is essentially reading matter, it is likely to be zero-rated. If its nature is more akin to stationery it is probably standard-rated. Letter headings, diaries, calendars and greeting cards are all standard-rated items. If tempted to argue that a particular item, such as a calendar, has extensive wording, remember that the test in law is whether it is a book, booklet, brochure, pamphlet, leaflet, newspaper etc. The reading matter test is merely a guide.

The above is a distillation of points from the numerous cases on what is covered by *Group 3*. The precise nature and purpose of the item are usually the key to whether something is or is not, for instance, a leaflet.

In *GNP Booth Ltd (EDN/01/129 No 17555)*, the Tribunal commented that the purpose is the key when deciding if an item qualifies as a leaflet. Items the size of a visiting card are too small but the weight of the paper is unimportant.

Books in electronic form

A book in electronic form is standard-rated, unless it is covered by the special relief for talking books for the blind — see *Group 4* below. This means that a cassette tape or a CD ROM is standard-rated despite the same material on paper being zero-rated. Unfortunately, the answer to this anomaly is to standard rate books. The zero rating in the UK is the exceptional situation, not the other way around!

Printed material supplied with other goods or services

Where printed material is supplied with a package of goods or services, Customs have often accepted that part of the supply is zero-rated. Examples include:

- a subscription, which includes a magazine;
- a book and a CD ROM sold together.

It is no longer safe to assume that the printed material is a separate zero-rated supply merely because it has a physical existence and would be zero-rated if sold on its own. See Chapter 12, *Have I Got One Supply or Two?* for comment on the numerous cases on whether there is one supply or two. If there is only one supply, the question is which one is dominant and therefore decides the rate of VAT applicable.

Talking books for the blind and handicapped and wireless sets for the blind — Sch 8 Group 4

This covers

- supplies to charities for the blind of specialist audio tape and specialised equipment for recording or reproduction of speech;

- supplies to any charity of radio receivers and cassette recorders/players.

Transport — Sch 8 Group 8

This group covers a large number of services connected with ships and aircraft and with the transporting of people or goods in them.
Examples are:

- sale of or repair of ships and aircraft except those below 15 tons/8,000kg respectively or which are designed or adapted for recreation or pleasure;

- lifeboats and associated equipment, such as tractors or winches;

- transport of people in vehicles, ships or aircraft taking 10 or more passengers, or by the Post Office or on a scheduled flight;

- transport of people to or from a place outside the UK;

- transport of goods to or from a place outside the EU;

- various services, such as pilotage, agency work, handling and storage connected with the import or export of goods.

Some of these zero-ratings cover only specific services in limited circumstances so, if you come across them, check both the law and Customs' interpretation of it.

For instance, 'fun' transport within such tourist attractions as a coal mine or a safari park, when supplied by the person who charges admission and recreational trips in aircraft are generally standard-rated.

Relevant Notices are 744A *Passenger transport* and 744B *Freight transport and associated services.*

Caravans and houseboats — Sch 8 Group 9

This Group zero-rates:

- caravans over legal towing size (ie residential);

- houseboats without own means of propulsion;

but not the supply of accommodation in them.

Thus, although the sale or renting of residential caravans or houseboats is zero-rated, short-term accommodation is not. This prevents a potential distortion of competition with hotel rooms or with other forms of holiday accommodation, both of which are standard-rated by exception from the exemption for licenses to occupy land in *Sch 9 Group 1.*

Notice 701/20 Caravans and houseboats refers.

Gold — Sch 8 Group 10

This zero-rating is confined to transactions involving a Central Bank.

Bank notes — Sch 8 Group 11

This is for the benefit of those Scottish and Irish Banks, which have the right to issue their own banknotes.

Drugs, medicines, aids for the handicapped etc — Sch 8 Group 12

This group has numerous items including some which zero-rate aids for the disabled, whether supplied to the handicapped person direct or to a charity. It covers for example:

- drugs and other goods when supplied on prescription by a chemist;

- goods designed or adapted for use in connection with medical or surgical treatment when supplied by order of a doctor;

- certain specialised equipment designed for use by handicapped people;

- certain work to facilitate use of a building by handicapped persons when supplied to:
  (i) a *handicapped person* in his private residence; or
  (ii) a *charity* if the building qualifies — see comment in brackets.
  The work is
    (a) building a ramp or widening a doorway or passage (in any building when supplied to a charity);
    (b) creating or adapting a bathroom, washroom or lavatory (in residential accommodation or in a day centre where at least 20% of the users are handicapped; or a washroom or lavatory (not bathroom) in any building used principally by a charity for charitable purposes);
    (c) installing a lift (in a permanent or temporary residence or day centre for handicapped persons);

- alarm systems for the handicapped when supplied to the latter or to a charity for making available to handicapped people.

See Notice 701/7 *Reliefs for disabled people*. To explain the law in detail here would mean virtually printing it verbatim since the 20 items in *Group 12* are carefully worded to cover limited circumstances only and are supported by numerous detailed notes. If you are involved, you will need to study these rules in detail. To cover that detail here would take more space than their specialist nature justifies.

However, the Group does potentially zero-rate a wide range of goods and many businesses have found themselves in the Tribunals in the process of trying to claim that zero rating. The comments on some of these arguments below illustrate its restricted nature. Often, a complete understanding requires reading the full decision.

The design problem

Where the law requires the goods to be specifically designed for use by handicapped people, that means what it says! In *Donald Bell (LON/83/147 No 1480)* standard fittings installed in a special kitchen for a disabled person did not qualify. They were merely fixed at a lower height than normal, not specially designed.

Compare that with *Softley Ltd (t/a Softley Kitchens) (LON/96/1810 No 15034)* in which the units, although made of standard components, had design features, such as special plinths, which made them unsuitable for use other than by handicapped persons.

In *Kirton Healthcare Group Ltd (LON/00/498 No 17062)*, a chair was found to be designed for the chronically sick and disabled but a second design only qualified when equipped with certain optional accessories.

In *Hulsta Furniture (UK) Ltd (LON/98/936 No 16289)*, an electrically adjustable bed was held to be designed for people temporarily or permanently suffering from disabilities. In *Tempur Pedic (UK) Ltd (LON/95/458 No 13744)*, a very high density foam mattress and pillow was held to be equipment designed solely for use by the chronically sick.

In *Medivac Healthcare Ltd (LON/99/1271 No 16829)*, bedding covers, a special vacuum cleaner, a dehumidifier and other products were accepted as designed solely for chronically sick and disabled on the basis of evidence that they were for use only by people seriously affected by allergy to house mites. An anti-allergen spray was also an *equipment or appliance*, the canister being essential to the use of the spray.

In *Royal Midland Counties Home for Disabled People (MAN/00/24 No 17010)*, a generator, which provided emergency standby power for essential aids for severely handicapped people, was held not to be an *accessory* to relevant goods. The generator, when in use, was the sole means of providing power, not an optional extra. The decision contains a useful review of the meaning of *accessory*.

In *Arthritis Care (LON/95/2611 No 13974)*, a specially constructed staircase, designed with extra fire protection so as to provide a rescue point at a hotel for arthritis sufferers for use by people unable to use the stairs, was not *equipment*. Even if it had been, it was not designed solely for use by handicapped persons.

In *Joulesave Emes Ltd (MAN/99/462 No 17115)*, radiator and pipe covers were held to be designed solely for use by handicapped persons on the basis of the designer's intention, how they were marketed and sold and to whom. It did not matter that they also provided protection to the able bodied.

In *Boys' and Girls' Welfare Society (MAN/96/1041 No 15274)* the design and installation of a hydrotherapy pool and its environmental control system, (heating, water cleansing, humidity control etc) at a residential home for handicapped children was held to qualify as *equipment and appliances,* being a separate element from the building in which it was housed. Although supplied by a sub-contractor to the main contractor, it was then supplied on as a separate element by the main contractor.

However the installation of special low surface temperature radiators in the residential unit was altering the heating system, not adapting goods.

Meaning of chronically sick or disabled

Note (3) defines *handicapped* as meaning *chronically sick or disabled*. Tribunals have interpreted this strictly. In *Benefoot UK Ltd (LON/98/942 No 17022)*, a man able to do a route march with the aid of an 'orthotic' appliance in his boot was held not to qualify.

In *Foxer Industries (LON/95/1452 Nos 13817 and 14469)*, single seater golf buggies did not meet the design requirement. In the second decision, the Tribunal decided whether the work of adapting individual buggies to special requirements did on the basis of whether each customer qualified as handicapped and on the nature of the modification.

The customer problem

The zero ratings in *Group 12* mostly include in their requirements that the supply is to a handicapped person or to a charity. This creates problems where another body is paying for the work. Thus, in *Cross Electrical and Building Services Ltd (MAN/99/1070 No 16954)*, the supply was held not to be to the tenant when a housing action trust ordered the work and received and paid the invoice. Similarly, in *Mrs DM Brand as Trustee of Racket Sports for Children with Special Needs (LON/95/2751 No 14080)*, the work of widening doorways etc to facilitate access for handicapped people was not supplied to the Charity which funded the work but to the tennis club owning the premises, which contracted with and paid the builder.

The premises problem

Some of the zero-ratings only apply if the goods are installed in a particular kind of building. For instance, items 16–18 between them zero rate to a handicapped person the installation of a lift in his or her house or to a charity in its home or day centre for handicapped persons. In *Union of Students of the University of Warwick (MAN/95/802 No 13821)*, the Union failed to get zero-rating for the installation of a lift at their premises. Although the lift was used mostly by handicapped students and although the Union's activities were charitable, the premises were a day centre for all students, not just handicapped ones.

Imports, exports etc — Sch 8 Group 13

This provides three specialist zero-ratings for:

- the sale of goods not yet cleared through customs;

- supplies of goods or services in connection with international defence projects;

- the supply to an overseas customer of jigs, patterns, templates, dies, punches and similar machine tools used in the UK solely to produce goods for export outside the EU.

The last of the above enables a manufacturer to zero-rate his charge for tooling required to produce the goods to the customer's specification, which are exported. He cannot zero-rate the tooling under the ordinary rules for the export of goods because it never leaves his factory.

Charities — Sch 8 Group 15

This zero-rates a variety of supplies either by a charity or to a charity including:

- the sale by a charity, or its trading subsidiary, of goods donated to it;

- the donation of goods to a charity, or its trading subsidiary, for sale or export;

- the export of any goods by a charity;

- the supply of relevant goods, primarily medical equipment of various kinds and vehicles designed or adapted to carry handicapped persons, either to an eligible body or for donation to one. 'Eligible body' means hospitals, NHS bodies of various kinds and certain others. The zero-rating enables, for example, a local appeal committee to get a piece of medical equipment for donation to a local hospital free of VAT or that hospital to buy it direct using any charitable funds which it may happen to have. Many National Health institutions benefit from trust funds dating from before the NHS was formed;

- advertising supplied to a charity.

The above is only a synopsis of detailed rules which cover several pages of the law. As with the rules on aids for the handicapped in *Group 12*, you will need to study the law in detail, if it affects you.

The following guidance has been issued by Customs:

- Notice 701/1 *Charities*.

- Information Sheet 8/98 (June 1998) (plus correction) *Charities: Supply, repair and maintenance of relevant goods — including adapted motor vehicles.*

- Notice 701/6 plus supplement Charity funded equipment for medical, veterinary uses etc.

- Notice 701/58 zero rating of charity advertising.

Donated goods

Donated goods can be created out of a variety of goods and services. For example, the calendars sold via the BBC 'Hearts of Gold' programme in 1993 on behalf of SOS for children qualified, having been produced from goods and services supplied without charge. The relief does not zero-rate all sales of a charity shop. Bought in goods are standard-rated.

A concession zero-rates the disposal of goods unsuitable for sale to the public because of poor quality (Notice 48 (March 2002) para 3.21)

Relevant goods

Relevant goods is defined in *Note (3)* and includes many of the items zero-rated as aids for the handicapped under *Group 12*. It includes:

- medical, scientific, computer, video, sterilising, laboratory or refrigeration equipment if it is:
  – for use in medical research, training, diagnosis or treatment; or
  – parts and accessories for use in or with the above.

A careful study of the above wording shows that it is not enough for goods to be used in medical training. They must be medical in nature. This prevents equipment, such as an overhead projector, being zero-rated merely because of the use to which it is put.

However, Customs used to argue that it was not enough for goods to be designed for medical training and that they must also be of a kind used for diagnosis or treatment. On that basis, resuscitation training models would not qualify but an extra-statutory concession was announced on 8/7/98, effective from March 1997. Further details were given in Business Brief 10/99 dated 22/4/99.

This 'concession' was probably unnecessary. In *Medical and Dental Staff Training Ltd (LON/98/1442 No 17031)*, I persuaded the Tribunal that 'phantom heads' used in training dentists, were *medical equipment*. 'Phantom heads' are specialist equipment , which reproduce the physical characteristics and limitations of a human head. My client's witnesses gave evidence that the heads were used to some extent in postgraduate training on actual patient cases in which the equipment was used to plan and practice the dental treatment to be later carried out on the patient. Thus, there was an element of use for treatment which blurred the distinction between training and treatment.

In *Anglodent Co (LON/2000/271 No 16891)*, a case concerning similar equipment, another Tribunal took an even firmer line, commenting that the words of the statute suggested that the words *for use in medical training* suggested that medical training equipment was intended to qualify as *medical equipment*. Whilst equipment with a variety of possible uses did not become medical merely because it was for use in medical training, the goods in question had a unique purpose at the time of supply and therefore qualified as medical.

See also under *Group 12* for notes on the numerous cases concerning aids for the handicapped, some of which also qualify as relevant goods.

Rescue equipment

Note (3)(g) says that *relevant goods* includes certain specialist equipment *solely for use for the purpose of rescue or first-aid services undertaken by a charitable institution providing such services*. In *Severnside Siren Trust Ltd (LON/99/88 No 16640)*, a siren system for alerting the public to danger from toxic gasses etc resulting from industrial accidents was held to be for the purpose of rescue services and thus to be *relevant goods*.

Evidence to justify zero-rating

The supplier must obtain evidence that the supply is to a charity and is eligible for zero rating. Where that zero rating depends upon the specific circumstances of the customer, the latter must provide a certificate to the supplier. Check on the precise terms of the certificate — see examples in the notices listed earlier.

Clothing and footwear — Sch 8 Group 16

The zero-rating is for children's clothing and protective boots and helmets, including cycle helmets, both motor and pedal, to private purchasers (not when supplied to a business for use by its employees).

Children's clothing is not automatically zero-rated!

The law requires the clothing or footwear to be:

* designed for young children; *and*
* not suitable for older persons.

The issue of size

Although Notice 714 (January 2002) *Zero rating young children's clothing and footwear* contains detailed guidance on and sizes for different items, which are accepted as qualifying for zero-rating, this is subject to the overall requirements of design and suitability. Mere size is insufficient, as a matter of law, despite the misleading suggestion otherwise in para 4.2 of the Notice!

The sizes are intended to provide a cut-off point on a child's 14th birthday. However, many small women can wear children's sizes and many children need adult sizes. Since, as soon as a child understands the difference between children's clothing and that for adults, it wants to wear the adult version, Customs have a control problem.

The result is an unsatisfactory situation in which retailers have a difficult problem differentiating between adult and children's clothing at the margin and where there is some revenue leakage because women wear children's sizes. On the other hand, some 12-year-olds need adult sizes and have to pay VAT.

If involved, take the design requirement seriously!

In *Brays of Glastonbury (CAR/78/95 No 650)*, moccasins were held to be standard-rated because there was no evident feature of design for young children. Evidence at the hearing included the point that 60% of UK women could wear shoes of size 5 or smaller despite the Notice stating that zero-rating was acceptable up to size $5\frac{1}{2}$!

In *Smart Alex Ltd (LON/01/1307 No 17832)*, the Tribunal said an XL size sweatshirt for an 11-year-old, to which a school logo and the pupil's name was added by the wholesaler to create a school uniform, was standard rated. The evidence of the design intention was the size of the item, not the age of the user.

Some questions to check your understanding. Review your answers with the text.

The following are general questions, not ones specific to the detailed explanations given above. This is because there is no point in trying to learn the contents of the zero rating Schedule in detail until you have a real problem to deal with. You need to know where to go to find the answer rather than to try to learn the law. In any case, this keeps changing.

- There are 15 Groups in *Sch 8, Group 14* having been deleted. How many can you remember? (It is not important to be able to list them all. However, to know the main ones is useful because this makes it easier to spot a situation in which there could be a zero-rated supply rather than a standard-rated one).

- Why should the question 'is it standard rated?' be banned?

- Why is it important to look at the law itself rather than at a Customs Notice or a book like this one if you need to decide whether a product is zero-rated?

11.   So What is Exempt?

As explained at the start of the zero-rating chapter, this book does not attempt to cover either zero-rating or exemption in every detail. The aim is to provide you with a good grounding in the rules so that, if and when you have to go into them in more detail in order to decide the correct treatment of a transaction, you will start with a basic understanding.

The contents of Schedule 9

Group 1	Land
Group 2	Insurance
Group 3	Postal services
Group 4	Betting, gaming and lotteries
Group 5	Finance
Group 6	Education
Group 7	Health
Group 8	Burial and cremation
Group 9	Trade unions, professionals and other interest bodies
Group 10	Sports, sports competitions and physical education
Group 11	Works of art etc
Group 12	Fund-raising events by charities and other qualifying bodies
Group 13	Cultural services etc
Group 14	Supplies of goods where input tax cannot be recovered
Group 15	Investment gold

Land — Sch 9 Group 1

The exemption for land is brief. It covers *the grant of any interest in, right over or any licence to occupy land* with a rider, which adapts that for Scottish land law.

'Grant' includes an assignment or surrender of a lease. It also covers a reverse surrender; ie a case where a tenant has to make a payment to a landlord in order to get out of obligations under an onerous lease (*Note (1)*).

Then come the words 'other than' at the start of a long list of exceptions in Items 1(a)–(n). Being exceptions to the exemption, they are standard-rated. Thus, Item 1(d) standard-rates hotel accommodation.

Note: Be precise in your language over land transactions. For instance, people routinely refer to the 'sale' of a property when they mean either a sub-lease or an assignment at a premium. The VAT status can be different.

The exemption

Thus, subject to the exceptions, the exemption is for:

* Any interest in land. This means a freehold or a lease, which must be in writing.

* A right over land. Rights of way and mineral rights are examples.

- Any licence to occupy land. Licences do not have to be in writing and they are often informal. A licence to occupy land can be for as short a period as an afternoon and for as small an area as that occupied by a market stall.

What is or is not a licence to occupy?

The precise definition of a licence to occupy was referred by the House of Lords to the CJEC in *Sinclair Collis Ltd ([1999] STC 701: [2001] UKHL 30: [2001] STC 989: [2003] STC 898*. This is an important case, which helps to clarify the borderline between exempt licences to occupy land and standard rated rights related to its use.

Sinclair Collis's agreement with each publican gave it the right to install its cigarette vending machine and to operate and maintain it in the premises for two years in a place decided on by the publican.

Article 13 (B)(1)(b), of the *EC 6th VAT Directive*, exempts *the leasing or letting of immovable property*, so that is the basis for interpreting any licence to occupy land. The CJEC held that the agreement with *SC* did not amount to a letting of immovable property. The publican could move the machine about, as necessary. *SC* had no right of possession of any specific area; moreover the public also had access to the machine. *SC's* right of access, limited to opening hours, was to the inside of the machine in order to service it.

The CJEC decision will not of course cover all possible licences. The House of Lords, which came to the same conclusion on a majority of 3/2 before referring the matter to the CJEC, commented that the mere right to occupy space is not exempt. Otherwise, that would cover permission to display a picture on the walls of a gallery. Thus, a key distinction made by both courts seems to be between the mere right to use a spot for a particular purpose and the right to exclusive occupation of a specific area. The right to place a public telephone in someone else's premises also seems likely not to qualify for exemption on the basis of *SC*.

Another example is whether the right to use a chair in a hairdressing salon, granted to a self-employed stylist, is exempt. The trend of decisions has been that this is a standard rated supply of the right to carry on a hairdressing business in the salon including the use of the chair and access to other facilities, rather than an exempt licence to occupy. See for example *Mrs SV Cranmer (LON/95/3120 No 17037)*.

However, in *DR Kirkman(MAN/99/958 No 17651)*, the Tribunal commented that, if the tenancy agreement had been correctly drafted, a licence to occupy land could have been achieved. It could have seen two supplies, a licence to occupy land and a supply of supporting services if the plan attached to the agreement had clearly identified the area to be occupied and if references to the ancillary services had been in the separate service contract rather than that for the tenancy.

Leases

Rent under a lease is exempt unless you opt to tax it, as explained in the chapter *Property*. Normally, service charges payable in addition are merely rent under a different name and are treated in the same way.

However, in *Canary Wharf Ltd (LON/95/2869 No 14513)*, repairs and maintenance, servicing common areas and car parking were held to be separate standard-rated supplies rather than part of the rent, when supplied by a management company direct to the tenants. The decision was based on the wording of the lease and the fact that the services supplied were more extensive than those necessary to ensure 'quiet enjoyment' of the property by the tenants.

Beware of any additional terms of the lease, such as that either side shall pay a premium or for work to be done. Usually, such payments will have the same character as the rent because they are paid as part of the conditions under which the property is occupied. For example, Customs used to argue that a premium was only exempt if paid by the tenant to the landlord. Then the CJEC held in *Lubbock Fine ([1993] ECR 1-6665, [1994] STC 101)* that a reverse premium, paid by a landlord to induce a tenant to take on a lease, was also exempt.

However, in *Cantor Fitzgerald International ([2001] STC 1453)* the CJEC held that the exemption applies to the grant of leases, not to transactions, which are merely based on them or are ancillary to them. Therefore, when *CFI* was paid by the existing tenant to accept the assignment of a lease, it made a standard rated supply to that existing tenant.

In *Mirror Group plc ([2001] STC 1453),* heard at the same time, the CJEC held that a reverse premium paid to *MG* by the landlord as an inducement to take up a lease was also not payment for an exempt supply. The Court also said that merely undertaking to become a tenant in such a case was not a supply of services to the landlord. However, the Divisional Court noted that the Tribunal had held that there had been a supply and refused to remit the case for a further hearing.

Thus, if a premium is charged by a landlord for granting a lease or by a tenant for assigning one, the supply is exempt. So are payments for surrenders and reverse surrenders, as noted at the start of the comments on *Group 1*. This is because, in each of those cases, there is the supply of an interest in land. Neither *CFI* nor *MG* had any interest in the land in question at the time of the payments to them; each was acquiring it, not supplying it.

Customs do accept, in para 10.5, Notice 742 (March 2002) *Land and Property* that variations to existing leases, such as changing the permitted use, altering the length of the lease or the property covered by it are exempt. Nevertheless, the *CFI* and *MG* cases have shown that the scope of the exemption for interests in land is not as wide as was previously thought.

Thus, an important planning point is that, before entering into any agreement concerning property, the parties agree on the VAT status of the transaction. In the most simple situation of an ordinary lease with no premium, the one supplying the interest in land will wish to waive exemption for (opt to tax) the rent so as to make it standard rated and the associated input tax recoverable. The VAT involved may be considerable if there has been expenditure on, for instance, refurbishing the building. However, a tenant, who is partly exempt or not even VAT registered will not wish to be charged VAT. Depending on the input tax involved, it may be better for the landlord to negotiate a higher rent with such a tenant rather than to opt to tax it.

As soon as the agreement becomes more complicated with payments other than rent, consider carefully whether they qualify for exemption. If they do not, the option to tax is irrelevant.

A planning point concerns any work needed on the property, which may seem obvious but which all too frequently seems not to be understood. If the rent is exempt and the landlord therefore could not recover VAT incurred on the property but the tenant can, leave it to the tenant to do the work. The tenant will be able to recover the VAT if the property is to be used for the purposes of a taxable business.

However, do not write into the terms of the lease a requirement that the tenant shall do the work or you will be in danger of increasing the value of the exempt rent by the value of the work done by the tenant. The same applies if a rent-free period is part of the formal terms of the lease, as opposed to merely arising from the fact that the rent only starts from a date subsequent to occupation.

Similarly, a landlord cannot recover VAT incurred on work done to meet the requirements of the tenant merely by including a provision that the value of the work will be invoiced separately. The work will be supplied by the builder to the landlord, not to the tenant and the onward supply can hardly be of building work. Thus, in *West Devon Borough Council (LON/97/549 No 17107)*, a contribution from a tenant towards the cost of refurbishing the property was held to be a premium for the lease, not payment for the work.

Property owned by the owners of a business

An associated point concerns the situation where a business occupies an office or factory owned by one or more of its directors or by their pension fund. In such situations, directors tend to take it for granted that their company can recover any VAT incurred on expenditure on the property, regardless of the fact that it does not own it. Of course, many 'leasehold improvements' will have little or no ongoing value in an industrial context; that is to say, work in adapting the fabric or altering the layout of the building for the purposes of the business occupying it may be irrelevant to the next user.

However, suppose a property was substantially improved at the expense of the occupying company and then sold on for a substantial capital gain; VAT recovered by the company on the cost of the improvement work would represent a significant saving to a property owner not registered for VAT. If Customs realised what had happened, they would obviously query it.

Neither the directors nor their pension fund are likely to be registered for VAT. The arrangements are probably informal but commonsense suggests a written agreement under which an initial rent is determined and the business is made responsible for all expenditure on the property needed for that business. I suggest making a note of the normal commercial rent payable for such a property at the time and the reduction due to the business assuming liability for repairs. However, do not build into the agreement a rent reduction or a rent-free period in return for a formal obligation of the business to carry out improvements.

Although, for arrangements not at arm's length, a formal lease and security of tenure may be unnecessary, it seems to me that something in writing is needed in order to confirm the basis for VAT recovery. Board minutes setting out the reasons for major expenditure as it occurs could also be useful evidence of why it was necessary for the purposes of the business.

The standard-rated exceptions

Items 1(a)–(n) standard-rate the following supplies.

(a) **Sale of the freehold** — (fee simple) in commercial and industrial buildings , whether still under construction or within 3 years of completion *(Notes (2) and (4))*. See Chapter 25, *Property*, for further comment.

(b) **Supplies under developmental tenancies etc** — now of no practical effect.

(c) **Sporting rights** — (shooting, fishing, etc) unless included in the freehold of the land in question. A lease, which includes sporting rights, must be apportioned *(Note (8))*.

(d) **Hotel accommodation.**

This is wider than it sounds because it covers a bed in a hotel, inn, boarding house or similar establishment, together with any room provided in conjunction with the sleeping accommodation or for the purpose of a supply catering, such as at a wedding reception.

Similar establishment also includes furnished houses and flats which are used by or advertised as suitable for use by visitors or travellers even if without board or facilities for preparing food *(Note (9))*.

Similar establishment has been held to cover a hostel for the homeless, even though, in order to obtain a place, the individual had to be on Social Security and the average stay was several weeks rather than the few nights more typical of a hotel (*Namecourt Ltd [1984] VATTR 22,1560*). A Tribunal reached the same conclusion in *Westminster City Council ([1989] VATTR 71 No 3367)* concerning a hostel called Bruce House in which the accommodation was basic cubicles. So did that in *Look Ahead Housing and Care Ltd (LON/00/1133 No 17613)*, a hostel providing accommodation mostly for homeless people.

However, in *International Student House (LON/95/3142 No 14420)*, the Tribunal observed that the 'predominant characteristic' of a hotel, inn or boarding house was 'the offer of use of accommodation for gain'. *ISH*, a charity, whose objective was to further international understanding by providing accommodation to students from the UK and overseas, was not operating a *similar establishment*.

Then, in *Dinaro Ltd (t/a Fairway Lodge) (LON/99/855 No 17148)*, a 42 room hostel for people with mental problems and in need of care was held not to be one either. This was because of the selectivity in the choice of residents — people with mental problems-, the high degree of care and supervision, most of the residents being in receipt of the middle rate care component of the Disability Living Allowance and the emphasis on the residents being part of a 'family'.

The hire of premises including catering is standard rated

If you provide catering in a place, which is not a hotel, the entire charge is likely to be standard rated even if you price the use of the venue separately from the food and drink. In *Leez Priory (LON/02/181 No 18185)*, the venue charge for the use for weddings of a period house set in parkland was held to be part of a composite supply with the catering and other facilities offered, which included overnight accommodation for guests. Even if that was wrong, it was a similar establishment despite the sleeping accommodation only being on offer to guests attending a wedding.

The 28-day rule for long stay accommodation

See *Sch 6 para 9* for a special rule, which reduces to a minimum of 20% the value of the supply to an individual once a stay exceeds 28 days. This means that, from day 29 on, the value reduces to that of the facilities provided, such as cleaning and linen. The minimum value for the latter is 20%. VAT must also be charged on the value attributable to any meals provided. The balance of the charges, up to 80%, are outside the scope of VAT, not exempt.

(e) Holiday accommodation.

This includes any in a building, hut, such as a beach hut or chalet, caravan, house-boat or tent if the accommodation is advertised or held out as holiday accommodation or as suitable for holiday or leisure use (*Note (13)*).

It also includes houses, flats chalets and the like:

* Where the lease prevents the tenant living there throughout the year. Timeshares are an example.

* Where living there throughout the year is similarly prevented by the terms of any covenant or planning permission. Seaside chalets are a possible example (*Note (11) via Sch 8 Group 5, Note (13)*).

However, if the building is more than three years old, neither the freehold nor a premium for a tenancy, lease or licence in it are caught. In other words, the sale of, say, a holiday flat is only standard-rated until it is more than three years old (*Note (12)*). Moreover, the rule normally only affects places in which there is no right to live all the year round since, if permanent occupation is possible, a place will not usually be marketed as holiday accommodation.

In *Livingstone Homes UK Ltd (EDN/99/88 No 16649)*, a tribunal held that houses could be principal private residences even though the terms of the planning consent were that they 'shall be used as holiday dwelling houses only and for no other purpose and shall never in any way be sub-divided'. There was nothing to prevent owners from living in them. Although Customs did not appeal this decision, they do not accept it and further argument on the point is likely.

(f)   Seasonal pitches for caravans and associated facilities at caravan parks.

(g)   Pitches for tents and camping facilities.

(h)   Parking facilities for vehicles.

Beware of any right over land which includes the right to park on it — including a lock-up garage. The nature of the land is important and the intention of the customer as to use is irrelevant. It is no good merely getting a statement from your tenant of a wish to park a sofa rather than a motor! To avoid standard rating the rent of a lock-up garage, the tenancy agreement must expressly prohibit the parking of a vehicle (*Trinity Motor Factors* [1994] *STC 504*).

In *Internoms Ltd (LON/98/1112 No 16257)* a sub-lease for 120 years of a piece of land, for which planning permission for two cars had been granted, was held to be a standard rated supply of the facility to park a vehicle, not an exempt interest in land. Then in *Venuebest (MAN/00/942 No 17685: [2002] EWHC 2870 (Ch): [2003] STC 433)*, it was held that a lease of land used as a car park was a supply of parking rights in the absence of an express term to the contrary in the lease. The Tribunal had been wrong to say that the rent was exempt merely because the lease granted unfettered use of the land with no reference to parking.

In Notice 742 (March 2002) *Land and property*, Customs say:

- a *freehold* interest in a car park is exempt, once it is over 3 years old — one on bare land presumably being seen as a civil engineering work;

- a *lease* for the purpose of car parking in various circumstances, including a car park to a car park operator, of a taxi rank and of storage for bicycles or touring caravans is standard rated;

- but that a lease of land, except for a garage, which says nothing about use for parking vehicles or of land on which a tenant will store its own property, such as the stock of a motor dealer, is exempt.

In the light of *Venuebest,* the last indent above seems doubtful if the land is laid out as a car park or planning permission has been granted for that purpose.

(i)   Deleted.

(j)   Timber rights; ie, the right to fell and remove trees.

(k)   Housing or storage of aircraft or the mooring or storage of ships and boats.

(l)   Boxes, seats or other accommodation at sports grounds, theatres, concert halls or other places of entertainment. This catches, for instance, a box at the Albert Hall or a season ticket at a football ground.

(m)   Facilities for playing sport or participating in physical recreation.

Note (16) puts back into exemption a grant of sports facilities for:
More than 24 hours; or
A series of 10 or more periods, no matter what the total time provided that:

- they are for the same activity at the same place

- at intervals of at least a day but not more than 14 days

- under a written agreement for single price

- for exclusive use of the facilities

- the customer is a school, club, association or organisation representing affiliated clubs or constituent associations.

There is no legal definition of 'club'. It can consist of an informal team formed just for a competition involving ten or more events.

For further comment on other rules concerning land, including those on the waiver of exemption or option to tax, see Chapter 25, *Property*.

(n)   Specific to Scotland. Rights under Scottish land law to be granted an interest or right covered by the above paragraphs.

Insurance — Sch 9 Group 2

See Notice 701/36 *Insurance* (May 2002) for additional specialist comment on the nature of insurance. The comment here relates only to the exemption for UK insurance risks. For international transactions, see Chapter 22, *Exports and Imports of*

Services re *Sch 5 para 5* and Chapter 23, *Partial Exemption* re *Your right to recover input tax* and *How the right to recover affects banking, finance and insurance* . Those chapters explain the rules under which a premium to an insured who belongs outside the EU or one which is related to an export of goods outside the EU, together with commissions thereon, changes to outside the scope of VAT with recovery of the associated input tax.

Items 1 and 2: Insurance premiums

Insurance is only exempt if it is provided by (*Items 1 and 2*):

(a)   A person authorised under the *Insurance Companies Act 1982* to carry on insurance business; or

(b)   An insurer who belongs outside the UK against any risks or other things described in *Schs 1 and 2* to the *Insurance Companies Act 1982*.

The CJEC ruled in *Card Protection Plan Ltd* ([1999] *STC 270*), that a Member State may not restrict the scope of the exemption for insurance to supplies by insurers, who are authorised by national law.

See later for more on *CPP*.

Of course, insurance offered by an unauthorised insurer is likely to be illegal under the *Financial Services and Markets Act 2000*. However, Customs accept that the following are exempt from insurance even though they are not seen as such for regulatory purposes under the *FSMA*:

- funeral plans written under contracts of insurance;
- vehicle breakdown insurance;
- recharges under block insurance policies.

The policyholder acts as a principal; ie as the insurer, not as an intermediary, when charging for the insurance. Thus, the entire recharge is an exempt supply.

The term *block policy* does not include delegated authority arrangements under which a broker enters into contracts on behalf of the insurance company. There, the broker is acting as an intermediary and his supply is the value of his commission.

Recharges under block insurance policies

A block insurance policy allows the policyholder, acting in his name, to buy insurance for third parties on terms with the insurer and the third parties under which he then recharges the insurance to those parties. The policy may include cover for the policyholder's own liability to its customers or members.

Examples are:

- a removal company which provides insurance against the risk of damage during the move;
- a sports organisation, which provides its members with cover against the risk of injury or liability to another person whilst taking part in an event.

Product guarantees and warranties

If a guarantee or a warranty is recognised as insurance by the *Financial Services Authority,* it is exempt, subject to the rules in *Note (3)* explained later under

Insurance commissions associated with taxable supplies. Those provided by manufacturers and retailers are not usually seen by the *FSA* as insurance and Customs regard them as standard rated. However, it is probably preferable to have a standard rated warranty if you are the supplier of the goods. This is because an exempt supply incurs *Insurance Premium Tax* at 17.5%; a standard rated supply at least lets you recover the associated input tax.

'Run-off' situations

If an insurer ceases to issue new policies, the business is in 'run-off' whilst it deals with claims under contracts already written. The treatment of any additional premium under those existing policies is the same as that of the original one.

If handling the 'run-off' is contracted out to a third party, a planning point arises over the contract. To qualify for exemption as an insurance related service, the third party must make a composite charge for all its services. If it separates that for administration, such as accountancy or the management of invested premiums, that part of the supply will be standard rated.

An insurer with contracts in 'run-off', which is using a partial exemption method based on premium values, may need to discuss its calculations with Customs if using the current output values would distort the position. For instance, Customs might agree the use of the percentage recovery achieved in the last three years of active underwriting.

Engineering insurance and inspection

Engineering insurance covers such plant as boilers, cranes and lifts. The contract often requires the plant to be inspected and this may be covered by the premium. In paragraph 4.5 of Notice 701/36 (May 2002), Customs require insurers to decide whether they are making a separate supply of insurance and inspection or a composite one of either exempt insurance or standard rated inspection. A key consideration will obviously be whether the premium is calculated and quoted in separate amounts.

Item 4: Insurance brokers

Item 4 exempts the services as an *insurance intermediary* of a broker or insurance agent if they are related to a supply, actual or proposed, of insurance covered by *Items 1–3*; and provided when *acting in an intermediary capacity*.

What are the services of an insurance intermediary?

A service qualifies as that of an insurance intermediary if it is within any of the following *(Note (1))*:

(a) The bringing together, with a view to the insurance of risks, of persons seeking insurance and those who provide it.

(b) Work preparatory to concluding insurance contracts.

(c) Assistance in administering and performing such contracts including handling claims.

(d) Collecting premiums.

Exclusion of market research and similar services

Note (7) excludes from the Item 4 exemption:

- Market research, product design, advertising, promotional or similar services.

- The collection, collation and provision of information for use in connection with market research, product design, advertising, promotional or similar activities.

To avoid being caught by the exclusion of advertising services, Customs say that an organisation which, say, inserts a leaflet in a customer mailing, must:

- be paid per policy sold;

- endorse the product or the insurer;

- target its own customer base.

The last point seems of doubtful validity. It would appear to make no difference whether the person mailed is a customer, a supplier or a blind date!

What is acting in an intermediary capacity?

Note (2) says that a broker or agent is acting in an intermediary capacity wherever he is acting as an intermediary, or one of them, between:

(a)   An insurer; and

(b)   An actual or prospective buyer of insurance.

The above wordings are an attempted simplification of the law intended to make it easier to follow. See the law itself for the actual wording.

Some cases on acting in an intermediary capacity

In *Teletech (UK) Ltd (EDN/02/52 No 18080)*, the Tribunal rejected Customs' argument that the services of a call centre cold calling to sell insurance by telephone were promotional. A successful call, which sold a policy, put the insurance company on risk so *Teletech* was an insurance agent supplying services related to insurance transactions. In *Business Brief 07/03*, Customs accepted this.

In *SOC Private Capital Ltd (LON/2000/0810 No 17747)*, the insurers in the *Lloyd's* market were held to be the underwriting Members, not the Syndicates. The Members' Agents were insurance agents, who supplied both insurance and reinsurance services and services related to insurance transactions. They were a part of the chain between the insured and the insurers and thus participated in insurance transactions. They were authorised to act on behalf of the underwriting Members, they introduced them to the Syndicates, entered on their behalf into commitments with the Managing Agents of those Syndicates and carried out work preparatory to the contracts of insurance.

However, setting up, training and maintaining a sales force of self-employed sales agents, who supplied their services direct to the insurance company was itself not an intermediary service *(Agentevent Ltd (LON/00/1331 No 17764)*. The *Insurance Intermediaries Directive 77/92,* to which it was permissible to refer in interpreting the *6th Directive,* appeared to regard an insurance broker or agent as having a direct relationship with the insured.

Insurance commissions associated with taxable supplies

Note (3) says that if insurance is sold:

- in connection with a standard-rated supply of goods or services; and

- by the supplier thereof or a person connected with him who deals directly with the customer,

the insurance-related services, apart from the handling of claims, are standard-rated unless:

- the amount of the premium; and

- any other amount that the customer must pay; ie the commission,

are disclosed in writing to the customer. This stops car dealers, for example, reducing the output tax due on their profit margins by attributing artificially large sums to exempt warranties.

In *C R Smith Glaziers (Dunfermline) Ltd [2001] STC 770: [2003] UKHL 7: [2003] STC 419)* the House of Lords overturned the ruling by the Court of Session and the Tribunal view that the above rule requires that the customer be told exactly how much is charged for an insurance service. A simple formula, such as 10% of the total price, was sufficient.

The Card Protection Plan case

Card Protection Plan (LON/90/282 No 5484; on appeal [1992] STC 797; affd [1994] STC 199, CA; revsd [2001] STC 174, HL: CJEC [1999] STC 270) is an important case:

- Because it decided that a credit card registration service was a supply of exempt insurance. This was contrary to my expectations and, I suspect, those of many others.

- As a decision that there was a single supply rather than a multiple one at different rates of VAT. See Chapter 12, *Have I Got One Supply or Two?*

CPP claimed to provide 15 benefits as shown overleaf:

1. **Confidential Registration of all Cards** — accurate computer records will be kept of all your valuable cards.

2. **£750 Insurance Cover** — against fraudulent use on any one claim, provided loss notification is received within 24 hours of discovery of loss.

3. **Unlimited Protection** — you have £750 cover up to the moment of your call to CPP. After that your protection against fraudulent use is unlimited.

4. **Immediate Loss Notification** — free 24 hour ACTIONLINE to receive your loss reports and act immediately to protect you. ACTIONLINE stickers provided for your phone, diary or wallet, so our vital ACTIONLINE number is always at hand.

5. **Replacement Cards** — can be ordered when losses are notified, thus minimising your inconvenience.

6. **Change of Address Service** — all card insurers can be notified before you move to ensure your cards don't get into the wrong hands.

7. **Lost Key Location** — key tags with your unique policy number and our FREEPOST address help ensure keys can quickly be returned to you in confidence, when found.

8. **Valuable Property & Document Protection** — register serial numbers of your property and details of policies, shares, passports, etc for your own security and to assist in notifying police or making insurance claims in the event of loss or theft. Through our insurance cover you can claim up to £25 on communications costs when assisting police or claiming against personal insurance in respect of items registered with CPP. Includes phone calls, correspondence, postage, etc but not travel costs.

9. **£500 Emergency Cash** — rushed anywhere in the world (upon approval) if you are stranded and have lost your cards. An interest free advance repayment within 14 days.

10. **Lost Luggage Recovery** — with CPP stickers lost luggage and other personal property such as briefcase or handbag can be quickly identified and owners advised of its location. Our special insurance cover entitles you to claim up to £25 on communications costs incurred arranging recovery of keys or luggage protected by CPP tags and stickers. This includes phone calls, correspondence, postage, etc, but not travel costs.

11. **Emergency Medical Cover Worldwide** — in the event of illness or an accident abroad you need professional help, fast. We provide 24 hour emergency cover and one phone call secures medical advice and assistance in English and other languages, anywhere in the world. If necessary, at your expense, a full consultation, and even medical repatriation by air — with all necessary specialist personnel — can be arranged for you.

12. **Emergency Airline Ticket** — if your credit cards and cash are lost or stolen and you're stranded overseas, CPP's travel cover means arrangements can be made, upon approval, to issue an air ticket to get you home. Cost repayable within 14 days.

13. **Computer Update Services** — confidential printout of your card details for you to check, annually.

14. **Medical Emergency/Warning Card** — dual purpose - to warn that all your cards are protected, and also to provide medical information that can save vital seconds in an emergency. Carry with you at all times.

15. **Car Hire Discounts** — you can claim valuable discounts on car rental from Hertz, Avis and Europcar worldwide.

The case went to the House of Lords, via the CJEC, the decisions being:

Tribunal: standard-rated, there being no supply of insurance.

Divisional Court: multiple supply of exempt insurance and standard-rated other services, which must be apportioned.

Court of Appeal: standard-rated card registration service to which the insurance elements were incidental.

CJEC: House of Lords must decide whether there were:

- Two supplies — of insurance and a card registration service; or

- One principal supply to which the other was ancillary.

The House of Lords commented:

- The CJEC's judgment showed that at least some of the supply was insurance.

- Whether there was a single supply with ancillary services or two separate supplies depended on whether the key features of the transaction were several distinct principal services or a single one.

- Take an overall view; avoid over-zealous dissection and analysis.

The judgment then said:

- Points 2, 3 and 8 were insurance. People joined the scheme to get insurance against loss due to mis-use of credit cards.

- Points 4, 9, 10, 11 and 12 were 'assistance' covered by class 18, point A of the annexe to the First Insurance Directive. That referred to *assistance for persons who get into difficulties while travelling, while away from home or while away from their permanent residence.* The Directive also said that the assistance could be in kind rather than in cash. That the emergency cash advance and air ticket had to be reimbursed did not prevent them being 'assistance'.

- The up-to-date record of cards and ordering replacements were valuable in minimising the loss. The luggage tags and medical warning card were useful in assisting in the administration of the scheme. Those services, which were not insurance, were ancillary to the main objective of financial protection against loss and some were minor features. They were preconditions to the client making a claim for indemnity or assistance or for the furnishing of insurance cover.

- Even if they could be seen as sufficiently coherent to be treated as a separate supply, it was ancillary to the insurance.

- To regard the insurance as ancillary or subsidiary to the registration of credit card numbers was unreal. The consequences for the client of being able to take protective action with CPP, with whom the cards were registered, were closely linked to the insurance service. One could not say that some elements of the transaction were economically dissociable from the others.

The outsourcing problem

- Outsourcing ordinary administration services, such as running the computer department, has long been recognised as standard-rated.

- But it now appears that administering the principal activity of an insurance company is also standard-rated unless

    – that work involves direct contact with the insured, or

    – is a service of a kind normally provided by an insurance broker or agent.

Outsourcing a mis-selling review is exempt

The requirement that the broker act in an intermediary capacity may have gone beyond the terms of *Article 13(B)(a)* of the *6th VAT Directive*. In *Century Life plc ([2001] STC 38, CA)*, a decision accepted by Customs, the Court of Appeal rejected Customs' argument that an insurance agent or broker must act as such in making a supply; ie that the service must be a kind normally provided by insurance brokers of agents. The nature of the services was already defined by the Directive as *insurance and reinsurance transactions, including related services*.

- It was sufficient that *CFS*, the provider of the services (a mis-selling review), was an insurance agent because of its other activities.

- The Court agreed that there must be a close nexus between the service and reinsurance transactions.

- However, a mis-selling review making sure that a policy complied with the regulations concerned its nature and was intimately related to it.

- That the policy had been sold made no difference since compliance was a continuing obligation.

Similarly, in *C & V (Advice Line) Services Ltd (LON/00/153 No 17310)*, operating a helpline and a service of screening claims and issuing claim forms, the claims then being handled by the insurer, was held to be provided in an intermediary capacity. The Tribunal based this on the definition of an insurance agent in the *Insurance Intermediaries Directive*.

Outsourcing insurance administration is probably standard-rated

The CJEC ruled in a Swedish case, *Skandia ([2001] STC 754)*, that charges by an insurance company for running the business of its 100% owned subsidiary would be standard-rated. This ruling was in response to a reference to it by the Swedish court, which was dealing with an appeal by *Skandia* against a preliminary opinion. The opinion concerned a proposal that the subsidiary would continue to write the business but would become, in other respects, a shell with all the activity carried out by *Skandia*.

Difference between Skandia and Century Life

- *Skandia* would have no relationship with the insured.

- *Century Life* dealt direct with the insured on behalf of the insurance company.

However, note that, for reasons of Swedish insurance law, *Skandia* said it was not acting as an insurance *agent* and the CJEC did not even consider this possibility.

Initial and annual management charges for personal pension schemes

In *Winterthur Life (UK) Ltd (LON/1787 No 14935),* personal pension schemes were held to embody contracts of insurance between Winterthur and the members of the schemes.

Administrative services incidental to implementing the contracts were part and parcel of the provision of insurance and therefore qualified for exemption:

- despite being provided by two subsidiaries, which were not authorised insurers and

- despite the member of each scheme controlling the investment policy.

If that were wrong, the two subsidiaries acted as agents for Winterthur in administering the schemes.

In a second *Winterthur* case, *(LON/98/1339 No 17572),* the outsourced administration of the self invested part of a pension scheme was held to be exempt under *Group 2, Item 4* as the services of:

- an insurance agent performing services related to insurance and;

- acting as an insurance intermediary providing assistance in the administration and performance of insurance contracts.

Having accepted that the personal pension plan was a supply of insurance, the Tribunal refused to separate the self invested part. It noted that *Article 2(1)(b)* of the *EC Insurance Intermediaries Directive 77/92,* which dealt with the rights of establishment of insurance agents and brokers, included in its definition of agents' activities the provision of such assistance. The outsourcing company was closely concerned with the administration of the part of the insurance transaction, which was the self-administered scheme. It acted as an intermediary in certain respects and had a direct relationship with scheme members.

For more cases on outsourcing, see under *Finance – Sch 9 Group 5* later in this chapter.

Watch the wording of commission agreements

A payment made by an insurance company or a broker to a third party is not necessarily exempt just because it is concerned with the provision of insurance.

In *British Horse Society Ltd (MAN/98/736 No 16204),* a 'contingent discount', earned on the society's own policies and on those taken out by its members, was held not to reduce the premium but to be payment for the standard-rated exclusivity in advertising to BHS members and promoting the broker's services.

In Notice 701/36, para 8.3, Customs accept that introductory services *can* qualify for exemption. However, the recipient of the commission has to do more than merely include advertising material in its mailouts.

Fees to the insured for advice are not exempt

Where a flat fee is charged to an insured instead of the usual commission to the insurer, its VAT status depends upon the service provided. It is as likely to be for consultancy services as it is for 'the services of an insurance intermediary'. Only the latter are exempt.

To charge a standard-rated fee rather than an exempt commission is advantageous because of the increased input tax recovery.

Handling a claim is also exempt but not other services

Checking and processing a claim is exempt (*Note 1(c)*). However, a service is not exempt merely because it is connected with insurance.

Note (8) excludes valuation or inspection services.

Note (9) excludes supplies by loss adjusters, average adjusters, motor assessors, surveyors or other experts except for:

- handling an insurance claim; and

- with written authority from the insurer to accept or reject it and to settle any amounts payable. This may be via a broker who has power to delegate such authority.

Note (10) excludes services provided to the policyholder and paid for by the insurer in settling a claim.

Example: The insured finds and pays a plumber. The plumber's services to the insurer do not qualify as handling a claim.

Postal services — Sch 9 Group 3

This only covers postal services by the Post Office. Although privatisation of the Post Office in the UK seems unlikely at the time of writing, postal services in the EU are increasingly open to competition. It is therefore probable the Post Office's privileged position on carrying letters will be reduced and that this exemption will then be restricted.

Betting, gaming and lotteries — Sch 9 Group 4

Item 1 exempts 'the provision of any facilities for the placing of bets or the playing of any games of chance'. That covers income from video races for instance.

Item 2 exempts 'the granting of a right to take part in a lottery', which covers tickets for raffles, tombola, etc.

The exemption covers the gambling itself, not:

- admission to the premises on which it takes place;

- a membership subscription;

- gaming machines.

Note (1) removes from the exemption charges for entry to premises where the gambling takes place and session or participation charges. In *Rum Runner Casino Ltd (MAN/80/33 No 1036)*, payments made by players to play games such as backgammon, poker, mahjong and bridge, were held to be participation charges even though they were distributed to the players as winnings.

In *Fakenham Conservative Association Bingo Club (LON/73/164 No 76)*, a 'jackpot participation fee' paid for the right to take part in the cash jackpot was also held to be a participation charge although a charge for the jackpot card was exempt.

In *United Utilities (MAN/01/146 No 17582; [2003] STC 223)*, an outsourced service of taking bets by telephone was held to be a standard rated call centre and information technology service, not the exempt services of a bookmaker's agent.

One amusing case concerned target shooting at a fairground (*W & D Grantham (MAN/70/102 No 853)*) in which charges by a shooting gallery were held to be gambling. In order to win a prize, one had to remove the entire bullseye. It was a matter of chance whether one did so because putting all one's shots into the black was no guarantee of success. In fact only about 30 attempts out of 18,000 by the public in an average year succeeded. In tests, expert marksmen could not make winning scores regularly. The Tribunal found it to be a matter of chance whether one removed the bullseye entirely, however good a shot one was, and that the fees were therefore indeed exempt as the right to take part in a game of chance.

Finance — Sch 9 Group 5

The comment here relates only to the exemption for financial services to UK customers. For international transactions, see Chapter 22, *Exports and Imports of Services* re *Sch 5 para 5* and Chapter 23, *Partial Exemption* under *Your right to recover input tax* and *How the right to recover affects banking, finance and insurance*. Those chapters explain the rules under which a financial service to a customer who belongs outside the EU or a service which is related to an export of goods outside the EU, together with commissions thereon, changes to outside the scope of VAT with recovery of the associated input tax.

Item 1: Dealings in money

Item 1 exempts 'the issue, transfer or receipt of, or any dealing with, money, any security for money or any note or order for the payment of money'.

Dealings with money — The issue or cashing of travellers' cheques is an example of an exempt dealing with money.

Security for money — A 'security for money' in this context means something like a bond or indemnity given as security, not the kind of stock exchange security or secondary security covered by *Item 6*. Examples are fees for:

- bank guarantee given to Customs as security for a trader meeting the liability for import VAT;

- performance bond guaranteeing the carrying out of, say, a construction contract;

- confirming house guarantee of payment by an importer to a foreign supplier.

Any note or order for the payment of money — A note or order for the payment of money includes:

- bills of exchange (local authority or commercial);

- instruments and paper negotiable for cash;

- trading paper coupons (from bearer bonds; ie the right to the dividend).

The value of the supply is the price paid both at issue and on any subsequent sale. Only at redemption is the transaction outside the scope.

In Notice 701/49 (March 2002) *Finance and securities,* Customs also accept as exempt under *Item 1:*

- The assignment of a debt.

- Charges for accepting payment of bills on behalf of another business.

- Foreign exchange transactions.

Item 1 does not cover work *preparatory to the carrying out of* an Item 1 service (*Note (1A)*).

Item 2: Loans and trade credit

Item 2 exempts *the making of any advance or the granting of any credit.* Loans and bank overdrafts are thus exempt, the value of the supply being the interest paid. The interest is payment for the service of making the money available. When goods are sold under a credit agreement, the interest charge is exempt if separate from the charge for the goods or services and it is disclosed to the purchaser (*Note (3)*). Any charge associated with the loan is also exempt. Thus, a commitment fee is exempt as part of the charge for the credit, albeit not called interest. So is a facility fee for an overdraft.

Item 2 also covers charges made by credit card companies (*Note (4)*):

- annually to cardholders;

- to retailers, made by deducting discounts from the sums paid to them; and

- interest on overdue balances charged to cardholders.

Penalties charged to holders of chargecards who fail to pay on time, are seen as outside the scope of VAT because there is no supply. The cardholder is not supposed to take extended credit.

Item 2A: The management of credit by the person granting it

This item was added from 1/8/03 and Notes (2A) and (2B) concerning the management of credit were deleted.

Item 3: Hire-purchase and credit sale agreements

Item 3 exempts hire-purchase interest if a separate charge for the facility is disclosed to the purchaser of the goods.

Do not confuse the exempt interest charge with the standard-rated supply of the goods themselves. The supplier charges VAT on the goods to the finance company which charges it on when it re-sells them to the customer.

'Lease-purchase' agreements are also accepted by Customs as being a supply of goods. Technically, lease-purchase is the hiring of goods for a fixed period at the end of which the hirer can buy them. The charges are based on the purchase price of the goods plus a finance charge.

Item 4: Option and documentation fees

Item 4 exempts option fees, documentation fees and similar charges in hire-purchase, conditional sale or credit sale agreements, provided that they do not exceed £10 per agreement. That limit only applies if the charge relates to the goods, as opposed to the credit. See the two cases quoted below, which illustrate the pitfall/planning point involved.

In a typical example of the pitfalls of not understanding one's own contractual terms, option fees exceeding £10, which *General Motors Acceptance Corpn (UK) plc (LON/97/1471 No 16137)* charged at the start of hire-purchase agreements, were held to be standard-rated, not ancillary to the charge for credit. They were for the right to purchase the car, which was exercised automatically if all instalments were paid.

On the other hand, a £65 'administration fee', charged at the start of a hire-purchase agreement, was held to be part of the charge for the facility of instalment credit finance. It was included in the 'total charge for credit' shown in the agreement signed by the customer *(Wagon Finance Ltd (LON/98/215 No 16288))*. The Tribunal rejected Customs' argument that it was, in part, related to the supply of the car.

Item 5: Commissions re transactions exempt under Items 1–4 and 6

Item 5 exempts:

- 'intermediary services … by a person acting in an intermediary capacity'; and
- in relation to a transaction covered by Items 1–4 and 6.

'Intermediary services' and 'acting in an intermediary capacity' are defined by Notes (5) and (5A).

Examples of exempt commissions are:

- hire-purchase commissions;
- the services of mortgage brokers and money brokers in arranging loans;
- building society commissions on investment and mortgage business.

Electronic dealing systems

Charges for carrying out transactions under an electronic dealing system, which allows subscribers to deal on it, are exempt as an intermediary service.

Advice is standard-rated

Do not confuse a standard-rate fee for investment advice with an exempt commission. A commission on a specific transaction is not the same as a fee for general advice.

Also standard-rated is advice from accountants, lawyers and merchant banks, which is connected with an issue of shares but is not in itself an intermediary service.

Item 5A: Underwriting fees re Items 1 and 6

Item 5A covers commissions and underwriting fees earned on transactions covered by *Items 1 and 6*.

A commission is only exempt if it is an *intermediary service* done *in an intermediary capacity*. Advertising and promotion are excluded by Note (5), which defines *intermediary services* as:

- bringing together seekers and providers of financial services;

- together with work preparatory to the conclusion of contracts,

but excludes:

- market research, product design, advertising, promotional or similar services or the collection, collation and provision of information in connection therewith.

Note (5A) defines *acting in an intermediary capacity* as:

- acting as an intermediary, or one of them, between providers and seekers of financial services.

Foreign exchange dealings create supplies

Although the exchange of one currency for another may not appear to involve a supply, it is a dealing in money. This may be good or bad news for a financial institution depending upon the extent to which its forex dealings are with counterparties outside the EU and thus outside the scope of VAT with recovery of input tax instead of exempt. See Chapter 22 on *Exports and Imports of Services* for transactions which are outside the scope, with or without recovery.

In *First National Bank of Chicago*, the CJEC held that the consideration is *the net result of the supplier's transactions over a given period of time*. As that consideration is either exempt or outside the scope of VAT, it is not necessary to identify that net result for output tax purposes.

Effect on partial exemption methods

The value of forex transactions could be included in an apportionment calculation for partial exemption purposes using the standard method. However, Customs say that this will 'normally be unacceptable' because they believe it unlikely to result in a fair and reasonable attribution of input tax to those supplies which are outside the scope with recovery. Their preferred approach is to isolate the input tax incurred on forex costs and to apportion this as a separate calculation within the partial exemption method. A possible basis is the proportion of outside the scope with recovery transactions to total transactions. However, they will accept any method, which appears to achieve a fair and reasonable result.

Foreign exchange activity which merely supports other activities

Large industrial companies often undertake forex transactions to fix the sterling value of future trading income and to ensure that currency is available to meet anticipated non-sterling liabilities. Banks also engage in foreign exchange trading purely to meet the needs of their customers, as opposed to trading speculatively for profit. Customs may be prepared to allow recovery of input tax related to such activities on the basis of 'looking through' the immediate transactions to those, which the forex activity supports.

Debt factoring

A business can finance its sales by assigning the debts due from its customers to a Factor. The latter takes over responsibility for collecting the debts. The Factor may provide various services such as advancing a proportion of the debts before they are collected and administering the client's sales ledger. *Recourse factoring* allows the Factor to reassign to the client any unpaid debts. *Invoice discounting* involves an advance to the client of a proportion of the debts. They are not assigned to the Factor and the client remains responsible for collecting the debts.

The assignment of the debt by the client is exempt under *Item 1*. So is any re-assignment back by the Factor. The interest or discount charged by the Factor is exempt under *Item 2*. Credit advice and sales ledger administration charges are standard rated. So are fees for collecting debts not assigned to the Factor.

On 26/6/03, the CJEC held in *MKG-Kraftfahrzeuge-Factoring GmbH (C-305/01)* that debt factoring, for which the German company charged fees totalling 3% of the face value of the debts purchased, is, like debt collection, excluded from exemption under *Article 13B(d)(3)*. This seems to mean that factoring charges should be standard rated, whether the basis is with or without recourse. At the time of writing, Customs have yet to comment.

The problems of outsourcing services

A prime reason for outsourcing services is to reduce costs. If you incur VAT on those outsourced services, which is not recoverable, much of the benefit will disappear.

When work is done in-house, the only VAT incurred is that on taxable expenses. The most important cost, salaries, is outside the scope of VAT.

Customs have argued in various cases explained in the following pages that outsourced financial services are standard rated. See also the comment on outsourcing under *Insurance – Sch 9 Group 2*.

Life assurance and investment are different to insurance

A commission on selling life assurance or an investment product is covered by the rules on finance, not insurance. For finance commissions, the key word in an intermediary situation is *negotiation. Article 13(B)(1)(d)(5)EC 6th VAT Directive* exempts the *negotiation* of transactions in securities.

Compare that with the exemption for insurance commissions in *para (1)(a)* for *related services performed by insurance brokers and insurance agents*. The difference has been important in a number of outsourcing cases.

Some outsourcing cases

The Sparekassernes case

If a service amounts to a dealing in money, it is exempt under *Item 1* provided that it is not merely preparatory. It must have the characteristics of a financial transaction. The *Sparekassernes Datacenter* case *([1997] STC 932)* demonstrates how fine the nuances are between a standard-rated and an exempt service. Sparekassernes Datacenter, a Danish company, provided back-office services in maintaining customers' accounts such as:

* cheque clearance and processing;

* calculating interest and crediting or debiting it to accounts;

* standing order payments and foreign exchange transactions;

* administration of cash cards;

* customer enquiry handling and other services.

The CJEC held that it was not necessary for the supply to be to the final recipient of the exempt service but the service, viewed as a whole, had to constitute a transaction listed in the *6th VAT Directive*. It was not sufficient merely for a service to be needed in order to carry out an exempt financial transaction. A distinction must be drawn between exempt services and the provision of a facility, such as a computing system. It was for the national court to rule on the nature of the services provided, including the extent of *Sparekassernes'* liability to the banks. The Danish tax authorities are said to have agreed a 60/40 split between exempt and standard-rated.

In *FDR Ltd (LON/95/2887 No 16040; CA [2000] STC 672)*, a tribunal held that similar services for credit card issuers and merchant acquirers were mostly exempt. FDR did carry on various activities in providing its services to card issuers and merchant acquirers. However, there was a single or core supply to both issuers and acquirers of processing all their card transactions and settling their liabilities and claims under these transactions to meet the obligations of the issuers and acquirers. This included opening and maintaining accounts, authorising transactions, ascertaining the credits and debits and statementing. These were either integral parts of the principal supply or necessary for its performance.

This was confirmed by the Court of Appeal. It held that:

* *FDR* made 'transfers', which were exempt under *article 13 B (d)(3)*;

* the Tribunal's analysis of the supplies made was correct. There was a single core supply;

- supply consisted of the movement of money between card-holder, merchant, issuer and acquirer.

Customs' argument that merely giving instructions for payment via BACS did not amount to a transfer of money was rejected.

In *CSC Financial Services Ltd (C-235/00: [2002] STC 57)*, formerly known as *Continuum (Europe) Ltd*, the CJEC ruled that *transactions*, in the context of Art 13B(d)(1), means:

Transactions liable to create, alter or extinguish parties' rights and obligations in respect of securities.

It commented that administrative services, which did not alter the legal or financial position of the parties, were not covered. Nor was the supply of financial information. The mere fact that a service was essential to completing an exempt transaction did not make that service exempt.

The CJEC said that *negotiation* means:

The activity of an intermediary, who does not occupy the position of any party to a contract relating to a financial product and whose activity amounts to something other than the provision of contractual services typically undertaken by the parties to such contracts. Negotiation is a service rendered to and remunerated by a contractual party as a distinct act of mediation. It may consist, amongst other things, in pointing out suitable opportunities for the conclusion of such a contract, making contact with another party or negotiating, in the name of and on behalf of a client, the detail of the payments to be made by either side. The purpose of negotiation is therefore to do all that is necessary in order for two parties to enter into a contract, without the negotiator having any interest of his own in the terms of the contract.

On the other hand, it is not negotiation where one of the parties entrusts to a subcontractor some of the clerical formalities related to the contract, such as providing information to the other party and receiving and processing applications for subscription to the securities which form the subject matter of contract. In such a case, the subcontractor occupies the same position as the party selling the financial product and is not therefore an intermediary who does not occupy the position of one of the parties to the contract, within the meaning of the provision in question.

Electronic Data Systems Ltd (LON/2000/91 No 17611: CA [2003] STC 688) ran a call centre at which applications for loans were recorded, validated under a credit scoring system and accepted or rejected; loans were paid out and repayments collected, early settlements dealt with, interest calculated, statements produced etc on behalf of *Lloyds Bank. Lloyds* merely advertised the loans and dealt with borrowers in arrears. *EDS* did everything else. The money was paid out and collected into accounts held by the Bank, which were cleared daily.

The Tribunal found *EDS's* services to be exempt as the granting of credit on behalf of the Bank. If that was wrong, they were exempt as being for *transactions, including negotiation, concerning deposits and current accounts, payments transfers and debts*. The Court of Appeal found them to be *transactions … concerning … payments, transfers …* It was sympathetic to the view that they were *negotiation* but would have referred to the CJEC on whether they were *the granting of credit*. Customs have applied to the House of Lords for leave to appeal.

Cases on intermediary services

BAA plc (LON/00/867 No 17377; [2002] STC 327) concerned a credit card co-branded with *Bank of Scotland*. *BAA* offered it to its customers, checked application forms and screened out applications not meeting the bank's requirements. It was paid a one-off introduction and processing fee and an ongoing commission fee based on the bank's interest income.

Customs argued that *BAA* was providing credit management in the form of promotional and similar services, advertising, credit checking and decision taking. They said that credit management and credit negotiation were mutually exclusive and any supply containing elements of credit management could not properly be described as *negotiation*.

BAA argued that *negotiation* had the wider dictionary meaning of acting as an intermediary. *BAA* was not involved with the management of credit. The decision on whether to issue a card was left to *BOS* and *BAA* did not do the credit checking.

The Divisional Court and Court of Appeal agreed in the light of the comments of the CJEC in *CSC*. The *negotiation of credit* within Art 13B(d)(1) was not restricted to the brokering of an actual exempt transaction by an intermediary who had power to affect the transaction itself. *BAA* performed an *act of mediation*. Without its services, the individual contracts for the issue of the credit cards would not take place. Its activities were not mere clerical formalities carried out as a subcontractor of the bank. Its role was not passive. Nor did it merely carry out promotional or marketing activities for the bank.

In *Debt Management Associates Ltd (MAN/01/0631 No 17880)*, the negotiation of extended payment terms for outstanding debts was held to be an exempt supply even though no revised contract was created.

In *Lindum Resources Ltd (MAN/93/784 No 12445)*, an application fee charged to a potential borrower by a broker was held to be exempt because it was the first stage in the exempt making of arrangements for a loan, even if a feasibility study showed the loan to be impractical.

The key point is the nature of the intended supply. The status of a fee cannot depend upon success in arranging a loan as the rate of tax has to be known when the tax point is created by payment of the fee at the start of the broker's work.

Item 6: Securities and secondary securities

Item 6 exempts the 'issue, transfer or receipt of, or any dealing with, any security or secondary security' as defined. See the text of *Item 6* in *Sch 9 Group 5* for the full definition. It includes:

- stocks and shares, bonds and debentures including allotment letters and warrants;
- certificates of deposit;
- Treasury bills;
- unit trust certificates.

Stock lending

Stock lending is the inaccurate description adopted by the financial markets to describe the borrowing of stocks or shares by market makers. If a market maker is short of a stock and is unable to buy enough in the open market to deliver what it has sold without moving the price against it, it may arrange to 'borrow' the holding held by another institution as an investment. It contracts to replace the holding in due course and to pay interest meanwhile equivalent to any dividends due plus interest on the value of the stock.

Although called lending, this involves:

(a) A sale of the stock by the lender to the borrower;
(b) In due course, a sale of the replacement stock by the borrower back to the lender;
(c) Interest to the lender on its loan, which is represented by the debt outstanding for the stock. To the extent that this substitutes for any dividend due, the lender's outputs (probably exempt) are increased.

Customs used to regard (a) and (b) as outputs at open market value even though no money passed. However, in *Scottish Eastern Investment Trust plc (EDN/99/211 No 16882)*, a tribunal held that the value of the output was the fee charged to the borrower. It was unreal to regard the transfer of legal title as creating an output. Customs have accepted this.

Global custody and safe custody

Global custody — a package of services, which includes the holding of stocks and securities, collecting dividends or interest on them and dealing with scrip or rights issues — is seen by Customs as exempt. Do not confuse this with the standard rated service of safe custody, which is primarily the physical safekeeping of stocks and securities.

Item 7 has been deleted and replaced by Items 5 and 5A

Item 8: Bank charges re current, deposit or savings accounts

This covers bank charges on account, as opposed to interest.

Item 9: Management of unit trusts

Item 9 exempts fees for managing:

* an authorised unit trust; or
* a trust-based scheme.

A requirement for the management to be by the operator of the scheme was held to be invalid in *Prudential Assurance Co Ltd (EDN/00/37 No 17030)* — it having been outsourced. The rule was then deleted from 1/8/03.

Item 10: Managing an 'open-ended' investment company

Item 10 exempts the management of the scheme property of an OEIC. A requirement for the management to be by an authorised corporate director was held to be invalid in *Abbey National plc (LON/00/928 No 17506)* and was then deleted from 1/8/03.

Education — Sch 9 Group 6

Item 1: The main exemption exempts the provision by an eligible body of:

* education;
* research if supplied to another eligible body;
* vocational training.

Note 1 says that 'Eligible body' means (paraphrasing):

* Schools, colleges, UK universities including any college, institution, school or hall thereof;
* Government departments, local authorities and health authorities;
* Bodies, such as charities, which are precluded from distributing profits. The body must plough back any profit made from *Group 6* education into that activity.

A trading subsidiary is not an eligible body.

The scope of 'education' is wide

The law does not define *education*. Nor does it say where the education has to be provided — only that it must be by an eligible body. The range of courses provided by educational institutions is so wide that one can find an argument for most subjects being 'education'. Customs acknowledge this in Notice 701/30 (January 2002) *Education and Vocational Training*, para 5.1 where they say:

Education means a course, class or lesson of instruction or study in any subject,

* whether or not that subject is normally taught in schools, colleges or universities; and
* regardless of where and when it takes place.

Education includes:

* lectures;
* educational seminars;
* conferences and symposia;
* holiday, sporting and recreational courses;
* distance teaching and associated materials, providing the student is subject to assessment by the teaching institution.

But does not include plays, concerts, sports meetings or exhibitions.

There is no need for any examination or diploma. Courses such as embroidery or basket-making are now accepted as being education.

See also the possibility discussed later for the course being vocational training.

In *TK Phillips (LON/90/862 No 7444)*, motorcycle training was held to be education.

In *Allied Dancing Association Ltd (MAN/91/84 No 10777)*, the Tribunal held that teaching ballroom dancing to juniors for the purpose of a test was education for life!

In *British Organic Farmers (LON/87/164 No 2700)* and *Buxton Civic Association (MAN/87/385 No 3380)* it was suggested that the teaching must be more than the provision of an occasional seminar or a one-off visit but Customs continue to accept that a single lecture can be 'education'.

In *Harrogate Business Development Centre Ltd (LON/98/569 No 15565)*, advice and information for people starting businesses was held to be training, when provided as part of the package which included training seminars. The services did not cease to be training merely because they included on the job advice.

There must be some structure to the education

In *North of England Zoological Society ([1999] STC 1027)*, admission to a zoo was held not to amount to education despite the efforts made to educate visitors. The key distinction here is that the average family at the zoo is looking for entertainment rather than education. The basic offer is of an afternoon out, not 'come and listen to lectures about the animals'. Having got them inside the gates, a zoo may make great efforts to teach them and many no doubt respond. However, the extent of that response will vary from a willingness to read a few explanatory boards to avid attention on an escorted tour. If this was education, many stately homes, for instance, could claim that they were educating their visitors.

Sport — the difference between education and the mere provision of facilities

Customs accept that a class which is *led and directed rather than merely supervised* counts as education. That includes instruction in the use of equipment and in warming-up techniques.

However, the mere presence of staff to supervise on health and safety or insurance grounds, such as in a swimming pool, is not sufficient.

Research

Research is standard-rated unless supplied by one eligible body to another such body. Much of the problem of distinguishing between exempt research and standard-rated consultancy disappears if both are standard-rated. However, the distinction sometimes allows the exemption of a charge to another eligible body, which is unable to recover VAT charged to it.

See Notice 701/30 (January 2002) *Education and Vocational Training*, para 5.6 for Customs' views on what constitutes research. Often, if the supply is to another eligible body, it is likely to be of research, possibly on a joint project. However, educational institutions do provide consultancy to each other in, for instance, designing courses, setting up computer systems and the like so care is needed.

Vocational training

'Vocational training' is defined by *Note (3)* as training or retraining for:

(a) Any trade, profession or employment; or

(b) Any voluntary work connected with —

- education, health, safety or welfare; or

- the carrying out of activities of a charitable nature

and includes the provision of work experience under training schemes for the unemployed.

Consultancy via a limited company

Educational institutions often put their consultancy and other trading activities through a limited company to preserve their charitable status for corporation tax purposes. The profit is then covenanted to the institution. Any education or training done by such a company cannot be exempt because the company is not an eligible body.

Trading companies can be grouped for VAT purposes with their parent institutions as these are corporations. This means that any management fees or other charges between them are outside the scope.

'English as a foreign language' courses

Courses teaching English as a foreign language are exempt, whoever provides them. *Note (2)* restricts the exemption to the teaching which means that part of the charges may be standard-rated. However, following *Pilgrims Language Courses Ltd ([1999] STC 874)*, Customs accept exemption for all elements integral to the course, together with closely related supplies of goods and services provided they are for the direct use of the student and necessary for delivering the education. This includes sports, recreational or social activities.

Item 2: Private tuition

Private tuition is exempt under *Item 2*, if it is *in a subject ordinarily taught in a school or university … by an individual teacher acting independently of an employer.*

In *C Clarke and E Clarke, A Clarke and H Clarke (LON/96/1446 No 15201)*, the partners in a dance teaching business were held to act independently as principals so their charges were exempt as private tuition.

However, in *John Page (t/a Upledger Institute) (EDN/99/14 No 16650)*, training in CranioSacral Therapy was held to be standard-rated to the extent of the 40% of income derived from fees for teaching by employees of Mr Page. This was not *private tuition by an individual teacher acting independently of an employer.*

Similarly, in *Brian Graham (t/a Excel Tutoring) (LON/98/213 No 16814)*, Mr Graham recruited teachers as needed to coach pupils. The teaching was done by them, not him. His services were therefore standard-rated.

Item 3: Examination services

Examination services are exempt under *Item 3*. *Note (4)* defines them as including the setting and marking of examinations and setting and maintaining of educational training standards. In Notice 701/30 (January 2002), para 7.1, Customs say that course accreditation services, validation and certification are covered.

The exemption applies if the supply is by or to an eligible body or to a person receiving vocational training which is exempt, such as at independent fee paying schools or non-business such as at local authority schools.

Item 4: The supply of any goods or services closely related to the education, research or vocational training

This is an important part of the exemption because it covers a multitude of supplies made by educational institutions to their students.

The supply must be:

- for the direct use of the student;
- by the eligible body which educates or trains them; or
- by a second educational eligible body to the one, which does.

An example is catering.

A *student* is anyone, who is being educated, whether through a full-time course or an individual conference or lecture. Customs accept that this includes a candidate for admission to the institution.

Not covered are goods sold from campus shops. It would be difficult to know which purchasers were students, let alone whether the item in question was related to that student's course.

Items 5 and 5A: Vocational training

Item 5 exempts vocational training and the supply of any goods or services essential thereto, which is funded under the *Employment and Training Act 1973* and similar law in Northern Ireland and Scotland.

Item 5A exempts both vocational training and education, which are funded by the Learning and Skills Council for England or the equivalent for Wales.

See the law for the precise wording of these items and section 13 of Notice 701/30 (January 2002) *Education and Vocational Training*.

Item 6: Youth clubs

Item 6 exempts the provision of facilities by a youth club to its members, or by an association of youth clubs to its member clubs or direct to their members.

Note (6) defines a youth club as a non-profit making body established to promote the social, physical, educational or spiritual development of its members, who must be mainly under 21 years of age.

Health — Sch 9 Group 7

Group 7, Items 1–3: Services of doctors etc

Items 1–3 of this Group cover the services of doctors, nurses, dentists, pharmaceutical chemists and other medically-qualified people including osteopaths and chiropractors. See the law for the various registers, such as that kept under the *Health Professions Order 2001,* membership of which is required. This creates a pitfall because, although the range of expertise covered by the registers is expanding, it is not all embracing. Thus *Lawrence Yusupoff (MAN/01/899 No 18152),* a clinical psychologist, found that his services were not exempt and had to register for VAT retrospectively. The exemption covers services in the branch of medicine in question related to the health of patients, rather than, say, royalties for writing a book on a medical subject. In *D v W (Case – 384/98; [2002] STC 1200),* the CJEC ruled that the services of a doctor in conducting a genetic test to establish parenthood did not amount to *the provision of medical care.* That phrase, in *6th VAT Directive Art 13A(1)(c),* only covered medical interventions for the purpose of diagnosis and treatment of diseases or health disorders. The Advocate General then said on 30/1/03 in *Dr Peter L d'Ambrumenil & Dispute Resolution Services Ltd (LON/97/951 No 15977: C-307/01)* that tests of blood and other bodily samples for viruses etc, done on behalf of an employer or an insurance company, were not exempt if the aim was not therapeutic but to obtain health-related information. Similarly, medical certificates and reports related to fitness to travel, entitlement to a pension or litigation were not therapeutic but the obtaining of an expert opinion.

The pitfall for general practitioners

Although, at the time of writing, the CJEC had not delivered its judgment in *d'Ambrumenil,* it seems probable that many medical practices will find that they have significant taxable income, which they have previously thought exempt. Even now, a variety of work is standard rated and I believe that Customs will extend this.

In Notice 701/57/02 (March 2002) *Health Professionals,* Customs accept as exempt:

- medical or dental reports written in connection with insurance, negligence or personal injury cases;

- certification of medical sickness or fitness, where this requires a medical assessment or the exercise of medical judgement by the health professional.

However, the above appears to conflict both with the CJEC comment and with that later in the Notice concerning legal services in that a mere assessment does not of itself involve a care element.

Customs say that the following are standard rated:

- services which do not require medical knowledge, skills or judgement;

- services not related to care, such as paternity testing and writing books or articles;

- services carried out for legal reasons such as:

  - negotiation or advocacy;

  - arbitration, mediation or conciliation;

- – investigating the validity of an insurance or negligence claim;
- – considering medical reports and other evidence to try to resolve disputes;
- – work carried out for lawyers and insurers;
- analytical testing services for medical trials which involve little or no contact with patients;
- countersigning passport applications, providing character references or photocopying medical records.

In the above summary of the comment in *Notice 701/57*, I have tried to make sense of some clumsy writing, parts of which are illogical and conflicting. If in doubt, check the Notice and then discuss the problem with Customs.

The exemption includes situations in which the work is done by someone not medically qualified provided that the service is *wholly performed or directly supervised* by someone who is. If this is relevant to you, check the terms of *Notes (2) and (2A)*.

In *Anthony John Lane t/a Crown Optical Centre (LON/97/162 No 15547)* a tribunal held that the supervision test was satisfied when a qualified optician did all the eye tests and was present five days a fortnight. Evidence showed there were a few problems for him to resolve and he was available by telephone when not present. Similarly, in *Personal Assistance (UK) Ltd (MAN/00/974 No 17649)*, a case concerning nursing care at home for seriously ill patients, part-time support provided by a qualified nurse, working six hours a week but on call the rest of the time, was held to provide the necessary supervision; on the other hand, the Tribunal held in the same case that the engagement as a 'consultant' of a nurse, who had a full-time job with the local health authority, did not. There was no appraisal of each new patient or allocation of a care worker to each patient and only a limited review of the care workers, most of the support being by telephone.

However, in *A & S Services (LON/97/812 No 16025)*, an unregistered optician was found to be not directly supervised by an ophthalmic medical practitioner when the latter referred people needing glasses to him but did not attend himself and merely checked that glasses previously supplied met his prescription if customers came back for further tests a year or so later.

Group 7, Item 4: Charges by hospitals

The exemption for charges by hospitals to patients is in *Item 4*. It covers *the provision of care or medical or surgical treatment and, in connection with it, the supply of any goods*. The supply must be in a hospital or state-regulated institution. The latter is defined in *Note (8)* and potentially covers such establishments as nursing homes. However, the more reliable source of exemption may be *Item 9*. This is because, in *Kingscrest Associates Ltd and Montecello Ltd (LON/2000/875 No 17244)*, a tribunal held that the association of the word *care* with *medical or surgical treatment* meant that the care must be medically or surgically related.

In *Business Brief 10/2001*, Customs said that residential care homes could continue to treat their supplies as exempt and the law was then changed from 21 March 2002 to expand the coverage of *Item 9*.

In *Gregg (C–216/97 [1999] STC 934)*, the CJEC ruled that the exemption covered individuals and partnerships running such institutions as well as corporate bodies.

How wide is 'care' ?

Customs interpret the word care as covering:

- the protection, control or guidance of an individual to meet medical, physical, personal or domestic needs;

- usually involving personal contact with the individual (Notice 701/31/02 *Health and Care Institutions* para 2.4).

That of course covers care under *Item 9* as well as *Item 4*. Customs say it includes:

- accommodation and meals for relatives staying with a sick child in hospital — but no other supplies to visitors, relatives or carers;

- assistance with daily tasks for residents of a home for disabled, elderly or infirm people;

- meals and accommodation for in-patients, residents or other care beneficiaries;

- supervising children in a day nursery or an after school club;

- entertainment, leisure and other organised activities where these are not separable from the main supply of care or treatment.

It does not include catering for staff.

Who has to provide the care ?

The person providing 'care' need not be medically qualified. The exemption covers supplies made by, for instance, a charity, which caters to patients in an institution or by an outside contractor which supplies nursing services.

In *Crothall & Co Ltd ([1973] VATTR 20 No 6)* a VAT tribunal held that services supplied by the company in hospitals, which involved personal contact with the patients, were exempt. Thus services on the ward in meeting patients on admission, making refreshments and delivering messages for them, escorting them about the hospital and arranging their discharge were exempt as were the services of the staff controlling and supervising such duties.

Only the services of people not in personal contact with patients, such as receptionists, telephonists and cleaners, were standard-rated.

Thus, there is a distinction between services supplied direct to patients and those supplied to a hospital to enable it to supply its own services.

Customs quote renal dialysis services in hospitals as one of a few examples of supplies by an outside contractor, which do qualify for exemption.

Supplies not amounting to care

In *MJ Coleman (LON/92/1274 No 10512)*, the provision of hearing aids in a hospital was held not to amount to 'care'. The Tribunal held that the care had to be such as would ordinarily be regarded as treatment in a hospital. This makes sense —

otherwise, the supply of goods like hearing aids would be exempt if made within a hospital but standard-rated if sold from other premises.

If you want exemption, make sure you are registered

Health care is only exempt under *Group 7 Item 4* or *Item 9* if the hospital or clinic is registered under the appropriate law, such as the *Nursing Homes Act*. Until you are so registered, your charges are standard-rated. You do not obtain a retrospective exemption by gaining registration.

Although this is a pitfall for, say, a clinic specialising in hair transplants, it might be possible to turn it into a planning point. If one set up such a business, registered for VAT and charged it to patients for the first few months, the input tax incurred on the initial capital cost would be recoverable. On obtaining the appropriate health registration, the charges would then become exempt. The VAT recovered would only be repayable to the extent that it was caught under the *Capital Items Scheme* for buildings costing more than £250,000. See Chapter 24.

In practice, commercial considerations might make it difficult to achieve the correct timing. The idea would be unlikely to work for a nursing or care home because one would have to obtain official approval before being able to accept patients.

Group 7, Items 5–8

These items are of limited application. *Item 5* exempts the services of a person deputising for a doctor. *Item 6* exempts human blood and *Item 7* products for therapeutic purposes derived therefrom. *Item 8* exempts human organs or tissue for diagnostic or therapeutic purposes or for medical research.

Group 7, Item 9: Welfare services by a charity, state-regulated private welfare institution or agency or public body

The scope of *Item 9* was expanded from 21/3/02 for the reasons explained in the comment on *Item 4*. It was expanded again from 31/1/03 to cover agencies providing care and domestic help to elderly, sick or disabled people, who cannot perform the task themselves, provided that the agency is registered or regulated as detailed in the law. In *Business Brief 1/03* Customs also said that various other agencies, such as those providing fostering, adoption or nursing could qualify. You must supply a welfare service, not just an introduction fee or a commission so beware the self-employment pitfall! A commission for supplying self-employed carers, as opposed to staff, is standard rated.

It exempts welfare services and goods supplied in connection with them including when supplied by commercial businesses.

Note (6) defines *welfare services* as those directly connected with the provision of:

* care, treatment or instruction designed to promote the physical or mental welfare of elderly, sick, distressed or disabled persons;

* care or protection of children and young persons;

* spiritual welfare by a religious institution as part of a course of instruction or a retreat, not being a course or retreat designed primarily to provide recreation or a holiday.

A state-regulated private welfare institution can only exempt those services in respect of which it is regulated.

Note (8) defines *state-regulated*. See the law for the precise wording. For an *agency*, see the start of the comment on *Item 9*. An institution is one which is either:

- approved, licensed or registered under the relevant social legislation; or
- exempted from obtaining such an approval or registration.

Customs quote as examples of such institutions:

- children's homes;
- residential homes for disabled, elderly or infirm residents;
- residential homes for people with a past or present dependence on alcohol or drugs, or a past or present mental disorder;
- nurseries, creches or playgroups;
- after school clubs or similar providers of non-residential care for children.

The latter two only need to be state-regulated if they exceed a certain number of hours of care to children under 8.

If you also provide care to children over 8 Customs say you can treat it as exempt too if:

- you are a commercial institution providing care to children both under and over 8;
- your hours of opening are the same for all age groups; and
- you provide activities which are comparable for both age groups.

The item covers, for instance, religious retreats — provided that they are not primarily designed to provide recreation or a holiday! See *Notes (6) and (7)* for the full definition of *welfare services*.

In *Trustees for the Macmillan Cancer Trust (LON/97/614 No 15603)*, charges to cancer patients and carers to stay for up to two weeks in an establishment run like a hotel with trained nurses in 24 hour attendance but without 'hands-on' nursing care were held to qualify as welfare.

Group 7, Item 10: Supplies by religious communities

This Item exempts supplies of goods and services incidental to spiritual welfare by a residential community to its residents in return for membership subscriptions. Again, it must be otherwise than for profit.

Group 7, Item11: Transport for the sick

This Item exempts the transport of sick or injured people in vehicles specially designed for that purpose.

Burial and cremation — Sch 9 Group 8

This group covers:

- the disposal of the remains of the dead;

- the making of arrangements for or in connection with the disposal of the remains of the dead.

This covers those charges which are strictly related to burial or cremation. 'Extras', such as flowers and headstones, are standard-rated.

For many years, this Group caused little or no trouble. However, there have been the following three cases in the last few years, which show that, even in undertaking, there is scope for argument on VAT!

Network Insurance Brokers Ltd ([1998] STC 742) concerned a commission on annual subscriptions paid at a rate per member by affinity groups, whose members were thereby entitled to a standard funeral service (retail value £1,000) provided by the Co-operative Wholesale Society. The commission was held to be standard-rated because it was earned in arranging payment for the disposal of the remains of the dead, not for the disposal itself.

In *Co-operative Wholesale Society Ltd ([1999] STC 1096)*, a fee of £150 per member for 'facilitating and administering' a general benefit scheme on behalf of the Leeds Hospital Fund was held not to be for the making of arrangements for or in connection with the disposal of the remains of the dead.

However, in *CJ Williams' Funeral Service of Telford (MAN/98/654 No 16261)*, the storage of bodies and the provision of a chapel of rest to other undertakers were held to be part and parcel of the making of arrangements for or in connection with the disposal of the remains of the dead, not one stage removed from it.

Trade unions, professional and other public interest bodies — Sch 9 Group 9

This exempts the membership subscriptions of:

- trade unions and similar bodies;

- professional associations whose membership is restricted to those qualified or studying for the appropriate exams;

- associations concerned with advancing a particular branch of knowledge or fostering the professional expertise connected with its members' work;

- associations whose primary purpose is to lobby the government on legislation and other matters affecting the business or professional interests of its members; ie, primarily trade associations;

- bodies with objects of a political, religious, patriotic, philosophical, philanthropic or civic nature.

Charges to non-members

Note (1) excludes admission charges to premises or events, which non-members have to pay. Other Notes contain various details or limitations to the different headings above. As always, check the law for the precise wording because I have paraphrased the law in an attempt to clarify it.

Goods covered by subscriptions

The exemption covers any goods which are covered by the subscriptions and which are referable to the aims of the organisation. In practice, this is most often a journal or magazine for which one wants zero-rating under *Sch 8 Group 3* in order to recover the related input tax.

> Although not strictly a planning point as such, the apportionment of part of the subscription as zero-rated is sometimes overlooked by associations and their advisers. It can be valuable. Sometimes, the cover prices of the journal or journals supplied to members come close to the entire annual subscription. However, the sales at these prices to non-members are often minimal. Clearly, the other benefits of membership are worth something and it is usually sensible not to be too greedy when negotiating an appropriate apportionment with Customs.
>
> Moreover, Customs see an apportionment as a concession: Para 3.35 of Notice 48 *Extra statutory concessions* says:
>
> *Bodies, that are non-profit-making and supply a mixture of zero-rated, exempt and/or standard-rated benefits to their members in return for their subscriptions, may apportion such subscriptions to reflect the value and VAT liability of those individual benefits without regard to whether there is one principal benefit. This concession may not be used for the purposes of tax avoidance.*

On the other hand, beware the pitfall that, if the subscription includes admission to any premises, event or performance for which non-members have to pay, it must be apportioned as partly standard-rated.

What is a trade union, professional or public interest body?

Numerous cases have concerned claims by organisations for exemption under *Group 9*. The only one concerning a trade union is *Institute of the Motor Industry (LON/96/224 No 16586:* [1998] *STC 1219)*. After a reference to the CJEC for guidance, the Tribunal decided that the *Institute* did not qualify as a trade union. The defence of the members' collective interests and representation of those interests in disputes was not a main aim. The Institute avoided taking sides in disputes between members and their employers.

Professional associations

Allied Dancing Association Ltd (MAN/91/84 No 10777) was a borderline case in which the Tribunal held that the teaching of dance by its members was a profession. The decision was based on the fact that the *Association* conducted its own examinations and had a code of conduct. However, whether an association qualifies as professional is usually obvious. The requirement for a membership restricted to people qualified in the profession or students limits the possibilities.

Meaning of fostering of professional expertise

The majority of the arguments have therefore been about whether the body in question was an *association concerned with advancing a particular branch of knowledge* or *the fostering of professional expertise* connected with its members' work. Customs have won the majority of the cases. This is partly because Tribunals have interpreted *professional expertise* in the traditional sense of that of a doctor, a lawyer or an accountant rather than someone doing a job to a professional standard. Thus, in *The Institute of the Motor Industry* mentioned above, the Tribunal concluded that the expertise in question was that *of the sort carried on in any profession, whether its members be self-employed professionals or professionals employed in, for example, industry, commerce or public bodies.* The Institute did not qualify because its primary purpose was *the improvement of the standard of work by the individual members in their various employments, the improvement of career structures within the different sectors of the industry and the consequent enhancement of the public perception of the industry and the people working within it.*

Advancement of a branch of knowledge

Customs have seen the advancement of a branch of knowledge as referring to knowledge of an academic nature, despite *British Organic Farmers (LON/87/164 No 2700)*, in which the Tribunal held organic farming to be a branch of knowledge — a branch of the science of agriculture. It was influenced by the fact that it was the subject matter of a course at 2 colleges. Similarly, counselling was found to be a branch of knowledge in *British Association for Counselling (LON/93/1494 No 11855)* — based on evidence of academic courses and the level of articles in the Association's journal.

However, *Permanent Way Institution (LON/01/585 No 17746)* has undermined the academic argument. I persuaded the Tribunal that the *PWI's* activities in furthering knowledge about the design, construction, inspection and maintenance of the permanent way of the railway amongst those who work on it amounted to the advancement of a branch of knowledge. *PWI* publishes a journal and a leading textbook, *British Railway Track* and runs conferences. *PWI's* role as a forum enables ideas not just to be put forward but to be discussed and refined. People from all levels of seniority within the industry meet on equal terms and, although there is some science and considerable engineering expertise involved, much of the knowledge being advanced is practical rather than academic.

Meaning of 'philanthropic'

In *Rotary International in Great Britain and Ireland (RIBI), ([1991] VATTR 177 No 5946)*, Customs argued that RIBI's functions were merely administrative and organisational. The Tribunal rejected that, commenting that what mattered was not what it did, but why. It did not perform its administrative services in a vacuum. Its purpose was to promote the purposes of Rotary International. That was philanthropic being redolent of a desire to promote the well-being of mankind.

Meaning of civic nature

In the *Expert Witness Institute (LON/99/1173 No 16842; [2001] STC 679; [2002] STC 42)*, the Divisional Court held that *EWI* had aims of a *civic nature. EWI* had argued that a meaning of *civic* was *citizenship* and that that included activities concerning the relations between the citizen and the state. The Court agreed. *EWI's* aims were fairly described as for the promotion and support of the proper administration of justice and that was not subverted or undermined by other objectives, which benefited its members. This was confirmed by the Court of Appeal.

Sport, sports competitions and physical education — Sch 9 Group 10

This exempts:

- Entry fees for competitions in sport or physical recreation where all the fees go towards prizes;

- Entry fees in such competitions charged by non-profit-making bodies;

- Fees for playing sport or for physical education charged by non-profit-making bodies to individuals. If there is a membership scheme, charges to non-members are standard-rated. The exemption is for services essential to sport or physical education in which the individual takes part so sales in the bar, for instance, are standard-rated.

Membership subscriptions

The key exemption is the third one for subscriptions charged by members' clubs for taking part in sport. It is very useful to local sports clubs of all kinds.

One planning point which arises is the need for careful negotiations with Customs on how much VAT is recoverable when a new clubhouse or other expensive facilities are constructed. The club's income will be a mixture of standard-rated bar sales, charges to non-members etc and exempt subscriptions. The appropriate attribution of VAT incurred on capital expenditure is often open to argument.

Unfortunately, owners of commercial businesses providing sporting facilities started to try to take advantage of the exemption by forming members' clubs, which charged the subscriptions and ran the activities, the profit being extracted by the owner of the business as, for example, rent. Anti-avoidance rules were brought in and, as a result, this Group has lengthy notes attached to it aimed at restricting the exemption to genuine members' clubs.

What is a non-profit making body?

In *Kennemer Golf and Country Club C-174/00 ([2002] STC 502)*, a Dutch case, the CJEC confirmed the UK's view that a non-profit making body can make surpluses provided that its constitution prevents it from distributing them to its members. 'Profits' in this context means financial advantages for those members, not merely surpluses which remain within the body to finance its future activities.

Works of art etc — Sch 9 Group 11

This exempts the handing over to the Treasury of works of art in lieu of payment of tax under the 'douceur' arrangements. This is not an option open to most people and appears never to have caused any trouble, possibly because it is not often used.

Fund-raising events by charities & other qualifying bodies — Sch 9 Group 12

Group 12 exempts the supply at a fund-raising event:

- of goods and services including advertising to sponsors;
- by a charity, or charities, a qualifying body or a combination thereof;
- in connection with an event whose primary purpose is fundraising and which is promoted as such.

There are various conditions including a limit of 15 events during the charity's financial year:

- at the same location,
- of the same kind,

but you can ignore an event if the gross takings from that kind of event in that location do not exceed £1,000.

'Charity' includes a company which the charity wholly owns and whose profits are payable to it, whether or not under covenant (*Note (2)*).

'Qualifying body' means one which is:

- non-profit making and is covered by the exemption in *Sch 9 Group 9* already explained (for political, religious, patriotic etc bodies);
- a non-profit making body supplying facilities for sports or physical education, which meets the definition of 'eligible body' in *Sch 9 Group 10*;
- an eligible body as defined in *Sch 9 Group 13, Item 2* re cultural services.

What kind of event?

The exemption covers any activity recognisable as an individual event — as opposed to the regular opening of a shop or a bar. Thus, events such as horticultural shows, marathons and sports competitions are eligible.

Excluded are:

- fund-raising holidays or day trips covered by the Tour Operators Margin Scheme; or
- any event including more than two nights accommodation (*Note (9)*);
- any supply, the exemption of which would be likely to so distort competition as to disadvantage commercial enterprises (*Note (11)*);
- social events which happen to make a profit (Customs' comment).

Cultural services etc — Sch 9 Group 13

Group 13 exempts charges by public bodies and eligible bodies for admission to:

- a Museum, Gallery, art exhibition or zoo; or
- a theatrical, musical or choreographic performance of a cultural nature.

In the case of a public body, exempting the supply must not so distort competition as to disadvantage a commercial competitor.

'Public body' means primarily a local authority but includes government departments and certain other non-departmental public bodies.

'Eligible body' means one which:

- is not allowed to distribute any profit it makes and does not do so;
- uses any profit from the exempted supply to continuing or improving the facility in question; and
- is managed and administered on a voluntary basis by people with no financial interest in its activities.

Although that typically means a charity, the requirement for voluntary management must be taken seriously.

In *Glastonbury Abbey (LON/95/2909 No 14579)*, a trust was held to be run on a voluntary basis despite having two paid employees. Customs' argument that the management must be wholly voluntary was rejected because the law refers to 'essentially', not wholly.

The *Zoological Society of London (LON/96/1766 No 15607: C-267/00: [2002] STC 521)* was also held to be managed on an essentially voluntary basis by its unpaid Officers and Council. The Tribunal distinguished between the management and administration of a body and the activities it carried out. The existence of paid officials did not preclude voluntary management — so to hold would risk distortion between small and large bodies. On appeal by Customs, the case was referred to the CJEC, which confirmed the Tribunal's views. If persons having a financial interest in the body did direct it (ie under its constitution as, for example, members of the Council), it was for Customs to consider whether the essentially voluntary character of the management or administration could be accepted.

In *The Dean and Canons of Windsor (LON/97/552 No 15703)*, St George's Chapel was held not to be run on a voluntary basis because the Dean and Canons received stipends and part of their duties was to manage the Chapel and other buildings.

However, Customs' argument that the Chapel was not a museum because it was the site of a living institution was rejected. On the other hand, a restored garden open to the public was held not to be a museum in *Trebah Garden Trust (LON/98/1372 No 16598)*.

Supplies of goods where input tax cannot be recovered — Sch 9 Group 14

The heading of this Group is a little misleading. It exempts the onwards sale of goods on which input tax was disallowed when they were bought under the rules for:

- business entertainment;
- non-building materials incorporated in a building;
- motor cars.

As there would normally be no VAT on such second-hand goods, the practical effect is to disallow tax on any sale costs, such as auctioneers' commissions.

Investment gold — Sch 9 Group 15

This group exempts the sale of gold and certain gold coins where the transaction does not involve a member of the London Bullion Market Association.

Some questions to check your understanding. Review your answers with the text.

The following are general questions, not ones specific to the detailed explanations given above. This is because there is no point in trying to learn the contents of the exemption group in detail until you have a real problem to deal with. You need to know where to go to find the answer rather than to try to learn the law, especially as this changes from time to time.

- How many of the 15 Groups in *Sch 9* can you remember? As with *Sch 8*, it is the main Groups which matter and the purpose of this question is just to reinforce your understanding of roughly what is covered by *Sch 9*.

- Why is it important to look at the law itself and not just to rely on a Customs Notice or a book like this one if you need to decide whether your company's service is exempt?

12.   Have I Got One Supply or Two?

This chapter discusses the possibility of making two or more supplies at different rates of VAT within a single price. This can have a big impact on consumer pricing.

For many years, the matter was relatively straightforward. The answer with goods was usually obvious. For instance, it was accepted that an audio cassette and a book sold together were respectively standard-rated and zero-rated. Equally, if goods with a separate identity were included in a price for a service, they were often treated as a separate supply. An example was a journal as one of the benefits for a subscription to a professional body.

Services, being intangible, it was more tricky to separate a supply consisting entirely of services. For instance, an airline ticket was held to cover a single supply of transport. A meal provided during the flight was not a separate supply.

The position is now much more complicated because the cases discussed in this chapter have overturned or challenged previous ideas.

The problem

Is there:

- a multiple supply at different rates of VAT; or

- a composite supply consisting of two or more elements amounting to a single supply with the dominant element deciding the rate of tax.

Some possible examples

Here are some examples of where there might be supplies at different rates of VAT. 'Might' because, as explained below, one cannot be sure in the present state of understanding of this subject.

- A home study course consisting of a manual and a cassette.

- A home study course consisting of books or booklets but the price of which also includes the right to submit work for a number of tutorials or critiques.

- A container which is clearly designed for use independently of the product it contains, such as marmalade in a porcelain pot.

- A subscription to a professional body which includes a magazine.

Business Brief 2/2001 issued by Customs and a number of Tribunal decisions conflict with previous understanding of the position and have, in effect, required the above and numerous other situations to be reconsidered. I believe that the answer will often depend on the precise facts of the case.

The linked supplies concession

In Notice 700/7 (March 2002) *Business Promotion Schemes*, Customs make what they call the linked supplies concession. If a minor item:

- is included with the main supply at a single price;

- costs no more than 20% of the total cost of the two items; *and*

- costs no more than £1, excluding VAT, if the goods are intended for retail sale or £5, excluding VAT, in other cases,

the minor item may be ignored. A typical example is the standard-rated CD-ROM on the cover of a zero-rated computer magazine.

Key questions

The CJEC in *Card Protection Plan* identified the following key points. These had all been discussed in previous decisions and thus were not new but *CPP* is one of the trickiest cases so far and, currently, the most often quoted. See Chapter 11, *So What is Exempt?* under the comment on *Insurance, Sch 9 Group 2* for the details of *CPP*.

I have translated the points from the somewhat tortuous wording of the CJEC into words which, hopefully, you will find easier to understand. If in doubt in applying them to a difficult situation, go back to the original wording and explanations in the judgment.

In order to determine whether a typical customer is being provided with several distinct principal supplies or with a single supply, consider the following:

- Identify the key features of the transaction. Normally, each supply is regarded as distinct and independent but, if a supply is a single one from an economic point of view, one must not artificially split it so as to distort the VAT system.

- If a supply includes different features and actions, consider all the circumstances in which the transaction occurs.

- If one or more elements make up the principal supply and the others are ancillary to it, that is a single supply.

- A supply must be regarded as ancillary if it is just a means of better using and enjoying the principal one, rather than being an aim in itself for the customer.

- An all-in price is merely suggestive of a single supply, not a decisive factor. If the circumstances of the transaction indicate the customer intends to purchase two distinct supplies with different tax liabilities, the single price must be apportioned.

- Any such apportionment should be done using the simplest possible method.

The above tests must all be considered in each situation. None is by itself decisive.

Further points from various judicial commentaries

- What is the legal effect of the transaction considered in relation to the words of the law?

- To decide that, one must ask what the trader has supplied for the payment made. Motive and intention are irrelevant; the test is objective.

- Having identified and defined that, there is, in substance and reality, more than one supply, could the alleged separate supply realistically be omitted from the overall supply? Is it 'economically dissociable' or is it an integral part or component of the whole?

- Supplies by different suppliers cannot be fused together to make a single supply.

- One should treat a zero-rated or exempt supply as separate from a standard-rated one, if it is practicable and realistic to do so and the general scheme of the legislation can be followed.

Characteristics of a multiple supply

In *FDR Ltd (CA [2000] STC 672)*, Laws LJ propounded the idea that a composite supply might be either:

- a single dominant supply forming an apex, other elements being merely ancillary to it; or

- several supplies, integral to each other but none predominant and forming a 'table top'.

In a table top case, one must ask what is the 'true and substantial nature' of the supply. If the tax treatment is not then evident, one must look again at those core supplies and decide, possibly on a numerical basis, whether the taxable or exempt elements predominate!

Summary of the above points

Probably the key point, of all those listed above, is whether the element of the supply, which one wishes to separate, can be seen as a key aim for the customer rather than merely enabling that customer to benefit from the main supply.

If you have understood all the above, congratulations! It is doubtful whether anyone else does! By that I mean that I believe that it will take some time yet before one can be reasonably sure of all the situations, which may be affected.

Even experienced VAT specialists have difficulty in understanding some of the cases on which I comment below, all of which took the above tests into account at least to some extent. Now, if VAT specialists have problems in applying these tests, so will traders and local Customs officers!

So why does all this matter?

It matters because some well-established situations have changed — or, at any rate, Customs think they have! In *Business Brief 2/2001*, Customs said that they required everyone to reconsider their position based on the tests laid down by the CJEC as to whether there was a single or a multiple supply situation. Any changes which were necessary had to be applied from 1 June 2001.

Customs claimed to be giving *advance notification of the need to apply the CJEC tests*. Yet, despite knowing that the circulation of a Business Brief is limited, they took no other steps to warn traders in general other than to mention the *Brief* in *VAT Notes*

1/2001. That warning did not reach some of them until May or June. Further information did emerge in *VAT Information Sheet 2/01* but that was not even on Customs' Web site by the end of June, let alone publicised.

I make the above points because I believe that some traders, who have relied on rulings given to them previously either individually or through their trade associations or on previous key Tribunal and Court decisions, will find themselves assessed up to three years later for VAT from 1 June 2001. In some cases, depending upon the precise facts, it may be possible to persuade Customs to withdraw at least a part of the assessment on the basis that the trader concerned had no means of knowing of the change of policy in time to do anything about it.

The *Brief* said that supplies previously accepted as zero-rated or exempt might become standard-rated. Alternatively, the entire supply could be exempt instead of partly zero or standard-rated or even zero-rated instead of partly exempt or standard-rated.

For instance, Customs questioned whether a journal supplied to members of an organisation as one of the benefits of a subscription was a separate zero-rated supply. They said in the *Brief*:

Where a membership body supplies, in return for its membership subscription, a principal benefit together with one or more ancillary benefits, it will normally have to treat the subscription as being in return for that principal benefit. This means that the body will have to ignore the liability to VAT of the ancillary benefits and account for VAT on the whole subscription based on the liability to VAT of that principal benefit.

The clumsy phrasing aside, that seems far too broad an assumption. The circumstances will vary from case to case and I think that there will be some in which there can be seen to be two or more principal benefits each of which is an aim in itself.

Presumably, Customs no longer accept the validity of *Automobile Association ([1974] STC 192)*, an early case in which the subscription to the *AA* was held to be part zero-rated on account of its year book.

For an extra-statutory concession for subscriptions to non-profit making bodies, see the comment on *Sch 9 Group 9* in Chapter 11, *So What is Exempt?*

So does an optician make multiple supplies?

Customs now again accept that, in addition to the eye test, which is exempt, the charge for spectacles can be apportioned between the exempt dispensing of the lenses and the standard rated supply of the frames.

Years ago, the Divisional Court upheld the apportionment in *Leightons Ltd/ Eye-Tech Opticians ([1995] STC 458)*. Customs wrote to the *Federation of Ophthalmic and Dispensing Opticians* requiring opticians to standard rate dispensing services from 1 June 2001. The resulting appeal by the same two companies was upheld *(LON/2001/0302 & 03 No 17498)*. Customs acknowledged defeat in *Business Brief 3/2002*.

In _O-Pro Ltd (LON/99/971 No 16780)_, the Tribunal held that mouthguards were a separate supply from that of the dental services of producing them. The selling price should therefore be apportioned.

Note, however, that the Tribunal found that the professional input involved in examining the child's mouth, taking an impression and making inferences concerning the way in which the mouth would develop required considerable skill and experience as did the work of the technician in making up the mouthguard. This meant that the price of _O-Pro's_ mouthguards was considerably higher than the lower quality ones available from sports shops. The Tribunal saw the professional input as by far the most important thing from the parent's point of view and thus very much an aim in itself. Does the average customer for glasses on prescription similarly see the dispensing skill as a key aim in itself?

Goods — one supply or two?

If goods at different rates of VAT are sold together, it is usually obvious. Attempts to reduce the output tax due on standard-rated goods by including zero-rated ones in the price are unlikely to work.

For instance, many years ago, a petrol filling station offered carrots at a high price together with petrol at a nominal one. This did not work because Customs pointed out that, if you could only have the petrol at the low price because you bought the carrots at a high one, that was non-monetary consideration for the petrol. The market value of petrol would therefore be substituted for the artificially low price charged.

However, an attractive biscuit tin was held to be simply packaging required for a presentation box of biscuits, not a container standard-rated because of the possibilities for subsequent use (_United Biscuits (UK) Ltd ([1992] STC 325)_). There is a distinction between packaging primarily intended for the product in question and that clearly intended for further use such as marmalade in an expensive porcelain pot. The fact that a pot can be bought separately without the contents is a strong indicator it is a separate product, not just packaging.

Kimberly-Clark Ltd (LON/01/1273 No 17861; [2003] All ER (D) 372 (Jun)) concerned a 'free toy box' containing 124 nappies, sold at the same price as a cardboard container of the same quantity. The Tribunal said it was a multiple supply of zero rated nappies and standard rated box. On 30/6/03, the Divisional Court reversed that. The dominant supply was that of the nappies, the box being ancillary to it. The value of the latter was the cost of buying it in. _United Biscuits_ was distinguished because supplying biscuits in a biscuit tin, which prolonged their shelf life, met a customer need.

Thus, in _MD Foods plc (LON/2000/899 No 17080)_, a cardboard package containing a pottery butter dish and cover plus two 250g packs of butter was held to be a multiple supply consisting of a standard-rated butter dish and zero-rated butter.

Services — one supply or two?

If either or both of the supplies for an all-in price are services, it is often more difficult to determine whether there is a multiple supply at different rates of VAT, or a compound supply consisting of two or more elements taxable at the rate applicable to the dominant element. Examples of decided cases are:

- providing grazing, water and general care for an animal is a single standard-rated supply of the care and supervision of it, not one partly zero-rated for the animal feed element (*Scott ([1978] STC 191)*);

- providing a meal on an air flight is incidental to the air transport and not a separately identifiable supply (*British Airways ([1990] STC 643)*);

- but catering on a luxury train, on a trip sold partly on the basis of the quality of the catering, was a separate supply (*Sea Containers Services Ltd ([2000] STC 82)*).

Some more recent cases

The Tribunal cases quoted so far in this chapter are mostly old ones and seem to me likely to remain valid. Of the more recent ones, however, some are not straight-forward to understand and the decisions seem distinctly odd. I quote them to show how difficult it has become to judge how a Tribunal will interpret a multiple or composite supply situation.

Medical care and drugs

Dr Beynon & Partners v C & E Comrs ([2002] EWHC 518 (Ch): [2002] STC 699: [2002] EWCA Civ 1870: [2003] STC 169) carries the authority of the Court of Appeal. It overturned a Ch D decision that there was a single exempt supply of medical care by an NHS general practitioner when drugs and other medical items were administered by the doctor, for example by injection.

The consultation and diagnosis leading to the medical decision as to treatment was an exempt supply. The drugs were a separate supply of goods dependent on the consent of the patient. If an element of medical care in the administering of the drug was involved, such as an injection, this was not a third supply of care because it was merely the means of enjoying the benefit of the drug. Thus, there was a multiple supply of consultation and diagnosis followed by the administration of the drug but the latter was a composite supply including any medical care involved.

In *Beynon*, the drugs qualified for zero-rating under *Item 1A, Group 12 Sch 8* but that is not always so and some doctors may find themselves making standard rated supplies. See *Business Brief 2/03* for more details. Customs have appealed to the House of Lords.

Negotiating extended credit and subsequent debt collection

In *Debt Management Associates Ltd (MAN/01/0631 No 17880)*, it was held that the negotiation of extended payment terms for client debtors and the subsequent collection and distribution to creditors of payments, separate fees being charged, were separate supplies.

Processing insurance claims and training the client's staff

In *Equitable Life Assurance Society (LON/01/372 No 18072)*, a contract to handle insurance claims, whilst at the same time training the client's staff who were to take over the work at a different location, was held to be a multiple supply. It was illogical to regard the claims handling, which took two-thirds of the resources, as ancillary to the training.

Correspondence courses or distance learning

What was once a *correspondence course* is now often called *distance learning*, much of it being based on electronic rather than paper communication. However, many courses are still supplied as manuals and the question is whether they are a supply of:

- zero rated books or booklets; or

- exempt education; or

- a multiple supply of both.

The following cases illustrate how the scope for argument depends upon the precise facts. *International News Syndicate Ltd (LON/96/130 No 14425)* sold courses in journalism, media studies and for cartoonists/illustrators. It offered the manuals at 15% discount if the customer did not want any tuition.

The Tribunal thought it important that:

- *INS* were publishers, not authors or teachers;

- one course was compiled by a related company and another was derived from a variety of sources, not written by *INS*;

- students did not receive tuition by submitting work after receiving each weekly 'tutorial'. Indeed, one course involved home assessment for almost its entirety and work was only seen at the end.

It held that the predominant supply was that of the manuals. Whilst undoubtedly anyone following a course could learn much from it, so would anyone who bought a teach yourself book but there was no question of standard rating that.

The Tribunal then held that there was a single zero rated supply of manuals to which the tuition was incidental because of:

- the small element of external tuition;

- 10% of customers chose not to pay for it.

In *International Correspondence Schools Ltd (EDN/01/180 No 17662)* courses consisting of a self-contained manual were also held to be a zero rated composite supply. A key point was that only about 15% of the students took up the offer of support .

However, in *College of Estate Management (LON/02/145 No 18029)*, a leading provider of courses for the property and construction professions with 2,300 students, of whom 35% were overseas in over 70 countries, was held to be making a single supply of exempt education. The printed materials were a means of better enjoying that education. The teaching element was substantial with face-to-face sessions compulsory for UK students and two overseas countries and the staff costs were far higher than those incurred in producing the printed material.

The golf course and the greenmower

You rent a golf course and clubhouse to the club, which uses it, together with various equipment such as mowers.

- Is this the single supply of a fully equipped golf club?

- Or is it an exempt licence to occupy; and

- the standard-rated hire of the equipment?

Here are the conclusions of the Tribunal in *Tall Pines Golf & Leisure Co Ltd (LON/99/0266 No 16538)*:

- The supplies were made simultaneously.

- They were made by the same supplier, the owner of the course.

- The right to use the name 'Tall Pines Golf Club' was ancillary to the principal supply of the licence to use the course.

- The kit could not be used anywhere else so the supply of it could not have been an aim in itself but just a means of better enjoying the use of the course.

- The owner had the right to refuse permission to bring further equipment on to the premises.

- That separate sums were charged for the use of the equipment and for the licence to use the course was unimportant, given the essential features of the transaction as a whole.

- The commercial reality of the transaction was the supply of a fully equipped golf club and course. The supply of the trading name and of the equipment was so dominated by the supply of the course itself that they lost all separate identity for fiscal purposes.

- The true and substantial nature of the supply was the exempt licence to occupy a golf course.

This decision could offer planning opportunities where VAT on equipment has previously been recovered against taxable supplies — but I suggest caution!

The helicopter complete with pilot

Is the provision of an air ambulance (helicopter) and pilot two supplies — of aircraft and of pilot or is it a transport service?

This mattered because, if there was a hire of goods, the helicopter, it was zero-rated to the two Air Ambulance Trusts. Key points were:

- The Trusts got control of and use of the helicopter as they desired, subject only to the pilot's right to refuse to fly on safety grounds.

- One of the two agreements did include the pilot in the price consisting of a standing charge and a flying charge per hour. However, there was provision for extra charges for additional pilots. Moreover, that agreement provided for the fuel to be invoiced directly to the Ambulance Trust.

The Tribunal therefore found it clear in both cases that there were multiple supplies of the helicopter and its repair and maintenance and of the provision of the pilot to fly it. It also commented that this was not a transport service just because a pilot was supplied. The machines and pilots were available on standby five days in a week. The Trusts supplied the transport to the NHS, not the helicopter company *Medical Aviation Services Ltd (LON/97/016 No 15308)*.

A book with a game

In *Games Workshop Ltd (MAN/98/1073 No 16975)*, *Warhammer* games in boxed sets, which included a 288 page book together with miniature plastic figures and various items used to play the game including some cards and dice, were held to be a single supply.

This is a worrying case if you zero-rate a book as part of a supply with other items. Besides the rules, the book contained extensive explanations and stories about the fantasy world of *Warhammer*. One had to read much of the book in order to understand what fantasy war games were about and how to play. *Games Workshop* had created a complete fantasy world, which amounted to a gaming cult for boys of 12 to 16. Despite the book being sold separately at £25, the Tribunal saw it as primarily a means of better enjoying the game.

A course, which includes a book

Where a course fee has included a published book available separately, the latter has in the past been accepted as a zero-rated supply. Indeed, in *Force One Training Ltd (LON/95/1594 No 13619)*, a tribunal held that the manuals supplied to course students were zero-rated because they were physically and economically dissociable from the tuition, despite the fact that they were not sold separately.

What is the difference between the *Games Workshop* and the *Force One Training* situations? You tell me!

Sailing down the river

You hire out a river boat for functions.The boat travels along the river whilst you provide catering and, if required, entertainment.

The customer chooses the date, length of the trip and the route.

There is no argument about the catering and entertainment.

- However, you say you are providing zero-rated transport.
- Customs say you are hiring functions suites on the water.

Surely, that was a single supply? Not according to the Tribunal in *Virgin Atlantic Airways Ltd (LON/94/1530 No 13840)*. It held that the supply was of transport, albeit in comfortable conditions. Only the separate charges for catering and entertainment were standard-rated.

Is stabling for a horse separate from the care of that horse?

In *John Window (LON/00/0011 No 17186)*, the provision of a stable for a horse and the care of that horse were held to be a composite supply, which was an exempt licence to occupy the stable. Customs had agreed that charges merely for the use of a stable to those customers, who looked after their own horses, were exempt. The dispute therefore concerned the full 'livery' charges, which included the care of the horse. The Tribunal held that the livery services, such as feeding and watering, cleaning out the stable, turning the horse out in a field or exercising it, were ancillary to the principle service of an exempt licence to occupy the stable. The level of livery service provided varied from owner to owner.

It distinguished *Scott*, one of the cases mentioned earlier under the heading *Services — one supply or two?* because the main purpose of the supply in that case had been for the mares to be served by stallions. The accommodation and care were incidental to that purpose. The mares only went to the farm to be served; in contrast, the horses did not go to *Mr Window's* premises to be looked after but to occupy the stables rented by their owners. Such livery services as were supplied were consequent upon that and incidental to it.

I find this decision difficult to understand: it is feasible that the provision of a stable can be an exempt part of a charge for full livery in an establishment which offers the option to an owner of looking after his or her horse but it is hard to see how the substantial additional service of care can be ancillary to that part. Indeed, in many cases, it would be a principal aim of an owner, who had a full-time job, to obtain that care. Only the provision of it would make it possible to own the horse.

It also seems to me that the reasoning in *Window* does not sit well with that of the House of Lords in *Sinclair Collis* and in the hairdressing salon cases, discussed in Chapter 11, *So What is Exempt?* under the heading *The arguments about licences to occupy.*

Does mail-order include delivery?

A separate charge for delivery made by a shop is standard rated even if the goods are zero rated. You can't isolate the postage element in order to make this an exempt supply by you — the exemption for postage is only for a supply by the Post Office. For the position of a mailing house see Chapter 6, *So What Must I Charge VAT on?*

However, if the contract includes delivery, there is a single supply. For milk or newspapers, it is zero rated.

In mail order situations, the price of the goods normally includes delivery taxable at the rate applicable to those goods. In *Book Club Associates ([1983] VATTR 34)*, it was held that the contract to supply a zero rated book by mail order included delivery to the customer's home.

I say 'normally' above because of *Plantiflor Ltd ([2000] STC 137: [2002] UKHL 33: [2002] STC 1132).*

Plantiflor said in its catalogue:

Collection and Delivery:

Orders collected incur no handling charges. If you require delivery by carrier then a nominal charge is made to cover mail order packing and handling.

We will happily arrange delivery on your behalf via Royal Mail Parcelforce if requested, in which case please include the Postage and Handling charge on your order. We will then advance all postal charges to Royal Mail on your behalf.

Plantiflor's argument that it disbursed the postal charges on behalf of its customer was rejected by the Tribunal and by the Ch D, accepted by the CA and rejected by the HL. The HL decision that there was a single supply of delivered bulbs so the delivery charge was part of the standard rated supply was by a majority of 3 to 2. Thus, as the 3 CA judges upheld the appeal, the 5 supporting *Plantiflor* were more senior than the 5 for Customs, even though the latter won.

The doubts which this provokes are reinforced by the lack of clarity in both the CA and the HL decisions. Whilst I believe the result was the right answer, there may well be a further challenge based on a more thoroughly drafted contract than that in *Plantiflor*. If you are interested, start by reading the CA and HL decisions!

So how do I apportion the price between each supply?

An apportionment of a price between two supplies at different rates of tax must be fair. It can be based either on a proportion of the cost of each item to total cost or on an assessment of the market value of each supply. Often, however, there is no obvious way of arriving at the market value because one or more of the supplies does not have a separate stated price.

In *Jarmain ([1979] VATTR 41 No 723)* the market value of a catalogue included with the entrance fee for an exhibition was calculated on the basis of the direct printing cost plus a percentage for overheads and a profit margin.

In the case of a subscription to a society, the cover price of the journal or journals included in the subscription sometimes covers all the latter or even exceeds it! However, these cover prices are often artificial — comparatively few copies are sold to non-members. In any case, one would expect the price to the members to be substantially discounted because of the bulk order they represent. Obviously, there is a value attached to the other benefits of membership. Even if the cover price of the several journals or magazines received by members exceeds the membership subscription, 75% might be a fair apportionment for the zero-rated element of the subscription, although of course circumstances vary.

If you claim a very high percentage for the zero-rated or exempt element of a multiple supply, you may have to argue the matter at a tribunal. If so, the tribunal is unlikely to support an artificial calculation. Moreover, there is always the possibility that it decides that there is, in reality, no separate supply at all.

In *Public and Commercial Services Union (LON/01/717 No 18102)*, admittedly a case in which the accounting evidence was poorly presented, the Tribunal upheld Customs' argument that the apportionment should be based on cost and even rejected the idea of a markup.

Some questions to check your understanding. Review your answers with the text.

- How many of the criteria for deciding whether there is a single or a multiple supply can you remember?

- What is the status of a professional subscription, which includes a journal?

- Why can one not achieve zero-rating for an expensive piece of porcelain by filling it with marmalade?

- Why does the same problem not catch a smart reusable biscuit tin containing biscuits?

- Why is a meal included within an air ticket zero-rated, whereas the same meal taken on a luxury train is standard-rated despite being supplied within an all-in price for the ticket?

- If you have to apportion a single prtrice covering two supplies, what are the two different approaches to doing this?

13. What Can I Recover Input Tax on?

This is a long chapter because the subject of what input tax is or is not recoverable is a big one. However, you may find that some of the later detail such as owning a racehorse or a powerboat as a means of publicising the business, is unlikely to affect yours and will be of limited interest.

The rules dealt with here are those affecting every business. For those related to partly exempt businesses, see Chapter 23, *Partial Exemption*.

Input tax recovery is not automatic!

A VAT registration does not get you an automatic right to recover VAT:

- the expenditure must be for the purpose of your business, not for private purposes, nor for the purpose of somebody else's business rather than yours;
- you must hold a tax invoice, which must be in your name (see Chapter 14, *What is a Valid Tax Invoice?* for more about this);
- the supply shown on the tax invoice must actually occur, and be made to the business reclaiming the tax;
- the VAT in question must not be caught by the rules specifically disallowing tax on:
  - (i)   entertainment (*Input Tax Order (SI 1992/3222), Art 5*)
  - (ii) cars (*Input Tax Order, Art 7*)
  - (iii) directors' accommodation (*VATA 1994, s 24(3)*)
  - (iv) goods not ordinarily installed by builders as fixtures in new houses (*Input Tax Order, Art 6*)
  - (v)   goods sold under a second-hand scheme (*Input Tax Order, Art 4*)
  - (vi) costs of a tour operator covered by the Tour Operators Order (*Tour Operators Order SI 1987/1806*).
- If you have exempt sales, you cannot recover the related VAT, only that attributable to your taxable sales.

The mere holding of a tax invoice is insufficient. There must also be a supply to you. A tax invoice received in advance of a supply provides only a provisional right to recover. An invoice in your name includes one in the name of a company within the same VAT group because input tax of all companies within the VAT group is treated as that of the representative member.

If you do not pay your supplier, you must repay Customs

For supplies received on or after 1/1/03, you can only keep the input tax you have recovered if you pay the bill within 6 months of the date of supply or, if later, that on which the payment became due. If you do not pay your supplier within that time limit, you must refund the input tax on the outstanding invoice to Customs (*s 26A* and *Regs 172F–J*).

You make the refund by deducting the VAT from that recoverable on the VAT return covering the date on which the time limit ran out. If you have made a part payment, the refund required is based on the outstanding proportion of the invoice.

If and when you do pay in whole or in part, you can then reclaim once again the input tax or such proportion of it as relates to the part payment. In practice, this of course means that you have a period of grace, between the date on which the time limit runs out and the end of the VAT period in which it happens, during which you can pay and thereby avoid having to make the refund and subsequent reclaim.

Although this rule is designed to prevent the recovery of input tax on invoices, which were never intended to be paid, it will also catch those cases where, for genuine business reasons, invoices remain outstanding for long periods. Accounting systems should therefore include a monthly review of all invoices still unpaid after 6 months.

Late reclaims of input tax

Customs accept in para 10.5.1 of Notice 700 (April 2002) *The VAT Guide* that you can reclaim input tax late at any time up to 3 years later. The return, on which you claim late, must be made within 3 years of the date on which was due the return for the period in which fell the tax point of the sum, which you are reclaiming.

The Notice only refers to claiming VAT late because you did not have the necessary evidence at the right time. Presumably, Customs would not usually object if the invoice had been held but was overlooked or, perhaps, if the VAT had been incorrectly thought to be not recoverable on an individual invoice.

Do not confuse that situation with a claim to recover sums, which have previously been disallowed by agreement with or on the instructions of Customs. In such cases, a voluntary disclosure is required in order to give Customs the opportunity of objecting and to avoid any question of a penalty. Moreover, such a disclosure establishes the sums on which interest is to be calculated, assuming that the original non-recovery was due to an error by Customs.

VAT laundering

A VAT registration must not be used to launder VAT on behalf of someone else, who cannot recover the tax. Examples of this include:

* expenditure incurred by an unregistered or partially exempt associate;

* expenses of a self-employed salesman;

* UK travel costs of executives from overseas who come to the UK on the business of affiliates abroad;

* goods bought for directors or staff and billed to their current accounts.

What if I pay a bill on behalf of another business?

See Chapter 6, *So What Must I Charge VAT on?* for comment under *Disbursements* and *What if the tax invoice is in the agent's name?* for more detailed comment.

If the invoice is in your name, either the input must not be recovered or the net expenditure must be recharged plus output tax. *If the invoice is addressed to the person to whom the supply was made*, you cannot recover the tax and must bill the gross cost to the other entity as a disbursement outside the scope of VAT. The other person can recover the VAT, subject to the normal rules, if you attach the original invoice to your bill.

The expense may be yours but is the input VAT?

The mere fact that you pay an expense does not of itself mean that it is incurred for the purpose of your business. You may be legally liable to pay but there may not have been a supply to you.

Thus, a credit card company is merely financing purchases of goods. The CJEC held in a Dutch case, *Auto Lease Holland BV (C-1 85/01)* that, when lessees of its cars paid monthly estimated amounts for the petrol they bought using a special card and settled the balance at the end of the year, the supply of the petrol was to the lessees, not to *Auto Lease*.

Example

> You rent premises, which you no longer need, so you wish to get out of responsibility for the rent by assigning the lease to another business. You cannot do this without permission of the landlord.
>
> Under the terms of your lease, the landlord is entitled to demand that, as a condition of granting permission to assign, you pay the legal costs generated by your request; ie the expense of checking the credentials of the proposed tenant and preparing the assignment.
>
> The solicitor's invoice may well be addressed to you and it will include VAT if the landlord cannot recover this because the rent is exempt. However, that VAT is not recoverable by you because the service was supplied to the landlord, not to you, even though you are required to pay it.
>
> It can be worse! Many leases entitle the landlord to claim from a previous tenant rent which the current tenant has failed to pay. Thus, you could be faced with a demand for rent plus VAT under a lease, which you assigned some years previously. The VAT on that lease would not be recoverable by you because you would merely be compensating the landlord, not receiving any supply of use of the premises.

Now think about this one.

> You are the developer of an estate of new houses. You say to prospective buyers that you will pay the fees of the estate agent for selling their existing house if they buy one of your new ones.
>
> Customs argue that the services of the estate agent are to the owner of the house, not to you and that you therefore have no right to recover the VAT on the agent's fees.

On the basis of what has been said so far on this subject, you might think Customs were right. However, in *Redrow Group plc (1999 STC 161)*, the House of Lords held that the company *could* recover VAT on the grounds that a supply was made to it. The details of these grounds are set out below.

The supply must be to you

In the *Redrow* case, the company was able to recover VAT on the following grounds:

1   One must first identify the payment, which included the VAT to be reclaimed. If the goods or services were paid for by someone else, the trader had no claim to the deduction. *Redrow* had paid for the supply. *Note: This is how the judgment was worded. It does not necessarily mean you cannot recover the VAT if another VAT registered person pays on your behalf and re-invoices to you.*

2   The Tribunal had found that the fees paid to the estate agents were incurred for the purpose of its business.

3   The question was then whether *Redrow* obtained anything — anything at all — used or to be used for the purpose of its business in return for the payment to the estate agent for which it was liable.

4   The Court of Appeal had been wrong in requiring there to be a 'direct and immediate link' between the agent's services and the sale of *Redrow's* houses. That was only relevant where, having incurred an expense for the purposes of its business, a trader had to make an attribution of that expense to either taxable or exempt supplies.

5   *Redrow*,

    •   chose and instructed the agent;
    •   agreed the asking price for the house on the basis of the agent's valuation and the house owner's expectations;
    •   kept in touch with the agent to ensure that maximum effort was being made to sell the house;
    •   paid the agent's fees once the house owner had bought a *Redrow* house; and
    •   advised the agent to have a separate agreement with the house owner in case the latter did not do so. Under the agreement, the house owner could not unilaterally instruct a second agent because this would increase the fees payable.

Thus, *Redrow* obtained the right to have the householder's home valued and marketed in accordance with its instructions and under its control. That was different to the ordinary service of an estate agent, which was what was received by the householder if the latter became liable to pay the fees.

The circumstances in which *Redrow* is important are those where the person who pays the bill is not the most obvious recipient of the supply. However, it is not authority for VAT being recoverable just because of a payment.

Contrast the example of the landlord's legal costs above with *Redrow*. *Redrow* didn't just pay the bill and get a tax invoice addressed to it; at the outset, it had instructed the estate agent and had said that it would be responsible for the agent's fees if, in due course, the house owner bought a Redrow house. Thus there was a clear basis for deciding that there was a supply made to it.

In contrast, a tenant cannot instruct a landlord's solicitor; only the landlord can do that and it would not be acceptable for the solicitor to have a duty of care to the tenant, let alone be supplying services to the latter.

Meals for passengers on delayed flights

An example of a *Redrow* situation is when an airline pays for food and drink supplied to passengers when a flight is delayed. In earlier cases, the supply had been held to be to the passengers, who consumed the food. Part of the reasoning for this was that the airline handed out vouchers for stated values rather than amounts of food. The passenger chose the food and had to pay any excess whilst not being given a refund if the items chosen did not reach the value of the voucher. The airline was therefore seen as merely handing out to passengers the equivalent of cash and not itself receiving the supply.

However, on the basis of *Redrow*, a tribunal held in *British Airways plc (LON/99/520 No 16446)* that the airline could recover. By prior agreement with the food outlets, it obtained the right to have its passengers fed at its expense.

A key test is intention at the time of incurring the expense

Your intention at the time you incur an expense is of fundamental importance. If you had genuine business reasons for doing so, the fact that they are subsequently frustrated does not affect your right to recover the input tax. Things go wrong in business. Whilst subsequent events may tend to support or undermine your assertions as to your intention when you incurred the cost, they do not change it.

In a number of important cases concerning expensive projects to start businesses, it has been held that input tax is recoverable even if the project fails and no income is ever generated. Thus, an inventor can register for VAT and recover input tax on the costs of developing the invention from the prototype stage. Customs cannot subsequently reclaim that VAT even if the idea is eventually found not to work. Of course, there must be evidence of a serious business intent. Part of the logic is that, if Customs could collect the VAT back from the inventor, individuals would be disadvantaged compared with companies, whose research and development expenditure is lost within departmental budgets.

Evidence of intention becomes particularly important when the expenditure is on something like a racehorse, which is normally owned for pleasure. See later concerning various cases in which it has been shown that a racehorse, powerboat or whatever can be used to advertise a business.

Employees' travel expenses

Another example of a situation affected by *Redrow* is employees' travel expenses. Customs have always accepted that input tax is recoverable on bills for hotel accommodation and meals even if they are in the employees' names rather than that of the company. However, this was queried many years ago by a Tribunal Chairman, who suggested that the supply of the accommodation or meal had to be to the person who used or ate it.

Given that a business acts through its employees, it never made sense to the author to argue that the supply to them of business travel was not to their employer. However, on 8 November 2001 in *Case C-338/98*, the CJEC said that Holland was wrong to allow as input tax a fixed percentage of allowances for motor expenses to staff, who used their own cars. The CJEC said, *under Article 5 of the 6th Directive, the supply of goods means the transfer of the right to dispose of* them as owner. It is clear that use by an employee of his own vehicle in connection with his employer's business cannot constitute a supply, in that sense, to his employer. Accordingly, neither the vehicle belonging to the employee nor the fuel consumed by that vehicle can be regarded as "supplied" to the taxable employer, within the meaning of article 17(2)(a) of the Sixth Directive, simply because depreciation of the vehicle and fuel costs linked to such use give rise to partial reimbursement by the employer.

The European Commission has also queried the UK's policy — presumably on allowing recovery on mileage allowances: see under *Less detailed invoices* in Chapter 14, *What is a Valid Tax Invoice?* Since the decision in the *Netherlands* case concerned lump sum allowances and the employee's own vehicle, the UK seems to have a stronger case when it refunds on the basis of actual business miles, especially if that mileage is done in a car belonging to the business.

Nevertheless, it is a sensible planning point to arrange, where possible, for the fuel to be bought on a company credit card or invoiced direct to the business. The same applies to hotel and restaurant bills.

Incidentally, you must have the actual bills when reclaiming VAT on staff subsistence costs. If you only pay a proportion of the actual cost, you can recover the VAT included in the sum, which you pay. What you *cannot* do is recover on the basis of a flat rate allowance without the supporting invoices.

Redrow strengthens the trader's position since there must be a supply of a hotel room or a meal to a trader, who books or orders it and undertakes to pay for it just as much as there is of an estate agent's services to a house developer.

Entertainment is a dirty word

You cannot recover VAT on the cost of entertaining someone who is not an employee. Entertainment is a dirty word in the sense that this is an aspect of VAT which you should expect your VAT officer to know about and which is sure to be looked at sooner or later. If it sounds like entertainment, it probably is!

Moreover, it is not easy for a business, which has a large marketing budget, to identify entertainment. Whereas you probably take some care to vet employees' travel expenses for various reasons, it is all too easy for a large invoice covering a marketing event to slip through without the entertainment element being noticed. Even if an event is primarily to promote products or services, such as at a trade exhibition, there is likely to be some entertainment involved. Typically, such invoices do not give full details of the event but merely refer to the quotation setting out the original proposals of the agency which organised it. Therefore, unless the marketing director or whoever approves the invoice for payment, is aware of the problem and codes the invoice as entertainment either in part or in full or provides to the accounts department the information needed to do so, how will the clerk processing the invoice spot the entertainment?

The wording of the law in *Input Tax Order (SI 1992/3222), Art 5* is 'entertainment including hospitality of any kind'. This is strictly interpreted by Customs. Examples of situations caught are:

- Travel expenses of anyone, who although working for the company, is not an employee, such as auditors, self-employed salesmen and consultants. Such people should pay their own way and invoice on the cost as part of their fees. Naturally this does not help if the person is not registered for VAT;

- Hospitality element of trade shows, training courses for self-employed salesmen and public relations events such as a reception to launch a product or open a factory. Although your staff are present, they are there to entertain the guests so none of the input tax is recoverable — in contrast to the staff party. Often in such cases, only part of the expense relates to the hospitality and entertainment. VAT on a cost, which can be shown to be of an *advertising nature*, such as the cost of visual aids supporting a presentation about the product being launched, is recoverable;

- The annual staff party. Input tax is disallowed in the ratio of guests to staff. If each employee brings a partner, 50% is disallowed.

Other cases, such as a day at the races and similar corporate entertainment events, are obvious.

That the entertainment is ancillary is no help

In *Shaklee International Ltd ([1980] STC 708)* the Court held that it is irrelevant whether entertainment is ancillary to some other business purpose. *Shaklee* had to put on training courses in product knowledge and selling skills for self-employed salesmen in order to run its business but the VAT on meals and accommodation provided was not recoverable despite it being ancillary to the training. Note that the cost of hiring a room in which to do the training is recoverable. It is the hospitality which is disallowed.

If you hold a reception to launch a new product, the input tax on the sustenance for the employees is disallowed as well as that of the guests because *Input Tax Order (SI 1992/3222) Art 5(3)* disallows VAT on the entertainment of employees if it is *incidental to its provision for others*.

Who counts as an employee?

In most cases, someone will only count as an employee if they are on your payroll or are a director, partner or, as a sole trader, he or she owns the business. Thus, pensioners, former staff and job applicants do not qualify because they are not on the payroll; nor does a shareholder, unless also an employee, nor an auditor.

However, in Notice 700/65 (May 2002) *Business entertainment*, Customs say in para 2.3 that *employee* includes *self-employed persons (subsistence expenses only) — treated by you in the same way for subsistence purposes as an employee*. No further explanation is provided and, to the extent that it is noticed by people in business, that statement seems to me certain to lead to trouble!

Firstly, Customs do not define *subsistence* but they obviously mean to restrict the concession to accommodation and meals used by the self-employed person and paid for by the client whilst travelling on its business. If that seems clear, think again! What about such expenses when incurred whilst working at the office at which the self employed person is normally based whilst working for you? That is equivalent to the office at which an employee normally works; yet a consultant will usually expect you to pay for lunch and, if required, the overnight stay; costs which you would not normally pay for an employee — except to the extent that you provide a canteen.

The phrase *treated by you in the same way for subsistence purposes as an employee* seems to restrict your recovery of input tax to those cases in which the consultant travels away from the base office. If so, the concession creates an unnecessary muddle because it means that a VAT registered consultant should pay all subsistence costs at the base office and include them on the fee invoice — thus turning them into a part of the price for the services supplied — whereas the client can recover on expenses paid direct when the consultant travels!

The May 1996 version of Notice 700/65 referred to a self-employed person, working for a single 'employer', who used tools provided and was paid on a fixed rate basis unassociated with the trading profits of the business. Thus, the concession was at that time intended to refer only to such circumstances as someone working under a long term contract or, perhaps, as a labour-only subcontractor on a building site. In those circumstances, it had a limited application and, usually, to small expenses anyway. The potential application of the wording now used appears much wider and likely to cause trouble!

The sporting events concessions

Notice 700/65 also says that *helpers, stewards and other people essential to the running of sporting or similar events* can be regarded as employees. In para 2.7, Customs extend that concession to a *recognised sporting body* which *provides through necessity free accommodation and meals to amateur sports persons and officials who attend an event.* They say *a concession allows full recovery of the input tax occurred — See Notice 48 Extra Statutory Concessions.* Unfortunately, that statement as it stands is inaccurate — para 3.10 of Notice 48 says that the concession does not allow recovery on alcohol or tobacco, cigarettes or cigars.

It also explains that the concession is not normally needed for ordinary members of amateur sports clubs since subsistence expenditure they receive can be regarded as paid for through their subscriptions. The concession is therefore intended to cover team members chosen from affiliated clubs by national bodies, together with committee members of those bodies. Presumably, the restriction on alcohol or tobacco is intended to cover drinking in the bar or, perhaps, champagne celebrations of success but, typically of this Notice, it ignores an obvious problem — drinks on invoices for meals. No doubt, in practice, input tax on such drinks is claimed as part of the meal and reasonable amounts would probably not be challenged by Customs.

A concession if you entertain whilst travelling

Tax incurred on subsistence expenses of directors or partners and staff travelling bona fide on business is recoverable.

In Notice 700/65, *Business entertainment* (May 1996), Customs said that para 3 covered tax on meals with guests provided that any entertainment was secondary to the main purpose of the trip. That comment was not repeated in the May 2002 version but I understand that the policy remains the same. So, if whilst travelling away from your office you invite a customer out to lunch, the entertainment element is the customer's meal. The VAT on your meal is recoverable because you are out on subsistence.

In contrast, no VAT on either meal is recoverable when you leave your office for a prearranged lunch. This concession is of limited value for head office staff because of the difficulty of persuading executives to keep reliable records concerning the circumstances of each meal. However, your salesmen are usually out on subsistence.

Meals close to the office

If your managers regularly lunch in a local hotel, where they can discuss problems free from interruptions, you can reclaim the VAT. Notice 700 (April 2002) says in para 12.1.2, 'If your business pays for meals for employees you can treat any VAT incurred as your input tax'. Presumably, that covers breakfast or an evening meal when staff work out of normal hours and working lunches out of the office.

That does not apply to sole proprietors, partners and directors. Customs say that they 'cannot recover the VAT on meals which are not taken for business purposes'. Although the wording is far from clear, it seems that, in the context of para 12.1.2, they are likely to dispute recovery by the *owners or directors* of businesses on meals in the vicinity of the office because these individuals can decide on their own expenses. If you think you have an argument of business purpose for, say, Board lunches, ask Customs.

Entertainment must be free

If you provide, say, meals or accommodation as part of a contractual arrangement, you are not caught under the disallowance for entertainment and hospitality because the provision is not free.

In *Celtic Football and Athletic Co Ltd ([1983] STC 470)*, the Court of Session held that, because *Celtic* was obliged under the *UEFA* rules to pay for its visiting opponents' board and lodging and would receive in return the same when visiting their country, the provision was not free. It was therefore not entertainment.

Similarly, in *Kilroy Television Co Ltd (LON/96/677 No 14581)*, food provided to participants in a television programme was held to be in return for their participation. It was part of the deal that a train ticket would be sent to them and a buffet meal provided on arrival at the studio.

However, such an argument may get you nowhere if Customs then say you have provided non-monetary consideration, the accommodation etc, in return for non-monetary consideration from the other party. Thus, arguably, *Kilroy* should have accounted for output tax on the supply to the participants, the value of the supply being the cost to it of the food. If you cannot collect the output VAT, the end result is the same as if the input tax was disallowed.

If the other party is VAT registered, it can of course recover the VAT charged. Since it is doing something in return, it is making a supply to you and it too should charge tax to you on the value of the food, accommodation etc — in addition to any money charged to you.

A typical example is where a contractor stays overnight near the premises at which he is working and hotel bill is paid by the customer as part of the arrangements. Another is the conference organiser who pays for meals and hotel accommodation for lecturers. If the organiser agrees to pay for these as part of the arrangements under which the lecturer speaks, I believe that the value is part of the supply by the lecturer to which VAT should be added. Frequently, both parties ignore the matter but, as a matter of VAT law, it is an addition to the value of the supply by the contractor or the lecturer.

That the amounts, which each party should charge to the other, would offset each other might not prevent Customs issuing an assessment, there being of course no guarantee that each side could recover the VAT charged to it.

Motor cars

VAT on a motor car is recoverable if the car is used exclusively for business purposes. That eliminates most cars bought by businesses because the users travel to and from work in them. Getting to work and going home is a private activity, not a business one.

Numerous small businesses have argued that one vehicle is used only for business and that others are available to the owner and his or her family for private use. Unfortunately, most private cars are insured for private motoring as well as for use by the policyholder for his or her business. If the vehicle is normally kept at home too, it is available for private use.

That was confirmed in *C Upton (t/a Fagomatic) ([2002] STC 640)*. The Tribunal's decision that a Lamborghini car was not *intended* for private use by a sole trader, who worked 7 days a week, and claimed not to use the car for shopping or social occasions, despite having no other car, was overturned by the Divisional Court. The key was whether the vehicle was *available*, not the *intention* as to its use. The Court of Appeal confirmed that as the correct test, even though it was difficult for a sole trader to prevent himself using a car for private purposes.

So, to recover VAT on a motor car for use in your business, you must insure it for business use only — difficult to arrange — and/or park it overnight at the business rather than at home.

In the larger business, the position is much the same with pool cars. If you can show that a pool car is only used during the day for specific business journeys and that it is returned to the pool at night, you can recover input tax on it. However, one reason for having pool cars is usually so that, when a senior executive needs one, a pool car can be made available temporarily. Inevitably, such use will include journeys to and from work.

In *Squibb & Davies (Demolition) Ltd (LON/01/653 No 17829)*, input tax recovery was allowed on a *Range Rover* and a *Jaguar* which were locked up at night in the company car park and for which journey logs were kept. The *Range Rover* was used for emergency calls, often at night and was equipped with fax and mobile phone points and carried tools, protective clothing etc. The *Jaguar* was used to transport clients. No director was allowed to use them privately and the Tribunal accepted that there was no intention to make them available for private use.

In practice therefore, VAT on a car is not usually recoverable except by:

- A motor dealer — because the dealer will charge VAT when the car is sold;

- A leasing company — because it does not even have possession of the vehicle. The corollary is that the lessee is only allowed to recover 50% of the VAT on the leasing charges;

- For use as a taxi;

- For use for self-drive hire;

- For use by a driving instructor.

Although the use for business purposes in general must be *exclusive*, that as a taxi, self drive hire or for driving instruction need only be *primarily*. Thus, a taxi driver can use his car for private purposes as well.

If a car, on which input tax has been recovered, is sold, VAT is due on that sale.

The detailed rules are in *Input Tax Order (SI 1992/3222) Art 7*.

Car leasing and hire charges

As mentioned above, 50% of the VAT on the leasing charges for a motor car is normally disallowed to the lessee. That does not apply if the use is as a taxi, for self drive hire or for driving instruction.

It does catch a hire whilst your normal car is off the road. However, Customs accept that, in other cases, the 50% disallowance only applies after ten days (para 4.4 of Notice 700/64 (January 2002) *Motoring expenses*). Thus, you can recover if, for instance, you travel on business by train or by air to another part of the UK and hire a car there for a few days.

The 50% leasing disallowance does not apply to the maintenance of the vehicle if the charge for this is shown separately on the lessor's invoice.

If, after disallowing 50% on the leasing payments, you receive a credit note from the lessor on early termination or at the end of the lease, you need only reduce your input tax by 50% of that credit.

Private use of a car from a motor trader's stock

Having recovered all the input tax on a new car held in stock, a manufacturer must account for output tax on its private use if it is provided free of charge to a director or employee. Customs have agreed with the *Society of Motor Manufacturers and Traders Ltd* a simplified method of calculating the VAT due. Details are published in an *Administrative Agreement* available from Customs, which quotes lump sums payable depending upon the value of the car.

A similar agreement with the *Retail Motor Industry Federation* quotes figures for motor dealers, who make demonstrator cars available for private use.

The definition of a motor car

Most of the time, it is obvious whether a vehicle is a motor car or not. However, people sometimes get it wrong because they have not studied the words of the law. They think that, for example, a four-wheel-drive vehicle used on a farm or by a service engineer visiting customers is no longer a car because of what it is used for. Not so! The key is the design of the vehicle as can be seen from the following.

Input Tax Order (SI 1992/3222), Art 2 defines a car as a vehicle which:

(a) is constructed or adapted solely or mainly for the carriage of passengers; or

(b) has to the rear of the driver's seat roofed accommodation which is fitted with side windows or which is constructed or adapted for the fitting of side windows;

But not if it is:

- capable of carrying 10 or more passengers;
- or a payload of 1 tonne or more;
- or has an unladen weight of 3 tonnes or more.

Special purpose vehicles, such as hearses and street cleaning vehicles are also excluded from the definition.

The one-tonne payload

Customs have an agreement with the *Society of Motor Manufacturers and Traders Ltd* under which manufacturers inform both dealers and Customs of the ex-works pay loads of their standard double cab pickup trucks. Accessories added by dealers can be ignored except for hard tops. Customs accept a standard weight for a hard top of 45 kg. Since this reduces the payload, it could convert a pickup truck with a pay-load of just over one tonne into a car.

Maintenance of cars

You can recover all the VAT incurred on *maintaining* a car. There is no restriction for private use even if the business mileage is only a small proportion of the total. This generous interpretation of the law by Customs takes into account the fact that no VAT is recoverable on the car itself if there is any private use. Thus, the owners of businesses can reclaim VAT on car maintenance invoices as long as the business pays for the work, even though the car itself is not a business asset (Para 5.1 Notice 700/64 (January 2002) *Motoring expenses*).

In theory, an employer could agree to pay the maintenance costs of cars owned by staff and recover the VAT thereon. In practice, the direct tax consequences and the extra administration may make this not worth doing.

Fuel for cars

If a business pays for *any* fuel used for private motoring by its owners, directors or employees, it has to pay VAT on the fuel charge as set by *s 57*. This works thus:

- *s 57* fixes a sum, which is VAT inclusive so you apply the VAT fraction to it;
- you pay on each return;
- there are 3 rates for petrol engines depending on engine size, and 2 lower rates for diesels.

If you have a car fleet, you will need to set up a spreadsheet on your computer and to administer this carefully for all changes in the cars. Notice 700/64 *Motoring*

Expenses explains the detailed rules in *s 56* concerning, for instance, what happens when you change a car in the middle of a VAT period.

A possible pitfall is that the fuel charge changes each year. In 2002, the effective date was altered to periods starting on or after 1 May. This means that, if your VAT return is quarterly and begins on 1 April, you do not alter the VAT due until the return for July–September. Check the current sums. It would be easy to overlook the change if your spreadsheet is based on monthly or quarterly sums of VAT per car. Although increased in 2003/04, for 2002/03 and 2001/02 the charge was *reduced* so you could have overpaid, if you overlooked the change.

The scale assumes private motoring 10–13,000 miles a year, depending of course on your engine size and mileage per litre. Remember that private motoring includes journeys from home to work.

If your private motoring is low, consider the alternatives:

- Not reclaiming input tax on fuel at all — although the gross cost of the fuel can be paid by the business. That means fuel for *any* of your vehicles, so it will not make sense if you run a commercial fleet;

- Reclaiming by calculating the proportion of business mileage to total mileage and reclaiming that proportion of the VAT on the total expenditure on fuel during the VAT period or for the year. To satisfy Customs, you will need detailed records, recorded journey by journey, not estimates, together with the actual fuel bills;

- Claiming from the business for specific business mileage only trip by trip, thus claiming only for the mileage readily identifiable on the basis of a mileage allowance. In Notice 700/64, Customs do not say how you should calculate the petrol element of the mileage allowance but the figures quoted by the motoring organisations are likely to be acceptable.

The difference between purpose and benefit

Expenditure is not for the purpose of a business merely because it benefits from it. The benefit may be incidental, as when you make a valuable business contact whilst on holiday, or it may be closely connected, as when a director is defended against a criminal charge arising out of the business activities but *benefit* is not enough. You have to demonstrate a business *purpose*. See later under *Legal costs* for more on this.

The business in question could be your existing one or a new one. For example, the ownership of racehorses may be justifiable:

- because the horse(s) help to promote another kind of business;

- because your breeding and/or dealing in horses itself amounts to a business.

The promotion of a business with a racehorse, power boat, yacht, etc

For obvious reasons, Customs look carefully at the ownership of such desirable assets as racehorses and yachts. In the earlier years of VAT, numerous tribunal cases established some ground rules.

- You must show a credible business purpose for incurring the expenditure such as that the horse, or whatever, will advertise your business to potential customers. Input tax is not disallowed merely because the decision was not a wise one. On the other hand, tribunals have been inclined to support Customs where the evidence showed that it was unlikely that the expenditure could have benefited the company.

- Evidence of the intention at the time of purchase is important, such as minutes recording the background to the decision to incur the costs.

- You should record the subsequent use of the asset, noting publicity received, sales leads obtained or other benefits.

Beware of the entertainment pitfall. If the expenditure is used for the purpose of entertainment, as opposed to advertising, the VAT will be disallowed. Thus, any advertising must be to racegoers generally. The cost of taking customers to the races is caught as entertainment.

In *Hillingdon Shirts Co (MAN/78/26 No 678)*, a shirt manufacturer recovered tax on the cost of running a racehorse mainly because he produced a mock-up of a shirt to be launched bearing the name of the horse when the latter won a race. In other words, the quality of the business decision is not in question, merely whether or not the evidence supports the directors' assertion that they made a genuine business decision to acquire the asset for the purpose specified.

In *AJ Bingley Ltd (LON/83/333 No 1597)*, a company making plastic bags used in supermarkets won its claim to recover input tax on the cost, exceeding £250,000, of 6 racehorses. The senior management of the supermarkets tended to be interested in racing. Some of them owned horses. Bingley's ownership of horses provided talking points which enabled its salesmen to obtain interviews at which they could make sales pitches. Plastic bags being a low value routine product, it was not easy to get in to see the buyer. Getting the interview was the crucial first stage and the horse ownership facilitated this.

In *Demor Investments (EDN/80/74 No 1091)*, a public house succeeded because its customers took an active interest in the horse. The pub was next to a betting shop and most of its business came from people who came in to watch the racing, which they could not do in the betting shop. There was evidence that they came to regard the horse as their own, with consequent loyalty to the pub.

Personal number plates

Customs are bound to see a personal number plate as being for the private satisfaction of the individual rather than for the purposes of the business. To claim for input tax on the cost, you must show that it is in some way promoting the business. In *Sunner and Sons (MAN/91/1205 No 8857)*, a Tribunal accepted that the number plate *7 SUN* was bought to promote the *SUN* name on own label goods sold in a supermarket called *Sun*.

Input tax on expenditure partly for private purposes

In *H Lennartz ([1995] STC 514)*, the European Court of Justice held that 'A taxable person who uses goods for the purpose of an economic activity has the right, at the time of the acquisition of those goods, to deduct the input tax in accordance with the rules laid down in Article 17, however small the proportion of use for business purposes'.

This means that only if you agree can Customs use the power they have in *s 24(5)* to require an apportionment of the VAT incurred on most goods used partly for non-business purposes. If you object, you can recover all the input tax but must then account for output tax on the cost to you of the private use.

That does not apply to a major interest in land, buildings, civil engineering works or goods installed therein bought from 10/4/03 onwards. If the use will be partly private, the input tax must be apportioned. See the loan of a business asset rules in Chapter 6, *So What Must I Charge VAT on?*

Input tax on clothing

VAT on work wear provided to staff such as overalls is recoverable but not VAT on ordinary clothes. The normal rule is that input tax is not recoverable on clothing. One must turn up dressed appropriately for work.

In *John Pearce (LON/91/1638 No 7860)*, an actor recovered all the input tax on clothing bought for use in his profession. Customs allowed in full, tax on items identified as stage clothes or uniforms. However, only 50% was allowed for clothing purchased from normal retailers suitable for ordinary use. The Tribunal overturned this. Customs had accepted that it was bought partly for professional use. Thus, the disallowance was wrong under the *Lennartz* principle explained earlier.

However, *Sch 4(5)(4)* makes the loan of an asset for private use a supply of services by the business. Then *Sch 6(7)(b)* makes the value of that supply the full cost of providing it. The rules are normally applied to such items as yachts and aeroplanes but would also catch clothing. So Mr Pearce may have incurred greater administrative cost in accounting for output tax on his clothes than if he had accepted a disallowance on the purchase.

A key element of the calculation must be whether, when the actor goes to work dressed for the part, his journey to work is treated as business. If his office is at home and the locations are all different, he may have a good case for this. However, Customs could then require him to keep adequate records of the date and reason for the use of each suit, including the calculations for the entries made in each return. Arguing the *Lennartz* principle is all very well but Customs have the means to get their own back!

A sale of the asset will be taxable

Remember too that, when the asset is sold, output VAT is due. Whilst of no account for a suit, that may mean that, taking direct tax into account, it is better to keep the asset private and charge the business for business use.

Customs may demand VAT on the full sale price. However, there is authority in *Armbrecht ([1995] STC 997)*, a judgment of the CJEC, for arguing that it is only due on that proportion of the asset which has been treated as business. In that case, when living accommodation, on which input tax had not been recovered, was sold as part of a business, the CJEC ruled that output tax was not due on the dwelling.

A jazz musician's wig

See also *JM Collie (LON/90/1382 No 6144)* in which a jazz musician recovered VAT on the cost of a wig used to promote his image as the 'wild man of jazz'.

An actor's health club membership

Anthony Anholt (LON/89/487 No 4215) recovered tax on a health club membership because he needed to stay fit in order to play a role in 'Howard's Way'.

Legal costs

VAT on legal costs is not recoverable if it is for the benefit of, say, a director rather than for the purpose of the business. The following cases illustrate the problem of establishing business purpose.

In *Wallman Foods Ltd (MAN/83/41 No 1411)*, a tribunal held that tax was not recoverable by the company on solicitor's fees for defending its managing director against a charge of handling stolen goods, which were sold in its supermarket. It was for the benefit of the company that expenditure be incurred in an attempt to prevent its managing director being imprisoned and thus unable to operate its business. However the Tribunal drew a distinction between expenditure for the benefit of a taxable person and that incurred for the purpose of a business actually carried on by him. The charge was against Mr Wallman personally and there was no liability on the company. The invoice was addressed to him and it was clear that the services were supplied to him, not to the company. There was insufficient nexus between the payment of his costs and the company's business of retailing groceries.

In *Britwood Toys Ltd (LON/86/280 No 2263)*, tax on the cost to the managing director of a successful defence against a charge of corruption in offering inducements to a civil servant was similarly held to be non-recoverable. Even though the company had been severely prejudiced by the cancellation by the Home Office of a contract, which the managing director hoped to have restored, and even though the judge had decided there was no case to answer, the Tribunal found that the expenditure was personal, not for the business of the company.

In *Rosner ([1994] STC 228)*, the Divisional Court held that there must be a clear nexus between the expenditure and the business. Although there was a connection between the school run by Mr Rosner and the criminal proceedings re immigration offences, in that the offences related to potential students, it did not relate to the carrying on of the business.

However, in *SR Brooks (LON/94/412 No 12754)*, *Rosner* was distinguished. The trader succeeded in his claim for tax on the cost of defending himself against a charge of conspiracy knowingly to acquire gold on which duty had not been paid. The nexus with the business existed here because every step in the alleged offence was one taken in the normal course of dealing in gold.

Libel actions

In *WG Stern (LON/84/416 No 1970)*, the cost to a consultant of obtaining his *discharge from bankruptcy* was held to be mainly personal. The Tribunal accepted that it would also assist his business by re-establishing his integrity but had no evidence on which to base an apportionment. Fees re *a libel action* were a business expense. The action arose out of Stern's appointment as a consultant to the administrator dealing with the disposal of Stern Group properties and, without the action, his activities as a consultant would have been prejudiced. The cost of *attending a Parliamentary Committee of Enquiry* was not for his business. Although he was vindicated, this was not for the purpose of his consultancy business, the reasoning being as in the *Wallman* case noted above.

Another libel action case was *Orrmac (No 49) Ltd (EDN/90/185 No 6537)*. The legal costs were held to be 25% for the company's business, 75% to protect the personal reputations of two directors.

The defence of its staff by a company can be a business expense

In *P & O European Ferries (Dover) Ltd (LON/91/2146 & 2532 No 7846)*, input tax on costs of about £3.5m spent defending 7 individuals against charges of manslaughter after the *Herald of Free Enterprise* disaster was held to be recoverable. *P & O* instructed the solicitors acting for the individuals because:

* It was advised that it could face a charge of 'corporate manslaughter' if two or more of its employees were found guilty of gross negligence;

* If *P & O* itself had been prosecuted and convicted, the limitations of its insurance liability in relation to cargo claims might have been no longer available to it and it might therefore have borne the excess of loss liability;

* It was essential for *P & O* to defend a name under which many group businesses operated.

P & O's instructions to the seven firms of solicitors required them to work with *P & O* in planning the defence and *P & O* approved both the choice of counsel and their remuneration. Customs argued that the supplies of legal services had been to the individual defendants who had instructed them. However, the Tribunal found the evidence to show that *P & O* was the client of each solicitor:

* It had instructed that solicitor and agreed to pay him;

* The solicitor would have had no right to recover his fees from the employee, had the company refused to pay.

Of course, the employee was also a client of the solicitor but that did not change the fact that the company was a client as principal in relation to each. The services were therefore provided to the company, not withstanding that the individual employee also received the benefit of the services. The Tribunal also rejected Customs' argument that the expenditure was only for *P & O*'s benefit, not for the purposes of its business. The size of the business and the serious consequences for it of conviction of those individuals were so great, that the financing of the costs of their defence could be seen as serving the purposes of the business despite a substantial benefit being conferred on each of the 7 men.

See Chapter 6, *So What Must I Charge VAT on?* under *Services bought in are taxed if put to private use* for comment on a possible output tax liability because of a subsequent change in the law.

VAT on legal representation for pension fund beneficiaries

In a case similar in some ways to that of *P & O*, the *Plessey Co Ltd (LON/94/254 No 12814)* failed to recover VAT on the cost of legal representation for 14 representative pension fund beneficiaries. The company wanted to wind up three pension funds but the trustees insisted on Court approval. This could not be had without the Court being advised as to the position of the beneficiaries who were not prepared to join the proceedings unless their costs were met. The input tax was disallowed because the advice was given to the beneficiaries, who were the clients, not to the trustees, let alone to the company, which sought the reclaim. The lawyers' invoices were addressed to the beneficiaries. Even though satisfied that the trustees had to meet the cost and that the services were used for the purposes of the company's business, the Tribunal found that they had not been supplied to it but to the beneficiaries. It distinguished *P & O* on the grounds that *P & O* had been the client of the solicitors whose services were supplied to both the employees and to *P & O*. The distinction may mean that the *Redrow* case, discussed near the start of this chapter, would not help in this kind of situation.

Legal action by a pension fund

However, *Ultimate Advisory Services Ltd (MAN/95/2550 No 17610)*, was held to be entitled to recover VAT on the cost of defending a claim against the trustees of the company's pension scheme, despite the controlling director being the only member. The company had an obligation under the trust deed to pay the costs of the administration and management and was therefore already liable for such fees before it instructed the solicitors. Although this was a one-person scheme, the provision by an employer of a pension scheme could properly be regarded as having been done in the course of the employer's business. The Tribunal saw the situation as similar to that in *Redrow*.

Apportionment of work on living accommodation used partly for business

If you work from home, input tax on part of the running costs of that home is recoverable. In practice, this is likely to be limited to a proportion of the VAT incurred on heat and light and on the telephone, if you do not have a business line, since the other costs, such as insurance and water tend not carry VAT.
The exception is when major maintenance or repair work is done on the property.

In *Sir Ian McDonald of Sleat (MAN/81/150 No 1179)*, Customs had accepted that one-third of the tax on the cost of repair work on a Queen Anne house could be recovered. Only the basement, one of three floors, ignoring the attics, was mainly used for business as offices, store-rooms, etc, though occasional meetings were held in the dining room and business guests stayed in the bedrooms. The gardens were open to the public from March to October but not the house. In addition an agricultural estate of 2,000 acres with holiday cottages and caravans was attached, though not managed by Sir Ian himself. About two-thirds of the input tax in question of £6,376 was incurred on repairing the roof and on architect's fees. Presumably this was seen as relating to the building as a whole but it is not clear from the decision why, on the above facts, the Tribunal increased the apportionment to 60% recoverable.

In *Eccles (EDN/85/71 No 2057)*, a cottage was renovated to make it suitable for a farm worker to live in but the farmer's son then occupied it. A farm worker was needed on hand 7 days a week and to be available at short notice. The 4 farm workers lived from 1 to 9 miles away. The Tribunal was satisfied that, without the son, an agricultural worker would have been installed in the cottage and would so be in a few years time when the son moved into the main farmhouse after Mr Eccles retired. The dominant purpose of the expenditure on the cottage was to provide, in the long term, suitable accommodation to enable 7 days a week supervision of the farm activities to be obtained. Though there was a useful subsidiary purpose in housing John Eccles and his wife, that was much less important. Taking into account the fact that their occupation was unlikely to be indefinite, 70% of the input tax was recoverable.

In *W A Patterson & Sons Ltd (LON/84/377 No 1870)*, 50% of the input tax was disallowed on the cost to a company of providing a flat above a newsagents in a property owned by it. The Tribunal found there was duality of purpose, the director having to live above the shop under the terms of its service contract, but it being convenient for him to do so as he had to start selling newspapers at 5 am. Even though the property was owned by the company, the test of user was still appropriate. The occupation was partly for business and partly private.

You cannot claim for accommodation merely because you live elsewhere

In *Bernheimer Fine Arts Ltd (LON/86/182 No 2265)*, a company had two businesses, one in Germany and one in the UK. The company claimed input tax on the provision of a small bedroom and ancillary shower room above an antique shop for the use of its controlling director when visiting its UK premises, the main business being in Germany. The claim was disallowed. The expenditure was on the business premises and was on a *pied-à-terre* rather than a proper flat. Yet the tribunal held it to be for domestic purposes, since it was the duty of the director to present himself for work.

There is now a specific disallowance in *section 24(3)* for VAT incurred on domestic accommodation for directors but that does not affect the normal right to recover VAT on hotel and other travel costs when away from the normal place of work, as explained earlier under *Employees' travel expenses*.

Is input tax recoverable on removal expenses of staff?

For moves due to employment, tax is normally recoverable on the charges by the removal firm and on fees of estate agents and solicitors for the sale and purchase of houses, even though supplied to the employee, not to the company.

In *SSL Ltd (LON/87/254 No 2478)*, Customs' argument that the supply was to the controlling directors personally and that there was no contract committing the company to pay the cost was rejected. The Tribunal did hesitate for lack of evidence, so issue written instructions to estate agents and lawyers and get invoices in the name of the business.

VAT is not recoverable on any soft furnishings allowance — VAT was not recoverable when the furnishings for the previous house were bought by the employee.

Cases where recovery has been allowed without a tax invoice

Normally, you must hold a tax invoice in your name, subject to the minor concessions explained in Chapter 14, *What is a Valid Tax Invoice?* under *Less detailed invoices* and *Authenticated receipts*. The other exception is where the supply was by someone who was not registered but should have been. In other words, at the time of supply, the supplier was a taxable person due to sales exceeding the registration limit. Since the unregistered supplier was not in a position to issue a tax invoice, you only need evidence that there was a supply made to you. You can then recover the VAT — as calculated by applying the VAT fraction to the price which you have paid, not the VAT rate on top.

That said, the key to recovering input tax is that you have received a supply. If you can demonstrate this but lack a tax invoice, ask Customs if they will allow recovery on the basis of whatever other evidence you have. Customs have power to do so under *Reg 29 (2)*. Note, however, that the power of the Tribunal to intervene has been held to be supervisory rather than appellate. A supervisory power means that the Tribunal can only overturn Customs' refusal to allow recovery if it decides that, in the circumstances of the case, that refusal was unreasonable. In other words, the Tribunal cannot send the matter back to Customs for review merely because it would have come to a different conclusion — as it would be able to do if it had an appellate power. See *Richmond Resources Ltd (LON/94/1496 No 13435)*.

Tribunals have occasionally upheld appeals outright when satisfied that a supply was made to the claimant. The following cases are examples but they were decided long before *Richmond*.

In *J E Morgan (t/a Wishmore Morgan Investments) (LON/86/165 No 2150)*, the Tribunal overruled a refusal by Customs to allow input tax on an invoice addressed to an associate company. It was satisfied that the supply was made to the claimant.

Similarly, in *Bird Semple & Crawford Herron (EDN/85/35 No 2172)*, tax on agents' fees re a lease held by a nominee company, which did not trade, was held to be recoverable by a firm of solicitors. The sole purpose of the trustee company was to act as the nominee of the firm and simplify the administration of the leases of a property partly occupied by it.

Beware of the unregistered business such as a self-employed person

An unregistered person cannot pass on VAT.

In *R Wiseman & Sons (EDN/84/11 No 1691)*, Wiseman paid the maintenance and fuel costs for the vans used by self-employed milk roundsmen. It nominated garages where the roundsmen bought the fuel and obtained receipts for it. Envelopes containing sufficient cash for the fuel for each round were given weekly to each driver. The Tribunal rejected an argument that the fuel was bought by Wiseman through the agency of the drivers, in favour of the Customs' contention that the supply was to the roundsmen as independent contractors who used the fuel for the purpose of the business sub-contracted to them.

Distinguish between a business and the ownership of it

In *Shaw Lane Estates (MAN/88/680 No 4420)*, tax was denied on the grounds that the legal action, on which it was incurred, concerned the ownership of the business rather than that business itself.

A similar principle disallows input tax incurred by individuals on costs incurred in raising finance to put into a business. In *Rushgreen Builders Ltd (LON/87/116 No 2470)*, a house was sold to raise money, not because of a move to another area. The fees were held not to have been incurred for the purpose of the business. The supply of the services was to the directors personally to enable them to invest money, even though the invoice was to the company.

In *Sally McLeod Associates (LON/94/1080 No 12886)*, the VAT was incurred in defending an action by the bank to repossess the house, which was used partly as the appellant's home and partly for her business. That 25% of VAT on repairs had been allowed for the business use element did not impress the Tribunal; nor did the claim that, for unspecified reasons, the business would not have been able to continue if the house had been lost.

Mobile telephones

In *Business Brief 14/99* dated 2/7/99, Customs said that, if a mobile phone is provided to an employee for business use, all input VAT on the purchase cost and on charges is recoverable *provided that they do not include any element for calls.*

- If you have clear rules prohibiting private use, all input tax on calls is recoverable even if, in practice, you tolerate a few private calls.

- Output tax is due on any charges for private calls, all input tax being recoverable.

- If you allow private calls, you must disallow the corresponding input tax on calls. Customs say it is 'inappropriate' to account for output tax instead. A ratio based on a sample of bills taken over a reasonable period of time is acceptable.

- If the phone is bundled with some call time, you must apportion the full charge.

Some questions to check your understanding. Review your answers with the text.

- What are the five key conditions on which depends the right of a business to recover input tax, which were listed at the start of this chapter?

- What is the importance of the *Redrow* case?

- What is the distinction between an expense which is incurred for the purpose of a business and one from which it benefits?

- If you pay the costs of a member of your staff who moves to work at a different location, on which expenses is the VAT recoverable?

- If a director or senior executive is prosecuted, why is it usually difficult for the company to recover VAT on legal costs which it has agreed to pay on the person's behalf?

- If you take a customer out to lunch, can you recover VAT on the cost?

- Can a taxi firm recover VAT on the new cars it buys?

14.　What is a Valid Tax Invoice?

This chapter explains the information which must be shown on a tax invoice, together with various other points about them. In theory, tax invoices, which are mostly produced by computer nowadays, should all comply with the law and should be easily recognisable. In practice, the infinite variety of layout on invoices complicates matters.

If your business receives a substantial volume of invoices, you are bound to be at risk for amounts big enough to lead to possible penalties. The sheer volume of transactions means there is a risk of documents slipping through, which are not tax invoices. To reduce the risk to a minimum, both managers approving invoices and clerks processing them through the accounting system, must understand the importance of a tax invoice and the details which it must contain. That requires training, which is not easy to carry out systematically, especially if there is a turnover of staff. Yet, untrained staff will break the law in your name!

So do I have to worry about my input invoices?

Yes, you do! If your staff are not trained in what is required on a VAT invoice and you do not have a good enough system for checking for the key information, you are at risk; it is inevitable that VAT will be recovered on some documents which do not qualify. When did you last check your input invoice files for:

- Supplier's statements which sometimes show VAT?

- Delivery notes, which are sometimes carbon copies of the invoice and could easily therefore show the VAT number if not the actual sum of VAT?

- Requests for payment which often contain either the VAT number or the amount of VAT?

- Pro forma invoices which may look much the same as an ordinary invoice?

Customs will certainly disallow input tax claimed on the basis of such documents even if they take a more relaxed view on those which fail to state, for example, the type of sale; ie whether it is a sale, a lease, on hire-purchase or whatever.

This does not mean that you have to check every input invoice for every detail — though, if you wanted to delay payment, a blitz on them might well produce a substantial number with minor defects. However, staff do need to confirm that:

- the document is a tax invoice; and

- the VAT is being recovered in the correct period.

You cannot recover on a VAT return for the period ended 30 April on an invoice dated 1 May!

Do not invent VAT!

If a supplier sends you an invoice on which the VAT is incorrectly calculated, do not alter it! If you do, you cannot then prove to Customs that the supplier has also corrected it. Strictly speaking, a document, which does not show the right amount of VAT, is not a tax invoice and Customs could therefore disallow the lot. So if the sum matters, return it to the supplier for correction. If the amount of the error is trivial, you may decide to ignore it — though requiring the supplier to correct it is an excuse for delaying payment.

Information required on a VAT invoice

A VAT invoice must show (*Reg 14*):

- an identifying number;
- the time of the supply;
- the date of the issue of the document;
- name, address and registration number of the supplier;
- the name and address of the person to whom the goods or services are supplied;
- the type of supply by reference to the following categories:

    (i) a supply by sale;
    (ii) a supply on hire-purchase or any similar transaction;
    (iii) a supply by loan;
    (iv) a supply by way of exchange;
    (v) a supply on hire, lease or rental;
    (vi) a supply of goods made from the customer's materials;
    (vii) a supply by sale on commission;
    (viii) a supply on sale or return or similar terms; or
    (ix) any other type of supply which the Commissioners may by notice specify;

- a description sufficient to identify the goods or services supplied;
- for each description, the quantity of the goods or the extent of the services, the rate of VAT and amount payable, excluding VAT, expressed in sterling;
- the gross total amount payable, excluding VAT, expressed in sterling;
- the rate of any cash discount offered;
- each rate of VAT chargeable and the amount of VAT chargeable, expressed in sterling, at each such rate;
- the total amount of VAT chargeable, expressed in sterling.

In theory, the rules are strict. If an invoice does not contain one or more of the above pieces of information, it does not qualify as the basis for recovering input tax. This was demonstrated in *ABB Power Ltd (MAN/91/201 No 9373)* where the Tribunal held that a document was not a tax invoice because it did not show the:

- type of supply — sale, hire-purchase, rental etc;
- correct tax point;
- rate of tax applicable.

The *ABB* argument was in fact about Customs' right to demand output tax on a document issued by ABB. However, if Customs cannot collect output tax in such a case, what do you suppose they will do? It stands to reason, that they will deny input tax to the recipient.

In practice, if a document is obviously intended to be a VAT invoice, Customs are unlikely to use minor deficiencies in it as a reason for disallowing input tax unless they have been unable to collect the output tax. However, they do insist on the key details, such as the name, address and VAT number of the supplier, enough information about the supply to identify it as something bought for the purposes of the business and the amount of VAT.

Standard EU invoices

EC Directive 2001/115/EC introduces standardised rules for VAT invoices throughout the EU. At the time of writing, Customs had not yet published detailed proposals but they are supposed to take effect on 1/1/04. The information needed mostly matches that already on a UK tax invoice.

The one key point to note is that, in cases where the supply is exempt, zero rated or outside the scope, you will have to justify this by referring either to the relevant EU law or to that of the UK. Anyone designing a computerised sales invoicing system should check for any guidance by then issued by the Customs and query any problems with them.

Less detailed invoices

Retailers are allowed to issue less detailed invoices up to £100 (*Reg 16*). Although certain information such as the name of the customer and the amount of VAT is not required, these still have to show key details such as the name and address of the supplier, the nature of the goods supplied and the rate of VAT applicable.

Petrol filling station receipts are the most common example of a less detailed invoice, which is used for VAT recovery. Credit card slips do not usually contain the right details, although the slips produced by modern tills often do.

No invoice is required for (Notice 700 (April 2002), para 19.7.5):

- telephone calls;
- coin operated machines;
- car park charges — except on-street meters;
- toll charges;
- petrol element of mileage allowances to staff. Notice 700/64/96 (January 2002), para 8.7 says nothing about invoices but, presumably, the statement in the 1996 version remains valid.

For the first 4, the value limit is £25 and the supplier must be VAT-registered.

These are concessions by Customs. No excuses are accepted in other cases because of the problem of whether the supplier is registered. That apart, the rule is no tax invoice, no VAT recovery!

Must the tax invoice be in my name?

A tax invoice is supposed to show the person to whom the goods or services are supplied. So, if an invoice is not in your name, it usually means that the supply was not to you. In principle therefore, you should not recover VAT on invoices in the name of third parties. Customs will sometimes allow this in circumstances in which they are sure that there was a supply made to the person claiming the input VAT and that that VAT has not already been claimed by the party to which the invoice was addressed.

However, it is far better to obtain an invoice in the right name in the first place. The one common exception to that requirement is expenses incurred by employees. Whilst it is always a good idea to obtain an invoice addressed to the employer if possible for, say, hotel accommodation, Customs do not insist on this. Naturally, the travel must be on business.

When part of an expense, such as business calls on a private telephone bill, is paid by an employer, Customs will allow recovery of the appropriate proportion of VAT provided, of course, that you obtain a copy of the bill in question.

What if I fail to get a tax invoice?

Customs are likely to disallow input tax for which a VAT invoice is missing. Usually, the solution is to ask the supplier for one or for a copy if the original has been lost and, for routine transactions, Customs are likely to insist on this.

For further comment, see Chapter 13, *What Can I Recover Input Tax on?* under the heading *Cases where recovery has been allowed without a tax invoice*.

The extent to which your business is at risk for failure to obtain tax invoices must depend upon how many suppliers it has, whether it deals with relatively few of them frequently or infrequently, with a large number of different ones and so on.

Customs have power to allow electronic invoicing, which assists those suppliers whose systems are closely integrated with those of customers. The rules have been around since long before the internet, although no doubt this is encouraging the transmission of documentation electronically. If you just use the internet instead of the post and you print the invoices from your suppliers off your computer, Customs may, in theory, have little concern. However, it might be wise to discuss the matter with them if only because of the risk that 2 copies of the document might be printed, without this being apparent. See the comments below from the supplier's point of view.

Issuing tax invoices electronically

Systems for invoicing with a computer range from merely producing the document, which is sent by post, to a full-blown electronic data interchange system, known as EDI. Before installing the latter, you must get approval from Customs. It is wise in any case to consult them when developing a new computer system of any kind because they may have useful comments to make about its design, quite apart from the risk that you fail to take care of some VAT point.

One point to consider is the control on duplicate invoices. Cheap modern printers mean that it is possible to print off a copy of an invoice without there being any indication that it is a copy. When planning a computer specification consider a requirement that the second or subsequent copies of a document are overprinted stating that they are a copy with the date of printing.

Invoicing in a foreign currency

You can invoice in any currency you wish but the document should show the sterling equivalent for the net sum subject to VAT and the VAT so as to ensure that the customer reclaims the same sum as you account for as output tax.

Foreign currency conversions

You can convert foreign currency at either:

- The market selling rate in the UK at the time of the acquisition. The rates published in national newspapers are acceptable; or

- The period rate of exchange published by Customs and available at your local VAT office; or

- At a rate agreed with your local VAT office. See para 5.5 of Notice 725 *The Single Market* for more details.

You can use a mix of the first two options for different kinds of transaction provided you note in your records the kinds to which each applies. If you then wish to change this mix, you must ask Customs.

Self-billing

Self-billing is the system under which the customer produces the supplier's tax invoice, though the latter remains liable for the output tax. It is used in such circumstances as:

- Construction, where the main contractor is better equipped to produce tax invoices than the subcontractors working on site;

- Royalties paid by a publisher to an author. The information needed to calculate the royalties is in the publisher's records.

Dangers of self-billing

You can only use self-billing with the agreement of both Customs and your suppliers — who must not issue tax invoices for the transactions. The danger, from Customs' point of view, is that the supplier de-registers without telling you and that you therefore pay the supplier VAT, which you recover as input tax but the supplier never accounts for as output tax. Customs may therefore impose conditions such as that you give them an annual list of the suppliers.

Authenticated receipts

Reg 13(4)) permits an authenticated receipt to be issued by the customer when paying a person supplying construction services. It then substitutes for a tax invoice.

- The authenticated receipt must show all the details required of a tax invoice;

- Reclaim the input tax when you pay the supplier but get back from the latter the authenticated receipt duly signed;

- If the supplier fails to co-operate, contact your local VAT office.

Can I recover VAT shown on an invoice from a supplier in another EU State?

The answer is obvious when you think about it. UK Customs cannot be expected to allow you to recover, say, French VAT at a rate different to our own when they have not collected the output tax from the French supplier.

There is a system under which, in limited circumstances, you can reclaim VAT incurred in another Member State under the *EC 8th VAT Directive*. See Chapter 26 on *Recovery of Foreign VAT: the 8th and 13th Directives.*

Some questions to check your understanding. Review your answers with the text.

- The information to be shown on a tax invoice is listed at the start of this chapter under eleven main headings. How many points can you remember?

- What is the value limit for a less detailed invoice?

- What is the difference between a self-billed invoice and an authenticated receipt?

- Can one invoice in a foreign currency?

15. Watch Your Credit Notes

Credit notes are mostly routine. However, this chapter explains one or two points you should know. One of the most important is that you cannot cancel output tax with a credit note simply because the customer will not pay!

Credit notes for genuine corrections must be backed by evidence such as correspondence, quality control reports, goods returned notes etc. In practice, Customs are unlikely to challenge a credit note provided that it is issued bona fide in the course of settling a complaint from a customer. However, if you issue large numbers of credit notes, check the documentary back up.

A credit note does not have to include VAT. This is a matter for agreement with the customer. However, a customer, who cannot recover all the input tax he incurs, will want you to include it.

The rules on credit notes are in the *VAT Regulations (SI 1995/2518)*. *Reg 15* provides for credit notes when the rate of VAT changes. However, the rules affecting day-to-day trading are confusingly entitled 'Adjustments in the course of business' in *Reg 38*. They apply where 'there is an increase in consideration for a supply or there is a decrease in consideration for a supply, which includes an amount of VAT and the increase or decrease occurs after the end of the prescribed accounting period in which the original supply took place'. Thus, they deal with price increases as well as decreases.

The supplier must adjust the VAT payable side of his VAT account up or down and the customer must do the reverse. The rules do not say this is to be via a credit note but this is of course the usual way. You adjust your VAT account for the period in which the credit note is issued. The exception is for an insolvent trader where the period of supply must be adjusted.

Are you ever asked to cancel and reissue an invoice?

The above rules do not cover the situation when you invoice the wrong person, such as when a consultant invoices a professional advisor, only to be asked to bill the client direct.

If an original invoice is returned to you within the same VAT period, don't destroy it and issue a corrected version under the same reference number. This is wrong in law and could be dangerous. Suppose the VAT were recovered in error by the original recipient and an officer then attempted to trace the invoice back to your records. Imagine his doubts about your accounting system if he found an identical invoice under the same reference number but issued to another trader, who had also recovered the VAT!

Of course, common sense normally prevails in such situations. If the error and the correction are genuine and only one amount of input tax has been recovered, Customs are likely to accept the cancellation of the original invoice. However, why put yourself at risk when you have no control over whether or not the recipient of the original document recovers the input tax shown on it?

Send the original, together with a credit note cancelling it, back to the person originally invoiced. On that credit note, cross-refer to a new invoice. Issue this under a fresh reference number, even if it is within the same VAT return period.

If you accept goods back from consumers, watch your terms!

If, in your business, you take goods back from customers in exchange for other goods, there is a potential pitfall in the circumstances. In *S J Phillips Ltd (LON/01/36 No 17717)*, the Tribunal said that a credit note can only cancel a supply and reduce your output VAT if the customer has the right under the sale contract to return the goods as unfit for the purpose agreed. If you have merely agreed a price, which you will offset against the value of a second sale, you have repurchased the goods, not cancelled the original sale. The value at which you repurchase from the consumer does not of course include any input VAT you can recover; nor does it reduce the value of the second sale on which you owe output tax.

VAT only credit notes

In *Robinson Group of Companies Ltd (MAN/97/348 16081)*, it was held that VAT incorrectly charged is not 'VAT'. This means that, in law, you cannot issue a VAT only credit note under *Reg 38*. You are supposed to make a voluntary disclosure — which Customs will of course refuse unless you agree to refund the VAT to your customer. However, in practice, Customs accept that errors in charging VAT can be corrected by credit notes issued by the supplier or debit notes from the customer, provided that it is done within 3 years of the end of the VAT period in which the original mistake was made.

Some questions to check your understanding. Review your answers with the text.

- Does a credit note have to show VAT?
- What should you do when asked to re-invoice to a different business?

16.   Bad Debt Relief

You can claim bad debt relief for VAT charged to your customers, which they have not paid to you. The law is in *s 36* and *VAT Regulations (SI 1995/2518), Regs 165–172J*.

For sales after 1/1/03, you no longer tell a *customer* that you are claiming relief. However, see Chapter 13, *What Can I Recover Input Tax on?* for the rule, which requires you to repay input tax on any invoice you have not paid to a *supplier* after 6 months.

Relief for bad debts can be claimed provided that:

- the debt is 6 months old from the date on which payment was due or, if later, that of the supply; and
- it has been written off in your accounts; and
- if the supply was of goods, ownership has passed to the customer.

Telling the customer of your claim for sales prior to 1/1/03

If the bad debt is on an invoice prior to 1/1/03, you must still tell the customer that you are making the claim because the customer must make a corresponding reduction in his input tax. Your notification must state:

- date of issue;
- date of your claim to Customs; ie the date you send the relevant return;
- date, number and amount of VAT reclaimed for each unpaid VAT invoice, the exception being a supply made under the *Second-hand Scheme* for which you will not have issued a VAT invoice;
- total refund claimed;
- a statement saying that the customer must repay the amount of VAT claimed until such time as he pays you. To say that is not a legal requirement, despite being included in the example of a notification in Notice 700/18 (December 2002). However, it is obviously both sensible and an explanation of why you are sending the statement. Naturally, you will also tell the customer of whatever collection action you are taking in order to dispel any idea that the bad debt relief notification means you are giving up on the debt.

Pointless though it may seem, you should notify even if the customer is in liquidation and the liquidator has already told you that you will receive nothing.

Time limits for customer notification

- Tell the customer within 7 days of making the claim to Customs.
- That claim must be made within $3\frac{1}{2}$ years of the date on which payment was due or, if later, that of the supply.

Writing off the bad debt

You must create a *refunds for bad debts account*. The description of this both in the VAT Regulations and in Notice 700/18 (December 2002) is confused. To comply with the law as written may be impractical because of the descriptive information to be kept in the account — beyond the capability of most computer systems. You need the dates and reference numbers of the original tax invoices, the sums of VAT charged, any payments on account received, details of the claim and (if applicable) a copy of the notice to the customer described above. Even with only one or two invoices outstanding and if your computer system will let you transfer the invoice detail, not just the outstanding balance, to a new account, will it allow the additional information and in a single account?

That word *account* in reg 168 may mean file — the commonsense answer. Attach copies of the original invoices to that of the notice to the customer.
In *Alpha Leisure (Scotland) Ltd (EDN/03/14 No 18199)*, a claim was held to be valid despite it having been discharged as valueless as part of an agreement when 2 businesses were separated. Customs had claimed that the agreement extinguished the debt.

The pitfall of subsequent payments

How will you avoid the pitfall of failing to account for VAT on any payment which is subsequently received against a bad debt on which you have claimed relief? Any money which comes in subsequently includes VAT. You need a system for picking this up, since you normally account for output tax when the invoice is issued.

- Either transfer the outstanding customer account to a bad debts section of your sales ledger; or

- Will your system let you mark the account in some way so that the computer triggers a query when a payment is credited to the account?

As dividends in a bankruptcy or liquidation can arrive years afterwards, it would be all too easy to forget that bad debt relief had been claimed and fail to pay output tax at the appropriate VAT fraction on the net sum received.

How you make the claim

You add the refund to the input tax, which you are reclaiming for the period in which you make the claim. It is not a reduction of the output tax.

The amount of your claim

You claim for the output tax originally charged. It is irrelevant whether the rate of VAT has subsequently changed. Similarly, you pay VAT on any sums subsequently received at that rate, not at the one applicable when you get the payment.

If the customer has paid you sums on account, you can only claim for the VAT included in the outstanding balance. A typical example of the pitfall in this point is where a garage does accident repair work for a registered trader under an insurance claim. The customer is that trader but the net amount of the invoice is often paid direct to the garage by the insurance company.

If the customer never pays the VAT, the garage naturally thinks that the outstanding sum is all VAT. Sadly, that is not so! The insurance company's cheque is a payment on account, which includes VAT. Bad debt relief can only be claimed on the outstanding sum at the VAT fraction.

Several tribunal cases confirm the point!

Enderby Transport Ltd (MAN/83/304 No 1607) sold goods for £10,200 plus VAT of £816. The customer only paid £10,200 and the company claimed bad debt relief of £816. The Tribunal held that the outstanding debt of £816 should be treated as a gross debt inclusive of VAT of which only the VAT element could be recovered.

In *AW Mawer & Co ([1986] VATTR 87 No 2100)* a firm of solicitors acted for a company in an action to recover damages following a fire at its premises. The company was awarded costs of £7,127 plus VAT of £709. The defendants' insurers only paid £7,127. The company did not pay the bill and went into liquidation. Customs only allowed relief at the VAT fraction of the outstanding debt. The Tribunal agreed. The £709 was a debt owed to the solicitors by the client, and relief could only be given on the VAT element of it.

Goods supplied on hire purchase or conditional sale

Supplies made by hire purchase or conditional sale have two components: a supply of goods and the exempt interest charges. When claiming bad debt relief, *Reg 170A* allows the allocation of payments from defaulting customers to goods and to finance in the same ratio as the total sums due — thus increasing the VAT reclaim. This was originally a concession announced in *Business Brief 19/2001* from 6/12/01.

Customs also allow you not to deduct the sum you get from selling any repossessed goods from the outstanding debt *if the sale of the goods themselves was standard rated*; that would be because the customer had acquired them for a business purpose or you changed their condition prior to selling them. If the sale was not subject to VAT, the proceeds must still be deducted from the debt.

The position if you assign or factor your debts

If you sell your debts without provision in the contract for reassignment of them back to you, bad debt relief is not available. If the contract does allow it, only once the debts have been reassigned to you can you claim relief .

The payment from the factor for your debts is exempt and is therefore ignored for the purposes of bad debt relief.

17.   What Records Do I Need?

Taking records seriously

The key point in this chapter is that taking your records seriously will keep you out of most trouble concerning the evidence you need to satisfy Customs.

Customs can tell you to keep whatever records they see fit to require (*VATA 1994, Sch 11 para 6(1)*). The main rules applicable to everyone are in *Reg 31* and in Notice 700 (April 2002) *The VAT Guide*, chapter 19. However, many of the Notices on detailed aspects of the tax also contain rules on records. Examples are those concerning the various Schemes such as those for retailers, cash accounting, annual accounting, second-hand goods and tour operators.

An example of how people get into trouble regularly over records is the rules on evidence to support the zero-rating of an export of goods. See Chapter 19, *Exports of Goods* for details. An invoice addressed overseas is not enough. Evidence is also required as to the physical departure of the goods from the UK.

Without records, you cannot recover VAT

Everywhere you go in VAT, there are rules as to the records you must keep in order to qualify for the relief you want. Most records problems stem from simple points like the VAT audit trail not linking prime records, such as invoices, to the VAT account, or a lack of evidence needed to justify the VAT treatment adopted.

Examples of situations in which particular records are required are:

- exports of goods;
- imports of goods;
- zero-rating for services under the International Services rules;
- claims for bad debt relief;
- input tax recovery;
- issue of credit notes;
- partial exemption;
- self-billing.

Consider too the evidence as to the volume of the businesses activity. Records attesting to this are often not of an accounting nature; yet they can be vital in supporting the accuracy of the recorded outputs, especially in cash businesses.

Examples are:

- an appointments book for a hairdresser;
- customer calls records or mileage figures for taxi firms.

You must retain records for 6 years

VAT records have to be kept for 6 years — despite the fact that, in the absence of fraud, Customs can only assess retrospectively for 3.

Is your accounting system self-checking?

Many common mistakes, even simple ones, could be avoided if only accounting systems included common sense checks to ensure, for instance, that:

- The output tax is the correct percentage of the outputs;

- The input tax is the correct percentage of the inputs. If your suppliers offer you cash discounts, the overall percentage will be slightly less than the standard rate because the tax is calculated on the amount net of cash discount, regardless of whether or not it is taken as explained in Chapter 8, *The Value of Supply Rules*.

It is not sufficient for your system to check the VAT on individual invoices. You should prove the total for each day or batch of postings. Ideally, the figures for both input and output tax should be checked for the full month or quarter. See Chapter 18, *VAT Housekeeping for Finance Directors* for a case where the VAT cheque got posted as if it were input tax.

Don't take your computer system for granted!

Since few computer programmers have much idea about VAT, it follows that computer systems can easily be deficient. For example, does your system incorporate a 'default' calculation of the input tax on an invoice? This means that you enter the net amount and the machine calculates the tax. You have to say if the figure is not correct. This is bad programming. The system ought to require entering both the net and the tax, and for the machine then to query the latter if it does not check calculate. Otherwise, it is all too easy to accept the default figure instead of entering the correct one.

One restaurant bought a computerised sales system, which summarised the daily sales by menu item. Unfortunately, it:

- produced only a customer copy of the individual bill — so no detail of sales customer by customer, was available in the records;

- calculated the VAT line by line of each bill instead of on the invoice total. It then rounded down the VAT calculated up to 0.59p.

The result was to understate the output tax over a fairly short period by several thousand pounds.

How durable are your records?

Nowadays, most records in all but the smallest businesses are computer-based. Computer-based systems tend to be upgraded or changed every few years. So what about that 6-year requirement for VAT records?

Yes, you can download and store the data but you need to make sure that the storage medium you choose is durable. You cannot take that for granted. Data on magnetic tape used to become unstable in storage if it was not re-run every 10–12 months. Moreover, will you be able to read that data if you need to, in 5 years time? Not many years ago, $5\frac{1}{4}$ inch floppy disks were standard but how many computers these days have a drive capable of accepting and reading anything stored on one? Not only do you need a means of storing the data, you have to conserve the equipment and operating systems needed to access it.

The anti-carousel fraud measures

FA 2003 amended *VATA 1994, Sch 11 para 4* and inserted *s 77A* to give Customs draconian powers to attack 'carousel frauds' involving computer equipment and mobile phones. Such a fraud involves acquiring the goods zero rated as an acquisition from another EU State, selling them plus VAT in the UK and disappearing without paying that VAT to Customs. Sometimes, the fraudsters have operated through 2 or more VAT registered companies in the UK and the goods have been sold on zero rated to a customer outside the UK. That resale price could be below the original purchase price while still allowing a fraudulent 'profit' because of the input VAT recovered, which was not accounted for as a tax. In some cases, the same goods have been bought and resold repeatedly.

The objective of the new powers is to enable Customs to attack such frauds more effectively by collecting the unpaid tax from any traders still around, who dealt in the goods, without Customs having to prove that those traders were themselves fraudsters. Customs hope to force reputable traders to take great care to check the credentials of those with whom they are trading because of the risk of having Customs pin responsibility for the unpaid VAT on them.

The legislation enables Customs to:

* Demand from you security:
  — in respect of any repayment claim by you concerning a *past* purchase of *any* goods; or
  — against the risk that VAT charged on a *future* transaction in *any* goods is not paid by another trader in the chain, whether that transaction was before you bought those goods or after you sold them on.

* Claim from you VAT not paid by another trader in *a past* chain of transactions in, specifically, computer equipment or components and telephones, which occurred either before or after you bought the goods and sold them on. This is under a principle of joint and several liability of any or all traders in the chain, *if they knew or had reasonable grounds to suspect that some or all of the VAT payable in respect of (their own) supply , or on any previous or subsequent supply of those goods, would go unpaid.*

You will be presumed to have had *reasonable grounds* for suspicion if the price you paid for the goods was below market value or less than the figure paid previously for those goods. The obvious problems of knowing what the market value is of, say, a computer chip and of distinguishing between an artificial price and one merely reflecting excess stock or obsolescence are but 2 of many questions about how the rules can be applied fairly in practice.

Customs quote a business paying £50k for computer chips, which it has not seen, to a supplier it does not know, who turns up at the door. It is of course hard to understand how a genuine business would operate like that but that is not the point. The law could allow Customs to demand VAT from businesses involved in genuine transactions, if fraud has occurred either before or after in the chain. Therefore, I suggest that, if you deal in either computer equipment, components etc or in telephones, you maintain supplier and customer files in which you keep careful records of:

- Their credentials — not just credit references but trade reputation, how long established and who owned/run by etc — information of the latter kind is available from the records publicly available at Companies House. If the name of a company is obviously one of those 'made up' ones like *Rangepace,* which are purchased from an off-the-shelf agency rather than a name related to the trade in which it engages, that is a possible clue to its background.

- The circumstances of individual deals including all correspondence, e-mails etc and details of each product specification. Depending on the nature of your business, you may need evidence that you bought specific products for an identified market — together with a note of how the price of each transaction was arrived at. Deals which involve the purchase and immediate resale of goods at a substantial profit are by their nature often suspect, given that the more normal kind of business requires one to buy for and sell from stock.

- Records of the receipt and inspection of each consignment. Be especially careful if the goods are held in a third party warehouse. How then will you verify that they are new items, not old ones in battered containers being sold and resold but never used?

- Your check of the VAT numbers quoted to you; see below for further comment.

Those files will usually be kept in your purchasing or sales departments but no such file should be destroyed without the agreement of the head of finance. Each should be kept for at least 3 years after the last transaction with the supplier or customer.

The significance of such records will depend on:

- the proportion of your business which is related to computer equipment and telephones;

- whether a significant proportion of your purchases are from 1 or 2 suppliers or of your sales are to 1 or 2 customers.

A case, which illustrates the problem, is *Bond House Systems Ltd (MAN/02/534 No 18100).* A business, which had been established for 10 years, was denied over £5m input tax incurred on 26 transactions in the following circumstances:

There was no evidence that *Bond House* was involved in the fraud or even aware of it.

- *Bond House* had files showing that it made the research referred to above into the credentials of the traders, with which it did business and it did co-operate in providing market information to Customs.

- In May 2002, the month for which its repayment claim was refused by Customs, 99.1% of its £95m sales were in 51 transactions and 32.5% of its sales by number were to customers in other EU States, almost always in Ireland.

- The bulk of its purchases were from 2 companies, both of which had only been in business for a year or so. One of them was owned and run by a 21-year-old woman, who a director of *Bond House* had met when they were both employed by another company and to whom he had made a personal loan to finance the start of her business.

- *Bond House*, an experienced trader, was buying monthly £30m–£40m worth of computer chips from *each* of them — the bulk of its purchases. The Tribunal commented that it did not appear to have wondered how those newly established companies could immediately have identified a source of supply from which they could buy in such quantities and earn a profit on the resale.

- *Bond House's* own turnover increased from £258m in 2001 to a projected £1.5bn in 2002. It was not apparent how it had achieved that increase in a static or declining market.

- Whereas its 2 little suppliers made margins of 25p and 50p per chip, *Bond House* made exactly £4 on purchases from the one and £3 per chip on those from the other. Combined with evidence which showed that, on the balance of probabilities, the chips were being circulated within the 'ring fence' of the carousel and that all the deals, both purchases and sales, were prearranged, these fixed margins suggested artificial transactions.

- That was reinforced by the fact that purchases from each supplier were always sold to the same 2 customers in Ireland; ie, goods from A were always sold to C and those from B always to D — obviously unlikely in an ordinary commercial situation.

The above points are a summary of just some of the evidence in this case. In essence, the Tribunal felt that *Bond House* should have recognised the artificiality of the business being offered to it and that fraud was probably involved. It held that, despite *Bond House's* innocence of any wrongdoing and its ignorance of the fraudulent objective, the transactions were devoid of economic substance and the VAT paid out on them was therefore not recoverable.

I see the practical importance of this controversial decision as being in the points I have listed. If you spot those kind of deals in your turnover, you have a potential pitfall!

Checking a VAT number

When you set up a new purchase ledger account, it is good practice to check the supplier's VAT number because, if it is invalid, so is the tax invoice. No doubt the majority of such cases are innocent errors, such as printing mistakes. However, the fraudulent use of another trader's number is prevalent in certain sectors of business so checking is potentially a valuable precaution.

I am not telling you here how to check that a number is valid because to do so does not prove that it belongs to that trader and such a check is therefore inadequate. To confirm both that the number is valid *and* that it belongs to the trader quoting it, ring the NAS. See page viii at the start of the book under *Contacting Customs*.

Unfortunately, the NAS will only tell you whether that number belongs to the trader whose name and address you quote. The *Data Protection Act* stops them giving you information about another trader.

Should I tell Customs about a possible fraud?

That Customs cannot tell you about another trader does not of course stop them asking you for further information — for example about an invoice which quotes an incorrect VAT number. Logically, they should do that since the value of the invoice and the nature of the supply would usually indicate whether this was an innocent error, say a printing mistake, or a possible fraud.

If the latter, it would also be logical to suggest that you fax to one of the specialist offices dealing with fraud a copy of the invoice together with any other information readily available about any other parties involved, the grounds for suspicion etc. One might hope that, if such information were provided promptly and confirmed in writing and you agreed not to alert the potential fraudster, Customs might promise not to disallow the input tax on the invalid invoice — provided, of course, that you could show you did receive the supply in question and were not yourself involved in the fraud. Naturally, the more prompt and complete the information was, the less likely it would be that the provider was a fraudster trying to achieve a whitewash, given that putting oneself forward would create a risk of being caught!

Unfortunately, at the time of writing, Customs have no such policy and you may gain nothing by providing information to them. However, if you have already bought from or sold to a trader of whom you are now suspicious, I think you should tell Customs. I explain the potential benefit below.

Since you are unlikely to get anything more than a bare acknowledgement, if that, provide the information in writing and keep copies of your letter and all attachments. If any discussions do result, whether by telephone or face-to-face, make a careful note of exactly what was said on each occasion, sign and date it and send Customs a copy.

The potential benefit of telling Customs

Evidence that you did contact Customs could be crucial in defending against any subsequent notification of joint and several liability for VAT unpaid if your business had done a deal in a chain of transactions, which included a carousel fraud. You would have only 21 days from the issue of such a notice within which to show that you had no reasonable grounds for suspecting that fraud.

As the notice could be issued to you years after the transaction occurred, a file of information which you had offered to Customs at the time of the fraud might well be your only protection. Hence my advice to be alert to unusual transactions and that, if you do spot something like a false VAT registration, tell Customs in writing.

Much the same applies to the risk of Customs using their power to demand security from you in respect of any future transactions. Customs have said they will do that if you ignore a warning to stop dealing with other parties they suspect of fraud. It is doubtful how this procedure will work in practice. A system of checking on your business partners and of notifying Customs of any doubts could be useful, should any mistake by the Department lead to a questionable warning to you.

Some questions to check your understanding. Review your answers with the text.

- Given that most well-organised businesses keep proper accounts, why is it so important to stop to think about the records needed for VAT purposes?

- How long must one keep such records?

- What is the potential pitfall in any form of an electronic record?

18. VAT Housekeeping for Finance Directors

If you are head of finance, you may see VAT as a routine responsibility, which you can delegate. When you can't; not entirely anyway!

This chapter explains why you need to take an interest in the subject yourself. It points out various aspects of it which may need your attention because of the problems which could result from getting them wrong.

VAT problems are capable of seriously damaging the financial health of your organisation. Tribunal decisions concerning major businesses, involving well-known names, numbered about 30 in one recent 12-month period. These cases involved sums from a few hundred thousand pounds to many millions. Of course, some of the companies won their battles with Customs but they still had all the disruption of a major dispute and will not have recovered all their costs, never mind the management time.

Many VAT errors are caused by poor housekeeping. Tribunal decisions show that many careless mistakes are not spotted because:

- both management and staff are unaware of basic VAT rules;

- systems are inadequate;

- simple checks or common sense points are ignored.

No head of finance can escape responsibility for such problems. Yes, you can delegate most of the work on VAT but you still have responsibility for it! This chapter discusses what those responsibilities are and suggests some practical precautions you might take, which could help keep you out of trouble.

You

It starts with you! The head of finance should take some interest in VAT because, in most organisations, he or she is the only representative of the accounts department who is in regular contact with the heads of other departments such as sales, marketing, research and development or production. Yet the heads of these other departments often take decisions on policy, sales or purchase contracts and so on, which have VAT consequences. If they do not ask for advice on the VAT aspects of what they propose doing, sooner or later it is inevitable that they will land the business with a VAT expense, which could have been avoided. Examples of pitfalls and planning points are highlighted throughout this book.

So, as head of finance, it is your responsibility to ensure that your colleagues in other departments are aware of the need to think VAT before they act! In fact, VAT is one of the best excuses an accountant has for getting out of accounts to go visiting other parts of the organisation. You probably already do this anyway in the process of working with your colleagues in running the organisation but does your deputy? If you have a tax department, does the specialist responsible for VAT also go walkabout? In a big business, there is too much going on for the head of finance to be able to keep track of all of it. You need other pairs of eyes and ears in support. The task is to make sure that other departments are aware of the VAT angles which might affect what they do in their respective responsibilities and how getting it wrong could hit their budgets.

Here's a story to illustrate the point. A delegate from a major food company told me at one of the seminars I present, how his boss, the head of the tax department, had spotted a pack of a new product, which was about to be trialled, whilst visiting one of their factories. It was the first he knew of this; yet the product was on the borderline between zero- and standard-rating with the latter the more likely. Now standard-rate VAT on a product makes a critical difference to the pricing and profit margin. Yet the tax department had not been asked about it.

It was good that the head of tax went out visiting, good that he spotted the problem — but bad that it was possible for a new product to get that far in development without anyone checking its VAT status. Could it happen in your business?

Your staff

It continues with the staff to whom you delegate the routine work. Have they had any training in those aspects of VAT, which affect the business? Who completes the VAT return? Is it an experienced clerk with a knowledge of the organisation or is this seen as a boring and unimportant job, which gets off-loaded onto the latest arrival in the accounts department? That really does happen — all too often.

For example, not just anyone can handle the VAT return of a banking or insurance business. The person doing so needs a reasonable working knowledge both of how the business earns its living and of the partial exemption rules which are one of the more complicated aspects of VAT.

When appointing someone to deal with the VAT returns, it is not enough to simply provide a file of calculations for past returns and send them off to a VAT seminar. The staff dealing with the detailed preparation of the return need to have some understanding of the business if the figures, with which they deal, are to mean anything to them. They need training and proper notes about the system before they are left to get on with the VAT return. Junior staff should be encouraged to visit other parts of the organisation to see how it works and to meet the people, who produce the information used to prepare the return.

Basic training for staff

The training, which your staff need, will vary to some extent according to the nature of the organisation. However, it may include such points as:

● what the business does and how it earns its income;

● the status of that income, whether standard-rated, zero-rated, exempt etc;

● where the figures for sales etc, on which the VAT return is based, come from and who codes or otherwise determines the data, which goes into the computer system to produce those figures;

- the basis for using those figures to produce the information for the VAT return. For example, is the business using some special scheme, such as that for retailers or is it partially exempt? In either case, there will be rules with which it must comply, which may be at least partly set out in a letter from Customs received some years earlier;

- the tax point rules as they affect the organisation and the difference between tax invoices and requests for payment, proformas etc;

- the rules on credit notes and copy invoices;

- VAT grouping if applicable — precise membership of the group and the consequences thereof.

The above points are just a few examples. The appropriate list varies from one organisation to another.

An instance of how poor training and/or systems got a business into trouble was *Uniroyal Englebert Tyres Ltd (EDN/90/197 No 5637)*. A junior employee assumed that an associated company was in the VAT group and failed to charge VAT on an invoice for services. Upholding the £39,899 penalty, the Tribunal criticised the lack of supervision of the clerk's work.

Permanent VAT file

A permanent VAT file is an important safety precaution. It should contain such information as:

- how the return is prepared for your organisation;

- where the figures for the return come from;

- rulings from Customs on which you rely, with emphasis on any conditions imposed by Customs when granting the business permission to do something;

- if applicable, the legal basis for zero-rating or exempting your outputs;

- any other VAT rules, which specifically affect your operations, such as the Special Schemes;

- advice from your advisors.

Actually, you need 3 files for VAT:

1   The VAT returns file containing copies of the returns and details of the calculations and backup schedules from which the figures for each return were taken.

2   A permanent file containing anything from Customs of long-term importance, such as the VAT registration certificate, correspondence, rulings etc.

3   An advice file for correspondence with your advisers.

The VAT returns file should be kept for 6 years because that is the requirement for keeping VAT records. However, you will not normally need to refer to copy returns and schedules more than a year or so old — although, if a dispute with Customs arises, the old figures may be important.

The other two files contain the information which your staff may need to refer to or about which they need to know. Obviously, these documents must not be buried amongst the routine VAT calculations.

The reason for the separate advice file is that you do not necessarily want Customs to see the advice you receive. Whilst most of this will be straightforward, it may concern matters on which there is some room for argument as to the correct interpretation of the law. In such cases, you are entitled to act according to your view of the matter but you would not want to draw Customs' attention to the point by including the advice on it in the permanent file, which officers are likely to see during visits.

Nor would you necessarily wish Customs to see, for instance, comment by advisers on possible weaknesses in your system. For instance, both internal and external audit reports may mention matters on which a judgment has to be taken. Officers have limited accountancy training and sometimes misinterpret comment on such matters.

Who should review and sign your return?

As head of finance, you will of course delegate the detailed preparation of the return but you should consider carefully who should sign it. See the comments under *So who signs your return?* in Chapter 5, *The VAT Return*.

This is one of the most important legal documents which your business submits to the tax authorities in the course of the year and someone senior should sign it. When doing so, they should review the figures to make sure that they reflect any exceptional transactions, which can create substantial amounts of output or input tax such as:

- dealings in property;
- corporate activities such as 'rights' issues of shares and other ways of raising capital;
- takeovers or sales of businesses.

Who is responsible for VAT reviews?

You must ensure that your affairs are reviewed from time to time to see whether they are still being dealt with correctly. Depending upon the business, it might only be necessary to do this every 2 or 3 years but, if VAT is never considered, it will go wrong!

- Have there been any changes in circumstances, which ought to be notified to Customs or which might affect how VAT law applies to your operations?
- How do you learn of any changes in VAT law affecting you and ensure that information about them is passed to those responsible for taking any action required? This is especially important in a VAT group. For instance, *VAT Notes*, which comes with the VAT return, will only be sent to the representative member of the group.
- Are any rulings from Customs still valid? Have the law, the facts or the circumstances so altered as to invalidate the agreed basis? Customs

frequently give 'rulings' which in reality are no more than agreement to a given basis for accounting on a point of detail. An example might be the basis for apportionment of a sale which includes supplies at different rates of tax.

A ruling can easily be invalidated by changes in circumstances. Moreover, if staff understand nothing of the basis, the local folklore soon becomes that the ruling is 'we charge x%', whereas this is merely the arithmetical result of the agreed calculation for one period. In the next, it may differ considerably.

Relationships with Customs

Your relationship with Customs needs careful management. For instance, who asks questions on your behalf? Many VAT problems are caused by a junior member of staff asking a half-baked question, getting back an inaccurate or incomplete answer and taking the wrong action in consequence.

Senior management should check all VAT queries to ensure that the correct facts are identified so that the right question can be asked. Junior clerks usually do not have enough understanding of the law or of the wider aspects of a problem to ensure that they ask the right question, let alone get a sensible answer. So if they are dealing with the VAT issues themselves, make sure they:

- write down the facts and the question;

- note the date and name of the person to whom they refer and the answer;

- agree the action to be taken with you.

Customs have a generous policy on misdirection. In Notice 48 (March 2002) *Extra Statutory Concessions*, they say:

> If a Customs & Excise officer, with the full facts before him, has given a clear and unequivocal ruling on VAT in writing or, knowing the full facts, has misled a registered person to his detriment, any assessment of VAT due will be based on the correct ruling from the date the error was brought to the registered person's attention.

That is only fair and reasonable. However, Customs often extend it to cover situations in which the officer has not given a specific ruling but has failed to point out an error, which should have been obvious to that officer. An example might be where a business has been incorrectly treating a part of its sales as zero-rated and officers on one or more visits have failed to spot the mistake. The problem is to show that the officer looked at the incorrect sales invoices in question and so must have been aware of them. Unfortunately, visits are not certificates of VAT health. In a business of any size, it is unlikely that Customs will check every aspect of the return each time they come.

So:

- keep records of visits you receive — name of officer, who he or she saw, what records were examined and for which periods;

- make a file note of any points discussed, sign and date it;

- confirm in a letter to Customs anything of significance making sure that you include all the relevant facts given to the officer, such as the precise nature of the transactions in question, the amount of money involved and so on.

That last point is especially important in situations where an officer queries something, you discuss it without coming to a firm conclusion and the officer agrees to look into it further, back at the office. If you hear no more, you do not know whether the officer has forgotten all about it, perhaps after mentioning it to a colleague, who also did not know the answer or has decided you are right but has simply done no more about it. Without such a letter, how will you prove that the matter was even discussed, let alone that you gave the officer the full facts if, a year or two later, another officer spots that you were wrong all along and assesses you?

The three-year time limit on claims for overpaid VAT

If Customs give you a ruling, which you think may be incorrect, dispute it in writing and submit a claim for any VAT you believe you have already overpaid. The three-year rule in *s 80* limits the period for which you can reclaim overpaid VAT. See under *The three-year cap* in Chapter 5, *The VAT Return* for more on this.

Even if the overpayment was within the last three years, Customs can refuse to repay you if to do so would *unjustly enrich* you. Broadly speaking, the latter means that, if you have charged on the VAT to a customer, you can only get the money back from Customs if you promise in turn to repay it to that customer under rules set out in the *VAT Regulations regs 43A–G*. This limit on repayment claims matches the three-year time limit for assessments by Customs, which is explained in Chapter 38, *Assessments and VAT Penalties* under *Time limits*.

Thus, there is a serious potential pitfall in accepting a ruling from Customs, which you do not like. If you have been overcharging VAT for three years already, time is now running against you. Moreover, all too often traders, who are shown to have overpaid, are denied repayment under the unjust enrichment provisions and therefore get no compensation for any commercial disadvantage they may have suffered in having to charge VAT.

For a useful review of unjust enrichment, see *National Westminster Bank plc (LON/01/1715 No 17962)* in which Customs were found to have breached the community law principles of effectiveness and equality of treatment by refusing to repay the Appellant when they had done so in similar cases of claims by its competitors.

The interest problem

Even if you do get a repayment, Customs may refuse to pay you interest on it. The problem with interest is that *s 78* only makes Customs liable to pay it on a mistake if it was they who made the error. If you misunderstand the law, that is an error by you, not Customs.

You might think that, if, say, an officer refused to allow input tax to be recovered on certain expenditure, this would be automatically seen as Customs' mistake. Unfortunately, that is not necessarily so. In *Switzerland Tourism (LON/99/0007 No 17068),* failed to extract interest from Customs on sums, which *ST* had overpaid when Customs told it to apportion its input tax between business and non-business activities.

After I had won *Netherlands Board of Tourism (LON/94/607 No 12935),* thereby demonstrating that a tourist board could be wholly 'in business', *ST's* then adviser claimed that it could recover all its VAT on the basis of *NBT*. The officer replied: *I do* not agree that your client is entitled to full input tax recovery based upon the decision in the Netherlands case. The decision was based on the particular circumstances of the Netherlands Tourist Board. It is inappropriate to compare separate organisations when seeking to establish the amount of input tax recovery of a particular organisation. When the adviser replied, *in our opinion the circumstances are no different but we will decide in due course about the amount of input tax recovery,* the officer said that the ruling in his previous letter must be followed on pain of financial penalties.

Several years later, I won *Austrian National Tourist Office (LON/96/0674 No 15561)* and was then contacted by *ST.* I advised a voluntary disclosure of the input tax disallowed over the previous three years. This was rejected but the consequent appeal forced Customs to consider *ST's* circumstances properly for the first time. After being provided with additional information, Customs repaid the sum claimed.

The Tribunal rejected the contention that, when Customs say 'no', they are to be presumed to have had all the knowledge required for them to make that decision unless they can demonstrate otherwise. The Chairman did find it hard to resist the impression that the officer was doing his best to deter the Appellant's accountants from pursuing the matter. Normally, if a Tribunal has such an impression, Customs are in trouble. However, the Chairman commented that the activities of tourist offices are not necessarily exclusively taxable as *Turespana (Spanish Tourist Office No 14 568)* had shown in 1996. It and the *NBT* and *ANTO* cases had shown that various matters must be considered.

Here, there was no clear evidence of reliance on a decision of Customs made with the relevant facts before them. The Tribunal held that the true cause of the failure to claim input tax in full was the decision by *ST* and its adviser not to pursue the view that its activities were covered by the *NBT* case. The officer had said that each case depended upon its facts *which was in effect throwing down the gauntlet to the accountants to establish those facts in the light of the approach of the NBT Tribunal.* Note that the officer had not asked for any information, let alone specified what facts were needed. Thus the *ST* decision might be thought to provide an incentive to Customs to make decisions upon the basis of the often limited information presented to them rather than to ask further questions!

This story seems to me to be a warning to everyone! I believe it to be a hard case and, possibly, a decision, which was wrong in law. However, assuming it to be correct, the inference is that you should dispute decisions of Customs, which you do not like.

In a case in which Customs are, in effect, refusing to discuss the matter, as the officer did in *ST,* you can obtain a formal ruling by submitting an application for repayment of the VAT, which you believe that you have overpaid. This must show the sums in question by VAT return period for the last three years, assuming that the matter goes back that far. At the same time, you should ask Customs what further information they need in order to review their decision. Supposing that Customs then reject your claim after being provided by you with whatever facts they may have asked for, you should at least get interest from the date of that rejection, if not from the start of the period covered by the claim, if you eventually win the argument.

Another tale of trouble

If you think this may be over stating the problem, consider an import duty case, *Nor-cargo Ltd (MAN/99/7038 No C133)*. The same Chairman as in *ST* upheld a refusal by Customs to refund duty on peeled prawns in brine, which had been paid because Customs thought that the import quota had been exhausted. The Customs office, through which the goods were cleared, said so on three occasions. The Chairman called that 'bad' errors but it did not justify the claim for repayment of the duty because the importer could have found the right information on three databases to which there was electronic access.

So, you have been warned! If the money involved is significant, never take what an officer of Customs & Excise says at face value. Always seek confirmation elsewhere.

Is your system capable of producing the right VAT figures?

Do not assume that your computer system is capable of producing the right figures just because the vendor assures you that it has been approved by Customs and/or has been sold to many other users. Ask exactly what the terms of any approval by Customs are. You will probably find that it is no more than an agreement that, at a given date, the systems specification met Customs' basic requirements. It may have been amended since then. In any case, it is unlikely that Customs have done any testing of the final version.

Here are some points to consider and some tests used by Customs, which you might like to try.

Avoid defaults in your computer programming

A 'default' is an action the computer takes unless it is specifically instructed otherwise.

Examples are:

- the system assumes that the entry is zero-rated unless the operator specifies standard rate;

- the system assumes that the input VAT for an invoice, which it calculates, is the correct figure unless the operator overrides it to input the amount actually on the invoice.

A default is often dangerous because, when processing large numbers of documents, it is all too easy to hit the return key to accept an incorrect entry.

Check your input and output tax figures

Do all purchase and sales invoice posting routines incorporate checks for each invoice or batch of invoices posted to prove that the VAT is 17.5% of the net? Cash discounts offered or received marginally affect the calculation but do not invalidate this important credibility check.

In *Frank Galliers Ltd ([1993] STC 284)*, a cheque to Customs for a quarter's VAT was inadvertently coded by a clerk to the 'input tax to be claimed account' instead of the VAT Control account. A simple check to compare input tax with total inputs and output tax with total outputs would have shown up such an error.

Computer interrogation checks

Sophisticated checks, where it is possible to interrogate computer systems, include searching for:

- high value input tax — say greater than £1,000;

- input tax that is more than 18% or less than 16% of the net sum — to identify transposition errors;

- the date of purchase invoices — to prevent early claims of input tax;

- a check that invoice sequences are complete.

Talk to Customs when designing a computer system

When designing a computer system, which involves financial transactions, it is wise to consult Customs. They may have useful comments about potential VAT hazards. It is probably better to write rather than to ring the *National Advice Service* since Customs will need detailed information about the transactions with which the system will deal. See under *Contacting Customs* on page VIII.

See Chapter 14, *What is a Valid Tax Invoice?* under *Issuing tax invoices electronically* for further comment.

The Subversive Spreadsheet

Spreadsheets are causing trouble in VAT! If you work out figures on paper, you check them by adding them up, visually testing them for credibility and so on. It seems that that is not being done when the figures are in the computer.

Customs' experience suggests that people think that spreadsheets can be taken for granted as straightforward substitutes for manual calculation. Customs say that the price for cutting out all the sweat of calculation is a requirement to exercise intelligent control of the end result. In part, that is of course a matter of checking whether it makes sense both in absolute terms and by comparison with previous numbers, just as it always has been. However, it also means controlling the mechanics of the spreadsheet, just as you maintain the roadworthiness of your car.

In an article in the *De Voil Indirect Tax Service (January 2001)* under the heading *The Subversive Spreadsheet*, an official from Customs' *Computer Audit Operational Policy Team* explained how Customs were finding material errors in 70–80% of spreadsheets used in calculating tax liabilities. The examples he quoted included:

- A line added to record the liability of a newly acquired subsidiary, which was not included in the calculation of the subtotal.

- A retailer, whose spreadsheet slowed down as the number of branches grew. When in a hurry on one occasion, they set it to manual recalculation. The next time they used it, they forgot to re-calculate the totals.

- Mistakes in programming calculations into the spreadsheet.

The article showed how easy it is for any spreadsheet to go wrong if it is not properly managed. For instance, less than 1 spreadsheet in 75 looked at by Customs had any documentation or instructions for use.

This is not just a VAT problem. Spreadsheets are used throughout business for calculating all kinds of figures. If those used to work out the legal liability for VAT are not being properly specified, designed, tested and maintained in a disciplined fashion, there are likely to be problems with the ones which are used for such purposes as management reporting, marketing and so on. That could mean that your business is being managed at least partly on the basis of false information.

Customs have produced an 18 page *Methodology for the Audit of Spreadsheet Models,* which sets out how one should tackle the problem. This can be downloaded from their website. They are also offering a spreadsheet Audit tool *SpACE.*

Whether you need *SpACE* or could manage well enough with some common sense and a more disciplined approach to your spreadsheets, the message from Customs is clear. Businesses in general need to approach the use of spreadsheets more carefully. That's not just because failure to do so may land you with a substantial VAT bill; errors in one used as a basis for managing the business could break it!

The possible impact of mistakes in handling spreadsheets goes far beyond your tax liabilities. How about requiring staff, as part of their training, to compile documentation for spreadsheets you use and offering a bottle of champagne for the person who finds the biggest mistake!

Errors

Naturally, your company complies with the VAT rules to the best of its ability. However, compliance involves more than just good intentions! Here are some points, which your staff must understand.

Errors over £2,000 cannot in law be corrected on the VAT return. They have to be disclosed separately to your local VAT office. Failure to disclose could earn a penalty of 15%, as explained in Chapters 38 and 39 on *Appeals* and *Penalties.* Interest also runs.

Does your VAT accounting identify errors for past periods so as to permit disclosure?

What if the correct treatment is in doubt?

Suppose you are unsure about the correct VAT treatment of a transaction such as whether it is standard-rated or zero-rated. Do you always ask Customs or do you sometimes wait to see whether they challenge it? This should be a decision taken at finance director level so do staff always raise the query with you?

Where there is doubt, it is legitimate not to query the point with Customs. However, companies sometimes indulge in wishful thinking for which there is no technical basis so take advice before deciding and record the basis of your decision in writing.

If Customs were to decide that an error was so crass that it might be deliberate, they might interview the finance director and whoever signs the VAT return under caution with a view to possible prosecution!

Do you trade in equipment, components or telephones?

FA 2003 gave Customs some draconian powers to attack the 'carousel frauds'. If your business trades in computer equipment, components, telephones or in sectors such as the fashion industry in which fraudulent transactions are prevalent, you are potentially at very serious risk. See Chapter 17, *What Records Do I Need?* for more details and for comments upon the records which a head of finance may need to arrange for other departments to keep.

Beware of the slippery slope!

Sooner or later a senior financial manager is likely to meet a situation in which care about ethics is required. In the stress of the moment, it can be all too easy to do something which is near the edge of legality and which, later, you have difficulty in defending. In numerous cases, people running companies have been prosecuted or penalised by Customs for actions which involved dishonesty.

Suppose the business is short of cash. Although the VAT return is ready, you cannot pay the sum due so you hold up the return. The Customs computer produces an estimated assessment then, as this is for a much lower sum, you pay it and continue to withhold the return. That goes on for another three returns before Customs come round to check up. They then realise that you knew the assessments were understated so, in addition to assessing the business for the underpaid VAT, they claim a 100% penalty from you personally.

Oh yes, they can! They did so in *Frank Thornber (MAN/98/65 No 16235)* in which the Tribunal agreed that paying an assessment, which you know understates the true liability, amounts to dishonesty. For more on the 100% penalty for conduct involving dishonesty, see Chapter 38, *Assessments and VAT Penalties* under *Dishonesty cases*.

Thornber shows how easy it is to do what is expedient when one is under pressure in business. What may seem the practical thing to do at the time can amount to dishonesty. I call this the *slippery slope* because, often, the first step is merely unwise/incorrect in tax law; however, rather than admit the initial mistake, the temptation is to go on doing the same thing or, perhaps, something nearer to being dishonest, thus getting oneself deeper into trouble.

I have seen more than one such situation in which it was necessary to stop, think and say 'no'. That is not always easy if you are under pressure from colleagues. If ever it happens to you, remember that most of your colleagues probably do not have a professional qualification to put at risk. If you have letters after your name, not only do you risk losing them if you start down the slippery slope; Customs will take a harsher view of your behaviour because of the very fact that you have those letters. They tend to make examples of us professionals, if they catch us failing to live up to professional standards. Between them, Customs and the Inland Revenue have put several barristers, solicitors and accountants in prison in recent years.

VAT avoidance

Most businesses of any size are now regularly approached by tax advisers with supposedly cunning plans for avoiding VAT. The result is a much increased emphasis by Customs on anti-avoidance, about which they show some signs of paranoia.

Broadly, there are three approaches to VAT avoidance:

- We'll have a go at anything which is legal.

- We like to know about schemes but are cautious about using them.

- We won't touch anything which doesn't smell right.

Agree with your Board a policy on how aggressive the Board is prepared to be. Don't risk being caught out trying something, which Customs hate, without the support of your Board.

If it's worth doing, you will have enough VAT at stake, by the time Customs find out, for it to make a dent in your budget, which you may have to report to the Board even if you give in without the publicity of a VAT Tribunal case.

Some considerations to bear in mind

There is a difference between straightforward planning using the law in the way in which it is intended to operate and doing so to achieve a result which was obviously not that intended.

Aggression tends to breed aggression. If you upset Customs by doing something, which they regard as not legitimate planning, they will not trust you in future. Worse, they might decide to get their own back by applying the rules strictly on, for instance, the need to have tax invoices containing all the details required by law in order to justify the recovery of input VAT. They have it in their power to make a considerable nuisance of themselves should they decide to do so.

Bear in mind that advisers may put forward ideas which are theoretically sound but which require careful implementation in practice. In many cases, this means that to apply them correctly over time will give you significant administrative aggravation. The more cunning the plan, the more likely it is that it must be applied precisely, no matter how artificial and administratively expensive it may be to do so.

Conclusion

Under the pressures of responsibility for such key tasks as financial control, budgeting, reporting to management against budgets and working with colleagues to achieve them, it is all too easy for a Finance Director to overlook VAT. It may seem a routine matter of no great financial significance provided that the return is completed and the tax paid on time.

Not so! Whilst the degree of risk varies from business to business, it is in most cases sufficient for a serious mistake to cost a significant percentage of net profit.

Just as your Production Director must assess the risk of the factory blowing up, so must you review how VAT could damage the financial health of the business.

19.   Exports of Goods

This chapter is relevant to all those businesses which move goods from the UK to another country. Usually, that means selling goods to customers abroad but it also includes taking them to your own branch or office outside the UK.

Beware of thinking that, if you export goods, zero-rating is automatic. Not so! You only get it if you meet Customs' requirements on evidence. Whilst that is often simple enough provided that you and your staff understand what is required, there are many situations which require care. If you take the zero-rating for granted, you will get caught out sooner or later.

See also Chapter 21, *EC Sales Lists and Intrastat Returns* for details of forms and records you may need to complete concerning EU trade:

- EC Sales Lists.

- Intrastat Supplementary Declarations.

- Register of Temporary Movements of Goods.

The law

Section 30(6)–(9) zero rate the export or removal of goods in various circumstances subject to Customs being satisfied that they have left the UK. Customs are given powers to make regulations about the evidence they require in order to create such satisfaction. They have done so in *regs 128–155* of the *VAT Regulations (SI 1995/2518)*, which say that zero-rating in a variety of circumstances is subject to such conditions as Customs may impose.

The main sources of information on those conditions are VAT Notice 703 *Export and removals of goods from the UK* and Notice 725 *The Single Market*. However, there are subsidiary Notices such as 703/1 *Freight containers supplied for export or removal from the UK* and 705 *Personal exports of new motor vehicles to destinations outside the European Community from 1 January 1993*.

Membership of the EU

For a list of the Member States of the EU, see page ix at the start of the book.

Exports versus removals

An *export* of goods means to a destination outside the EU. A *removal* of goods is to a destination within the EU. Do not confuse them! The distinction is not academic; nor is it just a matter of jargon. The two systems of zero-rating are fundamentally different. Many people in business do not understand either set of rules properly so, if you use the word 'export' to cover both situations, sooner or later you will cause a muddle, which could prove expensive!

Evidence is critical

All too often, people assume that a sale is zero-rated just because they themselves know that the goods have left the country. It does not occur to them to consider how they are going to prove that to a Customs officer up to 3 years later! Zero-rating is not automatic. Customs must be satisfied that the goods physically left.

Time limit for evidence

You have 3 months from the date of each export or removal in which to get the evidence appropriate to that transaction. This is extended to 6 months if the goods are delivered within the UK for processing or for incorporation into other goods before leaving the country.

A common pitfall is failure to collect the evidence systematically. Then, when a VAT Officer on a visit asks for the records, they are incomplete. The officer is entitled to assess straight away for VAT on all shipments for which the evidence is missing. Even if you are allowed, say, a month's grace, that is very little time when you are chasing up paperwork on transactions up to 3 years old: especially if the people from whom you are trying to obtain it are transport contractors or freight forwarding agents acting for your customers rather than you and who have no financial interest in assisting you.

Exports are checked by Customs

An export of goods outside the EU goes through customs controls at the point of exit and there is therefore official evidence stamped by the officer. The precise nature of this proof of export differs according to the means of transport used. See Notice 703 (November 1996) which, in para 5.2, also demands supporting commercial documentation.

Removals are not subject to frontier controls

Within the single market of the EU, there are no customs barriers. No official evidence of removal is therefore possible but you still need evidence that the goods have left the UK. This is not always easy to obtain. Suppose a haulier employed by your customer collects the goods; you have no control over the haulier and will have no evidence of removal unless you make sure that the customer provides you with it.

Every time you remove goods, you must therefore pause to consider what evidence will be available to justify zero-rating.

The evidence you need

Often, several pieces of commercial evidence, such as the haulier's invoice, ferry documentation and a goods received note signed by the customer, are needed to provide a complete audit trail for Customs. In *VAT Information Sheet 2/00*, they ask for such details as the vehicle registration number, name and signature of driver, route used and trailer or container number.

In Notice 703 (November 1996) *Exports and removals of goods from the United Kingdom*, in paragraph 8.7, Customs say you can use a combination of the following:

- commercial transport documents from the carrier;
- order from and correspondence with the customer;

- copy advice note, packing list and sales invoice;
- details of insurance and freight charges;
- evidence of payment, by which they presumably mean from the customer;
- evidence of receipt of the goods abroad;
- any other evidence you may have concerning the transaction.

All of this is somewhat vague but it is up to you to establish what evidence is available in the circumstances in which you remove the goods from the UK. This is a problem of records on which Customs have wide powers so, when they refuse to accept that goods have left the UK, Customs nearly always win! It would be possible to fill several pages of this book with stories of the numerous tribunal appeals against assessments by Customs resulting from inadequate evidence that goods have been removed or exported. Here is an example.

DW Munge (LON/84/166 No 1852) shipped wallpaper to Ireland in lorries, which were returning empty from the continent via Dover to Ireland. The lorry drivers were the agents of the purchasers. Despite a statutory declaration by the managing director of the shipping line that the lorries had indeed passed through Dover and bank documentation showing payments received from the customer, there was no evidence of the quantities of wallpaper, nor that the payments concerned such quantities. The Tribunal was satisfied that, on the balance of probabilities, the wallpaper had been removed to Ireland but it had no power to substitute its judgment for that of Customs. This case is typical of the problems which arise from a failure to think! You may know your goods leave the UK but how will you *prove* that in several years time?

The customer's VAT number

In addition to obtaining the commercial evidence of removal, you must show on your invoice the customer's VAT number in the other Member State. A sale of goods to another UK business is standard-rated even though you may have sent the goods to France! The same rules apply when you ship your own goods to a branch of your business in another Member State. That branch will be registered in that State. Your records need to include an internal 'invoice' or debit note showing the branch's VAT number together with the usual commercial evidence. If this sounds odd, consider the problem for Customs if you did not have the full paperwork. A fraudster could claim that the goods had been shipped to his branch abroad when he had in fact sold them within the UK.

The Intrastat jargon

As explained later, the Intrastat return records your EU movements of goods both out of and into the UK. The Intrastat jargon is not 'removals' but 'despatches', possibly because certain 'despatches' have to be recorded on the Intrastat Supplementary Declaration but are not 'removals' for the EC Sales List.

Removals include taking goods to a branch in another EU State

If you take goods to a branch in another EU State for sale there, that counts as a removal for VAT purposes. The normal rules apply for both invoicing and evidence of removal. Thus, in order not to account for UK VAT on the goods, you must create an internal 'invoice' as a record of the transaction for VAT purposes, which shows the registration number of your branch in that State. Of course, you are likely to have to register there in order to account for VAT on your sales in that State. If you are not so liable the distance selling rules will apply as explained below.

Call-off stock and sale or return or consignment stock

Call-off stock supplied to a customer is treated as a removal/acquisition at the time of delivery, not when adopted by the customer.

On the other hand, stock supplied on sale or return or on consignment is regarded as supplied when ownership passes. You may therefore be liable to register in the State of your customer.

Distance selling (mail order) to customers in other EU States

You can sell goods to unregistered customers by mail order anywhere in the EU but you must charge UK VAT until your sales in a calendar year in a State reach the distance selling limit of that State. Then you must register there.

At the time of writing, the limits are as follows. Check the current figures. €27,889 in Italy; €31,424 in Portugal; €35,000 in Belgium, Finland, Greece, Ireland and Spain; €100,000 in Austria, France, Germany, Luxembourg and the Netherlands; DKK280,000 in Denmark; SEK300,000 in Sweden; £70,000 in the UK. In a VAT group, each company is treated separately for the purposes of the distance selling limits.

There are no distance selling limits for *excise goods* — any sales at all to unregistered customers in another EU State make you liable to register in that State.

Registration of an EU mail order business in the UK

The UK law requiring a business based elsewhere in the EU to register here is in *Sch 2*.

New means of transport

There are special rules concerning the zero-rating of new means of transport (NMT) sold to buyers elsewhere in the EU. In addition to the normal rules, the NMT must be removed from the UK within 2 months of the time of supply. A means of transport is defined as:

- a ship more than 7.5 metres long (about 24.6 feet);

- an aircraft with a take-off weight exceeding 1,550 kilograms;

- a motorised land vehicle which:

  (i) has an engine of more than 48 cc; or
  (ii) is constructed or adapted to be electrically propelled using more than 7.2kw (about 9.65 hp).

However, the above are not affected by these rules if they are not intended for the transport of passengers or goods. A means of transport ceases to be new when:

- more than 3 months have elapsed since the date of its first entry into service; and

- it has, since its first entry into service, travelled under its own power more than:
    100 hours in the case of a ship.
    40 hours in the case of an aircraft.
    3,000 kilometres (about 1,864 miles) in the case of a vehicle.

Do you deliver in the UK but invoice an overseas customer?

Beware the pitfall of assuming that you need not charge VAT to a non-UK customer. The normal rules apply as to the evidence required. The goods must leave the UK to justify zero-rating. However sure you are of the ultimate destination of the goods, you must standard-rate a delivery in the UK unless a special concession applies. There are only a few of these. An example is the one applicable to components delivered to another UK business, which incorporates them into the other goods, which are then exported. If you believe you qualify for zero-rating under such a concession, check its precise terms carefully. See, for example, earlier in this chapter about evidence and time limits.

Triangulation

Do you buy goods from a supplier in another EU State and have them shipped direct to a customer in a third State? This is known as triangulation.

Example

UK Ltd buys goods from a German supplier (Gmbh) for shipment direct to its customer in France (FR SA). Common sense says that UK Ltd should be able to obtain zero-rating from its German supplier against its UK VAT number and to zero-rate on to its French customer against the latter's French VAT number. However, the normal rules do not allow this. They would require UK Ltd to register either in Germany or in France. Registration in Germany would mean that Gmbh charged German VAT to UK Ltd. UK Ltd would then zero-rate the removal of the goods from Germany to France against the French customer's VAT number. Alternatively, registration in France would enable UK Ltd to quote a French registration number to Gmbh and thus obtain zero-rating from Germany. UK Ltd would then charge French VAT to FR SA.

A simplification procedure avoids the need for UK Ltd to register in either country.

Conditions for using the simplification measure

You can only use the simplification measure if:

- You are VAT registered in an EU State — so a non-EU trader has first to register.

- You have no obligation to register in the State to which the goods go.

- Your customer is VAT registered in that State.

How the simplification measure works

- You quote your VAT registration number to allow zero rating for the dispatch of the goods from the supplier's State.

- You issue a zero rated invoice showing, as normal, the customer's VAT number *and* endorsed *VAT: EC Article 28 Simplification Invoice*. In the UK, the invoice must be issued within 15 days of tax point, which would have been applicable under a normal transaction.

- You record the supply on your EC Sales List — explained in Chapter 21, *EC Sales Lists and Intrastat Returns* — separately from any ordinary supplies to that customer and identified by the figure *2* in the indicator box.

- Triangular transactions are not recorded on the VAT return or Intrastat Supplementary Declaration of the trader using the simplification measure.

- But the customer receiving the goods must record the transaction under the Intrastat rules.

Notice 725 (October 2002) *The single market* says nothing about whether a UK trader, when invoicing to another EU State under the simplification rule, must comply with rules similar to the following, so check. In the UK, in addition to the above, a trader from another State must:

- Write to the VAT Business Advice Centre 050, Custom House, 28 Guild Street, Aberdeen AB9 2DY stating:

  (i)   name, address and the EU VAT registration number used to obtain zero rating for the supply of the goods;
  (ii) name, address and VAT registration number of the UK customer;
  (iii) date of delivery to the UK customer, actual or intended.

- Copy that notification to the UK customer, no later than the issue of the first invoice, saying that that customer must therefore account for acquisition VAT on the supply.

That notification covers all subsequent supplies to that customer but separate notifications are required for any other UK customers.

Do you install or assemble the goods which you sell?

If you install or assemble your goods on your customer's premises, the place of your supply is your customer's premises. If that is in another EU State, you may be liable to register there. That creates a pitfall for the unwary because suppliers typically think that they can zero-rate the goods as a removal from the UK, including in the price the installation charge and that they can get the customer to pay for the accommodation and meals of the staff who do the work. In practice, this is no doubt what often happens and, for one-off transactions, it is difficult for the fiscal administration of the customer's State to catch the transaction.

Trouble can arise if you try to get back VAT incurred locally through an 8th Directive claim, as explained in Chapter 26, *Recovery of Foreign VAT*. If the State from which you claim realises the situation, the claim will be refused — unless that State applies the same reverse charge rule as the UK. See below.

The UK law is in *s 7(3)*, which makes the place of supply of goods outside the UK 'where their supply involves their installation or assembly at a place outside the UK to which they are removed'.

This reflects *Article 8(1)(a)* of the *EC 6th VAT Directive* which says:

> *Where the goods are installed or assembled, with or without a trial run, by or on behalf of the supplier, the place of supply shall be deemed to be the place where the goods are installed or assembled.*

EU suppliers installing goods in the UK

Para 8.11 of Notice 725 *The Single Market* (October 2002) details a concession, which is not necessarily replicated elsewhere in the EU. The EU supplier can require the UK customer to reverse charge the VAT by:

- Endorsing the invoice, which must be issued within 15 days of each tax point, *Section 14(2) VAT invoice;*

- Notifying the addresses and VAT numbers of both supplier and customer and the date the work begins to Customs at VAT Business Advice Centre 050, Custom House, 28 Guild Street, Aberdeen AB9 2DY;

- Copying the notification to the customer.

Some questions to check your understanding. Review your answers with the text.

- What evidence do you need to justify zero-rating an export of goods?

- What evidence do you need to justify zero-rating a removal of goods?

- What are the key rules concerning distance selling?

- How do the rules concerning New Means of Transport differ from the normal ones?

- What is triangulation and what are the special rules which apply to it?

- You obtain a contract to supply and install a computer system in France. Where is the pitfall in this situation?

20. Imports and Acquisitions of Goods

This chapter covers rules which are largely administrative routine for fully taxable businesses which bring goods into the UK. However, misunderstanding them could cause problems. Moreover, VAT on goods bought outside the UK by a partly exempt business may not be recoverable. Failure to account for it correctly could lead to an assessment with interest and a penalty. Just as there are important differences between an export and a removal of goods, an import is different from an acquisition. Goods are *imported* from outside the EU. They are *acquired* from within it; ie from suppliers in other Member States.

See also Chapter 21, *EC Sales Lists and Intrastat Returns* for details of forms and records you may need to complete concerning EU trade:

- EC Sales Lists.
- Intrastat Supplementary Declarations.
- Register of Temporary Movements of Goods.

The law

Sections 36A, 37 and 38 and various statutory instruments contain the rules. Of the latter, *The VAT Regulations (SI 1995/2518) Parts XII, XVI, XVI(A) and XVII I* and *The Imported Goods Relief Order (SI 1984/746)* contain the main rules.

Notices 702 (October 1998) *Imports*, 702/4 (January 2002) *Importing computer software*, 702/7 (June 1993) *Import VAT relief for goods supplied onward to another country in the EC* and 702/9 (October 1998) *Warehouses and free zones* refer.

Imports from outside the EU

Import VAT and, if applicable, duty are assessed on goods at the port or airport by Customs. They have to be paid either:

- under the deferment approval system; or
- in cash or by bankers' draft.

Alternatively, your import agent may be prepared to pay on your behalf.

The Channel Islands and the Isle of Man

The Channel Islands are not a part of the EU for fiscal purposes and import VAT is therefore due on goods brought into the UK from there.

On the other hand, the Isle of Man is treated as part of the UK, although it has its own customs authority.

Do you use an import agent?

Most importers use an import agent to clear the goods through Customs. Obvious reasons for this include the time saved in not attending at the point of entry in order to make the import declaration oneself and the specialist knowledge of import procedures which the agent is supposed to possess.

Do not assume that your agent possesses that knowledge! It is a complex subject and complying with the rules properly often requires a precise understanding of the nature of the goods being imported. That requires efficient communication between the agent and the importer and an understanding by the latter of the key rules affecting the goods in question and thus of the information which the agent needs. The tribunal decisions which I see concerning appeals on duty matters regularly reveal serious losses suffered by importers who have relied entirely on the expertise of their import agents only to find that the latter have made mistakes resulting in subsequent post-clearance demands for underpaid duty or import VAT. Admittedly, many of the problems concern import duty rather than import VAT and duty is not a subject covered in this book. However, it seems appropriate to warn readers of the potential pitfalls. For a horrendous example of the latter from which I had to rescue 2 clients recently, see later in this chapter under *The VAT-free import of goods shipped on immediately to another EU State.*

Are you an import agent?

The above remarks concerning mistakes made will be no great surprise to most import agents, given the complexity of the rules with which you have to cope. Most of those rules concern import duty rather than VAT and are not covered by this book. However, the case referred to above, which I explain later, illustrates the need for agents to put considerable ongoing effort into maintaining and expanding their specialist expertise.

A pitfall specific to VAT for import agents is the situation arising if you pay import VAT and then fail to recover it from the importer. Only that importer has the right to reclaim it as import VAT. You therefore need to take some care in obtaining a bank guarantee or some other assurance of the financial stability of your clients before you pay VAT on their behalf.

Only in very limited circumstances will Customs repay to you the VAT. These include that your client is in liquidation or administration and that the goods in question remained under your control, were not used and were then re-exported in the same state as they were imported. Obviously, those circumstances are unusual. See para 2.5 of Notice 702 (October 1998) for the full conditions applicable.

The deferment approval system

Under the deferment approval system:

- you provide security to Customs — usually a bank guarantee — to cover your expected maximum monthly liability for import VAT and import duty. Customs will relax their requirements for security for VAT only from 1/12/03 for approved importers, who must apply individually;

- you are allocated a Deferment Approval Number (DAN) which you or your import agent quotes in respect of each 'entry' of goods;

- the total of VAT and duty due on imports during the month is deducted by direct debit from your bank account on the 15th of the month following that in which the import occurs.

(Continued on page 204)

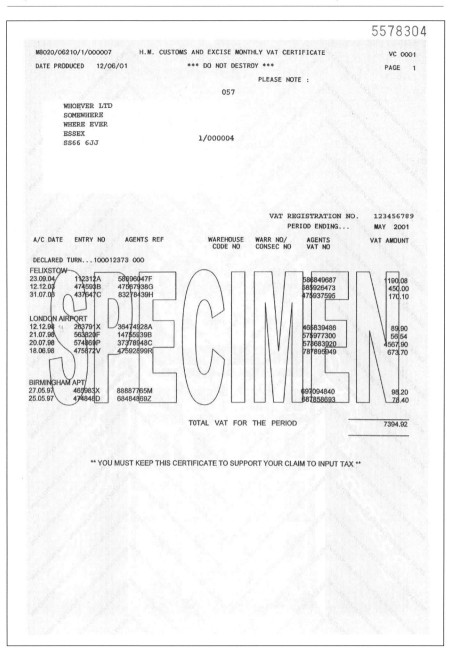

A monthly computer-produced certificate (see example following) is the evidence required to justify the recovery of the sums paid as input tax. That the money has been deducted from your bank account by direct debit under the deferment approval system is insufficient by itself. Nor is it safe to assume that the amount collected by direct debit is the same as the input tax shown on the certificate. The latter might include duty as well as VAT.

Moreover, the certificate will show the VAT assessed on all the goods imported by you during the month. This includes any amounts settled at the time of entry rather than under the deferment approval system — perhaps because the security provided to Customs is insufficient this month.

This creates a pitfall. Some traders have recovered the sum shown on the documentation covering the tax paid on entry and, later, the amount shown on the computer certificate, not realising the duplication.

The risk of something going wrong could be higher if your imports are only occasional rather than regular and staff are therefore not used to the system.

Acquisitions of goods from suppliers in other Member States

Goods 'acquired' without VAT from suppliers in other EU countries are not checked by Customs and no VAT is assessed by them. It has to be self-assessed by the trader. This may seem simple but problems include:

- Acquisition tax must be entered in box 2, which is thus part of your total output tax in box 3. The reason for this is that the supplier will not account for it to Customs, so you must do so instead.

- The corresponding input tax must be entered in box 4 with the rest of your input tax *if and to the extent that* it is attributable to taxable activities. You cannot recover any part of it which relates to exempt ones.

- Identifying all the deliveries of goods received from EU suppliers if you trade from various locations.

- Accounting for the input and output tax on the correct VAT return. This is the one covering the month *following* the date of dispatch or, if earlier, the date of the supplier's invoice.

- Assessing the VAT on the correct valuation for the goods — normally the invoiced price plus any freight and insurance if charged separately.

If you acquire goods elsewhere in the EU, check whether these rules are understood and are being complied with by your organisation.

The main pitfalls are:

- Failing to account, in box 2 of the VAT return, for acquisition VAT which is not recoverable as input tax in box 4 because it relates to exempt outputs, not taxable ones.

- Worse still, claiming the input tax without accounting for the acquisition tax!

Special reliefs for certain imports

The Imported Goods Relief Order (SI 1984/746) allows relief in the following situations:

- Hologram, multimedia kits and materials for programmed instruction produced by the United Nations or a UN organisation.

- Capital goods and equipment imported when a business is shut down abroad and transferred into the UK — provided the business only makes taxable supplies.

- Advertising materials, such as samples, catalogues and goods imported solely for the purpose of demonstration at an event. See the law for the definition of *event,* which does not include a show at which the goods on display are sold.

- Goods imported for examination, analysis or testing in the course of industrial or commercial research.

- Animals sent free of charge for laboratory use, human blood, certain goods imported for specified purposes, such as human organs and reagents and pharmaceutical products for the use of persons or animals participating in an international sporting event.

- Certain goods imported for charitable purposes including fundraising events.

- Printed matter for use in a variety of situations.

- Articles imported in situations such as copyright applications, evidence to a court or an official body, photographic material sent to the media, recorded media for the transmission of information, honorary decorations, cups, medals etc awarded to UK residents, gifts from one body to another and goods up to £18 in value.

- Works of art and collectors' pieces imported by approved museums, galleries etc other than for sale and for non-business purposes. Fuel and lubricants for the use of the vehicle carrying them, litter, fodder and feed accompanying animals and disposable packaging.

- Goods for war cemeteries, coffins and urns containing human remains or ashes.

The above descriptions only cover the key points. If the relief appears relevant, check the precise wording of the law.

The value on which import VAT is payable

Import VAT is due on the total of the invoiced price *plus* incidental expenses such as commission, packing, transport and insurance up to the first destination of the goods in the UK — and on to a further destination in the EU if that is known at the time of import *plus* any customs duty, levy or excise duty payable.

5% for works of art, antiques and collectors' items

Works of art, antiques and collectors' items are subject to a reduced import VAT rate of 5%.

Temporary imports and re-imports

If you are importing goods temporarily for reasons such as:

* to have work done on them;

* works of art, antiques or collectors' items for exhibition in the hope of a sale;

* second-hand goods for sale at auction,

or you are re-importing goods, which have previously been exported, you need to understand in advance the relevant detailed rules. It may well be possible to avoid having to pay import VAT — and import duty — if you comply with the rules set out in such Notices as 200 *Temporary importations*, 221 *Inward processing relief* and 235 *Outward processing relief* .

The VAT-free import of goods shipped on immediately to another EU State

An import agent or freight forwarder can clear goods through Customs free of import VAT if:

* the goods are removed to another EU State within a month; *and*

* the agent or freight forwarder invoices the goods — zero rated under the usual rules for removals from the UK to another State — to his client's customer in that State; and

* records the 'sale' in the EU sales box on his VAT return and completes the EC Sales List and, if required, the Intrastat return.

The big advantage is that no import VAT has to be paid anywhere since the customer in the other EU State merely treats the purchase as an acquisition. This therefore makes it much easier for an agent or freight forwarder to handle the transit of goods through the UK on behalf of a non-EU supplier. There are at least 2 pitfalls!

In a case I handled, both the import agent, who made the import entry and the freight forwarder, who shipped the goods on, failed to think! It did not occur to them that such an unusual procedure must have special conditions as to records. Part of the problem was that the explanation in the *Customs Tariff* of *Customs Procedure Code 42 00 00* said nothing about those conditions or the need to study Notice 702/7 (June 1993) *Import VAT relief for goods supplied onward to another country in the EC* in which the rules in *Reg 123*, made under *s 30(8)*, are (inadequately) explained.

That explanation is inadequate because it does not say how business could invoice goods which it does not own. In the course of the dispute, which involved post-clearance demands for £2.8m — enough to put my clients out of business — Customs accepted the special wording I proposed for the invoices stating that they were issued for VAT purposes only and that payment should be made to the overseas supplier. Unfortunately, as I write, Notice 702/7, which also quotes out-of-date legislation, has still not been revised and therefore remains a minefield for an unsuspecting trader.

Some questions to check your understanding. Review your answers with the text.

- What is the difference between an import and an acquisition?
- How is import VAT collected by Customs?
- What is a Deferment Approval Number?
- How do you account for acquisition VAT?

21. EC Sales Lists and Intrastat Returns

This chapter briefly describes the special returns which must be completed by those who remove goods to, or acquire them from, other Member States of the EU. As explained in Chapter 5, about VAT returns, there are special boxes on the VAT return in which you show the value of the goods which you have sold to customers elsewhere in the EU and of your purchases from suppliers in other EU States. However, that is not the end of it! You also have to complete:

- An EC Sales List. This shows your sales to customers in other EU States.

- An Intrastat Supplementary Declaration, which shows movements of goods both sent out to, or brought into the UK from, other EU States. This is only required once the value of the goods exceeds a de minimis limit.

Section 14 of Notice 725 (October 2002) *The Single Market* provides a detailed explanation of EC Sales Lists. Notice 60 (June 2002) *Intrastat – General Guide* covers Intrastat returns.

The EC Sales List

The EC Sales List (ECSL) covers your sales of goods to 2 EU customers, not services. It is due for each calendar quarter — but you can ask to submit monthly returns if that suits you. If you have non-standard monthly or quarterly accounting periods for your VAT returns — such as to match 12 or 13 week accounting periods — you can also apply for your monthly or quarterly ECSLs to cover the same periods.

Small trader concessions

If you use the *Annual Accounting Scheme*, you can ask to submit an *annual* ECSL if:

- your *total* taxable sales do not exceed £145,000; *and*

- your annual sales to other EU States do not exceed £11,000; *and*

- your sales do not include new boats, aircraft or motorised land vehicles.

You can ask for permission to complete an *annual simplified* ECSL, which just lists the VAT registration numbers of your EU customers, if:

- your *total* taxable sales do not exceed £72,500; *and*

- your annual sales to other EU States do not exceed £11,000; *and*

- your sales do not include new boats, aircraft or motorised land vehicles.

Information required

The information required includes the total value of your sales to each EU customer — identified by registration number including the alpha prefix, not by name. See the sample form on the next page.

(*Continued on page 211*)

Value Added Tax

EC Sales list

For the period

To

Branch/subsidiary Calendar

GB

Due date:

For official use D O R

Your VAT office telephone number is
Before you fill in this form read the notes overleaf.

	Country Code	Customer's VAT Registration Number	Total value of supplies in pounds sterling (£)	p	Indi- cator
1				0 0	
2				0 0	
3				0 0	
4				0 0	
5				0 0	
6				0 0	
7				0 0	
8				0 0	
9				0 0	
10				0 0	
11				0 0	
12				0 0	
13				0 0	
14				0 0	
15				0 0	

Number of pages completed

Lines completed (this page only)

Contact name

Telephone Number   Date

Full name of signatory in BLOCK LETTERS

Signature

VAT 101 (Full)   IB(January 2001)

NOTES ON COMPLETION

These notes provide guidance on filling in this form. You will find more detailed information in VAT Information Sheet, VAT: Filling in your EC Sales List and in Notice 725, VAT: The Single Market and Notice 703 VAT: Exports and removals of goods from the United Kingdom.

If you have not been involved in any intra-EC transactions during the period specified overleaf, DO NOT return this form. If no transactions have taken place you will not be liable to a financial penalty.

Do not write on or amend details in the green area of this form. If you think any of the pre-printed information is wrong, or if you need any help, contact your local office. The telephone number is shown overleaf.

Country Code

Enter your customer's country code, which can **only** be from the following list:

Austria	AT	Ireland	IE
Belgium	BE	Italy	IT
Denmark	DK	Luxembourg	LU
Finland	FI	Netherlands	NL
France	FR	Portugal	PT
Germany	DE	Spain	ES
Greece	EL	Sweden	SE

Customer'a VAT Registration Number

Enter your customer's VAT registration number in the spaces provided, starting from the extreme left hand side.

Do not repeat your customer's country code in this column or include any spaces, dashes or commas. Underline alphabetical characters.

Use one line only for each customer UNLESS you are an intermediate supplier in intra-EC triangular transactions. Show the total value of these supplies on a separate line and enter the figure '2' in the indicator column.

One of the conditions for zero-rating supplies of goods to other EC countries is that you must provide a **valid** VAT number for each of your customers. Once advised by HM Customs & Excise that a VAT registration number is invalid you must not continue to use it to zero-rate your supplies.

Notices 725 and 703 and VAT Information Sheet VAT: Filling in your EC Sales List all contain a table which details the **only** acceptable format of EC VAT numbers.

Total Value of Supplies

Only include the value of goods and related services supplied to customers who are registered for VAT purposes in *other* EC countries where the goods are moved between EC countries. Related services are services which form part of the price of the goods, such as freight and transport charges.

Add up the value of goods and related services supplied to your customer, deduct credit notes, and enter the total, rounded to the nearest pound sterling in the space provided.

Do not include the pounds sterling symbol (£), decimal points (.) or commas (,). The figure must then be entered **right** aligned.

If the value of credit notes is greater than the total value of supplies enclose the figure in brackets. **Do not** use a minus sign.

Indicator

Leave this column blank, UNLESS:

you have made supplies as the intermediary in intra-EC triangular trade. Enter **'2'**, with the details, on a separate line from your other supplies.

Lines Completed (this page only)

Enter the number of lines completed for this page only in the box provided.

Number of Pages Completed

Enter the number of pages completed in the box provided. Include all continuation sheets.

Common Errors

Before filling in this form, please take note of the list of common errors on page 5 of VAT Information Sheet VAT: Filling in your EC Sales List. This will help to ensure that we do not contact you unless absolutely necessary as every error you make has to be corrected. The information sheet is available from your local office.

Declaration

You or someone on your behalf **must** sign the form to declare that the information provided constitutes a true and complete statement.

VAT 101A (Continuation Sheet)

If you run out of lines on this form, contact your local office for a VAT 101A (Continuation Sheet). When you receive the VAT 101A complete the top of the form with the same information pre-printed on this form.

VAT 101B (Correction Sheet)

If you need to correct any data supplied in a previous period or supply any previously omitted data, contact your local office for a VAT 101B (Correction Sheet). When you receive the VAT 101B complete the form with the appropriate information.

Where to send this form

You must ensure that the completed form is received by the due date. Return it in the white pre-paid envelope provided, to:

The Controller, VAT Central Unit
H M Customs and Excise
21 Victoria Avenue
Southend-on-Sea X, SS99 1AN

Data Protection Act 1998

HM Customs and Excise collects information in order to administer the taxes for which it is responsible (such as VAT, insurance premium tax, excise duties, air passenger duty, landfill tax), and for detecting and preventing crime.

Where the law permits we may also get information about you from third parties, or give information to them, for example in order to check its accuracy, prevent or detect crime or protect public funds in other ways. These third parties may include the police, other government departments and agencies.

VAT 101(Full)   Reverse(01/01)

Intrastat Supplementary Declaration

The Intrastat Supplementary Declaration (ISD) is a monthly return intended to provide trade statistics.

De minimis limit for ISD

You are liable to submit the ISD if your sales or your purchases exceed the de minimis limit. This was set by the *Statistics of Trade (Customs & Excise) Regulations (SI 1992/2790)*, as amended, at £233,000 for the calendar year 2000 and was not increased for 2001–2003.

The limit applies separately to goods despatched and received, so you may have to submit an ISD for your sales but not your purchases or vice versa.

Dispatches and Arrivals

Dispatches and *Arrivals* are the jargon used for ISD purposes rather than *removals* and *acquisitions*, the terms used under the Single Market rules described in Chapter 19, *Exports of Goods*.

Separate returns are required for goods despatched to and received from EU countries. They cover movements of goods, not just sales and purchases. For instance, you include goods transferred to or from a branch elsewhere in the EU and movements of goods for processing or repair.

The example of the form for Dispatches shows what is required. That for *Arrivals* is the same, bar its title but the two sets of information must be reported separately.

If your 'acquisitions' of goods from the EU are delivered to various locations or even to such scattered points as construction sites, you need the cooperation of your shipping department and of such people as site managers, who may not normally liaise closely with accounts. An *Acquisition* for VAT return purposes occurs when you:

- Import goods from a supplier in another EU State;
- Bring goods into the UK from a branch of your business in another EU State; or
- Receive goods under a hire-purchase or a lease purchase agreement.

In addition, the following are also treated as Arrivals for ISD purposes:

- Goods received for processing by you;
- Goods of which you receive possession under an agreement by which ownership is intended to pass to you in due course. Thus a finance lease is an acquisition but an operating one is not.

Due date

The ISD is due with Customs by the end of the month following the month to which it relates.

(Continued on page 214)

INTRA EC TRADE STATISTICS

DISPATCHES

Supplementary Declaration

For Official Use

Period (mm/yy)

No of lines

Trader

HM Customs and Excise

INTRASTAT

VAT No:GB

Branch ID:

Agent

VAT No:GB

Branch ID

	Commodity code	Value £s Sterling	Delivery terms	Nature of transaction	Net mass (kg)	Supplementary units	Goods sent to (country)	Trader reference
1								
2								
3								
4								
5								
6								
7								
8								

When complete return to:

HM Customs and Excise
Sort Section, Alexander House
21 Victoria Avenue
Southend-on-Sea
Essex SS99 1AA

Have you considered sending in your data via the Internet? For details of this easier and more convenient method please contact the EDI Helpdesk, Tel: 01702 367248 or e-mail us at < helpdesk.edcs@hmce.gov.uk>.

Name of signatory: .... (in BLOCK LETTERS)

Signature: ....

Telephone No: ....

Date and Place: ....

PT(March 2001)

C1501

Notes on the completion of INTRASTAT supplementary declaration (SD).
Detailed advice on how to complete this form and on Intrastat generally can be found in The Intrastat General Guide, Notice 60.

	Separate forms must be used for Arrivals (C1500) and Dispatches (C1501). Continuation sheets are available.
Period (mm/yy)	The period is the month and year to which the declaration refers, e.g. 11/01 for November 2001. For special periods see Notice 60.
No of Lines	Show the number of lines of data entered on each declaration. If you are declaring more than 176 lines, please submit in batches containing no more than 14 continuation sheets to each header sheet (C1500 and C1501).
Sheet No. **Continuation Sheet**	Show the order of the sheets ie. 03 05 for continuation sheet three of a total of five.
Trader	Enter the name, address and post code of your business, quoting your UK VAT number. The three digit Branch ID should be completed if you are providing data on a branch basis and have already advised the Information Management Division of Customs & Excise.
Agent	This field should only be completed if an agent is completing the SD on behalf of a trader.
Commodity Code	You must classify goods using the appropriate code from the current Intrastat Classification Nomenclature (ICN). If you need advice, contact the Tariff Classification Helpline on **01702 366077.**
Value £s Sterling	Show the value, as used for VAT purposes, in £s sterling rounded up to the nearest pound. **Do not show the £ sign or pence.**
Delivery Terms	See Table opposite. Not required if below delivery terms threshold. See Notice 60.
Nature of Transaction	See Notice 60.
Net Mass	If required, should be shown in kilograms, rounded up to the next whole kilogram. The current ICN gives details of those commodity codes where the provision of net mass is optional. **Only show the figure, not kg letters.**
Supplementary Units	Complete this box only when the current ICN indicates that supplementary information is required.
Goods sent to/ Goods from (country)	See Table opposite.
Trader reference	The completion of this box, with an invoice number for example, may assist in resolving any queries raised. Completion of this box is **optional**.

C1501 reverse(03/01)

CODES FOR USE IN COMPLETION OF INTRASTAT DECLARATION

Delivery Terms	Code	Goods sent to/Goods from Country	Code
Carriage Paid to	CPT	Austria	AT
Carriage Insurance Paid to	CIP	Belgium	BE
Cost and Freight (C&F)	CFR	Denmark	DK
		Finland	FI
Cost, Insurance and Freight	CIF	France	FR
Delivered at Frontier	DAF	Germany	DE
Delivered Ex Quay	DEQ	Greece	GR
Delivered Ex Ship	DES	Irish Republic	IE
Delivered Duty Unpaid	DDU	Italy	IT
Delivered Duty Paid	DDP	Luxembourg	LU
Ex Works	EXW	Netherlands	NL
Free Alongside Ship	FAS	Portugal	PT
Free On Board	FOB	Spain	ES
Free Carrier	FOA	Sweden	SE
Other terms not listed above	XXX		

Useful e-mail addresses:

Intrastat: intrastat.hmce@gtnet.gov.uk
Electronic Data Interchange (EDI)
helpdesk: helpdesk.edcs@hmce.gov.uk
Tariff Classification helpdesk: classification.tso@hmce.gov.uk
Information Management Division (General enquiries):
statistics.tso@hmce.gov.uk
Complaints: complaints.tso@hmce.gov.uk

Data Protection Act 1998

HM Customs and Excise collects information in order to administer the taxes for which it is responsible (such as VAT, insurance premium tax, excise duties, air passenger duty, landfill tax), and for detecting and preventing crime.

Where the law permits we may also get information about you from third parties, or give information to them, for example in order to check its accuracy, prevent or detect crime or protect public funds in other ways. These third parties may include the police, other government departments and agencies.

NOTE: YOUR DECLARATION MUST REACH THE ADDRESS OVERLEAF BY THE 10TH WORKING DAY AFTER PERIOD END.

Information required

The Intrastat requires information not by customer but by international commodity code. Thus, if a despatch is of goods covered by different commodity codes, the value, in sterling, must be split by code. The same applies to incoming goods. Also to be shown are:

- delivery terms — if the value of despatches in the previous calendar year exceeded £13.5m. The same applies for arrivals;
- nature of the transaction code (NOTC);
- net mass in kilograms (optional for some commodity codes);
- the supplementary units (certain commodity codes only);
- the country the goods are despatched to or came from.

You can add your own reference if you wish.

Nature of transaction code (NOTC)

The code has two functions:

- the first digit identifies the nature of the transaction for statistical purposes; and
- the first and second digits together identify reasons for differences between values declared in boxes 8 and 9 of your VAT returns and ISDs.

The codes are as follows:

1st digit

1 = Sales or purchases including stock moved within the same legal entity and financial leasing.
2 = Returned goods and replacement goods.
3 = Free of charge transactions involving permanent change of ownership.
4 = Goods sent for processing or repair (other than within code 7).
5 = Goods returned following process or repair (other than within code 7).
6 = Movements of goods without transfer of ownership for hire, operational leasing and other temporary use. For process or repair, see codes 4 and 5. However, most temporary movements are not required to be declared.
7 = Joint defence projects or other joint inter-governmental production programme (eg Eurofighter).
8 = Supply of building materials and equipment as part of a general construction or engineering contract. The value is that of the goods, not that of the contract.
9 = Other transactions.

2nd digit

0 = In all cases where codes 6, 7 or 8 below do not apply.
6 = Credit notes.
7 = Transactions included on ISD but not shown in boxes 8 or 9 of the VAT returns for the equivalent period.
8 = Transactions included in boxes 8 or 9 of the VAT return but not required on ISD.

Commodity codes

Deciding the correct commodity code is often not a simple task. The International Standard Classification is a complex manual, even in the simplified version. For imports, you may want your suppliers to quote, on invoices as well as on shipping documents, both codes and such information as the net mass of the goods — needed even if the item is a single machine. Customs use it for a crude check on the value per kilo!

Low value transactions on the ISD

If your invoice includes goods classifiable under two or more commodity codes with a total value not exceeding £80, you can declare them against a single low value code (99500000). This optional simplification applies regardless of the value of other goods on the invoice.

The register of temporary movement of goods

If you despatch goods, which are to be returned within 2 years, to another EU State, or receive such goods from another EU State, you have to keep a 'Register of Temporary Movement of Goods to and from other Member States'.

Notice 725 says that this applies to goods:

Despatches

- sent for processing, repair or alteration; or
- moved to another State for use in making supplies in that State.
- sent to other States under what would be Temporary Import Relief conditions if they were imported from outside the EU.

Receipts

- received for processing.

Information required

The information required is:

- date of the initial despatch or receipt of the goods;
- date of their subsequent return;
- description of the goods;
- the reason for the movement;
- the price charged for the processing or other work done on them, whether in the UK or elsewhere in the EU.

Format of register

The register can be in any convenient form which provides the information required.

Some questions to check your understanding. Review your answers with the text.

- What is the information required on the EC Sales List?

- How is that information organised?

- What is the information required on the Intrastat Supplementary Declaration?

- How is that information organised?

- What is recorded in the Register of Temporary Movements of Goods?

22.   Exports and Imports of Services

This chapter discusses the rules applicable when you supply services to a non-UK customer or you do the work outside the UK. Services being intangible, the rules bear no relationship to those for goods. They are one of the most complex parts of VAT law. Various rules deal with different services in different ways.

If your business has any international operations, you will meet these rules sooner or later even if you sell goods rather than services. For instance, if you make management charges between companies in different countries, you need to understand enough to know how you can justify not charging VAT on them.

This chapter is called *Exports and Imports of Services* to distinguish it from that on *Exports of Goods*. However, the subject is often called 'International Services'. Either name will do as a general title for the subject but neither is strictly correct. Although *Sch 8 Group 7* is called *International Services*, it zero-rates only certain supplies in somewhat specialist circumstances. The most important rules are those on the *Place of Supply of Services*. If the place of supply of a service is outside the UK, it is outside the scope of UK VAT — not zero-rated. It may be outside the scope either with recovery of the associated input tax or without recovery. These two categories are equivalent to zero-rating and exemption within the UK.

If you find this chapter heavy going, take heart! Everyone finds these rules difficult at first. The best way to learn them is to understand the basic idea; then leave the detail until you have a real situation to which to apply the rules.

The law

Thus, in order not to charge VAT to a foreign customer, your supply must be:

- outside the scope of UK VAT because the place of supply is made outside the UK by the *Place of Supply of Services Order ('POSSO') (SI 1992/3121)*; or

- zero-rated under *Sch 8 Groups 7, 8* or *13* or the Terminal Markets rules in *s 50* re commodities; *or*

- covered by *concessions* made by UK Customs; *or*

- *exempt* in the UK anyway — such as insurance or finance.

Membership of the EU

For a list of the Member States of the EU, see page ix at the start of the book.

So can I recover my input tax?

Not having to charge VAT to a foreign customer is only half the story. The other half is whether you can recover the input tax you incurred in making the supply. A supply standard-rated in the UK, will be outside the scope with recovery of the associated input tax if the place of supply is outside the UK.

A supply which is exempt in the UK, will be outside the scope when the place of supply is outside the UK:

- with recovery if the customer belongs outside the EU;
- without recovery in most cases if the customer belongs within the EU.

See Chapter 23, *Partial Exemption* under *Your right to recover input tax* for a fuller explanation.

The starting point for the place of supply

If the place of supply is the UK, you must standard-rate a transaction unless it happens to be zero-rated under the rules noted above, or it is exempt.

The starting point for deciding on the place of supply is that, if the supplier belongs in the UK, the place of supply is here. This is the *starting point* because, in practice, the place of supply often changes under specific provisions. Customs call it the *basic rule*. However, that may imply that it is the usual position. That is not so because, in the majority of cases, one of the various reliefs applies.

Why does the place of supply matter?

The place of supply matters because, if it is the UK, you must charge UK VAT to the customer even if the latter is in a country on the other side of the world.

If the place of supply is not the UK, the supply is not subject to UK VAT. In other words, it is 'outside the scope'.

Some supplies are always standard-rated. There is no automatic relief just because the customer is in another country or the work is done outside the UK.

In practice, there often is a relief enabling you not to charge UK VAT but it is not automatic; you must find a specific rule covering your particular supply.

Examples of standard-rated supplies:

- *Travel costs* are always standard-rated, no matter who the customer is. People from overseas, even those here on business, have to pay VAT on hotel and restaurant meals, car hire and similar travel expenses here. Those who are in business overseas can then reclaim it under the 8th or 13th Directive rules described in Chapter 26, *Recovery of Foreign VAT*.

- *Running repairs to vehicles, light aircraft and the like*. There is a relief for work on goods which are either bought here or brought into the UK, in either case for export once the work has been done. However, if a visitor's car breaks down on a motorway, that does not apply!

- *Services related to land* within the UK are standard-rated, no matter who owns it.

- *Training courses* held in the UK. A non-UK delegate has to pay UK VAT but may then be able to make an 8th or 13th Directive claim to reclaim it.

Transactions on the Internet

Taking orders via the Internet does not of itself change anything. If you then deliver goods in physical form, the normal rules will apply.

It is when you deliver over the Internet in electronic form that there are changes. For instance, computer software bought from a shop is a supply of goods but, downloaded from a web site, it is a supply of services. Such a download might be from a supplier outside the EU or from one EU State to another. Treating the supply as one of services enables it to be taxed as a supply of copyright under licence to a business customer under the reverse charge rules explained later in this chapter.

If a UK business sells a product via a download to a private customer in another EU State, it must charge UK VAT.

If the seller is not VAT registered anywhere in the EU, the supply is dealt with under the *VAT e-commerce Directive 2002/38/EC* and the accompanying *Regulation 792/2002*. These were agreed on 7 May 2002 to come into effect on 1 July 2003 and require the non-EU business to register in one of the Member States.

For the rules on registration in those circumstances, see Chapter 3, *Should I or Must I Register for VAT?* For details of the services in question, see later in this chapter under *Electronic supplies of services to unregistered customers in the EU.*

If your customer is outside the EU, you do not charge VAT, just as, under the rules explained in this chapter, you do not for any other Schedule 5 service.

Schedule 5

The most common reason for not having to charge VAT to a customer outside the UK is that the service is covered by *Sch 5*. This is therefore the logical place to begin studying the place of supply rules.

Actually, *Sch 5* does not contain the relief. It is just a list of services, most of which are taken verbatim from *Article 9(2)(e)* of the *EC 6th VAT Directive*. It is based on what lawyers call a purposive approach and is therefore much more loosely drafted than would be the case if it had originated in UK law. The idea is to ensure common treatment throughout the EU for a range of services typically traded across international frontiers. Examples are royalties, advertising, the services of accountants and lawyers, provision of information and supplies of staff.

A prime objective of the rules is to prevent people avoiding VAT by buying services from a supplier in another country rather than from one in their own. This is achieved in the UK by the rules in *Article 16* of the *Place of Supply of Services Order* ('POSSO'):

Supplies to business customers outside the UK

- *POSSO, Art 16* makes the place of supply the country in which your customer 'belongs'. Your invoice is thus outside the scope of UK VAT.
- If the place of supply is thereby another EU State, tax is collected there through the customer's VAT return in that country at the rate of tax applicable to the supply in that country. This is under the reverse charge rules which are explained later.

Supplies to private EU customers outside the UK

- If a private customer belongs in another EU State, you must standard-rate your supply — the customer has no VAT return on which to pay the tax.

- If a private customer belongs outside the EU, the supply is outside the scope, just as it is for a business one.

The effect of these rules in *POSSO, Art 16* is as follows:

- A business customer in another EU State must account for VAT in that State under the reverse charge — explained on the next page — at the rate applicable in that State, no matter where the supplier is.

- A private customer in the EU has no VAT return so must pay VAT on a Sch 5 service at the rate applicable in the country from which he or she buys it.

So what does Sch 5 cover?

VATA 1994, Sch 5 covers the following services. See the law for the precise wording.

1 Transfers and assignments of copyright, patents, licences, trademarks and similar rights.
2 Advertising services.
3 Services of consultants, engineers, consultancy bureaux, lawyers, accountants and other similar services; data processing and provision of information — excluding services relating to land.
4 Accepting an obligation not to pursue a business activity or to exploit rights within 1 above.
5 Banking, financial and insurance services including reinsurance but not safe deposit facilities.
6 The supply of staff.
7 The hire of goods — except for means of transport.
7A Telecommunications services.
7B Radio and television broadcasting services.
7C Electronically supplied services.
8 Agency services in procuring for another person any of the above services.

Later in this chapter is an explanation of what *paras 1–8* do and do not cover. For the moment, it is sufficient that you have a rough idea of what is in the list.

Sch 5 also contains *paras 9* and *10* but these are not relevant to your *supplies*. They extend the 'reverse charge' on services, which you *purchase* in certain circumstances dealt with later.

Electronic supplies of services to unregistered customers in the EU

The *VAT E-commerce Directive 2002/38/EC* has added new rules from 1/7/03, put into *Sch 5* as *para 7C* and applied in relation to unregistered customers by *POSSO, Art 16A*.

The *e-commerce Directive* sets out the rules under which non-EU businesses are to register in a Member State of their choice and charge VAT on services to private customers at the rate applicable in the State in which the customer belongs. See Chapter 3, *Should I or Must I Register for VAT?* under *Registration due to electronic supplies via the Internet* for more details of the system.

That does not apply to *para 7B*, broadcasting services. A supplier of these to UK consumers must register under the normal rules.

The rules only affect non-EU businesses. A trader in the EU charges VAT to customers in his own State and to private customers in other Member States under the rules explained in the rest of this chapter.

See later for the services covered by *para 7C*.

Communication by e-mail does not of itself mean that a service comes within the above list. Presumably, that means that a lawyer or an accountant could provide professional services by e-mail without the fact of electronic transmission meaning that the supply is caught. Thus, a private customer can continue to buy legal or accountancy services from outside the EU without having to pay VAT thereon.

However, a subscriber to an information service will have to, if the new system is effective in persuading the non-EU supplier to comply with it. In theory, the larger suppliers will comply because they will wish to maintain a good relationship with the EU because of other possible ramifications. That will give a competitive advantage to any smaller one, which believes that the EU will not be able to force it to register and is prepared to risk any possible action against it. It remains to be seen what will happen. The system is temporary for 3 years from 1/7/03, although past experience of such temporary rules suggests that it may well be extended.

The reverse charge (VATA 1994, s 8)

As explained above, a registered trader can buy a Sch 5 service from a supplier in another Member State without paying VAT in that State. Having done so, the reverse charge then applies: VAT is due in the trader's own State and at the rate applicable in that State.

The reverse charge:

- taxes only Sch 5 services; but

- bought from anywhere in the world, not just elsewhere in the EU.

This prevents unregistered or partially exempt traders from avoiding UK VAT by, for example, buying accountancy services from the Channel Islands. It makes no difference whether you buy those accountancy services from within the UK, from another Member State or from outside the EU. You have to account for VAT at the UK standard rate, and you can only recover this if it is attributable to taxable, rather than to exempt outputs.

The way it works

- You self-assess yourself for *output tax* on the sum you pay for each Sch 5 supply — assuming of course that it is standard-rated in the UK.

- You include the VAT in your output tax on your VAT return in the VAT period in which you pay for the supply.

- The corresponding input tax can only be included with your input tax on the return if it is attributable to taxable supplies you make. If it relates to exempt supplies, you cannot recover it. That puts you in the same position as if you had bought from a UK supplier.

The other POSSO services

In addition to the Sch 5 services, *POSSO* makes certain others outside the scope of UK VAT in some circumstances. The rules on these differ from those applicable to Sch 5. If the place of supply is outside the UK, it does not matter who the customer is or where he belongs, and the customer's VAT number is unnecessary. However, the supply of such a service in another EU State will often make you liable to register there — the registration limits in other States tend to be low or non-existent. The services in question are explained later.

The reverse charge created by Sch 5 paras 9 and 10

The UK has added the other *POSSO* services to the reverse charge rules via *Sch 5, paras 9 and 10. Para 9* reads: *Any services not of a description specified in paragraphs 1 to 7 and 8 above when supplied to a recipient who is registered under this Act.*

This does not mean any service at all because it is then restricted by *para 10* to those services, the place of supply of which is the UK under *POSSO*.

The three sources of reverse charge

The difference between the reverse charge:

- applied by *s 8* to *Sch 5, paras 1–8* (but not *para 7A*) services;
- that created by *paras 9* and *10* on the other *POSSO* services;
- and that created if you quote your VAT number for certain other services,

often confuses people. The following explanation may help.

For *paras 1–7 and 8* supplies imported from an EU supplier;

- the place of supply is originally the State of the supplier ;
- but changes to the UK if you buy for the purposes of your business (*s 8*).

For the other *POSSO* services; ie those not covered by *Sch 5* via *Art 16, paras 9 and 10* apply the reverse charge when the place of supply is the UK.

Example

- The place of supply of a service relating to land in the UK is the UK;
- so, if you use an interior designer from another EU State to re-vamp your London offices, that interior designer is potentially liable to register in the UK;
- but, if you account for VAT under the reverse charge, the designer need not register here.
- You quote your VAT number to your supplier, the designer, as evidence that he is not liable to account for UK VAT.

The above applies only to *imports* of para 9 services. Some other EU States have a similar rule but not all of them. Thus, a UK supplier of a service relating to land in another State may have to register there for lack of a reverse charge rule applicable to the supply.

In addition to the above, *Art 14* in certain cases enables you to quote your VAT number to an EU supplier in order to avoid the need for that supplier to charge you his country's VAT.

Example

If a French transport contractor moves your goods from France into Germany, the place of supply is France because the journey begins there. However, it switches to the UK if you quote your VAT number. You then reverse charge the supply.

So, *paras 9* and *10* apply the reverse charge to:

- Various services, such as those related to land and cultural, artistic, sporting and other services if the place of supply is the UK but the supplier is not registered here.

- Transport and agency services supplied outside the UK. They are reverse charged where the supply is treated as made in the UK because you quote your registration number in order to avoid being charged VAT from the supplier's State.

The non-Sch 5 services covered by *POSSO* are, in outline, as follows. See later for more details.

Services relating to land

These are taxable in the State in which the land is (*Art 5*).

Transport services and services ancillary thereto

These are taxable where the transport occurs or the service is performed, but where the transport begins, if that is within the EU (*Arts 6, 7, 8, 9, and 10*) but see below re *Art 14*.

Agency Services

Agency services are taxable in the State in which is taxed the supply on which the commission is earned (*Arts 11, 12 and 13*) but see below re *Art 14*.

Certain services supplied where performed

- artistic, sporting, scientific, educational or entertainment services;
- services relating to exhibitions, conferences or meetings;
- services ancillary to, including organising, any supply of the above;
- valuations of or work on goods.

These are taxable in the State in which the services are physically carried out (*Art 15*) but, for valuations of or work on goods, see below re *Art 14*.

Hire of goods, including means of transport and telecommunications services

The supply of these services is (*Arts 17 and 18*):

- outside the EU if the effective use and enjoyment is outside the EU;

- in the UK if that use is here. If the supply is from a non-UK supplier, the customer then has to account for VAT under the reverse charge rules.

For more on how *Articles 17 and 18* work, see the detailed comment on *Sch 5, paras 7 and 7A* later in this chapter.

Use of customer's registration number under Art 14

If your customer quotes a VAT number to you, the place of supply of the following services changes to the Member State which issued that number.

- intra-EU transport of goods and some agency services;

- valuations of or work on goods which then leave the UK;

- services ancillary to the intra-EU transport of goods.

Liability to register

The value of *paras 1–8 services* received counts towards the registration limit. An unregistered organisation therefore might have to register for VAT purely in order to account for reverse-charged services.

This applies only to *paras 1–8*. Receiving services for which the place of supply is the UK under other parts of *POSSO* does not make you liable to register.

Do I need my customer's VAT number?

For services within *Sch 5 paras 1–8*, a VAT number is not necessary in law. However, getting the number is evidence that the customer is in business. You do need the VAT number as a matter of law for those services covered by the rest of *POSSO*.

The rules on belonging

Where you or your customer *belongs* is often important. Although it is usually obvious, that is not always so.

Suppliers

Article 9(1) of the *6th Directive* says that the place where a service is supplied shall be deemed to be the place:

- where the supplier has established his business; or

- has a fixed establishment from which the service is supplied.

Customers

Article 9(2)(e) says that, for *Sch 5* services, the place of supply is:

- where the customer has established his business; or

- has a fixed establishment to which the service is supplied.

UK law

Section 9, which puts that into UK law, says that, in both cases, a trader belongs in a country if:

- he has there a business establishment or some other fixed establishment and that;
- if he has such establishments in more than one country, it is the establishment:
  – which is most directly concerned with the supply in the case of a supplier;
  – at which or for the purposes of which the services are most directly used or to be used in the case of a customer.

Section 9(5) says that a person carrying on a business through a branch or agency in any country shall be treated as having a business establishment there.

The belonging rules may sound simple but here are some of the arguments, which they have caused.

Services to a Jersey company owning a London flat

WH Payne & Co ([1995] V & DR 490) concerned accountancy and tax advice in respect of letting a London flat, which Payne supplied to a company registered in the British Virgin Isles but managed from Jersey. *Payne's* client, Trafalgar, was held to have *established its business* in one of the latter places.

It did not belong in the UK at its flat. The flat was what it supplied, not a fixed establishment from which it made supplies.

In *Berkholz ([1985] 3 CMLR 667)* a CJEC case concerning gaming machines on a ferry, the Advocate General commented that a fixed establishment must be of a certain minimum size and that the human and technical resources necessary for the provision of the services must be permanently present.

There were no such resources at Trafalgar's flat to enable it to receive Payne's services.

A subsidiary can constitute a fixed establishment of its parent

DFDS A/S was a Danish company supplying package tours. These were marketed in the UK through its subsidiary *DFDS Ltd* which acted as the UK central booking office and provided administration services. The contracts were in the name of the Danish company. The UK subsidiary received 19% commission and was reimbursed its UK marketing costs. It had premises and staff in the UK.

The European Court of Justice (*Case C-260/95*) held:

- *DFDS Ltd* was wholly owned. In the contractual circumstances it was not independent, merely an auxiliary organ of *A/S*.
- It possessed the necessary human and technical resources to make the supplies in the UK.
- It was to be regarded as a fixed establishment of the parent and as the establishment from which the supplies were made.

The Court commented that:

- where a business was established; and
- where it had some other fixed establishment,

were both primary criteria for deciding the place of supply. The first preference was normally the place where the business was established. However, if that did not lead to a rational result or if it created a conflict with another Member State, the possibility of the supply being made at a fixed establishment must be considered.

DFDS is an important constraint on any cunning plan to escape charging UK VAT by setting up in another country and using a UK agent to carry out whatever might need doing here.

In *RAL (Channel Islands) Ltd, RAL Ltd, RAL Services Ltd, RAL Machines Ltd (LON/01/1979 No 17914)*, the place of supply of gaming machines in UK amusement arcades was held to be the UK. The arcades were fixed establishments of a Channel Islands company formed for the purpose of renting the sites and the machines and which arranged for their maintenance by companies in the same group as itself. The services company was acting as a mere auxiliary of the Channel Islands company which was therefore making supplies from the arcades.

A company can belong at its registered office

In *Binder Hamlyn ([1983] VATTR 171), Jamaica Sugar Estates Ltd* was held to belong at its registered office in *Binder Hamlyn's* offices for the purpose of receiving company registration services including maintaining the UK share register. This was despite *Jamaica* having no trading activity in the UK and it meant that *Binder Hamlyn's* services were standard-rated.

Similarly, in *Vincent Consultants ([1988] VATTR 152)*, handling a company's statutory and tax returns was held to be standard-rated because the establishment at which the services were used was its UK registered office.

Usual place of residence of an individual

In *USAA Ltd (LON/92/1950 No 10369)*, which sold motor insurance, the 'usual place of residence' of US officers on three-year tours of duty in the UK was held to be the UK even if they still owned houses in the USA. However, in *SA Razzak and M A Mishari (LON/97/754 No 15240)*, it was held that:

- 'Usual place of residence' in *s 9(3)* gives effect to the *EC 6th VAT Directive, Art 9(2)(e)* wording 'the place where he has his permanent address or usually resides'.
- 'Permanent' means the antithesis of purely temporary and having a sufficient degree of permanence.

An Indian domestic servant had been brought to the UK under a domestic workers concession. After leaving her employers, she stayed in Asian women's refuges for four years with temporary visa extensions until her action for damages for mistreatment was settled. She only remained in the UK in order to pursue the case and for lack of money to return to India to look after her children. Her usual place of residence was held to be India.

USAA Ltd was distinguished because the officers were in the UK voluntarily on three-year tours of duty, which might be extended. The Tribunal was obviously sympathetic to the unfortunate circumstances of the case and therefore stretched that logic to its limit.

Beware of multiple belonging

A customer could belong in the UK as well as elsewhere in the EU. If he belongs here in the capacity in which he receives the services, your supply to him is standard-rated.

Where does an individual belong, who owns homes in London and Bermuda and spends six months of the year at each? The nature of the services provided may suggest one country or the other.

Is your EU customer in business?

If your customer belongs in the EU, that customer must receive the supply for the purpose of a business carried on by him *(POSSO, Art 16(b))*. Otherwise, your supply is standard-rated.

To check the VAT number, name and address of an EU trader, ring the *NAS*. See page viii. The electronic checking systems on the EU and Customs websites are pointless because they can only confirm the validity of the number, not that it belongs to the trader whose name and address you quote.

Usually, it will be self-evident that your customer is in business. However, do not take that for granted. Here are some examples of possible pitfalls.

Government bodies, municipal authorities and similar bodies

In para 11.7 of Notice 741 (March 2002) *Place of supply of services*, Customs say that government bodies, municipal authorities and similar bodies are not in business. Although they add the proviso 'unless the services are specifically received for the purposes of a business activity', I think that the statement is misleading. UK local authorities engage in numerous businesses, such as the running of car parks and leisure centres.

This may be less so in other Member States and I understand that most of them do not register their local authorities. Customs' view is presumably based on *Omnicom UK plc (LON/93/2441 No 12605: [1996] STC 398*) heard in the Divisional Court as *Diversified Agency Supplies*. On the basis of the available evidence, which showed that the Spanish Tourist Office in Spain appeared to be not an independent body but under the control of a Government Ministry, Omnicom's customer was held not to be in business. The Divisional Court confirmed that a customer must not just be VAT registered but must receive the supply in question for the purpose of a business. However, that seems to me to be judicial theory!

Common sense suggests that, provided that the organisation can quote you a VAT number, your supply should be outside the scope of VAT: it should then be for the fiscal authority of the other country to determine whether your client was in business in the capacity in which it bought your services. Only that authority is in the position to gather all the necessary information. However, the Divisional Court rejected that argument. There is therefore a pitfall in such situations.

Is a tourist office in business?

There have been three UK tribunal cases concerning whether tourist offices are in business. In *Turespana (Spanish Tourist Office LON/96/002 No 14568)*, which followed on from the *Omnicom* case discussed above, the London office of the Spanish Tourist Office failed in an argument that it was in business in the UK and therefore entitled to recover all its input tax.

The Chairman in *Turespana* questioned the decision in *Netherlands Board of Tourism (LON/94/607 No 12935)*, which I had previously won. However, I then won *Austrian National Tourist Office (LON/96/0674 No 15561)*, thus confirming that it is possible for a tourist office to be in business.

Customs have continued to question the status of tourist offices case-by-case. Although they have given in in two more cases, where my client's appeal did not reach a formal hearing, this has been after a detailed examination of the facts of each case. It follows that Customs might well dispute whether a tourist office in another Member State was in business.

International research establishments

A similar problem arises with research bodies, which are largely funded by government. In the UK, these are legally independent in most, if not all cases. In the ones where I have advised, there has been substantial business income so they have been registered for VAT. Nevertheless, most of the input tax incurred relates to non-business fundamental research rather than to the making of taxable supplies.

Suppose you are supplying services to such a body in another Member State. How will you persuade Customs that your client is buying your services for the purpose of its business activities rather than its non-business ones? The same comments apply as those made above concerning local authorities.

Electronic services

If you supply electronic services covered by *Sch 5 para 7C*, take extra care if your sales to a customer exceed £500 either per transaction or in total per quarter. Customs expect you to check with them the VAT number quoted to you.

They also expect you to check if you have any reason for suspicion of a number quoted to you — including that your supply is of an item such as music, a computer game, a film etc, not normally sold to a business customer.

Detailed comment on the Sch 5 services

Below are some detailed comments on the Sch 5 services based partly on Customs' published guidance in Notice 741 *Place of Supply of Services* and partly on some important court decisions.

Be careful how you interpret *Sch 5*. In the past, everyone has tended to assume that headings, such as the professional services in *para 3*, can be interpreted broadly. Two CJEC decisions explained later in this chapter, *Hoffmann* concerning arbitration and *Lindthorst* on veterinary services, show that one must not take it for granted that a service is covered just because it seems as if it ought to be.

Customs have always maintained that the reference in *para 3* to *engineers* means professional engineers, not people who work on machines such as motor mechanics. Now, there are warning signs concerning the services of accountants. Anyone can call themselves an accountant and much accountancy work is relatively low level book-keeping whether or not it is done on a computer. Customs already say that clerical and secretarial services, office facilities and archiving services are not covered by *para 3*. I have doubts about the status of book-keeping charges, as opposed to those for accounting expertise and advice.

So, do not take *Sch 5* for granted. It is not all-inclusive. Consider carefully the nature of the service which was supplied and make sure that the wording on your invoice explains it properly. Note: *paras 7B* and *7C* were added from 1/7/03.

Management charges

The phrase *management charge* is an example of the kind of superficial wording sometimes seen on invoices, which is potentially dangerous! It is used to cover different things in different circumstances; often it is merely a means of moving profit from one legal entity to another. Of course, corporation tax rules and their equivalent in other countries mean that you have to justify a management charge. You do for VAT too.

Management charges are not mentioned in *Sch 5*. However, they are generally accepted as covered by it provided that you can show that at least some element of a Sch 5 service is provided. Para 3 services of consultancy, accountancy, data processing etc are amongst the most obvious but advertising, the supply of staff and interest on inter-company loans are other possibilities.

Sch 5 para 1: Transfers and assignments of copyright, patents, licences, trade marks and similar rights

Examples:

- royalties from granting limited rights, ownership of copyright remaining with originator;

- a franchise fee;

- producing a cinema film for a distributor;

- a licence to use computer software.

Sch 5 para 2: Advertising services

This covers:

- all actual advertising on TV and radio, in press, on internet etc;

- sponsorship — payments in return for publicity in relation to an event or activity;

- trade events, demonstrations and public relations activities in promoting the business of an individual client as part of a campaign;

- the means of advertising; ie master films and tapes, photographs and printing blocks.

It does not cover supplies to people providing advertising services: ie actors to producer of an advertising film.

In *Phil Lawrence (LON/94/1233 No 13092)*, the distribution of envelopes was held not to be advertising. The tribunal distinguished between an advertising service and services, such as distribution, which enabled it to be provided.

Para 2 may also cover arranging an advertising exhibition or meeting. If the essential purpose is advertising, public relations and other services included in supply are covered though not services used by individuals such as hotel meals or rooms. The authority for this is the decision in *EC Commission v France (case C-68/92)* in which the CJEC said that it was possible for a social function, such as a cocktail party, to qualify as advertising.

However, in *Austrian National Tourist Office (LON/96/0674 No 15561)*, I failed to persuade the Tribunal that, when *ANTO* organised an informal workshop and promoted it to the UK travel trade, it was supplying advertising services.

The Tribunal rejected this saying:

- The CJEC had merely decided that France (and Luxembourg and Spain) were wrong to distinguish between pure advertising and promotional activities, such as meetings. The latter *could* be advertising.

- The CJEC had in mind promotional activities for a single client.

- There was a distinction between a meeting, which enabled a client to put across a message as part of an advertising campaign and providing businesses with an opportunity to attend an event at which they did the work of promotion themselves.

Schedule 5 is not all-inclusive!

Sch 5 para 3: Services of the following

- consultants (not medical consultants);

- engineers (usually professionally qualified);

- consultancy bureaux;

- lawyers;

- accountants and other similar services;

- data processing and provision of information;

- but excluding any service relating to land.

Paragraph 3 is seen by Customs as covering professional type services. Thus an accountant using professional skills is covered but routine bookkeeping may be thought borderline — see below re clerical services. Similarly, engineering services are seen as those of qualified professionals rather than of mechanics.

The comments below represent Customs' views. The law contains none and there have been few tribunal cases. These comments therefore cannot be definitive.

Consultancy services

These include:

- management services if essentially of a type covered by *Sch 5*;

- market research;

- research and development;

- written translation services. For oral interpretation services, see later under *Services supplied where performed*;

- testing and analysis of goods such as drugs, chemicals and domestic appliances, etc on the basis that this is the analysis by experts who use the test results as the basis for a professional opinion about the goods;

- writing scientific reports;

- designing, updating or maintaining computer software. But maintaining computer hardware is work on goods.

Not included are:

- management services unless essentially consultancy in nature;

- clerical and secretarial services, office facilities and archiving services.

Customs also say in Notice 741 (12.4.7), that clerical or secretarial services include the keeping of financial records. Presumably, they see this as routine work not requiring professional skills — though see also Fiscal agents under *Similar services*, below.

Consultancy - Arbitration Services

Would you expect services of arbitration provided by a lawyer to qualify either as legal services or as consultancy?

In *Bernd von Hoffmann (Case C-145/96: [1997] STC 1321)*, the CJEC ruled that they did not. The arbitrator, a member of a tribunal sitting in Paris, must charge German VAT! Though he was a law professor who drew upon his legal expertise when acting as an arbitrator his services were not those of a lawyer. A lawyer normally provided services presenting or defending the interests of a particular client whereas those of an arbitrator were principally settling a dispute between two or more parties.

The services were not those of a consultant because consultants did not habitually settle disputes between two or more parties.

The Court overruled the Advocate General who had noted that lawyers habitually provided advice to clients and negotiation on their behalf as well as legal representation. In rejecting that view, the Court disagreed with the AG's opinion that the services of an arbitrator chosen for his legal expertise were similar to those of lawyers. 'Similar' meant 'to serve the same purpose'. Negotiation depended on expediency and weighing-up of interests whereas arbitration was based on justice or equity.

Accountancy services

In *Aspen Advisory Services Ltd (LON/94/2773 No 13489)*, services of managing property and collecting rents under a contract to act as 'managing agents of the property' were held to be a single supply relating to land. It would be artificial to separate a part as accountancy so the place of supply was where the land was.

Engineers' services

Customs regard this as meaning 'intellectual' services. They include editors and sound engineers making a master tape or disk but not physical work such as by mechanics or in installing goods.

In *Component Holdings Ltd (LON/92/906 No 10371)* the provision of an editing suite to process confidential material was held to be the hire of goods, the engineering service of setting it up and maintaining it being merely an element of the hire service.

In *Mechanical Engineering Consultants Ltd (MAN/93/1074 No 13287)*, the services of a consulting engineer concerning an incinerator complex were held to be services relating to land. Even though much of the plant was moveable, the complex had to be looked at as a whole. In consequence *para 3* did not apply and the place of supply was where the land was.

Similar services

Customs say that this covers services of:

- loss adjusters and assessors — except where the claim relates to land;
- architects and surveyors not relating to specific sites;
- fiscal agents in completing VAT returns (where the customer does not belong in the UK);
- design;
- creative or artistic services of specialists or technicians;
- film directors or producers;
- management services amounting to the corporate or strategic guidance of another company.

Provision of information includes

- tourist information;
- private enquiry services;
- weather forecasts;
- telephone helpdesk services such as for computer software;
- satellite navigational and locational services;
- on-line information by computer including non-fiction publications. Examples are academic articles, biographies, educational material, encyclopaedias, maps, news services and travel guides.

Sch 5 para 4: Acceptance of obligation not to exercise para 1 rights

One does not often come across *paragraph 4*; it would cover a non-competition agreement by the vendor of a business.

Sch 5 para 5: Banking, financial and insurance services (including reinsurance, but not including the provision of safe deposit facilities)

Most banking, financial and insurance services are exempt in the UK under *Sch 9*.

Thus, the change in status to outside the scope only affects the *output tax position* of those which are standard rated in the UK. However, the impact on *input tax recovery* can be important. See *How the right to recover affects banking, finance and insurance* in Chapter 23, *Partial Exemption*.

Para 5 excludes safe deposit facilities — but see *Article 9(e), EC 6th VAT Directive*, which reads *hire of safes*.

Definition of 'financial' services

A rent collection service is not a financial service. In *Culverpalm Ltd ([1984] VATTR 199)* a tribunal held that a property management service was not a financial service in the context of 'banking, financial and insurance services'; nor was the rent collection element. Financial services meant primarily those 'relating to money, foreign currency and securities therefor'. This conclusion was reinforced by the exclusion from *para 3* of services relating to land.

Fees for work which has a financial flavour, such as investment advice, portfolio management and merger or takeover advice, may qualify under para 3 as consultancy services.

Standard-rated services which become outside the scope under para 5

Not all financial services are exempt. Here are some examples of standard-rated ones, which become outside the scope under *paragraph 5*.

- commodity brokers' commissions on futures and options in those cases where zero-rating under the Terminal Markets rules does not apply;
- debt collection services;
- portfolio management services;
- trustee services.

Exempt financial services becoming outside the scope under para 5

- Interest charged to a foreign borrower;
- Storage of gold bullion or gold coins by a bank or by a dealer, which is a subsidiary of a bank — this is seen as a banking service. (see Notice 741 (March 2002), para 12.6.2);
- Sale of securities as a principal — normally but not necessarily on a stock exchange — to a buyer who belongs outside the UK;
- Underwriting of share issues and stockbroking commissions;
- Sale of *unallocated* gold, gold coins, silver, platinum or palladium. 'Unallocated' means that specific goods are not designated as the property of the purchaser,

who merely has a claim to an unidentified part of the total stocks of the vendor. The supply is therefore one of services, not goods (*Sch 1 para 1*). Customs accept that the service is financial because of the nature of these goods.

Sch 5 para 6: The supply of staff

Paragraph 6 does not cover work done in your office by your staff. Do not confuse the provision of staff with a service provided by you, such as using your employees to maintain records for a client.

'Staff' means people under the general control and direction of your client. They will usually work on his premises, not yours, and take their instructions from him, not you.

Sch 5 para 7: The letting on hire of goods other than means of transport

Paragraph 7, via *POSSO, Art 16*, makes the hire of goods, *other than a means of transport*, outside the scope of VAT on the same terms as the rest of *Sch 5*. *Articles 17 and 18* then qualify the *Sch 5/Art 16* rules to provide that:

- A hirer of goods, *including a means of transport*, is making a supply in the UK if the services are effectively used and enjoyed here. A non-EU hirer is therefore liable to register here.

- Where the services are effectively used and enjoyed outside the EU, the supply is outside the scope of UK VAT even though the supplier or the customer may belong in the UK.

If an operator is supplied to operate a machine, the supply depends on the nature of the work done. It is not the hire of goods.

Para 3.6 of Notice 741 (March 2002) says that a *yacht hired for racing* is a means of transport as is a *train leased to a railway museum*. So is a *road tanker hired separately from its tractor unit* because it has wheels.

However, Customs do not regard a *freight container* as a means of transport. Containers are therefore covered by *para 7*, which covers the hire of other goods. Notice 703/1 deals with freight containers.

In *IDS Aircraft Ltd (LON/93/2864 No 12452)* the effective use and enjoyment of a light aircraft used by a lessee based in Jersey was held to be in the countries visited or flown over, not where the lessee belonged.

In *Derry Bros (LON/00/1323 No 17701)*, refrigerated trailers were held to be means of transport.

Sch 5 para 7A: Telecommunication services

See the law for the detailed wording. It covers the sending or receiving of material by electronic or similar communications systems, ie:

- telephone services including calls, switching, leased lines etc;

- satellite transmission services;

- fax, telex and multi-messaging;

- access to global information networks;
- charges for transmission capacity

Sch 5 para 7B: Radio and television broadcasting services

Para 7B was added from 1/7/03 by *SI 2003/86*. An example is a subscription for satellite or cable television. Transmitting the programmes for the broadcaster is covered by *para 7A*, not *para 7B*.

Sch 5 para 7C: Electronically supplied services, for example —

(a) website supply, web hosting and distance maintenance of programmes and equipment;

(b) software including updates;

(c) pictures, text, information and databases;

(d) music, films and games including gambling games;

(e) political, cultural, artistic, sporting, scientific and entertainment broadcasts including broadcasts of events;

(f) distance teaching.

The above services are intended to be those which are supplied automatically with little or no human intervention. Thus, distance teaching would not include a course in which there was significant contact between the student and the teacher, the Internet being a communication tool. Similarly, the professional services of an accountant or a lawyer are not electronic merely because the advice is sent by e-mail. *Para 7C* was added from 1/7/03 by *SI 2003/86*.

VAT Information Sheet 4/03 (April 2003) provides further detailed comment, which may help if you are in doubt about the coverage of *para 7C*.

The use and enjoyment rules applicable to paras 7A–C

Paragraphs 7A–C work via *POSSO Art 16* in the same way as the rest of *Sch 5*. However, the *effective use and enjoyment* rules in *Arts 17 & 18* then qualify the *Sch 5/Art 16* rules to provide that:

- a non-EU provider of telecommunication, radio or TV broadcasting services is making a supply in the UK if the services are effectively used and enjoyed here and is therefore liable to register here;
- where the services are effectively used and enjoyed outside the EU, the supply is outside the scope of UK VAT even though the supplier or the customer may belong in the UK.

That applies to the *para 7C* electronically supplied services only if received by the customer for the purposes of a business. However, since Customs recognise that a non business customer will normally use the services where he belongs, they say in *VAT Information Sheet 1/2003* that, if an existing accounting system is set up to tax supplies where they are effectively used and enjoyed, this can be applied to electronically supplied services, provided that it does not lead to abuse.

The meaning of *use and enjoyment*

Customs define *use and enjoyment* as occurring where the customer actually consumes the service irrespective of contract, payment or beneficial interest. They say that it only changes the place of supply as between the UK and outside the EU. If the place of supply of a service is in the UK or elsewhere in the EU, that does not alter if it is used and enjoyed in a different Member State.

Customs quote the example of a web hosting service supplied to a business in the USA. Although the supply is received in the USA, it is subject to UK VAT to the extent that it is used in the UK.

On the other hand, an electronic information service supplied by one UK business to another is used and enjoyed outside the EU to the extent that it is used in a non-EU country. In such situations, keep a record of how you arrive at any apportionment you make.

Sch 5 para 8: The services rendered by one person to another in procuring for the other any of the services mentioned in paras 1 to 7C above

Note the pitfall in *procuring for*, which appears to mean obtaining a supply for the customer, not getting an order for a supplier. If charging a commission to a *supplier*, consider whether the place of supply rules for agency services in *POSSO, Arts 11, 12 and 13* help.

More on the rest of POSSO

POSSO, Art 16 covers the Sch 5 services. As noted earlier, other articles change the place of supply for a variety of other services. Here are some more details.

Services relating to land

POSSO, Art 5 makes a service related to land taxable in the State in which the land is. It covers, for example:

- holiday property lettings;

- work on buildings and civil engineering work;

- services of estate agents, architects, surveyors and the like including, for instance, seismic survey and associated data processing services.

Work on buildings can include installing or dismantling a machine.

If the land is in the UK, a supply relating to it is standard rated to a foreign customer. In *McLean and Gibson (Engineers) Ltd (EDN/01/119 No 17500)*, dismantling a massive paper making machine 50–60 yards long and weighing 4–500 tons, a task which took three months, was held to be a supply relating to land. The charge to the foreign buyer for the work, including packing and delivering it to the port, was therefore standard rated. *Note:* the possibility that the work could have been zero rated under *Sch 8, Group 7, Item 1* as work on goods, which are then exported, does not appear to have been considered by the Tribunal. See later in this chapter.

For a case about the services of a consulting engineer concerning an incinerator complex, see under *Engineers' services* in the commentary concerning *Sch 5, para 3* earlier in this chapter.

A service is not caught by *Article 5* just because it involves land. Administering a deceased's estate which includes land or the advertising or insurance of overseas property are not covered. Nor is general advice re the property market as opposed to services concerning a specific property.

Legal services are often in relation to a contract term, rather than to the land to which the contract related and are therefore covered by *Sch 5, para 3* via *Article 16*, not *Article 5*. An example is legal advice to a mortgagee concerning a mortgagor's default. The hire of space at an exhibition is covered by *Article 15*. See below.

Transport services and services ancillary thereto

Articles 6, 7, 8, 9 and 10 deal with the transport of passengers or goods in a variety of situations. Normally, the place of supply is where the transport takes place or the service is performed. However, the transport of goods within the EU is treated as made in the State in which it begins (*Art 10*).

A pleasure cruise is treated as the transport of passengers, which includes any education or training during it (*Arts 2 and 8*).

If the journey is between two points in the same country without visiting another, the entire supply is made there even if part of the journey is outside its territorial limits (*Art 7*).

Examples of ancillary transport services are:

- Loading, unloading, or reloading;

- Stowing;

- Opening for inspection;

- Cargo security services;

- Preparing or amending bills of lading, airway bills and certificates of shipment;

- Storage.

Services supplied where performed

EC 6th VAT Directive, Art 9(2)(c) says that *the place of supply of services relating to:*

- *cultural, artistic, sporting, scientific, educational, entertainment or similar activities, including the activities of the organisers of such activities, and where appropriate, the supply of ancillary services …*

- *ancillary transport activities such as loading, unloading, handling and similar activities,*

- *valuations of moveable tangible property,*

- *work on moveable tangible property,*

shall be the place where those services are physically carried out.

POSSO, Art 15 is not in precisely those terms. For instance, it does not mention *similar activities* although it does cover *services relating to exhibitions, conferences or meetings* which the UK has interpreted *similar activities* to include.

Examples quoted by Customs in Notice 741:

- Singer or actor performing before a live audience — but work in a recording studio is a *Sch 5 para 1* supply of rights.

- Services ancillary to a live performance, such as make-up or hairdressing.

- Oral interpreters working at an event, such as a conference.

- Sale of a nomination to a stallion standing at a stud.

Where the *Art 15* services are performed outside the UK, they are outside the scope of UK VAT. If the place of supply is in another EU State, the supplier may have to register there unless, like the UK, the State has extended the reverse charge rules to cover these supplies when made to VAT registered persons.

Work on goods

Physical work is required, not mere inspection. However, in *Banstead Manor Stud (LON/78/412 No 816)* the care and handling of a mare attending a stallion was held to be an essential adjunct to the services of the stallion.

Sporting services

In *John Village Automotive Ltd (MAN/96/1384 No 15540)*, charges to sponsors of a racing team were held to be predominantly supplies of advertising rather than sporting services.

Ancillary services

An example of an *ancillary service* is that of an organiser of an exhibition, who works on behalf of the exhibition owner. The place of supply of the organising service is where it is performed. This is not necessarily the event location.

In *J Dudda v Finanzamt Bergisch (C-327/94)*, the CJEC ruled that an engineer, who provided the sound amplification at a public event, performed an ancillary service because it was a pre-requisite to the performance of the artists at the event. The place of supply was thus the country in which the event took place.

In *Sugar and Spice on Tour Catering (MAN/99/1053 No 17698)*, a tribunal adopted that purposive approach in holding that catering was also ancillary. Thus, the place of supply of catering at events to performers and the touring organisation, arranged by the tour manager but paid for by each promoter, was the State in which the event took place.

Veterinary services

Suppose a Dutch vet supplies services to cattle farmers in Belgium. Where is the supply taxed? In *Maatschap MJM Linthorst, KG Pouwels en J Sheres (C-167/95: [1997] STC 1287)*, the CJEC ruled that the place of supply of the services of a veterinary surgeon is the place where he has established his business or has a fixed establishment from which the services are supplied.

The service was the scientific assessment of the health of animals, taking preventative medical action and treating sick animals. Presumably this was not seen as a scientific service. Nor did it qualify as 'consultancy'.

Thus UK VAT must be charged on veterinary services performed in another EU state for a non-UK client.

Conferences and exhibitions

As noted at the start of the comments under *Services supplied where performed,* the wording of *Art 9(2)(c)* of the *EC 6th VAT Directive* has not been applied precisely in *Art 15* of *POSSO . Similar activities* has been interpreted as *services relating to exhibitions, conferences or meetings*.

Conferences, meetings etc come in all shapes and sizes ranging from major international conferences and exhibitions to company meetings, training courses and public relations events such as product launches and press conferences. Organising them requires a wide range of services by various types of business.

For a public conference at which places are sold, the place of supply *by the promoter/owner* must be where it is held. On the other hand, Customs accept in para 5.7 of Notice 741 (March 2002) *Place of supply of services* that someone, who organises an event on behalf of the promoter/owner, may be supplying those services from the office where the work is done rather than at the event location. Similarly, Customs say that a trade organisation, which provides a package of services, such as exhibition space, consultancy, design of the stand and so on, supplies those services *where they are physically carried out.*

That is inadequate comment, as is revealed by the next paragraph, which says that a comprehensive package of services is supplied at the exhibition in question. That does make sense on the grounds that a package, which includes stand space, must be essentially a supply of that space. Such a supply can only be at the event, even though other services, such as stand design, are supplied. However, Customs then say that, if the event is in another Member State but the UK supplier does not have to account for VAT there and the services are otherwise physically carried out here, the supply is in the UK.

I question whether that is correct. It is not practicable for the place of supply to depend upon whether an individual Member State enforces the rules correctly!

Then there is the problem of the public relations company, which arranges an event on behalf of its client. An instance I met was the organisation, in another Member State, of a conference for distributors of the products of a non-EU company. My client merely did the organisation, including selecting the location and most of this work took place in the UK. Places at the conference were sold by the non-EU company on whose behalf it was organised.

Representatives from the PR company did attend but were there only in a supporting role, everything on the day being handled by the non-EU company. Arguably therefore, the main supply took place in the UK, not at the event. The VAT authorities in the other Member State initially demanded VAT on the PR company's services but then accepted that the place of supply was the UK.

However, in the light of the *Dudda* case on ancillary services, explained above, the position must be doubtful where there is any attendance in the other country. If a public relations company organises an event, it may be in charge of the organisation with the executives of its client company merely responsible for the technical content of the presentation. Of course, organising a press conference might qualify as a supply of advertising and therefore be subject to the place of supply rules for *Sch 5* suppliers rather than that for a service relating to a meeting.

A further point is when a service becomes ancillary to an event rather than merely a supply to the promotor or organiser in the latter's country. The answer is likely to depend on the precise facts — as so often!

If you sell a package of services for delegates attending an event including travel and hotel accommodation, the *Tour Operators Margin Scheme* might apply. See Chapter 36.

Training

Art 15 makes the place of supply of education where it is performed. This means that a commercial training course in the UK is standard-rated, no matter where the delegates come from. Those from outside the UK have to make *8th* or *13th Directive* claims to recover the VAT, as explained in Chapter 26.

Do not confuse standard-rated commercial training with that provided by universities and other eligible bodies, which is exempt under *Sch 9 Group 5* as explained in Chapter 11, *What is Exempt?*.

Para 3.17 in Notice 48 (March 2002) *Extra Statutory Concessions* allows zero rating where the charge is to a foreign government. The conditions are:

- The supply must be for the purpose of the sovereign activities of the foreign government;
- The supplier must obtain a written statement from the government or its accredited representative that the trainees are employed in those activities.

The relief is intended to cover training in the UK of officials, public servants, armed forces, police, emergency services and similar bodies answerable to the government concerned.

It does not apply to staff of state-owned businesses or sponsored commercial organisations such as state airlines for which claims must be made under the *8th* or *13th Directives*.

Means of transport — use and enjoyment rules

For comment on *Arts 17 and 18* and the use and enjoyment rules, see earlier re *Sch 5 para 7*.

The zero-ratings in Sch 8

As mentioned earlier, *Sch 8 Groups 7, 8 and 13* zero-rate specific services.

Group 7 'International Services'

Item 1 zero-rates work on goods, which are subsequently exported from the EU. The work must be prearranged but the goods can be either imported into the EU or acquired within it with a view to doing the work.

Item 2 zero-rates agency services in arranging for:

- an export of goods outside the EU;
- work on goods where the work is zero rated under Item 1;
- any supply of services made outside the EU, except those insurance and financial services which would be exempt in the UK under *Sch 9 Groups 2 and 5*. This is because these are dealt with under the *Sch 5* rules.

Thus an agency commission to a UK manufacturer on a sale of goods dispatched to an EU customer is standard-rated because the goods have not been exported. Of course, the UK manufacturer will recover VAT on the commission.

If you do not understand why the goods were not exported, see Chapter 19 on *Exports of Goods* for the difference between an export and a removal.

Group 8 'Transport'

This Group covers a variety of services as noted in the chapter on zero-rating. They include services connected with movement of goods in or out of the EU.

Group 13 'Imports, Exports, etc'

This Group covers three miscellaneous cases, which are concerned primarily with goods although one does cover services connected with international defence projects. See Chapter 10, *So What is Zero-rated?* for more comment.

VAT groups — Sch 5 anti-avoidance rule

An anti-avoidance rule in *s 43(2A)* affects you if:

- The UK branch of an overseas company is included in your VAT group; and
- That overseas affiliate supplies the UK companies in your VAT group, via its branch, with Sch 5 services, which it has bought in.

Such a situation is not caught by the reverse charge because there is no supply of services between branches of the same legal entity. Customs were worried that international groups might arrange for services, such as telecommunications, to be billed to an overseas company rather than to the one actually using the services and that the charge could then be passed back through the UK branch. As there would be no VAT on a charge between the branch and another company in the same VAT group, non-recoverable VAT could be avoided.

Some VAT advisers thought that such a scheme would not work because the supply was to the user company in the first place and addressing the invoice overseas would not change that. However, Customs decided to take no chances so we have an anti-avoidance rule.

The rule is not confined to services sourced in the UK. It catches, for instance, legal services from a US lawyer bought by a US company, A Inc and re-charged to a UK subsidiary B Ltd via the UK branch of A Inc. Thus, this is a classic example of aggressive tax planning leading to anti-avoidance measures, which have a wider impact than the original problem.

The rule taxes the Sch 5 service by creating a self-supply by the representative member of the group, the tax point being the date of payment for the supply. The output tax thereby created is only recoverable to the extent that it can be attributed to taxable supplies. You can reduce the value of the supply if the service in question is made up partly of bought in Sch 5 services and partly from in-house resources, such as the overseas company's legal department.

Remember that the problem only arises when the branch of the overseas affiliate, through which the charge from the overseas company is passed, is a member of the UK VAT group. If the affiliate's UK branch is not VAT grouped, any onward charge by it to other UK companies will be standard-rated.

The rules affect all businesses, not just those which are partly exempt though, of course, there is no loss of VAT if the reverse charge tax can be attributed to a taxable supply.

That is just an outline of the rules intended to help you check whether you are affected. If you are, you will need to study the law.

Some questions to check your understanding. Review your answers with the text.

- How many supplies on which VAT must be charged to customers from outside the UK can you remember? Four were mentioned at the start of this chapter.

- Including *para 7A*, there are nine categories of service covered by *Sch 5*. How many can you remember?

- In addition to the Sch 5 services, POSSO contains rules on the place of supply for five other main categories of service. How many can you remember?

- If you are selling a Sch 5 service to a customer, who has offices in two or more countries, how do you establish where that customer belongs for the purpose of your supply?

- When selling a Sch 5 service to a customer within the EU, what fact about that customer do you have to establish in order not to charge UK VAT?

- Does the reverse charge apply to the services of a lawyer in Japan when bought by a UK business?

- The reverse charge does not only apply to Sch 5 services bought from non-UK suppliers. It also applies to two other kinds of situation under various articles of POSSO. What are they?

- In what circumstances does the anti-avoidance rule apply to imports of Sch 5 services?

23. Partial Exemption

This chapter explains the situation called partial exemption which occurs when a business has both exempt and taxable outputs. Such a business calculates the VAT, which it can recover, using a partial exemption method. Although they can be straightforward, partial exemption situations are often amongst the more complex aspects of VAT.

Do not confuse partial exemption with business/non-business situations. An example of the latter is a charity, which raises money through a business activity, such as retail shops. Its main charitable activity is non-business and the VAT related to that is not even input tax, let alone recoverable input tax. However, the charity can recover the VAT related to the business side. Chapter 27, *Am I in Business?* deals with some situations where at least a part of an activity does not amount to carrying on a business.

In practice, the method of arriving at the VAT related to the business side of an organisation is often the same as for partial exemption. Anyone involved in a business/non-business situation should therefore read this chapter.

Incidentally, partial exemption is one of those subjects where the main principles are relatively straightforward but applying them in practice is much more complicated because of the infinite variety of situations in the numerous kinds of business affected. There is a limit to the amount of detail into which one can go in an explanation of partial exemption without producing a detailed case study. Yet such a case study would be of limited relevance to many readers. For example, even within banking and insurance, businesses vary greatly in the kinds of financial activity they undertake, the types of insurance they write and so on.

The law on partial exemption

Articles 17 and 19 of the *EC 6th VAT Directive* are the basis for the rules, which each Member State must implement. However, they only state general principles. *Section 26* outlines those principles in UK law and gives Customs power to make the detailed rules. The latter are in the *VAT Regulations, Part XIV (SI 1995/ 2518)*.

What kinds of business are partially exempt?

Examples of partially exempt businesses are:

- banks, finance houses, building societies and finance brokers;
- insurance companies and insurance brokers;
- betting shops, bingo halls and casinos;
- hospitals, nursing and care homes;
- opticians;
- pawnbrokers;
- professional associations;
- property investment companies — unless they have opted to tax all rental income;

- schools;

- undertakers.

Other businesses are at risk of partial exemption. Some only occasionally have exempt outputs. Others do so regularly but the related input tax is below the de minimis limit. In either case, they may become partially exempt because of irregular or exceptional exempt outputs. Builders and property developers are the most common examples.

What is 'exempt input tax'?

'Exempt input tax' is the VAT which relates to your exempt activities. This includes any tax on your overheads, which has to be apportioned, not just that which is directly attributed. The full definition in *Reg 99(1)(a)*, as amended from 18/4/02, refers to VAT on supplies used or to be used in making exempt supplies.

The de minimis limit

You are partially exempt if your exempt input tax exceeds the de minimis limit. At the time of writing, this is:

- £625 per month on average — £7,500 a year; and

- your exempt input tax must be less than 50% of your total input tax.

How the limit works

Reg 106 says where in any (VAT period) or in any longer period the exempt input tax . . . does not amount to more than £625 per month on average . . . The use of the word *average* means that, if you first incur exempt input tax on the last day of a monthly VAT return, the limit is £625 for the period. If it is on the last day of a quarterly one, the limit is £1,875 because the average is for the whole 'prescribed accounting period', meaning the period of your VAT return.

If you have a case where regular subjective judgements concerning the amount of your exempt input tax have to be made and the figure is close to the limit, it would be wise to inform Customs of your calculations and the basis for them. The coding of a single invoice might make the difference between being partly exempt and being below the de minimis limit.

Your 'longer period' or 'partial exemption year'

Your 'longer period', otherwise known as your partial exemption year, runs to 31/3, 30/4 or 31/5 depending upon your VAT periods or to any other date to which Customs agree. Thus, it can be aligned with your financial year end, provided that this coincides with the end of a VAT return.

Both the de minimis calculations and the apportionment ones for your ordinary returns are only provisional and are re-worked for your 'longer period'. This is normally a full year.

There are special rules for applying the de minimis limit in the year in which you first have exempt outputs. Whether you escape under the limit in that first longer period depends upon these rules. They vary slightly depending upon whether you are newly registered or are an established trader. See Notice 706 *Partial Exemption*.

If in subsequent partial exemption years, your exempt input tax is below the de minimis limit for the full year, you can reclaim the input tax previously provisionally disallowed on your VAT returns during the year.

Your right to recover input tax

In order to understand partial exemption fully, you need to know the basis of your right to recover input tax. By this I mean the rules on which outputs create recoverable input tax and which do not. These rules are the basis of partial exemption calculations.

Section 26(2) lists the supplies in relation to which input tax can be recovered as:

- Taxable supplies;

- Supplies outside the UK which would be taxable if made here;

- Such other supplies outside the UK and such exempt supplies as are specified by Treasury Order.

The Treasury has duly made the *Input Tax (Specified Supplies) Order (SI 1999/3121)*, which details the supplies in question as:

Services:

- Supplied to a customer, who belongs outside the EU; or

- Directly linked to the export of goods outside the EU; or

- Agency services concerning either of the above,

Provided that the supply is exempt, or would have been exempt under the rules for insurance (*Sch 9 Group 2*) or finance (*Sch 9 Group 5, Items 1–7*), if it had been made in the UK:

Goods

- Together with sales of *investment gold (Sch 9 Group 15, Items 1 and 2)*.

Thus, you can recover input tax on insurance and financial services, or on commissions earned on them, provided that:

- Your customer belongs outside the EU; or

- Your services are directly related to the export of goods outside the EU.

How the right to recover affects banking, finance and insurance

The above rules tie in with those on the Place of Supply of Services, which are explained in Chapter 22 on *Exports and Imports of Services*. Thus:

- Banking and financial services are covered by *Sch 5, para 5*.

- *POSSO, Art 16* makes those supplies outside the scope of VAT to business customers within the EU and all customers outside it.

- As set out above, the *Specified Supplies Order* makes the input tax recoverable on certain supplies, which include some to non-EU customers, which are exempt in the UK.

If you are not already familiar with *Sch 5* and *POSSO*, see Chapter 22, *Exports and Imports of Services*.

If you wonder why, of those services exempt in the UK, only banking and financial services become outside the scope of VAT with recovery when supplied to customers outside the UK, consider what other exempt services might benefit from such a rule anyway. Usually where a UK business incurs UK VAT in relation to them, it relates to supplies made to customers in the UK.

Partial exemption methods

In order to calculate your exempt input tax, you have to use a partial exemption method. You can use either:

- the standard method; or

- a special method — which means anything, which you can persuade Customs to agree to.

Whatever method you use, there are always two stages to it.

Stage 1: you directly attribute

The first stage of a method is always to directly attribute as far as possible the input tax you incur to either your taxable or your exempt outputs. Direct attribution means attributing input tax as far as possible to the outputs, *past, present or future*, to which it relates. That means to:

- existing outputs;

- a project, which will produce outputs at some future date;

- outputs which occurred in the previous year.

The words in *Reg 101 used or to be used* make it clear that whether or not any outputs have occurred is irrelevant; the question is whether the input tax in question has been incurred in respect of an activity likely to result in exempt outputs, in taxable ones or in ones outside the scope with recovery.

If your expenditure is being made some time in advance of any income resulting, it might seem more accurate to refer to *activities* rather than to *outputs*. However, there must always be an output in prospect, however distant, so that is the word used throughout this chapter.

Stage two: you apportion

The tax not directly attributable, called the *residual tax* or *the pot* must be apportioned either using the standard method based on your outputs or using a special method agreed with Customs.

The direct attribution stage always comes first. Apportionment under either the standard or a special method only affects the residual tax.

The standard method

The standard method apportions residual tax to taxable outputs in the ratio of taxable outputs to total outputs. Thus, if you have taxable outputs of £1m and total outputs of £3m, you can recover one-third of your residual tax. The outputs method has the virtue of relative simplicity. Information on outputs is often more readily available than other data. However, if the output values vary significantly between kinds of output or the ratio of taxable to exempt swings about, this may distort the recovery of input tax either for or against you.

Any ratio is potentially dangerous if you do not understand it properly. There is not necessarily a direct relationship between output values and the input tax incurred in creating them. Output values for different transactions in the same business can vary considerably but the underlying costs do not. For instance, a financial institution may have relatively small standard rated fees for managing portfolios and exempt outputs of securities in much larger values but on tiny profit margins. In such a situation, a special method will have more chance of providing a fair apportionment than would the standard method.

An example of a standard method calculation

		Taxable outputs	Exempt outputs
Total input tax for the period			£100k
		£	£
Stage 1: Attribute as far as possible the input tax directly related		10k	20k
Stage 2: Apportion the residual tax of £70k in the ratio taxable outputs/total outputs	$\dfrac{£1m}{£10m}$	7k	63k
		£17k	£83k

Thus, on those figures, £17k is recoverable and £83k is disallowed.

Note that there is not necessarily any correlation between the ratio of recoverable input tax at the direct attribution stage and that calculated at the apportionment one. There is no law of accountancy or mathematics which entitles you to expect that, merely because you recover one third under direct attribution, you should get a similar proportion at the apportionment stage.

For instance, this business might be selling both standard-rated goods, on the cost of which it recovers directly attributable input tax and a mix of standard-rated and exempt services for which there is relatively little directly attributable tax because most of the costs are overheads, which relate to both. Thus, there is nothing surprising in the ratios in this example of one-third and one-tenth.

Note also that the proportion of the total input tax, which is directly attributable, varies widely, depending upon the kind of business. In many of those, which sell financial services, most of the VAT is incurred on non-attributable overheads.

So far, only the standard method has been outlined. There are various detailed rules commented on later in this chapter.

See also the end of this chapter for the anti-avoidance rules known as the *standard method override*, which were introduced from 18 April 2002.

Special methods

You do not have to use the outputs ratio. You can use any special method of apportioning residual tax, which Customs will accept as fair. Under *Reg 102* they have power to approve a method which you suggest. They can also direct you to use one based on their own ideas, if they think that the standard method is distortive and they cannot agree a special one with you. Examples of special methods of apportionment are:

- staff numbers engaged on different activities;
- transaction counts for each activity;
- floor areas occupied by activities.

Possible financial criteria are:

- the ratio of input tax directly attributable to taxable supplies to total directly attributable input tax;
- the ratio of the cost of the supplies used exclusively in making taxable supplies to the cost of those used exclusively in making taxable or exempt supplies.

Large organisations tend to use cost centre accounting to produce management accounts. That being so, this is also the logical basis for splitting up the expenses amongst the different activities for VAT purposes. Such a method will involve:

- allocating costs to each department;
- re-analysing the support departments costs to those departments which generate income;
- attributing and apportioning the total VAT thus allocated to each income generating department to the supplies which it makes.

Different methods may be suitable for the various activities. For example, one might use a transaction count for one department and output values for another.

You may find that a two stage apportionment gives you a better result than a single ratio. For instance, the running expenses relating to a building used partly for taxable and partly for exempt activity might be apportioned on the basis of the respective floor areas. This would be desirable if it enabled more tax to be recovered than under the overall apportionment of residual tax.

Customs will consider any combination of bases of calculation which you propose. Although they have power to dictate the nature of a special method, it is rare for them to use it. You know your business far better than they do and it is therefore for you to suggest the right method. An example of a cost centre based method is on the next page.

An example of a special method based on cost centres

Stage 1— Code input tax by department

	Sales CC split	£ VAT
Support depts		
Accounts	33.3% each	30,000
Overheads such as rent, telephone/audit fee (unless each invoice is to be multi-coded)	40%, 40%, 20%	40,000
Management & Administration (MD & non-exec. directors, personnel, receptionists, cleaners etc)	1/3 each	10,000
Back office (Such as policy admin. or contract notes/ settlement depending on the business)	50%, 50%	20,000
Sales Dept		
Sales 1		40,000
Sales 2		50,000
Sales 3		20,000
		£210,000

Stage 2 — Apportion the support departments

		£
Sales 1 Directly incurred		40,000
Support Depts	10,000	
	16,000	
	3,333	
	10,000	
		39,333
Total Sales 1		79,333
Sales 2 Directly incurred		50,000
Support Depts	10,000	
	16,000	
	3,333	
	10,000	
		39,333
Total Sales 2		89,333
Sales 1 Directly incurred		20,000
Support Depts	10,000	
	8,000	
	3,334	
		21,334
Total Sales 3		41,334
TOTAL INPUT TAX NOW SPLIT BY SALES DEPARTMENT		£210,000

Stage 3 — Apportion the sales departments

			Non-recoverable	Recoverable
	1.	£		
Sales 1	All outputs exempt		79,333	
Sales 2	Part taxable outputs: Apportion using transaction count 55.2% OS(R) 44.8% OS(NR)		40,021	49,312

Sales 3 Part taxable outputs:
Apportion using sales value

		£		Non-recoverable	Recoverable
	Taxable	300,000			
	OS(R)	200,000			
		500,000	33.33%		
				27,557	13,777
	Exempt	1,000,000	66.67%		
	Total	£1,500,000			

Non-recoverable £146,911 Recoverable 63,089

Total £210,000

A cost centre accounting problem

If you are using cost centre accounting as the basis of your special method, how do you post the input tax? The options are:

- Charge the invoice totals gross to the relevant expenses in each cost centre. How do you then identify the VAT to be apportioned? Some businesses do this by estimating the VAT included within each expense heading. Customs may accept this but can you identify any entries, which do not include VAT and which find their way for one reason or another into expense listings, which appear to be all standard-rated?

- Have a VAT code for each cost centre. The VAT not recovered then appears as a cost unless you spread it back to the underlying expenses.

- Charge invoices gross and record the VAT as a memorandum total. Some computer software includes this facility. This then leaves a credit to the cost centre for the VAT recovered. Often, this is too small a figure for it to be worth bothering with spreading it back over the expense accounts.

The outside the scope supply problem

In the cost centre example problem above, outside the scope supplies are included at stage three, in the apportionment for sales department number 3 which is based on turnover. Customs may not allow you to do this because *Reg 103(1)* requires *use* to be the basis.

In *Liverpool Institute of Performing Arts ([2001] STC 891, HL)*, the House of Lords said:

- The standard method under *Reg 101* calculates the VAT relating to supplies made within the UK.

- *Reg 103(1)*, based on use of the inputs in question, decides the VAT relating to supplies made outside the UK.

This prevented *LIPA* obtaining full recovery of input tax on its overheads at a time when it had *out of country supplies* but had not yet made *exempt* ones although much of its activity was devoted towards preparing to.

What does Regulation 103(1) do?

Reg 103(1) covers two categories of outside the scope supplies:

- *Out of country supplies* — those for which the place of supply is outside the UK, which would be taxable if they were made here.

- *Specified supplies* — those which would be exempt if the place of supply was in the UK and for which the related input tax is recoverable because they are covered by the *Specified Supplies Order* — mainly finance and insurance supplies made from the UK to a customer who 'belongs' outside the EU.

Input tax is to be attributed to those supplies and thus identified as recoverable *to the extent that the goods or services are so used or to be used expressed as a proportion of the whole use or intended use.*

How do I deal with 'non-specified' supplies?

'Non-specified' supplies are those:

- for which the place of supply is outside the UK;

- which would be exempt if made here; and

- which are not covered by the *Specified Supplies Order.*

Ie, they are Outside the Scope without recovery. The main example is financial services to EU customers.

These supplies must be treated the same as exempt ones made in the UK.

- The VAT incurred in making them cannot be deducted:

- Their value must be included in a standard method calculation.

What if I make UK supplies as well as outside the scope ones?

If you make taxable and exempt supplies in the UK as well as outside the scope ones:

Stage 1   Start by calculating the VAT that relates to *out of country* and *specified* outside the scope supplies on the basis of use under *Reg 103(1)*. You can deduct this.

Stage 2   Deal with the VAT which relates to *taxable* and *exempt UK* supplies and *non-specified exempt* ones under either a standard method or a special method.

At Stage 2, the standard method calculates the recoverable % as the value of *taxable* supplies divided by the total value of *taxable, exempt* and *non-specified* outside the scope supplies. You cannot include *out of country* and *specified* supplies. The input tax related to the latter has of course been dealt with at the first stage.

Is the above practical?

It is up to you to decide how to attribute on the basis of use. Customs will accept any method whose result seems fair.

If all your supplies are made from the same offices and with the same people involved, it may not be practicable to attribute or apportion separately the VAT relating to different kinds of supply. If you have a problem, discuss it with Customs. They may agree that you can use a turnover calculation based on all your sales, including those covered by *Reg 103(1)*, but you must ask. If they do agree, it will be a special method, not the standard one.

The annual adjustment

As explained near the start of this chapter in the comment under *Your longer period or partial exemption year*, your quarterly apportionments of residual tax are only provisional, whatever the method you use. The figures must be reworked on an annual basis for your partial exemption year in order to eliminate any distortions in individual quarters.

The annual adjustment is done on the return for the quarter following the end of your partial exemption year, thus giving you a little extra time in which to do it. Naturally, the direct attributions do not change, just the apportionment of residual tax.

See also the *Partial exemption over-ride* at the end of the chapter, which requires larger businesses to consider whether the standard method has produced a fair result.

Rounding up

Having calculated the percentage for the annual adjustment under the standard method, you round this up to the next whole number. Thus, 22.1% would become 23%. You are not allowed to do this under a special method unless the method includes it. Indeed, Customs may require a calculation to 4 decimal places. This is because, for a major financial institution, even a fraction of 1% can amount to a sizeable sum of money.

Provisional claims based on previous year

If you wish, you can use for your quarterly calculations during the year the % recovery of residual tax for the previous year, which you arrived at when making the annual adjustment for that year. You correct this to actual when you do the annual adjustment. Thus:

- For the year to 31 May 2002, you calculate, say, 19% recovery rate when you do the annual adjustment on the return to 31 August.

- You then use 19% throughout the year to 31 May 2003.

- You calculate 21% for that year when you do the return to 31 August 2003 and reclaim the extra 2% on that return.

The three-year cap

In Notice 706 (October 2002), para 10.8 Customs say you can only use the annual adjustment to correct your calculations to the extent that the annual adjustment would do this anyway; ie where the use of goods or services has changed during the year and to apply the annual average for ratio calculations.

You cannot get round the cap by including in the adjustment the correction of an error made in a period outside the three years. However, when doing the adjustment, they say you must use the correct figures, not those reflecting the error.

Certain outputs must be excluded from the standard method

When using the standard method, you have to leave certain outputs out of the turnover figures (*Reg 101 (3)*). This is because they are likely to distort the calculations. The list includes taxable transactions, which would distort in your favour, not just exempt ones.

You must exclude:

- *Any sum receivable* by you for a supply of capital goods used by you for the purposes of your business. There is no definition of *capital goods* but Customs will only be concerned about sales large enough to distort. In *JDL Ltd (MAN/98/297 No 17050: [2002] STC 1),* demonstrator cars were held to be *capital goods* of a motor dealer. The sales of them, exempt under *Sch 9 Group 14,* therefore qualified for exclusion.

- The following *if they are incidental* to your business activities. That they be 'incidental' is the only requirement. *Incidental* is not defined in the law but see later.

  (i)   Zero-rated interests in property (dwellings and those intended for relevant residential or charitable use) covered by *Sch 8, Group 5, Item 1* (new buildings) or *Group 6, Item 1* (reconstructed listed buildings).

  (ii) Surrenders of interests in, rights over or licences to occupy land.

  (iii) Rents or sales of land and property, exempt under *Sch 9, Group 1.*

  (iv) Sales of 'new' buildings, or civil engineering works, which are standard-rated under the exception in *Sch 9, Group 1, Item 1(a).*

  (v)   An interest in property, which is standard-rated as a result of a waiver of exemption under *Sch 10, para 2.*

  (vi) Those financial transactions, such as interest, financial commissions and sales of securities, which are exempt under *Sch 9, Group 5.*

- Sales of goods on which input tax has previously been disallowed such as cars. These are now exempt under *Sch 9, Group 14*.

- Self supplies such as of stationery and of imported services (the reverse charged services) (*Reg 104*). This prevents an artificial improvement in the ratio as a result of having these notional standard-rated outputs.

- On page 13 of Notice 706 (October 2002), Customs say that you must also exclude the transfer of a business as a going concern.

Meaning of 'incidental'

The sub headings (i)-(vi) above are only excluded if they are incidental to your business activities. Neither the *6th Directive* nor UK law define 'incidental'. Customs say that transactions cannot be incidental if they are carried out:

- on such as scale and with such regularity as to constitute a business in their own right; or

- in such as way as to constitute, in substance and reality, an integral part of the main business.

In *CH Beazer plc ([1987] VATTR 164; affd sub nom Customs and Excise Comrs v CH Beazer (Holdings) plc [1989] STC 549)* the President defined incidental as *occurring or liable to occur in fortuitous or subordinate conjunction with*.

Much of the time, it is obvious whether or not transactions are incidental to the way the business earns its profit. However, do not take it for granted that you can exclude, say, interest earned on client deposits.

In *Régie Dauphinoise — Cabinet A Forest Sarl (Case C-306/94 [1996] STC 1176)*, the CJEC ruled that interest earned on sums held by a property management company on behalf of the property owners was the *direct, permanent and necessary* extension of its taxable activity. It was therefore to be included in total income for the purpose of the standard method of calculating deductible input tax.

Interest charged by holding companies to subsidiaries

In contrast to the *Régie Dauphinoise* case noted above, the CJEC ruled in *Floridienne SA and Berginvest SA ([2000] STC 1044)*, that, where loans to its subsidiaries did not amount to an economic activity, a holding company could ignore interest on those loans when using the standard method.

Think carefully about your attributions

You might think that direct attribution of input tax is usually obvious. Indeed, much of the time it is apparent that a particular expense relates either entirely to taxable or entirely to exempt outputs. However, a flow of cases in recent years has shown that there is plenty of room for argument in the more borderline situations. The following comments demonstrate the problem.

Compare the wordings:

- Tax on supplies which *are used or to be used . . . exclusively in making taxable supplies (Reg 101(2)(b))*.

- Tax on supplies which are *used or to be used by him in making both taxable and exempt supplies (Reg 101(2)(d))*.

Any element of use for taxable supplies or for those outside the scope with recovery means input tax incurred in making an exempt supply is part of your 'residual tax'. It is not directly attributable as non-recoverable. The reverse applies to tax mostly attributable to taxable supplies.

For instance, *Dial a Phone Ltd (LON/01/14 No 17602)*, sold mobile phones and airtime contracts. Customers were given 3 months free insurance and *Dial a Phone* received exempt insurance commissions on those policies, which were not cancelled. Its advertising and marketing costs were held to relate to both its standard rated and its exempt income.

VAT related to sales of securities

The law in *Reg103* requires that, for a supply covered by *Sch 9, Group 5, Items 1 or 6* (primarily securities), the related input tax shall be attributed on the basis of use: ie, that it shall only be recoverable in the ratio that its use in making supplies, in respect of which VAT is recoverable, bears to total use.

This rule automatically applies even if Customs have approved a method which purports to allow another basis such as applying your residual VAT %.

Example

A company makes a 'rights' issue of shares to shareholders, some of whom belong outside the EU. It can only reclaim input VAT related to the rights issue in the proportion of shares sold to non-EU buyers. It cannot claim that the tax is part of its residual VAT and apportion this with the rest of the tax on its overheads, even if its special method would allow this.

So, persuading the Chairman's grandmother to retire to live on an island in the Pacific will only enable you to recover such proportion of the VAT incurred on an issue of shares as is represented by the shareholding, which she purchases. It does not move all the input tax related to the issue from VAT directly attributable to exempt transactions – the share issue – to residual tax. In other words, a small non-EU shareholding does not ensure that VAT related to a share issue is apportioned in the proportion applicable to ordinary overheads.

Holdings by UK nominees do not count

In *Water Hall Group plc (LON /00/1308 No 18007)*, it was held that, where a nominee holds shares, the supply of a rights issue is to that nominee. Thus, if the nominee is in the UK, the place of supply is here even if the beneficial owner belongs outside the EU.

Input tax relates to the immediate output

Input tax must be attributed to any output directly resulting from it. Arguing that you should be able to recover it because of a wider purpose will get you nowhere. Various cases have demonstrated aspects of this problem.

The need for a direct and immediate link

Two decisions of the CJEC, *BLP Group plc ([1995] STC 424) and Midland Bank plc ([2000] STC 501)* have affirmed the need for a *direct and immediate link* between the input on which you reclaim input tax and the output on which you base your claim to the deduction. That does not mean that input tax in general has to have a direct link to a taxable output — there is no such link for many overhead expenses. It means that, when, for partial exemption purposes, an input is attributed, there must be such a link, be it to a taxable or to an exempt output. Without such a link, the VAT must be apportioned as part of residual tax.

That is fundamentally important when the difference is between, on the one hand, full recovery or nil recovery and, on the other hand, recovery on the basis of the % calculated for residual tax.

The share transaction situation illustrates the problem. If a company raises money through an issue of shares to UK shareholders, that creates an exempt output. The argument that an issue of shares is not a supply for VAT purposes, which I tried long ago in *CH Beazer plc (1987 VATTR 164)*, has now been rejected by the Court of Appeal in *Trinity Mirror plc (formerly Mirror Group Newspapers Ltd) ([2001] STC 192, CA)*. The related input tax on, for example, professional advice concerning the issue is disallowed even though the purpose of raising the money may be to invest in machinery so as to expand production of standard-rated goods.

There is some lack of logic in this, given that, if money is raised through a loan or increasing the bank overdraft, VAT on professional advice is recoverable because there is no exempt output. However, as I explain above, the wider purpose argument gets one nowhere, as confirmed by several cases.

In *Swallowfield plc (LON/91/479 No 8865)*, VAT on the costs of an issue of shares was held to be attributable to that issue, even though it financed the purchase of a warehouse and the acquisition of a company, both related to taxable supplies.

In *BLP Group plc ([1995] STC 424)*, the Tribunal took the same view, rejecting the wider purpose argument and holding that tax on the costs of a sale of shares must be attributed to that sale. When the point was referred to the CJEC, it stated the need for a direct and immediate link to a taxable transaction and that the ultimate aim of the trader was irrelevant.

That principle was repeated by the CJEC in *Midland Bank plc (LON/94/117 No 14144: Case C-98/98: [2000] STC 501)*. £315,000 input tax was incurred on legal costs in defending proceedings brought by *British and Commonwealth Holdings plc* against the bank's merchant banking subsidiary, *Samuel Montagu & Co Ltd*. The latter was accused of a negligent misrepresentation made when it had advised *Quadrex Holdings Inc* in a deal with *British and Commonwealth*. The Tribunal held the costs to be directly linked to the taxable supply of the fees charged by *Samuel Montagu* to *Quadrex*. By defending the proceedings, *Samuel Montagu* sought to reduce the claim for damages and thereby quantify its exposure under its contract to supply services to *Quadrex*. The Tribunal accepted that there was a direct link with those services.

When, on appeal by Customs, the Divisional Court referred the matter to the CJEC, the latter again stated the need for a direct and immediate link. It said:

> . . . the right to deduct the VAT charged on such goods or services presupposes that the expenditure incurred in obtaining them was part of the cost components of the

taxable transactions. Such expenditure must therefore be part of the costs of the output transactions which utilise the goods and services acquired. That is why those cost components must generally have arisen before the taxable person carried out the taxable transactions to which they relate.

It follows that, contrary to what the Midland claims, there is in general no direct and immediate link in the sense intended in the BLP Group judgment, cited above, between an input transaction and services used by a taxable person as a consequence of and following completion of the said transaction. Although the expenditure incurred in order to obtain the aforementioned services is the consequence of the output transaction, the fact remains that it is not generally part of the cost components of the output transaction. . . . Such services do not therefore have any direct and immediate link with the output transaction.

The Court has therefore seen a distinction between expenditure incurred in the course of making a supply and that which arises afterwards merely as a consequence of that supply. Further arguments appear likely about what seems to be a fine dividing line between what is a cost component and what is merely a consequence.

Remember, none of this affects the right to recover VAT on the expense as a cost of the business; merely whether that recovery can be by direct attribution or must depend on the position concerning residual tax. It is therefore irrelevant for fully taxable businesses.

In *Deutsche Ruck UK Reinsurance Co Ltd ([1995] STC 495)*, a tribunal held that the VAT on legal fees incurred in disputing liability to pay claims under policies, for which the premiums were outside the scope with recovery, was held to be attributable to those premiums, not a part of the pot of overheads. Whilst this decision is now perhaps suspect, it seems arguable that disputing liability to claims is a cost component of providing the insurance in return for premiums. Obviously, dealing with and negotiating the value of claims is. Whether disputing liability altogether was a cost component might perhaps depend on the extent to which the insurance company in question could show that this was typical of the way it conducted its business, as opposed to a one-off dispute!

Sheffield Co-operative Society Ltd ([1978] VATTR 216) is a more straightforward example of where the wider purpose argument fails. Tax on the refurbishment of a restaurant was held to be related to the exempt rents charged to the caterer, who had been granted a licence to occupy the area. It could not be attributed to the outputs of the store generally. That the cost was incurred to promote the store by having a smart restaurant was irrelevant.

Similarly, in *Brammer plc (MAN/90/123 No 6420)*, VAT on 'reverse consideration' paid in order to assign a lease was held to relate to the exempt sale of the land, which it made possible. The transaction was part of a complicated series aimed at freeing *Brammer* from its obligations under a potentially onerous lease. It enabled *Brammer* to procure a transfer of that lease to the company to which it paid the reverse consideration and to which it also sold the freehold reversion. The VAT on the reverse consideration was thus attributable to the exempt freehold sale. The argument that it was incurred for the general benefit of the company was rejected.

Two cases in which there was no immediate output

Before jumping to conclusions on attribution, check the precise facts! If you were asked about recovery on the cost of producing and screening a series of four TV commercials with a mortgage storyline, your first reaction would probably be that the VAT was attributable to the exempt mortgage interest resulting from the business obtained.

Well, in *Britannia Building Society (MAN/96/174 No 14886)*, the evidence established that the commercials were designed to remind viewers of the existence of the Britannia Group and that it provided a variety of financial services. They did not advertise individual financial products. They were designed to modernise the image of the Society and were held to be part of general overheads, not directly attributable to the Society's exempt mortgages.

When a holding company buys a new subsidiary, Customs say the input tax is residual. *UBAF Bank Ltd (LON/91/2623 No 9813: [1996] STC 372, CA)* was not a normal holding company, all its subsidiaries being dormant. *UBAF* itself conducted the business. The day after acquiring three companies, it itself took over their business, the subsidiaries becoming dormant like the others. VAT on the acquisition costs was held to be directly attributable to the taxable supplies of leasing which *UBAF* acquired and which it itself made from then on.

The Tribunal said the question was the purpose for which the three leasing companies and their businesses were bought. What were the supplies used for? The transactions were intended to enable the bank to add substantially to its existing leasing business. There was no need to distinguish between tax related to the share purchases and that on the subsequent transfers of the businesses. They were so closely linked that there was one purpose only, not a mixed or wider one.

A key point in both the *Britannia* and the *UBAF* cases was that there was no directly related exempt output — not the same situation as in *Sheffield Co-operative Society* for instance.

Nevertheless, advice on a share issue could be residual

Two planning points arise in share issue situations. Firstly, do your advisers' invoices identify properly the nature of the work done? In *RAP Group plc ([2000]STC 980)* the input tax on an invoice from a firm of solicitors, which had advised over an issue of shares, was held to be residual. The detail on the invoice indicated that part of the advice had concerned:

- service contracts;
- a due diligence report on the company being acquired;
- investigating title to its properties;
- preparing papers for its AGM following the acquisition.

Thus, it was not all related to the issue of the shares and was therefore residual. Invoices from other advisers gave no details so the question could not be considered.

The second point is whether your advisers could exempt their services as intermediaries under the rules in *Sch 9, Group 5*, which are explained in Chapter 11, *So What is Exempt?*

In *Southampton Leisure Holdings plc (LON/99/0466 No 17716)*, it was held that, when a company issued shares in order to acquire another company, the costs were attributable as follows:

Partly to the business as a whole and therefore residual

- merchant bank's services in advising and negotiating, making arrangements for due diligence investigations and co-ordinating the work of other advisors;

- valuing properties of company being acquired;

- investigating title to the properties and drawing up service contracts for directors;

- advice on financing the offer and due diligence investigation of the financial affairs of the company being acquired.

Wholly to the exempt issue of shares

- printing the offer documents and press release;

- public relations services aimed at maintaining support for the offer.

In *Business Brief 23/02*, Customs accepted the above concepts in relation to a merger, an acquisition or a management buyout but claimed that the position was unchanged where an initial public offer or a rights issue to shareholders was made. In the latter cases, the transaction only involves cash, not the acquisition of a business.

Input tax on the transfer of a going concern is residual

The sale of a business, or part of one, to a taxable person as a going concern is outside the scope of VAT, as explained in Chapter 37, *Buying or Selling a Business*. Customs say that the related input tax should be treated as residual and must be apportioned under the method in use for overhead VAT, if the vendor is partly exempt.

This was accepted by the Tribunal in *Abbey National plc (LON/94/2245 No 14951)*, which saw no grounds for singling out property, or the letting of it, as a separate business activity or as the underlying business activity to which the input tax on the sale costs should be attributed. The underlying business was life assurance.

On referral by the Divisional Court to the CJEC *(Case C-408/98: [2001] STC 297)*, the latter agreed that the input tax was residual, there being no directly related output. However, it commented:

> *However, if the various services acquired by the transferor in order to effect the transfer have a direct and immediate link with a clearly defined part of his economic activities, so that the costs of those services form part of the overheads of that part of the business and all the transactions relating to that part of the business are subject to VAT, he may deduct all the VAT charged on his costs of acquiring those services.*

In *Business Brief 8/2001* dated 2/7/01, Customs said they would see the input tax incurred on the sale of part of a business as an overhead of that part and thus recoverable or not according to the nature of the supplies made by it.

The pitfall of costs on an abortive property project

Property developers often incur costs on a potential project before acquiring the site; examples are legal fees in negotiating with the owner, surveying the site and applying for planning permission. In many cases such projects then have to be abandoned. In *Beaverbank Properties Ltd (EDN/02/150 No 18099)*, it was held that the VAT on such speculative costs was attributable to the intended taxable supplies. The Tribunal accepted that it had been intended to opt to tax if the site had been acquired, as any ordinary and prudent businessman would. It rejected Customs' assertion that, in the absence of an option, the input tax had to be attributed to exempt supplies as the only possible ones.

I do not think that this carefully argued decision can necessarily be relied on in all abortive cost situations. Much may depend upon the precise circumstances. For instance, see later in this chapter under *What happens if the use of an asset changes?* about the *Royal and Sun Alliance Insurance Group* case concerning the situation in which input VAT was being incurred on leased property prior to it being sublet. Although not directly related, I think that case illustrates the need to create evidence at the start of a project of the nature of the intended supplies. An obvious answer would be to opt tax the property. As explained in Chapter 25, *Property*, you can do this before you own it. If you do not opt, at least the owner or senior management should date and sign a memorandum of the intention to do so.

Examples of direct attribution to minor outputs

There are various minor taxable outputs to which the associated input tax can be directly attributed and thus recovered in full. This prevents a double charge when output VAT, which cannot be charged to anyone, must be accounted for. The input tax can be offset in full instead of being partly disallowed in residual tax. Examples are:

Canteen

The input tax is attributable to that declared as output tax on any charges made. This applies even if the meals are free because there is still a taxable supply even if the value of it is nil. (*Sch 6, para 10*)

Petrol and gifts of goods

If staff are allowed to claim for petrol used privately and the scale charge is applied, the equivalent input tax on petrol is recoverable in full rather than being subject to apportionment.

The position is:

- output tax on scale charge is payable;

- input tax on fuel use for private purposes is recoverable in full — but must of course be identified;

- input tax used on business mileage is caught under your partial exemption calculations.

The same applies to goods given away on which output tax is accounted for under the gifts rules or which are caught as promotional items handed out in return for consideration.

Staff magazines

In *Post Office (MAN/95/1322 No 14075)*, three staff magazines were held to be gifts of zero-rated goods to staff, on which the input tax was recoverable, despite two being about management and technical matters.

Charges for use of company cars

The same principle applies where staff make contributions towards the running cost of the cars they drive. Some of the tax on maintenance costs is attributable to these contributions.

Payments for the *use* of cars are outside the scope of VAT assuming that input tax was not recovered on the purchase or, if the cars are leased, that the 50% disallowance applies.

Beware of management charges

Making a management charge will not necessarily improve your input tax recovery in a partial exemption situation — especially if it is for the services of one or two individuals. Charges for the time of people do not justify much input tax recovery by direct attribution. Even accounting and other office services do not necessarily generate direct costs, as opposed to general office overheads.

The only tax attributable to a management charge might well be a share of the VAT on those overheads which could be argued to relate to the charge as well as to the exempt activities.

Thus, a property company with exempt outputs resulting from the redevelopment of property will not recover input tax incurred on the redevelopment costs merely by making charges for the services of its managing director to other associated companies.

In *Neuvale Ltd and Frambeck Ltd ([1989] STC 395)*, the Tribunal found there to be two activities, the renting of property and the supply of the managing director's services. The input tax had to be attributed accordingly.

Customs say that a company cannot supply the services of a director to another company of which he or she is also a director. This was disapproved as a categoric statement in *Withies Inn Ltd (LON/95/1778 No 14257)* but Customs won on the facts. Those included that the charge was made to its subsidiary by a holding company which had no other income.

In *TS Harrison & Sons Ltd (MAN/91/1178 No 11043)* after a management charge had been invoiced and paid, a further invoice was raised for an additional charge in order not to have to pay back surplus pension fund contributions collected. The tribunal held this extra charge did not represent any supply made. The VAT on it was therefore not recoverable by the company to which the charge was made.

Though perhaps a 'one off', this is a warning against too glib an assumption that one can create a supply by raising a management charge at any time and for any reason.

What happens if the use of an asset changes?

If the initial attribution or apportionment of tax on an asset proves inaccurate it must be corrected. Thus, if the project, for which the asset is purchased, is to be expected to produce taxable outputs but intentions alter and, within six years, exempt or non-business ones result, *Reg 108* requires the attribution to be corrected. The correction must be made on the VAT return for the period in which the use occurs or the intention changes.

Reg 109 provides for a similar correction if the use turns out to be taxable rather than exempt. An application for refund of the tax previously disallowed must be approved by Customs before it is claimed on your VAT return.

In *Really Useful Group plc (LON/91/136 No 6578)*, VAT was incurred on a building intended as the company's offices. It was then realised that it would be inadequate and an exempt sale resulted. There had not been any use for taxable purposes by the company so the provisional attribution of the refurbishment costs to its taxable outputs had to be corrected and the VAT repaid.

In *Cooper and Chapman (Builders) Ltd ([1993] STC 1)*, a house was converted into 10 flats, which were advertised as holiday accommodation. Holiday lettings were achieved for only 4 of them. All 10 were then let for a year to a single tenant. *Reg 108* did not apply to those flats, which had been let for holiday accommodation because a taxable supply had occurred. However, it was held that an apportionment was required because the VAT attributable to the 6, which had remained empty before being let for an exempt rent, had to be paid back to Customs.

Thus, a single week's standard-rating letting of a flat meant the input tax apportioned to that flat was recoverable. Without a standard-rated letting, none of it was. The *Curtis Henderson* situation described below did not apply because there was no possibility of a zero-rated sale.

However, *Royal and Sun Alliance Insurance Group plc (MAN/97/916 No 16148: [2000] STC 933:CA [2001] STC 1476: HL 22/5/03)* held that *Reg 109* does not apply if a property has been vacant and available to let for some time. Opting to tax the lease eventually achieved does not create a right under *Reg 109* to recover input tax incurred on rents and service charges paid to the superior landlord during the vacant quarters. Such input tax is therefore treated as an overhead cost — recoverable according to the partial exemption calculations for those quarters.

The House of Lords upheld the Tribunal's view that opting to tax a sub-lease did not allow reallocation to taxable supplies of input tax incurred on the superior lease in VAT periods long gone, even though there had been no exempt sub-lease. There was no direct and immediate link between the rent paid to the head landlord before the option to tax was exercised and that charged to the sub-tenants in later periods.

To put it another way, just as the *failure to make a taxable supply* does not *prevent* the recovery of input tax related to the attempt, a *failure to make an exempt supply* — in this case by letting a property — does not *create* the right of recovery.

This was a majority decision 3/2 and, since the Divisional Court and the Court of Appeal, also by a majority, had supported *RSA*, the judicial support for Customs was 5 in favour, 5 against! However, I believe it to be correct.

In *Wiggett Construction Ltd (MAN/99/1047 No 16984: [2001] STC 933)*, VAT incurred on land was reclaimed because of an intention to construct houses on it. Wiggett then made an exempt sale of the land to a housing association and at the same time contracted to build flats on it. As explained in Chapter 25 on *Property*, a sale of bare land to a housing association is exempt because the option to tax is disapplied.

Customs disallowed the input tax incurred on the land because:

- It had been consumed in the sale of the land.

- There was no connection between the sale of the land and the subsequent construction works.

- The supplies were separate, at separate values and on separate invoices.

The Tribunal commented that:

- The agreements were entered into at the same time and formed an integral deal.

- Wiggett would not have sold the land at only a tiny profit without the construction contract.

- It had never intended to sell the land undeveloped.

- The time of construction of the buildings was a matter of mechanics, not substance, if the property was sold as part of the deal.

- Therefore, the input tax incurred on purchasing and improving the land had been used in making both taxable and exempt supplies.

Customs lost again in *Southern Primary Housing Ltd (LON/01/637 No 17770D; [2003] STC 525)*. Neither decision dealt with the apportionment thereby required.

See Chapter 24, *The Capital Items Scheme* for the rules requiring an adjustment once supplies have been made but the use of property and computers changes.

The zero-rated house/exempt rent problem

If you cannot find a buyer for a house you have built, an obvious possibility is to let it for a year or two. Unfortunately, that creates exempt, not taxable outputs. Customs have argued in a number of cases that the original attribution must be corrected because the exempt output meant that VAT was not recoverable.

In *Link Housing Association ([1992]; 1992 STC 718)* each house had first to be let for two years before the tenant could acquire the right to buy. Nevertheless, the sales to tenants by *Link* were held to be zero-rated and input tax on the costs of sale, presumably legal fees, was thus recoverable.

In *Briararch Ltd ([1992] STC 732)*, a listed office building was renovated. Under the old rules, a zero-rated major interest lease was possible at the time but a tenant could only be found for a four year one. An apportionment to the exempt rent of 4/29ths of the input tax on the renovation cost was made by the Tribunal on the basis that it was still hoped to grant a lease exceeding 21 years in due course. At the time, this would have been zero-rated but *Briararch* would now have to opt to tax it.

Curtis Henderson Ltd ([1992] STC 732) acquired a building plot in 1988. Customs granted registration in the usual terms which required the repayment of input tax should taxable outputs not result in due course.

The house was completed in April 1989 just in time for the housing slump. The house was let for nine months. Customs assessed for the entire £6,378 input tax incurred on its construction. The house was eventually sold in September 1990.

The Tribunal rejected Customs' argument that the input tax was 'used' to grant the lease. It had been used to construct the building which then put the trader in a position to grant the lease and, later, to sell the freehold. In that sense, the goods and services were 'used' to make both supplies. The tax should be apportioned accordingly.

Both the latter cases seem to fit in with the principle of a direct and immediate link, which was explained earlier in the comment on the *BLP* and *Midland Bank* cases. The link of the original expenditure in such a case is more strongly to the intended taxable output than to the short-term letting.

Similarly, the Tribunal found duality of purpose in *Scottish Homes (EDN/99/126 No 16444)* when houses were improved by major repairs or improvements, such as to kitchens or to central heating systems, for which there was no contractual obligation under the leases. The expenditure was partly for the purpose of the exempt rents and partly to encourage tenants to exercise their right to buy.

Importance of a proper systems file

My experience is that, all too often, junior staff are given responsibility for the VAT return in partially exempt businesses. Sometimes, it is the latest arrival in the accounts department!

The problem is that, to handle partial exemption properly, one needs firstly to understand what the organisation does and how and, secondly, how some complex rules apply to the resulting transactions. Without that knowledge, mistakes are all too likely. You therefore need to make sure that:

- Your system is set up by someone who thoroughly understands how the business works. That means how the profit is earned, not just how the accounts department records it.

- The staff, who operate that system, know both what they are supposed to do and why.

- There is a systems file to which anyone with no knowledge of partial exemption could refer to find out how and why it works in your organisation.

Detailed notes on how your partial exemption system works are vital. If you lack a proper file on it, mistakes are inevitable sooner or later when, due to staff changes, illness or whatever, new or inexperienced staff have to cope with what is one of the more complex aspects of VAT.

Moreover, without such a file, how can you or your successor review the system to see whether it is operating effectively and that you are recovering the maximum possible input tax?

More detail on special methods

Under *Reg 102*, Customs can approve or direct the use of a special method of apportioning residual tax. A special method is any alternative to the standard method which Customs will accept as fair.

See earlier in this chapter for some preliminary comment on possible methods. In the next few pages, some disputes are explained, which have arisen concerning the detailed operation of special methods.

You may need a special method without realising it

The standard method is rigid. Any deviation from it is a special method requiring Customs' approval. You can't just do your own thing!

In *Credit Risk Management Ltd (MAN/94/416 No 12971)* the Tribunal upheld a refusal by Customs to allow part of the input tax to be apportioned 50% to taxable activities as an intermediate stage instead of in the residual ratio. This would have kept the exempt input VAT below the de-minimis limit — but the company had not applied for a special method.

Agreement by Customs in writing

The agreement of Customs to your special method should be in writing. Usually, one writes to Customs with a detailed explanation of the method requested. Customs then reply in a letter, which is primarily made up of standard paragraphs, despite being several pages long. In essence, it says that one may operate the special method proposed subject to the conditions, which it sets out.

There is a pitfall in this. Be careful about the wording of your request. There have been several tribunal cases concerning the interpretation of agreements on special methods. So far, the cases have tended to show Customs' problem in setting out the terms of methods to cope with changes of circumstances or exceptional transactions. However, traders must also be vulnerable to suggestions that the method proposed was in some way inadequate or has been incorrectly applied

In *Kwik-Fit (GB) Ltd* ([1998] *STC 159)*, the Court of Session found ambiguous the words *Where goods and services are procured by one member of the VAT group for use in whole or in part by another member of the VAT group, any input tax incurred is to be recovered in accordance with the recovery percentage of the group or company benefiting from the goods and services*. In the context of the legislation, use meant physical use by the other member. That excluded overhead expenses of the procuring member, such as telephone calls which related to the business of another member.

Customs' interpretation of the wording as covering such indirect costs did not remove the ambiguity. A special method under *Reg 102* containing an ambiguous direction was not 'fair and reasonable', as required by *s 26(3)*.

In consequence, Customs could not enforce use of the special method. *Kwik-Fit* was entitled to use the standard method until a new special one was agreed.

Labour Party (LON/2000/0337) further emphasises how important is the precise wording of a special method agreement. That one assumed that affiliation fees were non-business and could therefore be left out of the partial exemption calculation. When it was realised that they were exempt, including them in the calculation increased the input tax recoverable! Of course, it ought to have made little or no difference since VAT related to non-business or exempt transactions was not recoverable in either case but the defective wording of the method had the opposite result.

The Tribunal rejected Customs' argument that a partial exemption method could not cover the apportionment of input tax between business and non-business supplies. Thus, until a new method could be agreed or directed, the existing defective one remained valid.

In Barclays Bank plc (LON/89/787 No 5616) the assessment exceeded £4m. *Barclays* used a special method agreed by Customs with the Committee of London Clearing Banks. The dispute concerned the assignment of third world loans under swap arrangements. Since the assignees belonged outside the EU, the related input tax was recoverable. The value over the three years exceeded £226m.

Customs referred to the condition in the special method requiring that:

Any supplies whose output value is disproportionately greater than the related input tax or vice versa are excluded from the (calculations)

and that any related input tax should be determined separately.

In upholding the appeal, the Tribunal noted that the wording was part of the preamble which said that a clearing bank could adopt the method if three conditions, including the one quoted, were met. The way the document was drafted meant that the conditions in the preamble were matters of which Customs had to be satisfied before a bank was allowed to use the method.

If that were wrong and they were part of the detailed terms, para 7(IV) of those terms read:

Supplies whose output value is disproportionately greater than the related input tax or vice versa. Such supplies, which will be kept under regular review as set out in the 'review' section on page 2, are set out in annexe III.

This was unambiguous. *Such supplies* could only refer to the previous sentence. Services not included in annexe III did not have to be excluded and there was no mention of assignments of debt in that annexe. Customs argued that the objective was to calculate the recoverable tax in a manner fair and reasonable. The Tribunal applied the principles of construing taxing acts under which intention is irrelevant. One must not read things in or imply terms; one must look fairly at the language used.

The agreement did not say how one decided whether the value of supplies affected the calculation 'disproportionately' to the related input tax. Therefore, this was not intended to be a substantive provision of the method. That the question was to be kept under regular review indicated that, if Customs thought a particular supply was disproportionate, they could add it to the list in annexe III, thus changing the method from then on.

Beware of changes in circumstances

An important condition imposed by Customs is likely to be that you notify them of any material changes in circumstances. This may require careful attention, especially as such a notification might be necessary several years later. How will you know if the circumstances of your organisation change?

In *Union Bank of Switzerland (LON/86/713 No 2551)*, the change was favourable. Customs had required UBS to inform them of 'a significant change' in its business. UBS started to do gold/currency swap deals without telling Customs.

The Tribunal held that commencing these transactions was not a significant change. That had to be considered in relation to the business of the London branch, not to that of the bank as a whole, but evidence showed that they were only a small part of its activity.

The Tribunal thought Customs had meant *any transactions which would significantly alter or affect the proportion of the input tax which the Bank can deduct*. That was not the same and Customs should have said so clearly. A trader should not be required to account for tax on a self assessing system on the basis of vague general words of which varying views could honestly be taken!

Changing from one partial exemption method to another

You must obtain the agreement of Customs to a change of method. Although you can use the standard method without their approval, any change to it or from it will involve a special method.

Reg 102(3) says that a trader using a special method must do so until Customs approve or direct a change. Any such approval is often from the start of the next tax year although they usually permit it from the beginning of the one in which they received your application. 'Tax year' is defined in *Reg 99(1)*. Normally, it is the year ending 31/3, 30/4 or 31/5 depending upon your VAT quarters.

Customs have power to permit a change of method after less than two years. *Reg 109(2)* empowers Customs to withdraw use of a special method or of the outputs pro rata method from such future date as they may specify.

Customs also have power to permit a retrospective change (*AJ Barrett as provisional liquidator for Rafidain Bank (LON/92/2732 No 11016)* and *PL Schofield Ltd (MAN/91/878 No 7736))*. However, they can (and usually do refuse to do so). In *Chartered Society of Physiotherapy (LON/97/185 No 15108)*, the Tribunal held that it had only a supervisory jurisdiction over a refusal by Customs to allow a retrospective change. Broadly, this means that it will only interfere if it finds the refusal to have been unreasonable.

Arguments about use of special methods

In *Merchant Navy Officers Pension Fund Trustees Ltd (LON/95/2944 No 14262)* it was held that:

- the effect of a direction to stop using a special method is to impose the standard method unless an alternative special method has been agreed;

- though the appeal was upheld because the effect of the standard method was even more distorted than the special method, approval of which Customs had withdrawn.

In *Glasgow Indoor Bowling Club (EDN/96/75 No 14889)*, it was held that Customs were entitled to withdraw the use of a special method which gave a 97% recovery following a change of subscriptions from standard-rated to exempt. The standard method, which became applicable, produced 47% recovery. If it seems too good to be true, it probably is!

Similarly, in *Aspinall's Club Ltd (LON/99/540 No 17797)*, Customs were held to be justified in withdrawing a floor area method which produced up to 55% recovery when taxable turnover was only 1%. One reason for the latter figure being so low was that the price of a meal was often not charged to a member who used the gaming facilities.

Correcting the application of a special method

In *Sovereign Finance plc (MAN/97/778 No 16237)* a tribunal held that special method calculations could be corrected by voluntary disclosure. Hire-purchase transactions had been treated as wholly exempt.

Distortion is the key word

Customs' main concern when considering a special method is to ensure that it arrives at a fair result and does not distort the position so as to recover more tax than is justified. For instance, they would be unlikely to permit a hire-purchase company to use an input tax ratio which included in the directly attributable tax that on the goods bought and resold. These large sums of tax are incidental to the way the business earns its profit by the charging of exempt interest.

Special methods agreed by trade associations

Notice 700/57 *Administrative agreements entered into with trade bodies*, (March 2002) gives details of special arrangements agreed by trade associations with Customs. Those concerning aspects of the partial exemption situations of their members are:

* ABI/Lloyds of London/ILU/BIIA
* Association of British Insurers
* Association of Investment Trust Companies
* Association of British Factors and Discounters
* Brewers Society
* Finance Houses Association
* Association of Unit Trust and Investment Companies
* MAT Insurance Underwriters

The effect of grouping on partial exemption

Grouping a partly exempt company with a taxable one does not of itself increase the input tax recoverable. Normally, the advantage of grouping is in not creating an inter company transactions output tax, which is not recoverable as input tax by the company being charged.

Grouping for VAT purposes means that transactions between members of the group are ignored. All the third party inputs and outputs are treated as being those of the representative member of the group. However, for partial exemption purposes, input tax is normally attributed and apportioned in the first instance in the accounting records of each company. This is convenient and usually reflects the use to which the expenditure is put.

If there are inter company management charges and some of the recipient companies are partially exempt, one must consider whether some of the input tax of the company making the charge should be disallowed as being related to the exempt outputs of the other company. One must 'look through' the outside the scope management charge and consider the nature of the supplies by the other company, which the charge supports.

Each case depends upon its facts. The principle is that one cannot recover input tax merely by incurring it in another company in the same VAT group.

In Notice 706 (October 2002), para 11.1 Customs say that a Group has only one partial exemption method. Presumably, they mean that a single method is supposed to include separate sections for each company.

Self supply of stationery

The *Self supply of Stationery Rules in the Special Provisions Order (SI 1995/1268, made under VATA 1994 section 5(5))* were repealed from 1/6/02. The following is only an outline of them. For more detail, see Notice 706/1/92. They created output tax, which had to be paid to Customs. They did not have anything to do with partial exemption calculations as such. However, they only affected organisations which:

- were partly exempt; and

- had their own printing department, which produced printed matter, the annual cost of which exceeded the registration limit; and

- which printed matter was used in the business rather than supplied on or incorporated in other goods.

Output tax was due on the standard-rated stationery produced, such as letter heads. The value of zero-rated booklets, leaflets etc counted towards deciding whether the registration limit had been exceeded but did not of course create any output tax.

Printed matter was defined by *Art 2* of the *Special provisions* Order as including printed stationery but not anything produced by typing, duplicating or photocopying.

Two planning points for partially exempt businesses

The following are a couple of straightforward planning points for partially exempt businesses.

A company with exempt outputs should employ its own staff.

A partially exempt company should employ its own staff or be VAT grouped with the employer. Otherwise, non recoverable VAT will be incurred when their salaries are charged to it by the employing company.

If staff work for several companies and you cannot group them, have the one with the most exempt business employ them and re-charge part of the cost to the others. Even if the others are not fully taxable, this reduces the lost VAT.

Buy fixed assets in a separate company and lease them

If you are about to incur substantial input tax on computers or other equipment, consider buying them in a separate company, which is not in the same VAT group. That company can then lease the goods to those which have exempt outputs. Although VAT on the leasing charges will be disallowed at least in part, recovery of VAT on the original purchase cost can give a useful cash flow advantage. This idea no longer works for property as there are elaborate anti-avoidance rules.

Be reasonable about the rate of return to your in-house leasing company! Customs have powers to direct the substitution of market value for an artificially low price, as described in Chapter 8, The *Value of Supply Rules — How Much You Must Pay*. They used them in *RBS Leasing & Services Ltd (No1–4) (LON/98/1005 No 16569)* in which the Tribunal upheld a direction substituting market value when *RBS* sold to a leasing subsidiary equipment it had bought and leased it back at a margin of about 1%.

The standard method override

What Customs call the *standard method override* is an anti-avoidance measure, in force from 18/4/02 *(Regs 106A, 107A-E)*. It is intended to stop VAT being recovered under a standard method calculation, when the latter does not reflect the intended use of the costs in question; ie where:

- the costs relate to both taxable and exempt supplies and are therefore part of residual VAT;

- but the standard method % recovery, in the partial exemption year in which they are incurred, does not reflect the expected use in a later year.

Although the override is primarily an anti-avoidance measure, it may help if your situation is the other way round; ie if the standard method is unfavourable to you because it does not reflect the expected future use of the inputs to support taxable supplies.

How the override works

The override only applies if the adjustment required to correct the distortion exceeds:

- £50k; or

- 50% of the residual input tax and £25k.

Thus, an adjustment under £25k can be ignored. Between £25k and £50k, it can also be ignored if it is less than 50% of your residual input tax.

Pro rata limits apply to part periods starting from 18 April 2002 until the end of that partial exemption year.

You review the position in the quarter after the end of your partial exemption year at the same time as you do the ordinary annual adjustment explained earlier in this chapter. You have to consider whether, in addition, an override adjustment is required if:

● your residual tax exceeds £50k a year;

● or £25k if you are a 'group undertaking' as defined in *Companies Act 1985, s 259*: in this context, that means a company which is required to be included in the consolidated accounts of the group or which is exempt from that requirement and which is not in the same VAT group as all its fellow undertakings.

How you work out the adjustment will depend upon the facts of the case.

In *VAT Information Sheet 4/02*, Customs quote the following examples:

● You incur costs in setting up a new activity, the outputs from which will significantly alter the % of exempt supplies in future tax years. You calculate the adjustment by applying the expected % of taxable use to the VAT on those particular costs instead of using that calculated under the standard method.

● Exceptional high-value transactions, which do not generate proportionate input tax, distort the standard method recovery %. Remove the exceptional transactions from the standard method figures and recalculate the %.

● The nature of the business is such that the ratio of the output values of taxable and exempt transactions does not reflect the use of the supporting inputs. Customs say you should *apply another suitable measure*. The legal basis for this seems doubtful. A trader is entitled to use the standard method unless a special one is imposed or agreed and a special method is not normally retrospective. If normal output values create an over favourable recovery on normal inputs, it is arguably up to Customs to require use of a special method. Presumably, they will argue that they have done that by making it a general requirement for all traders to apply the override.

VAT Information Sheet 4/02 contains some more detailed points and a number of examples — though, in some of the latter, the input tax figures quoted are unrealistic in relation to the sales.

Customs claim that, apart from businesses which have undertaken artificial planning schemes, the override will affect very few businesses. That may prove to be so in practice but many companies, which are not in a VAT group but are part of a group for *Companies Act* purposes, will have more than £25k residual VAT and will therefore have to consider their position each year. The representative member of a VAT group, though benefiting from the higher limit of £50k, will have the added complication of having to review the position of each company within the VAT group.

Some questions to check your understanding. Review your answers with the text.

- Numerous kinds of business, which are partially exempt, are listed at the start of this chapter. How many can you remember?

- What is the difference between the standard method and a special method?

- What two stages are included in every method?

- When can you round up the percentage of recoverable input tax calculated at stage 2?

- What is the jargon phrase describing the relationship which must exist between an input and an output if the input is to be directly attributed to the output?

- If you make a rights issue to shareholders, some of whom belong outside the EU, how is the input tax dealt with?

- What examples of the basis for a special method are quoted in the chapter?

- Why is it important to think carefully about the wording of your proposal of a special method to Customs and of their reply agreeing it?

- How does the standard method override work?

24. The Capital Items Scheme

This chapter describes a situation which only arises when you spend more than £250,000 on a building or £50,000 on a computer. Although that means that many very small businesses do not have to worry about the Capital Items Scheme, the figure for property is not large. If you work in or you advise a business of any substance, you will probably come across the Scheme sooner or later.

Purpose of the scheme

The Scheme requires the adjustment of input tax recovered by partially exempt traders on property and computers. The objective is to correct the recovery when, in subsequent years, the use for making taxable supplies varies from that in the year of purchase. That can be either good news or bad news; ie you may be able to reclaim more VAT or have to pay it back, depending on whether your taxable use has risen or fallen. The law is in Part XV of the *VAT Regulations (SI 1995/2518)*.

The items affected

The Scheme affects:

- Land and buildings costing £250,000 or more, whether the purchase of a freehold or of a lease at a premium, including the cost of standard-rated services 'for or in connection with' the construction of the building or work. This includes parts of buildings, enlargements, alterations, extensions or annexes which increase the floor area by 10% or more, refurbishments of existing buildings, and civil engineering works.

- Computers and items of computer equipment costing £50,000 or more.

Note that the law refers to *capital items*, not just goods, so that it catches standard rated construction services which you buy, not just finished buildings.

Note also that 'for or in connection with' is interpreted widely by Customs to include, for instance, professional services and landscaping (Para 4.4, Notice 706/2 (January 2002) *Capital goods scheme*). Only capitalised expenditure counts as a *refurbishment*.

'Computers' means individual machines or pieces of equipment, not the complete cost of an installation and it means only hardware, not software.

The adjustment period

This is:

- for land and buildings, approximately 10 years (5 years if the leasehold interest acquired is under 10 years);

- for computers, approximately 5 years.

The adjustment periods are not necessarily a full 5 or 10 years. Strictly, the adjustment is for 'intervals' and the first such interval runs from the date of acquisition to the end of the current tax year (*Reg 114 (4)*).

The initial adjustment starts in the period in which falls the tax point, not when you start using the asset. Thus, if you occupy a building in March and your partial exemption year ends on 31 March but the final invoice from the builder is received in April, the VAT on that invoice is subject to the partial exemption calculation for the coming year, not that just ended (*Witney Golf Club (LON/01/657 No 17706)*).

The annual calculations

A calculation is done each year so as to reflect the usage of the asset in that year.

Thus:

- in year 1, input tax is recovered in the usual way, subject to any partial exemption calculations applicable;

- in year 2 and later, the recovery is adjusted for any variance in the partial exemption percentage recovery.

Example

	£
Computer bought in year to 31/3/03 for £100,000.	
Input tax thereon	17,500
In year 1, partial exemption recovery percentage for 2003/4 = 50% recovery	8,750

In year 2, partial exemption recovery percentage is only 20%. So recovery is adjusted thus:

Input tax £17,500 over 5 year adjustment period equals £3,500 per year.

Recovery in year 1 at 50% of £3,500 was	1,750
Recovery entitlement in year 2: 20% of £3,500	700
Adjustment on VAT return to repay:	1,050

If, in year 3, the recovery percentage rose to 60%, there would be a clawback from Customs of an additional 10% of £3,500 and so on.

Changes during the year

If the use changes during the year, the adjustment must reflect the number of days for each use. Thus, if, after 274 days, the use alters from 100% taxable to 80% taxable for the remaining 91 days, the calculation is:

$$\frac{(100\% \times 274) + (80\% \times 91)}{365} = \frac{274 + 72.8}{365} = 95\%$$

A pitfall for industrial companies

Suppose you buy or construct an office or factory on which you recover the VAT because you use it for the purposes of your taxable manufacturing business.

If in year 2 or later up to year 10, you let surplus space in it without opting to tax the rent, the Scheme kicks in. The letting might be to an associated company and it might never occur to you that there was a problem with the recovery of VAT achieved several years earlier. Considerable sums of input tax might have to be repaid — plus interest and a penalty when Customs discover the position.

A pitfall re residential or charitable use

If a building was originally zero-rated because it was intended for relevant residential or charitable use, any change can create a self-supply on which output tax is due. See Chapter 25, *Property* under *The change of use pitfall*.

When the adjustment is due

Capital Items Scheme adjustments are due on the second return following the tax year to which the adjustment relates; ie, on the return ending either 2 months or 6 months after the end of the partial exemption year. This allows any partial exemption calculations to be made for the first return after the tax year so that the percentage recovery is available for use in the capital items adjustment, if required.

Sale of a capital asset

During the 'interval' in which the asset is sold, the use until the date of sale determines the adjustment for the entire interval even if the asset is sold only a few days after it begins. The remaining intervals are treated as either taxable or, in the case of property, exempt if the option to tax is not exercised.

If the sale is standard-rated, the tax, recoverable for this period of notional taxable use, *cannot exceed the output tax charged on the sale (Reg 115(3))*. That is another pitfall in this draconian rule. Customs will disapply it by concession if they are satisfied that the result is fair — but you have to ask. If you failed to do so and they subsequently refused to apply the concession, any right of appeal in law, which could be found, would be indirect and with, at best, a limited prospect of success.

Sale of the item as part of a going concern

The Scheme does not cease to apply merely because the asset is sold in a transaction which is outside the scope of VAT because it is the transfer of a going concern. The purchaser of the business must continue the annual adjustments for the balance of the adjustment period (*Reg 114 (7)*).

This means that the purchaser must ensure that the records transferred include the necessary details of the date of acquisition, the input tax incurred at that time and the percentage of that tax which was recovered by the vendor. It also means that the purchaser may be able to reclaim or have to pay some of that tax with a consequent reduction or increase in the effective cost to him of the asset.

Some questions to check your understanding. Review your answers with the text.

- What assets are caught by the Capital Items Scheme?
- What are the monetary values applicable to these assets?

- What is the objective of the Scheme?
- Various property transactions are listed as covered by the Scheme. How many can you remember?
- Can you remember the three pitfalls I mention?

25.   Property

To cover all the rules on property in detail would take a book in itself. Anyway, they change from time to time. The purpose of this chapter is therefore to demonstrate, by outlining the rules and explaining the more straightforward traps for the unwary, why property transactions are the quickest way of losing a really large sum of VAT.

Property is an important minefield. It is important because every business occupies property either as owner or as tenant. It is a minefield because there is a wide range of possible transactions; there are several sets of rules in different parts of the law; and those rules are very complex.

If you do not know VAT law on property thoroughly, get advice from someone who does. In order to get good advice, you need to explain the facts of a proposed transaction properly. You can't do that if you do not have any idea of the rules which might apply and therefore the facts which might be relevant. Thus, anyone with senior accounting responsibilities needs to have some idea of the key rules on property so that they can spot situations on which they need advice.

This chapter reviews complex rules, concentrating on the main points and highlighting the danger areas. It does not, for example, explain the anti-avoidance rules in any detail. Check the law before acting.

The law

VAT law on property comes under six main headings:

1   The zero-ratings in *Sch 8 Groups 5 and 6* for:

- the construction and sale or long lease of dwellings and certain other buildings;

- the conversion of non-residential buildings into dwellings and certain other buildings;

- alterations to listed dwellings and certain other buildings.

2   The reduced rate of 5% on certain conversion and renovation work.

3   The exemption for sales and leases of existing property in *Sch 9 Group 1*. See Chapter 11, *So What is Exempt?*

4   The standard-rating for new commercial buildings; ie those up to 3 years old by exception from that exemption in *Group 1*.

5   The waiver of exemption or option to tax for sales or leases of land and commercial property in *Sch 10 paras 2 and 3*.

6   The DIY builders and Charity self-build rules in *s 35*.

Although these main headings are in different parts of the law and they could in theory be discussed separately, one often needs to consider two or more of them in relation to a situation.

Note: there are also several items of *Sch 8 Group 12*, which zero rate certain alterations work on buildings, such as facilitating access, when supplied to a handicapped person or to a charity. See Chapter 10, *So What is Zero-rated?*

Overview of the property rules

The rules listed above break down into the following main areas:

- constructing new buildings — standard-rated except for dwellings and certain others;

- working on existing buildings — standard-rated with limited exceptions, of which the most important are the zero-rating for altering a listed dwelling and the 5% rate on certain conversion or renovation work;

- sale, or lease for over 21 years (20 years or more in Scotland), for the first time of a dwelling or of certain other buildings, by its constructor — zero-rated;

- sale by subsequent owners of that dwelling or the rental of it (including by the constructor) — exempt;

- sale by its converter of a dwelling, which has been converted from a non-residential building, such as a barn or a shop — zero-rated;

- sale by its reconstructor of a listed dwelling and certain others — zero-rated;

- sales of new commercial property — standard-rated if within 3 years of completion;

- sales of older commercial property and rent of any commercial property — exempt unless opted to tax.

- recovery of VAT incurred by individuals and charities on non-business projects to construct or convert a dwelling and certain other buildings.

The very length of that list demonstrates the complexity of this subject. Moreover, each category is subject to detailed rules, which are explored in the following pages.

The construction and sale of zero-rated buildings

Sch 8 Group 5 zero-rates both the construction of and the sale or long lease of a zero-rated building. It also contains some of the rules on conversions. These and those on sales and long leases are dealt with later in the chapter. This section starts with construction services.

Construction services

Building something from scratch in general is standard-rated. To be zero-rated under *Group 5, Item 2(a)*, it must be the construction of a zero-rated building.

Demolishing a building, including a house, is standard-rated but Customs allow zero-rating if the demolition is done as part of a contract for the construction of a new house.

Altering or enlarging an existing building is also standard-rated unless:

- a conversion for a housing association of a non-residential building into a zero-rated one; or

- an alteration of a listed building which is either a zero-rated building or which becomes one.

- reduced rated as a conversion or renovation under *Sch 7A Groups 6 and 7*. See later in this chapter for the definition of a non-residential building.

The construction or demolition of a *civil engineering work* is standard-rated unless it is:

- necessary to develop a permanent residential caravan park *(Group 5 Item 2(b))*;

- done in the course of constructing a zero-rated building (concession).

Professional services

The various zero-ratings only cover the work on the building. The services of architects, surveyors and the like are standard-rated.

Zero-rated buildings

The phrase 'zero-rated buildings' is used in this chapter to describe buildings for which the construction, sale or alteration is zero-rated under various parts of *Sch 8 Groups 5 and 6*. This avoids having to keep repeating the same descriptions. The phrase covers buildings:

- *designed* as a dwelling or number of dwellings; or

- *intended* for use solely for a relevant residential or a relevant charitable purpose.

Note the difference between design and intention.

See later under *What is a dwelling* and *The existing house/granny flat pitfall* for more comment on houses.

What is a dwelling?

Both the construction and the subsequent sale of a dwelling only qualify for zero rating if that dwelling meets the conditions in *Group 5, Notes (2)* and *(16)*. *Note (2)* requires that:

- the dwelling consists of self-contained living accommodation;

- there is no provision for direct internal access from the dwelling to any other dwelling or part of a dwelling; an internal fire door, which can only be opened in an emergency, would not count.

- the separate use, or disposal of the dwelling is not prohibited by the terms of any covenant, statutory planning consent or similar provision; and

- statutory planning consent has been granted in respect of that dwelling and its construction or conversion has been carried out in accordance with that consent.

Note that the points in *Note (2)* are conditions which a dwelling must meet, not the definition of it. Various tribunals, such as in *Amicus Group Ltd (LON/01/0309 No 17693)*, have held that they apply to the *completed* building. Thus, they are not relevant to:

- the status of an existing building, which must be non-residential if the subsequent sale of it after conversion or that conversion work, when supplied to a housing association, are to qualify for zero rating. In those cases, the building must have been neither designed nor adapted for use as a dwelling (*Sch 8 Group 5, Notes 7 and 7A*).

- the definition of an existing dwelling in relation to the reduced rate for work in changing the number of dwellings in the building (*Sch 7A, Groups 6 and 7*).

Note also that, in *Hopewell-Smith*, a Tribunal held that, even though the planning permission contained a restriction on the *use* of the property, that did not prevent its separate *disposal*. See later in this chapter under *Alterations to zero rated listed buildings*.

Note (16) says that the construction of a building does not include:

- the conversion, reconstruction or alteration of an existing building; or

- any enlargement of, or extension to, an existing building except to the extent the enlargement or extension creates an additional dwelling or dwellings; or

- the construction of an annexe to an existing building.

In *Amicus Group Limited (LON/01/0309 No 17693)*, bedsitter type accommodation was held to be dwellings so conversion of the building into flats did not qualify for relief from standard rating.

What is a 'relevant residential purpose'?

Note (4) to Group 5 defines *relevant residential purpose* as use for:

(a) a home or other institution providing residential accommodation for children;
(b) a home or other institution providing residential accommodation with personal care for persons in need of personal care by reason of old age, disablement, past or present dependence on alcohol or drugs or past or present mental disorder;
(c) a hospice;
(d) residential accommodation for students or school pupils;
(e) residential accommodation for members of any of the armed forces;
(f) a monastery, nunnery or similar establishment; or
(g) an institution which is the sole or main residence of at least 90% of its residents,

but *not* a hospital, prison or similar institution; or a hotel, inn or similar establishment.

Some cases on the meaning of 'relevant residential'

A student accommodation block probably qualifies as dwellings following the *Amicus* case. See above under *What is a dwelling?* The alternative of relevant residential accommodation for a university will not apply if it is let to third parties in the vacations (*University Court of the University of St Andrews (EDN/96/182 No 15243)*).

However, the length of stay of the students does not matter. In *URDD Cobaith Cymru (LON/96/1528 No 14881)*, use for accommodation for students on short courses qualified as a relevant residential purpose. Similarly, in *Denman College (LON/97/756 No 15513)*, 2 blocks, each containing 8 study bedrooms, were 'residential accommodation' despite having no cooking facilities and despite being for students on short courses of 3-6 days. The phrase meant residential in contrast to, say, office accommodation. It was unnecessary for there to be a degree of permanence as the person's home.

In *St Dunstan's (LON/01/1069 No 17896)*, a residential care centre was held not to qualify because the building was not used *solely* for a relevant residential or a relevant charitable purpose. Some people only came during the day. Others were short-term visitors on holiday rather than receiving care so the use was partly as an establishment similar to a hotel.

A building can be for use for a relevant residential purpose even if it does not include sleeping accommodation. In *Hill Ash Developments (LON/99/537 No 16747)*, turning a building into an administration block was held to be part of the zero rated conversion of several listed farm buildings into a nursing home.

Beware of the exclusions for hospitals, prisons or similar institutions

In *General Healthcare Group Ltd (LON/99/916 No 17129)*, a home for the care and rehabilitation of people with brain injuries, at which the average stay was 700 days, was held not to have the characteristics of a 'hospital'. In contrast, the Tribunal found in *Wallis Ltd (LON/98/1516 No 18012)*, that a building for use as a low security unit for mentally ill persons, who typically lived there for 1–2 years, qualified as a hospital under the *National Health Service Act 1977* and the *Mental Health Act 1983*. A proportion of the patients were detained there under hospital orders. There is thus a fine line between a residential care home and a clinic, which qualifies as a hospital.

What is a 'relevant charitable purpose'?

Relevant charitable purpose is defined by *Note (6) to Group 5* as use by a charity,

- otherwise than in the course or furtherance of a business; or
- as a village hall or similarly in providing social or recreational facilities for a local community.

See later under *What is a dwelling* for *Note (17)*, which provides zero rating for an annexe for use for a relevant charitable purpose.

See also later under *The Certificate pitfall* and *The change of use pitfall*.

Some cases on 'relevant charitable purposes'

It is not easy for a building to qualify as used for a *relevant charitable purpose* since any use at all for business will, in law, disqualify it. See below re a concession by Customs. The alternative use as a village hall has been interpreted narrowly in a number of cases.

In *Business Brief 8/2000* dated 31/5/00, Customs announced that they would in future accept calculation of the 10 per cent business use concession on the basis of the time the building is available for use or the use of floor space or the number of people using the building for business purposes.

In *St Dunstan's (LON/01/1069 No 17896)* referred to above under the meaning of *relevant residential*, use for a *relevant charitable purpose* did not apply either because charges were made — albeit only 15–20% of the estimated cost of the accommodation and care and there was some use by outside organisations for meetings and conferences.

In *St Dunstan's Roman Catholic Church Southborough (LON/97/1527 No 15472)*, a garage was found to be for relevant charitable use by a parish. It housed cars provided to the priests. That the cars were used partly for private purposes by the priests was not relevant.

The two cases, *Jubilee Hall Recreation Centre (LON/95/549 No 14209: St Dunstan's Educational Foundation (LON/96/838 No 14901); [1999] STC 945)*, heard together before the Court of Appeal, illustrate the village hall problem. Both tribunal decisions were overturned. The area of Covent Garden was not a local community of the kind served by a village hall and use *similarly* did not cover the wide variety of commercial activities run in the *Jubilee Hall*.

In *St Dunstan's*, a sports hall built by a charity was not used by it because it was leased to the local authority. Use by a fee paying school was not use similarly to a village hall in providing social or recreational facilities for a local community.

However, in *Bennachie Leisure Centre Association (EDN/96/60 No 14276)*, a leisure centre serving various parishes within a six mile radius was held to be similar to a village hall and to serve a local community.

Then, in *Ledbury Amateur Dramatic Society (LON/99/634 No 16845)*, a tribunal found that a hall, so constructed that it could be used as a theatre or as a single or several meeting rooms, which was run by *LEDS* not for profit, was similar to a village hall. It was used by a variety of local organisations.

In *Southwick Community Association (LON/97/1703 No 17601- heard after remission of decision 16441 back to a new Tribunal)*, the construction of a self-contained annexe to existing buildings forming a community centre was held to be zero rated. It consisted of :

- two large workshops used primarily by three local amateur theatre groups;
- a large meeting room used by various organisations;
- a small room used as a committee room and rehearsal area for one of the theatrical groups;
- various storerooms on the ground floor;
- a smallish room above housing 6 computers and used by a local college for adult classes.

The Tribunal found that 95% of the membership of the affiliated groups, by far the largest users of the annexe, lived within 6 miles. The business use by the adult education college and a commercial disco did not exceed 10% of the overall use and was therefore covered by the extra statutory concession on this point. The 3 theatre companies were charities, whose activities did not amount to a business. The charges made by them for performances and to them by the Association were set merely to cover costs. There was a diversity of use by other organisations, which was sufficient to meet the requirement in *Note 6 (b)* for use *similarly in providing social or recreational facilities for a local community.*

Customs have appealed.

In *Yarburgh Children's Trust (LON/98/1426 No 17209:* [2002] *STC 207)*, a building constructed for a charity and let by it at a low rent to another charity for use for a children's playgroup was held to be built for use for a non-business purpose by the charity. It might not have been possible to ignore the rent if the end user was not relevant but it was here because the purpose of constructing the building was for that user. The law required the intention to be for a relevant charitable use, not that the supply must be made to the user; nor did it require the purposes of that user to be taken into account rather than the use of the building.

The building also qualified as a village hall despite its use by other groups, restricted because of the Children's Act, being only occasional. Although the Divisional Court approved the decision, some of the reasoning seems questionable. Unfortunately, Customs' comments in *Business Brief 4/2003* are of little practical help.

The limited application of *Yarburgh* was shown in *South Aston Community Association and IB Construction Ltd (MAN/00/0797 No 17702)*. A centre built to provide facilities in a deprived community was not used solely for non-business purposes because part of it was let to an educational charity, providing free adult education. Though the latter was itself a charity, it was in the business of education — publicly funded and the letting to it was business.

What is an annexe?

Note (16) excludes from zero rating the construction of an annexe. *Cantrell (t/a Foxearth Lodge Nursing Home) (LON/98/195 No 17804:* [2003] *EWHC 404 (Ch):* [2003] *STC 486)* is the lead case on interpretation of *annexe*. The subject was a nursing home unit for 'Elderly severely mentally ill' patients, self contained with its own facilities and staffed separately from an adjoining 'Elderly Medical' unit. The only access to the Elderly Medical unit was an emergency fire door.

After its original decision was sent back to it by the Divisional Court for reconsideration, the Tribunal found for Customs a second time. This was then reversed by the Divisional Court, which held that an annexe was an adjunct or accessory to something else. In relation to a building that meant a supplementary structure, whether a room, a wing or a separate building. The Tribunal's view that any association sufficed was wrong. The unit was a new relevant residential building, not an annexe.

In *Amicus Group Ltd (LON/01/0309 No 17693)*, bedsitter type accommodation was held to be dwellings so conversion of the building into flats did not qualify for relief from standard rating.

Annexes for relevant charitable purposes

Note (17) restores to zero rating the construction of an annexe which:

- (a) is intended for use solely for a relevant charitable purpose; and
- (b) can function independently from the existing building; and
- (c) the only or the main access to the annexe is not via the existing building (and vice versa).

From 1 June 2002, *Note (17)* was amended to allow zero rating where only part of an annexe qualifies: *Note (10)* then applies to apportion the work.

Solely means no business use at all but see earlier under *Some cases on relevant charitable purposes* for a concession by Customs.

Another case on annexes for relevant charitable purposes

In *Grace Baptist Church (1MAN/98/798 No 16093)*, a community building attached to a church, which replaced a smaller one, was held to be zero-rated as an annex. See this case for a useful review of *Note (17)* concerning self-contained annexes as opposed to entire buildings.

Specific exceptions to zero-rating

The following transactions are standard-rated (*Group 5, Note (13)*):

* Sale of a timeshare — though a sale of the dwelling itself may be zero-rated.

* A sale or long lease of a dwelling, which cannot be occupied throughout the year. An example is a holiday chalet, the planning permission for which limits the period of occupation to prevent it becoming a permanent home.

The reason for these exceptions is to prevent new holiday accommodation from benefiting from zero-rating. Since holiday accommodation is also excluded from the exemption for land in *Sch 9 Group 1*, it is therefore standard-rated.

The existing house/granny flat pitfall

As stated in the conditions above, enlarging a house is standard-rated unless it happens to be a listed building so that the zero-rating for an alteration can apply. That means that adding a granny flat to an unlisted house is standard-rated. Rebuilding an existing house is also standard-rated, no matter how comprehensive the work may be, because the law says that the reconstruction of a building is standard-rated unless it produces an additional dwelling (*Note (16)*). That means that it could be cheaper to demolish an existing house rather than to reconstruct it.

Note (18) says that the building only ceases to exist when:

* it is demolished down to ground level; or

* the part remaining above ground level is just a single facade or, on a corner site, a double facade, the retention of which is a condition of planning consent.

The above comments relate to the zero-rating for constructing a new building. See later concerning the reduced rate on certain conversion work to existing houses.

Angus MacLugash (t/a Main & MacLugash) (EDN/97/146 No 15584) illustrates the problem of obtaining zero-rating if *anything at all* remains of the existing building. The modernisation of an uninhabitable croft was held to be the alteration and enlargement of an existing building. The floor space was increased from 50m^2 to 120m^2. The front and rear walls were retained, the others being demolished. This is only one of numerous cases over the years in which such projects as barn conversions have been held to be standard-rated.

The same rule applies if you include an existing building in, say, a new house. In *Co-work Camphill Ltd (LON/99/1351 No 17636)*, a building was held not to qualify as 'new' because it incorporated a barn, the footprint of which was about a quarter of the total.

With the introduction of the reduced rate for conversion work, the financial problem is much reduced, though there is still a difference between zero and 5% on work which does not qualify as the construction of a new dwelling. Moreover, not every project will qualify for the 5% rate. Study the rules explained later to check whether your conversion or renovation project does.

Conversion work for housing associations

The only zero-rating for the work of converting a non-residential building, as opposed to the subsequent sale of it, is where the client is a registered housing association and the project is to produce (*Sch 8 Group 5, Item 3*):

(a)   a building designed as one or more dwellings; or

(b)   a building or part thereof intended for use solely for a relevant residential purpose.

Again, the zero-rating does not cover the services of architects, surveyors and the like.

For an explanation of *non-residential*, see towards the end of this chapter under *What is a non-residential building?*

The contract variation pitfall

If, in the course of constructing a zero rated building, such as a house, it is decided to add an outbuilding or alter it internally, make sure that work starts before the building is completed. Once a certificate of practical completion is issued or the house is occupied, Customs will probably say that it is finished and that any additional work is therefore a standard rated alteration. See below re garages and last-minute choices for examples of the trouble this has caused.

Garages as part of zero-rated projects

Note (3) says that the zero-rating for building a dwelling or converting a non-residential building into one (for a housing association) covers the construction of a garage if:

●   the garage is constructed or converted at the same time as the dwelling; and

●   it is intended to be occupied with it.

Normally, this causes no trouble. However, in *Chipping Sodbury Town Trust (LON/97/943 No 16641)* a Tribunal held that the construction of a pair of semi-detached garages was standard-rated because they were built under a separate planning permission and construction had not started until shortly after the date on which the Tribunal found the two semi-detached houses to have been completed. It found that the fact that access paths and garden fencing were only done whilst the garages were being constructed was irrelevant. It referred to these as 'external works'.

The decorations and other last-minute choices pitfall

Beware of work done either just before or just after the house is occupied. When a house buyer chooses final finishes, kitchen units etc, the work is of course usually done by the builder. However, in *C McAllister (LON/02/408 No 18011)*, the buyer ordered special flooring and a cooker hood, which were installed by the respective suppliers, not the builder and invoiced to him direct. The Tribunal confirmed Customs' refusal to repay him the VAT under the DIY builders scheme because neither work was part of the construction of the house. I believe that reasoning to be faulty since, if done by a builder before the house was finished and included in the final price, work of that kind would be seen as zero rated. However, having paid for it direct, the buyer could not claim he was himself constructing the house and entitled either to zero rating for the work or to a DIY builders repayment.

Similarly, if you are having a house built on your own land and, for one reason or another, you want to move in before it is completed, make sure the contract includes provisional sums for all work such as decorating. Moving in is evidence that the house is completed. Whilst Customs might not challenge zero rating for work which continued under the original contract, they probably would for anything done as additional work. They would claim that work to be an alteration to a completed house, never mind its state when you moved in.

Residential caravan parks

In Notice 708 Customs say that the zero-rating for civil engineering work in constructing a permanent residential caravan park covers pitches, roads, drains, sewers, mains water and electricity but not such facilities as a swimming pool or a shop. Sites which cannot be occupied for the full 12 months of the year do not qualify as permanent (*Group 8, Note (11)*).

Alterations, enlargements and repairs are standard-rated (*Group 8, Note (9)*).

Civil engineering work — access roads and site preparation

As noted earlier, Customs accept that civil engineering work done in the course of constructing a house is zero-rated. However, it appears to me that work on access roads, mains drainage and the like could hardly be said to be part of the construction of the individual houses on a site and that it is therefore standard-rated. This seems likely to catch out small subcontractors.

In *RD Gazzard (L0N/89/1391 No 6029)*, a Tribunal confirmed that work to clear building plots ready for inspection by prospective buyers, who would then choose the design of house, was not done in the course of constructing those houses.

The certificate pitfall

In those cases in which zero-rating depends upon intention as to use, the purchaser must provide a certificate of that intention. *Note (12)* requires this to be in the form published in Notice 708.

Note (12) also requires the certificate to be held prior to the supply in question being made. Whilst Customs might allow retrospective zero-rating once a certificate had been obtained, an officer would undoubtedly assess for tax and interest if you could not produce it at the time of the visit.

The change of use pitfall

If the intended or actual use of a relevant residential or relevant charitable building changes, tax is due. It would be easy to overlook the provisions in *Sch 10 para 1* for collecting tax subsequently from the customer where:

- the intended use does not materialise; or
- within 10 years, the use changes from a relevant to a non-relevant use; or
- the person, who benefited from the zero-rating, sells, leases or grants a licence to occupy the building to someone else, who does not intend to use it for a relevant purpose.

A change of use need not necessarily be complete. Exceeding the 10% de minimis limits for residential homes (*Sch 8 Group 5, Note 4(g) via Group 10 para 9*) or for the indiscriminate business use of charitable buildings (concession by Customs) will trigger a liability under *Sch 10, para 1* if either of them occur at any time during the 10-year period.

From 1/6/02, the VAT due is reduced for each complete year of use for the purpose intended by 10%.

A pitfall for subcontractors

A subcontractor can only zero-rate work on a dwelling. Work on other zero-rated buildings is standard-rated because only the main contractor holds the certificate of intention needed to justify zero-rating. See also later for a similar problem with work in renovating a house at the 5% rate.

Building materials included in the zero-rating

If the service of construction work is zero-rated, so are the materials and other goods via *Sch 8 Group 5, Item 4*, if they are supplied by the contractor who installs them and are *building materials*.

Building materials are defined in *Note (22)* to *Group 5* as *goods of a description ordinarily incorporated by builders in a building of that description, (or its site), but does not include —*

(a) *finished or prefabricated furniture, other than furniture designed to be fitted in kitchens;*
(b) *materials for the construction of fitted furniture, other than kitchen furniture;*
(c) *electrical or gas appliances, unless the appliance is an appliance which is —*
   (i) *designed to heat space or water (or both) or to provide ventilation, air cooling, purification or dust extraction; or*
   (ii) *intended for use in a building designed as a number of dwellings and is a door entry system, a waste disposal unit or a machine for compacting waste; or*
   (iii) *a burglar alarm, a fire alarm, or fire safety equipment or designed solely for the purpose of enabling aid to be summoned in an emergency; or*
   (iv) *a lift or hoist;*
(d) *carpets or carpeting material.*

Where the builder installs non-building materials, it is only VAT on the goods themselves which is standard-rated. That on the installation service is zero-rated.

The disallowance for house builders pitfall

A similar rule achieves the same result for speculative housebuilders. VAT on goods, which do not qualify as *building materials* is disallowed to developers, who put up zero rated buildings for sale (*Art 6* of the *Input Tax Order (SI 1992/3222)*). This affects any building, the sale of which is zero-rated under *Group 5* or *Group 6*. In practice, it is only houses which are constructed speculatively. Relevant residential or relevant charitable buildings are constructed for individual clients because their status depends upon the intent as to their future use.

Although the house builder zero-rates the sale of the completed house, the disallowed input tax is part of his costs. The objective is to prevent the inclusion in zero-rated houses of luxury fittings such as music systems.

A builder, who installs goods in both new and existing houses which do not qualify as *building materials*, may have to keep special records to decide how much input tax he can reclaim if the goods are taken from a common stock or their use is uncertain when bought. He will only be able to reclaim tax on those units on which he has charged output tax.

Planning points for private clients

Only the supply of excluded goods themselves is standard-rated. The service of installing cupboards, carpets, etc in the course of constructing a zero-rated building is zero-rated provided that it is separately identified.

If you are having a house built or a listed one altered, think carefully before you buy articles, such as bathroom fittings or kitchen cupboards, yourself. You will incur VAT on them whereas, if the contractor bought them, they would be zero-rated together with the charge for installing them — so long as they meet the rules for *building materials* explained earlier.

Admittedly, there is the possibility of making a DIY builders claim if you are building a new house or converting a non-residential building into a dwelling, as explained elsewhere in this chapter. However, you will avoid paying the VAT in the first place, together with the administrative problem of having to make the DIY builders claim, if you obtain the goods through your contractor.

Meaning of 'ordinarily incorporated'

F Booker Builders and Contractors Ltd ([1977] VATTR 203 No 446), an early case on a previous version of the law, concerned heating. Although that point is no longer in issue, the principles remain relevant. The Tribunal said that the correct question was firstly whether some form of heating was ordinarily installed — the previous wording. Having decided that it was, the Tribunal then held that radiators and fires were within the genus of heating appliances. It was not necessary to consider whether a particular type of heating was commonly installed. This illustrates the reasoning required for other kinds of goods.

In any case concerning whether an item is ordinarily incorporated, evidence is vital. A tribunal is likely to refuse to make suppositions based on its own experience or on statements made by the appellant. It will require evidence on which it can make a finding of fact that the goods in question are widely incorporated by builders in that type of building. In *GE Joel (LON/88/403 No 3295)*, a safe was held not to be ordinarily installed in a dwelling.

Bedroom cupboards

There have been numerous cases concerning bedroom cupboards. In Appendix D of Notice 708 *Buildings and construction*, Customs provide detailed guidance on what they will accept as *building materials* and what they regard as *furniture*. A cupboard made by fitting doors right across the end of a room or by enclosing two walls of the house and a 'nib', which forms the end of the cupboard, is acceptable. On opening the doors, the back and inside walls of the house should be visible. Rear panelling or any internal fittings beyond a shelf and a hanging rail, are said to turn the cupboard into *furniture*. See the Notice for full details.

Customs also say that using a prefabricated panel for its end, instead of a nib projecting from the wall of the house, turns a cupboard into *furniture*. This was supported by the Tribunal in *Moores Furniture Group Ltd (MAN/97/142 No 15044)* which also agreed that the addition of a floor converted even a cupboard enclosing the entire end of a room into *furniture*.

Thus, as soon as you smarten it up, even the most basic kind of cupboard is likely to change from *building materials* into *furniture*.

Is it goods or an appliance?

Electrical items are not necessarily *appliances,* in which case they are *building materials* so long as they are goods of a description *ordinarily incorporated*.

In *Garndene Communication Systems Ltd (MAN/86/373 No 2553)*, concerning sheltered housing, alarm switches were held to be merely electrical goods, not appliances. In *FH Milan (MAN/87/89 No 3857)*, special blinds installed as an integral part of the windows of a house and which were controlled by a light sensor and thermostat as an energy saving system, were held to be an electrical appliance on the principle that the goods were fixed and were operated by electricity.

Customs accept in Notice 708 that fixed amplification equipment in churches — relevant charitable buildings — can be zero-rated.

Carpets do not qualify for zero rating

Of all the various forms of flooring, carpeting is the one singled out for disallowance. In *McCarthy and Stone plc (LON/91/382 No 704)*, *Sonicord*, a material bonded to the concrete floor in order to meet the requirements of building regulations for sound proofing corridors in sheltered housing, was held to be caught. There is no problem with a permanent flooring, such as wood block. By definition, a building must have a floor but some finishes are neither permanent nor ordinarily installed. Linoleum and cork are not carpet but they still have to meet the test of being ordinarily incorporated in the type of building in question.

In *KC Eftichiou (MAN/86/337 No 2464),* a dense material made of fibres bonded together with resin was held to be 'indistinguishable in principle from carpeting' and 'more akin to carpeting than to linoleum, vinyl or cork'. The appeal failed for lack of evidence that it was ordinarily installed (now *incorporated*). That it had been specified by the architects for a number of similar halls was insufficient.

Alterations to zero-rated listed buildings

Apart from the limited zero-rating for converting a non-residential building for a housing association, the only zero-rating for work on an existing building is that for work on listed zero-rated ones in *Sch 8 Group 6*. For practical purposes, 'listed' means a Grade I or Grade II building although *Group 6* uses the term 'protected', which includes an ancient monument. *Group 6* only zero-rates work:

- where the building is a zero-rated one or is converted to one as a result of the work. The definition of a zero-rated listed building is the same as for a new building, as explained on the second page of this chapter.

- which qualifies as an alteration, not repairs or maintenance;

- which both requires and receives listed buildings consent.

Many of the *Notes* to *Group 5* also apply to *Group 6* so, for instance, the requirements for the apportionment of mixed supplies and the provision of certificates of intended use by customers affect listed buildings.

The new building and outbuilding pitfalls

The status of work in the grounds of a listed dwelling is easily misunderstood. Putting up a separate new building in the grounds of a listed house is not, by its very nature, an *alteration* to that house. It will only qualify for zero rating in its own right if it meets the definition of a dwelling, explained earlier in this chapter under *What is a dwelling?*, including that it can be sold separately.

Similarly, work on converting, say, a barn, which is separately listed, will not qualify, the listing being as an agricultural building, not a dwelling. The reduced rate rules, explained later, may apply to the conversion work but not the zero rating.

Thus, altering an outbuilding, such as a stable, is only zero rated if that building is covered by the listing of the dwelling. Customs may argue that it is not if it is not attached to the house.

In *Zielinski Baker & Partners (MAN/98/950 No 16722: CA [2002] STC 829)* a listed building was held to include structures not fixed to it but within its curtilage. The work of converting a separate outbuilding into a changing room, plant room and games room and with a covered swimming pool attached was therefore zero rated. This was overturned by the Divisional Court, restored by the Court of Appeal and was under appeal by Customs to the House of Lords as this edition went to print.

Regardless of the outcome of *Zielinski Baker*, there may remain an argument as to whether a building, such as a barn, is a part of the dwelling, even though it is covered by the listing of the latter. In *D & L Clamp (LON/98/1316 No 16422)* work to convert a barn 20 yards from the house into ancillary accommodation was held to be standard rated because the original building had not been a domestic building. Curiously, that point was then not argued in *Nick Hopewell-Smith (LON/99/947 No 16725)*, in which work in similar circumstances was held to be zero rated. The decision was not appealed, possibly because the Tribunal held the converted building to qualify as a dwelling in its own right because, although the planning permission forbade separate *use*, it did not prevent its separate *disposal*.

Listed building consent is vital

It is often difficult to anticipate in advance all the work which will be required on a listed building. If, having started the project, you realise that additional work is necessary or you change your ideas, it is vital to obtain listed building consent for the change before you carry out the work. Otherwise, as numerous tribunal cases have established, zero-rating cannot apply. Therefore:

- Provide detailed plans and specifications when applying for consent so that you can demonstrate that it was given for particular work. The wording of a consent is usually so brief and general in nature that it is not evidence of what was or was not approved.

- Obtain what evidence you can at the time that the work, especially interior work, did require consent. Local planning departments tend to have different opinions but it is often questionable whether interior work needs consent.

- If the nature of the work changes or additional work is undertaken, apply for consent for this.

What is an alteration?

Numerous cases have dealt with the difference between an alteration and mere repair and maintenance. Most of these date back many years when the zero-rating for alterations was much wider. For example, in *Viva Gas Appliances Ltd ([1983] STC 819),* the House of Lords held that hacking out a fireclay fireback in order to install a gas fire was an alteration to the fabric of the building. Trivial though that might seem, it was held not to be so minor as to be de minimis. It is therefore necessary to examine in great detail the specification for work in order to obtain the maximum zero-rating for VAT, which counts as alterations. For instance, an alteration to a room involving changing a window or a doorway is likely to require complete redecoration. Redecoration work is normally repair and maintenance but, when required to make good after structural alterations, it can be included in the value of the latter. *Note (6)* says that *approved alteration* does not include any work of repair or maintenance or any incidental alterations to the fabric of a building.

My recent experience has been that Customs have been taking much too narrow a view of what amounts to an alteration. It is as if the people currently in charge of policy are unaware of the long line of cases. This creates a double pitfall. Understandably, builders are likely to base their views on rulings given to them, which may well be wrong. It is then difficult for the customer to argue because Customs will refuse a ruling, which that customer can appeal. Despite my protests, they maintain that only the supplier is entitled to a ruling, not the customer. Of course, that makes it all too easy for a builder to take the line of least resistance, especially if he has already collected the tax — and could encourage fraud.

As I write this, I have an appeal to the Tribunal on behalf of a client who I believe to have been incorrectly charged VAT by 4 contractors, 3 of whom ignored my letters.

Luckily for my client, I managed to get an (unintended) ruling on which I could appeal, thus forcing Customs to look at the matter properly.

By the time you read this, the policy on alterations may have altered but the following recent case is an example of a tribunal correcting misjudgment by Customs. In *Mrs A W Adams (LON/02/340 No 18054)*, the construction of a new retaining wall to stabilise the foundations of a house and replacement of the drainage and septic tank were held to be zero rated alterations. The Tribunal said that if you repair or maintain something that thing must still exist. The new wall was in a different position, much bigger and in many ways different from the old one. The case for the septic tank is less clear from the decision but it was in a different place and the system included new soakaways.

The reduced rate for certain work on property

The reduced rate for certain property conversions and renovation work took effect from 12 May 2001 and was extended to cover certain additional projects from 1 June 2002. I believe that these rules are sure to cause trouble especially for small builders. They are complex and the relationship of them to the zero ratings discussed elsewhere in this chapter is easily misunderstood. It is advisable to confirm your view of each project with Customs — especially as I believe the coverage in Notice 708 (July 2002) *Buildings and Construction* to contain mistakes.

Do not confuse:

- The reduced rate for *work on converting various kinds of property;* with

- The zero-rating for the *sale or long lease* of a converted non-residential building.

The only zero-rating for the *work* of conversion is that on a non-residential building for a housing association. Those zero-ratings are discussed elsewhere in this chapter under *Granting a major interest in a converted non-residential building* and *Conversion work for housing associations*.

The key rules in Sch 7A, Groups 6 and 7

A reduced rate of 5% (at the time of writing) *applies to conversion work which:*

- Changes the number of dwellings in a building, including creating one where none existed previously by converting a non-residential building.

- Converts a house containing one or more dwellings into one or more multiple occupancy dwellings, or vice versa. *Multiple occupancy* means a self-contained dwelling designed for occupation by persons not forming a single household. See later for some comment on the guidance on this provided by Customs.

- Converts one or more buildings or parts thereof containing only dwellings, including multiple occupancy ones and any ancillary outbuildings and, from 1/6/02, any building into a building intended solely for a relevant residential purpose.

- Renovates or alters, including extends, a dwelling, currently a single household, which has been empty for at least three years. It can remain a single household. *Empty* means not lived in, so past use for another purpose, such as storage, is okay. From 1/6/02, this rule was extended to cover relevant residential buildings and multiple occupancy dwellings, which have been empty for 3 years.

- Converts a relevant residential building into a dwelling or dwellings — and, from 1/6/02, into a multiple occupancy one.

The work eligible for the reduced rate is more or less the same as that zero-rated under *Sch 8 Group 5* in constructing dwellings. However, the wording is different and site works, such as landscaping, may not be covered. See later under *Limitations on the work eligible for the reduced rate.*

The complications of the term *non-residential*

The term *non-residential* appears in various places in this chapter with different meanings, which it is all too easy to confuse.

In relation to the zero rating under *Sch 8, Group 5, Item 1(b)* for the sale of a completed conversion project, it means a building not designed or adapted for living in or not used as such in the last 10 years. For the full definition in *Notes 7 and 7A* to *Group 5*, see later in this chapter under the comments on the zero rating for a major interest in a converted building.

In relation to most of the rules for the reduced rate for work on property, there is no such definition. Since the reduced rate applies to a *Changed number of dwellings conversion*, it is not necessary for the building to be non-residential in the first place. The requirement is that the number of dwellings in the building alters. Of course, that includes creating a dwelling out of a building, which was not designed as a dwelling.

The only definition of non-residential in *Sch 7A, Group 6* is in *Note 9(4)* in relation to the conversion of such a building into a garage. See later in this chapter under *Garages as part of a reduced rate project.*

In cases where an existing dwelling is renovated or altered but remains a single dwelling, *Sch 7A, Group 7* requires it to have been empty for the 3 years, not the 10 needed to justify zero rating for an onward sale under *Sch 8, Group 5, Item 1(b).*

Adding an extra dwelling

Adding a *single household dwelling* does not include making a 'granny' flat or annexe. The same requirements, such as self-contained living accommodation and no direct internal access to another dwelling, apply just as they do for the zero-rating of the construction of a new dwelling (*Sch 7A, Group 6 Note 4(3)*).

The part of a building trap

Where work is done to a building but the number of dwellings changes in only a part of that building, only the work in that part qualifies for the reduced rate (*Sch 7A, Group 6 Note 3(3)*).

Customs quote the example of a four-storey block of flats with 4 flats on each floor. A lift is installed, which requires alterations to the layout of each flat on the first 3 floors. On the top floor, the 4 flats become 3.

- Only the work on the top floor qualifies for the reduced rate because it is only in this part of the building that the number of dwellings has altered.

- If the 4 flats on a different floor were changed to make five smaller ones, the work on that floor would also qualify. It would not matter that there were still 16 flats in total because each floor is treated as a separate part of the building.

This rule is intended to prevent the deliberate planning of renovation projects so as to obtain the lower rate for an entire block merely by changing the number of dwellings in one part of it. However, it seems a pitfall, especially where extensive modernisation work is being done in large buildings.

Always check the plans for the precise facts. Projects have to take into account practical realities. For instance you cannot necessarily just refurbish a flat when, on the same floor, you are altering the fabric of the building. In *Note 3(3)* to *Sch 7A Group 6* the problem is the extent to which the word 'part' is to be interpreted as relating to floor space. I believe that what Customs say is much too simplistic.

Consider a block of flats with an empty roof-void. A developer engages a contractor to build a number of additional flats within the existing roof-void. To my mind, this is the conversion of a non-residential part of a building — eligible for the reduced rate on the work and for zero rating of a subsequent sale of a major interest.

Now suppose the existing roof was removed and raised so as to provide more space than merely the existing roof-void. Is that the zero rated enlargement of the building to create additional dwellings — as it would be if an additional storey was built on an existing flat roof? In para 3.2.4 of Notice 708, Customs appear to interpret *Note (16)* to *Sch 8 Group 5* as meaning that a new dwelling created by an enlargement or extension of an existing building cannot use any part of the existing space.

The pub conversion pitfall

When a developer converts a pub into a house, the sale of the completed result often does not qualify for zero rating under *Sch 8 Group 5, Item 1* because it previously contained a dwelling. In *Calam Vale Ltd (LON/99/977 No 16869)*, a tribunal decided that *Note 7*, which defines *non-residential* as not *designed nor adapted for use as a dwelling*, is not subject to *Note 2*, which says that a *dwelling consists of self-contained living accommodation*. *Note (2)* only applies to the finished dwelling.

Without the self-contained rule, bedsitter type accommodation qualifies, as subsequently held in *Amicus Group Ltd (LON/01/0309 No 17693)*. It is now established that a dwelling is where someone lives. Thus, in *Kingscastle Ltd (LON/01/47 No 17777)*, the room used by the manager of a pub as a bedroom was held to be a dwelling despite the fact that the shower and toilet facilities were communal for 7 bedrooms, the rest of which were used to accommodate travellers and the kitchen was that of the pub on the ground floor. The sale of a converted flat, which included that room, was therefore exempt.

That self-contained rule also appears in the definitions of a *single household dwelling* and a *multiple occupancy dwelling* in the reduced rate rules for conversion work explained later and again applies to the finished result.

The difference between what amounts to a dwelling at the start of the conversion work and what qualifies when it is finished thus creates a pitfall. This is worsened by Notice 708 (July 2002) *Buildings and construction*, which contains a mistake, not yet corrected as I write this. Customs say in para 7.3 that a *qualifying conversion includes the conversion of … living accommodation, which is not self-contained, such as a pub containing staff accommodation, which is not self-contained*! Beware!

Does a house converted to another use count as non-residential?

Customs say that a dwelling, which has been converted into, for example, a dental surgery, is a non-residential building and that, therefore, changing it back to a house qualifies for the reduced rate.

They mean that the use of the entire house has been non-residential. Here are two examples which would not qualify:

- An osteopath practises from the front room of his house. Customs say that the entire house is still designed as a dwelling even though a part is in non-residential use. Therefore, work to convert the front room back again would be standard-rated.

- The ground floor is a dental surgery. A self-contained flat is on the first floor. Conversion back to a single house would be standard-rated because, just as for a pub with a self-contained flat, the work would enlarge the existing dwelling, not create a new one.

In *Mr and Mrs Emberson (LON/00/963 No 17604),* a house, which had been converted 60 years previously into a hotel, was held to have reverted to residential use when lived in for 5 years prior to conversion into two dwellings.

Houses in multiple occupation

The terms *house in multiple occupation* and *multiple occupancy dwelling* both appear in the law and seem to be interchangeable.

From 1/6/02, the reduced rate applies to the conversion of any building, which does not already include a multiple occupancy dwelling, into a building containing only one or more such dwellings *(Item 5)*. Up to that date, the work only qualified if it was the conversion of a single household dwelling.

A multiple occupancy dwelling means *(Item 4(2 – 4))*:

- a dwelling which was and remains designed, or has been adapted, for occupation by persons not forming a single household;

- that is not to any extent used for a relevant residential purpose;

- which consists of self-contained living accommodation and with the same requirements of no direct internal access to another dwelling and no planning restrictions as for the construction of a new dwelling.

Similarly, the conversion of a multiple occupancy dwelling into a single household dwelling qualifies for the reduced rate *(Note 3)*.

Not covered are alterations to a multiple occupancy dwelling, which is already in multiple occupation — such as the addition of extra bedrooms.

Customs give as examples:

- Bedsit accommodation, presumably with shared facilities such as bathrooms.

- Shared houses or flats.

- Bed-and-breakfast establishments with a mix of short and long stay residents.

Customs say the relief is meant to encourage the provision of private accommodation for people who cannot afford a mortgage or cannot obtain one.

They say that the phrases do *not* cover:

- Hotels.

- Dwellings with attached granny annexes.

- Accommodation for au pairs, guests or lodgers.

By *shared house* Customs mean one occupied by several unrelated people, such as students. The scope for argument may be restricted by the need for the conversion work to have received any planning permission or statutory building control approval, which it needed *(Note 10)*. However, would it be needed if an ordinary house was being done up in order to let it to students, let alone for long-term occupation by, say, people living together as friends rather than as a family?

A bed-and-breakfast establishment is to be distinguished from a hotel in this context by the source of its funds. Usually, it will provide accommodation for homeless people on housing benefit. The exclusion in the guidance, not the law, of accomodation for *guests or lodgers* is intended to prevent one claiming that one is creating an HMO by adding a room for such a purpose.

Conversions into relevant residential buildings

The law refers to a conversion for a *qualifying residential purpose*, which has a similar meaning to that of *relevant residential purpose* in connection with the zero-rating for the construction of new buildings; ie, it means such communal buildings as homes for children, students and old people.

There is one difference in the reduced rate rules. The premises being converted must be intended to form the entirety of the institution in question, such as an old people's home, unless the use is to be as accommodation for students, school pupils or members of the armed forces. In those latter cases, the accommodation would of course often be part of a university, school or a military camp and could not be the entirety of the institution.

Up to 1 June 2002, the conversion had to be from one or more dwellings, either single household or multiple occupancy, although ancillary outbuildings occupied together with the existing dwelling(s) could be included. From that date, the conversion can be of any building provided that it is not already being used *to any extent* for a relevant residential purpose.

The use immediately prior to the conversion must not have been, even in part, for a relevant residential purpose *(Note 7(4))*.

The conversion of a qualifying residential building back into a dwelling is also eligible for the reduced rate, being the change of the number of dwellings in a building from none to one.

Certificates of intention to use for a relevant residential purpose

The reduced rate only applies when the supply is to the intending user of the premises for a relevant residential purpose. The builder needs a certificate confirming the intention of use *solely* for that purpose, signed by a responsible person on behalf of the home or institution (*Group 6, Note 8: Group 7, Note 4A(1)* from 1/6/02 for renovations — see below).

The renovation of empty residential buildings

Group 7 reduced rates renovating and altering the following buildings, which have been empty for at least 3 years up to the start of the work *(Item 3)*:

- a single household dwelling — but, if it is now occupied again, see below for conditions under which the reduced rate can still apply;

- a multiple occupation dwelling;

- a building or a part of a building which, when last lived in, was used for a relevant residential purpose.

The reduced rate does not apply to an empty building, which is within an operating relevant residential unit, such as a care home and which was part of that unit when it was last lived in. In such a case:

- the rest of that unit must also have been empty for at least 3 years when the work starts *(Note 3(2) as amended)*;

- you do not have to renovate or alter every building which formed the original unit but those which you do must form a unit solely for use for a relevant residential purpose;

- *Note 4 A(2)* provides that, where several buildings on the same site are renovated/altered at the same time, each of them shall be treated as intended for use solely for a relevant residential purpose to the extent that it otherwise would not be.

If a dwelling, which has been empty for 3 years, is now occupied (*Note 3(3)*):

- The supply of the conversion work must be to the person, whose occupation ended the empty period.

- No renovation or alteration must have been done during the 3 years preceding that occupation.

- That person must have acquired, at the time of occupation, a major interest in it *(Note 3(5))*.

- The work must be done within 12 months of that major interest being acquired.

That creates a pitfall for anyone buying a property which has been empty for under two years. Delaying the work until the property has been empty for three years is no help because, by then, it will be outside the 12-month period.

Planning permission

The requisite planning permission and, if required, statutory building control approval for the work must have been obtained (*Group 7, Note 4*).

Evidence of the unoccupied period

There is a pitfall for builders in the need to obtain evidence that the building was unoccupied for at least 3 years. A letter from an *Empty Property Officer* confirming this will suffice. A best estimate of the empty period is required if the officer is unsure of it and Customs may then require other evidence such as electoral roll and council tax data.

Only *building materials* qualify for the reduced rate

As with the zero rating for constructing a new dwelling, materials are included in conversion or renovation work taxed at the reduced rate, provided that they qualify as *building materials (Group 6, Note 12; Group 7, Note 6)*. Ie, the same restrictions apply, as for new work; thus, for instance, kitchen cupboards and very simple bedroom wardrobes qualify but elaborate wardrobes, much electrical equipment and carpets do not. See earlier in this chapter under *Building materials* for the full definition.

The pitfall in installing non-building materials

The service of installing non-building materials is not reduced rated, in contrast to the zero rating available when a new house is being constructed — as explained earlier in the chapter under *Building materials* (*Note 11(3)*).

Subcontractors

A subcontractor must standard-rate for his services to the main contractor in the case of:

- Conversion for a qualifying residential purpose — only supplies direct to the intending user of the building are eligible for the reduced rate (*Group 6, Note 8*).

- Renovation of a dwelling, which was empty for 3 years but is now occupied — only supplies direct to the occupier are eligible (*Group 7, Note 3 (3)(d)*).

There are at least two pitfalls here. There has long been one for subcontractors working on projects for which a certificate of intention as to use is required. Main contractors have had to understand that they must accept invoices at standard-rate from subcontractors. That is now extended to the conversion situation.

The second pitfall is that a subcontractor should charge at the reduced rate for renovating a dwelling, which has been empty for at least three years and is still unoccupied but must obtain the same evidence as the main contractor, as explained above. However, the subcontractor's work is standard-rated if the empty period has been terminated by occupation. The difference may not be apparent; the new owner may have moved in for a few months whilst planning permission was obtained and a building contract agreed but have had to move out again because of the extensive nature of the work. How will a subcontractor, who is only brought in after the work has begun, be aware of that distinction? Of course, one who understands the law will check the facts but that is not the point.

Garages as part of a reduced rate project

Conversion work includes the construction of a garage or the conversion of a non-residential building, or a part thereof, into a garage if carried out at the same time as the main conversion work and the resulting garage is intended to be occupied with the main building *(Group 6, Note 9)*.

The *non-residential* building converted into a garage has to be a building neither designed nor adapted for use as a dwelling nor for a qualifying residential purpose. Of course, that will be the usual situation but beware the pitfall of creating a garage out of part of what was previously a dwelling, as opposed to an outbuilding!

That is not a problem with a renovation/alteration project under *Group 7* where the building has been empty for three years. *Note 3A*, from 1/6/02, covers the construction of a garage, the conversion of a building or part of a building into one or the renovation or alteration of an existing garage. Again, the work on the garage must be done at the same time as the rest of the project and it must be intended to be occupied with the main building(s) The previous omission was not deliberate so, for work prior to that date, Customs might accept the reduced rate.

Limitations on the work eligible for the reduced rate

The reduced rate applies to a *supply of qualifying services* to convert or renovate, which is defined as (*Group 6, Note 11; Group 7, Note 5*):

- Work on the fabric of the building; or

- Within the immediate site of the building in connection with providing for the building water, power, heat, access, drainage, security or waste disposal.

The landscaping and outbuildings pitfalls

The eligibility for the reduced rate is narrower than that for zero-rated construction work, which includes simple landscaping.

This creates a pitfall for builders, who are used to including in their zero-rated invoices the cost of cleaning up the site. Whilst finishing it off with such basic features as paths to the front and back doors are covered by their reference to *access*, Customs say that the reduced rate does not cover landscaping, such as a simple lawn.

Similarly, they say that work to outbuildings that remain outbuildings is standard-rated. Suppose that a pub is converted into a house. There might be various outbuildings, such as a store used for empty barrels and bottles. Customs say, in relation to the conversion of a dwelling for a relevant residential purpose, that stables and barns are not part of a dwelling. That seems likely to be so in many cases, given that the normal usage is not domestic in nature. On the other hand, a fuel store is surely a part of a dwelling since its purpose is essential to heating it.

Although the dividing line may usually be obvious, it seems likely that there will be cases where work is done on outbuildings to tidy them up or make their use more practical and Customs may argue that this does not convert them into a part of the dwelling. An example might be a barn, which is converted into a workshop in which the house owner can practise a hobby, such as wood turning.

DIY builders

The DIY builders rules in *s 35* allows someone acting in a private capacity, who does certain building work him or herself, to reclaim the VAT incurred on *building materials,* which are incorporated into the building. So can a charity, which uses voluntary labour. The idea is to put the individual or the charity into the same position as if a contractor had zero-rated the work including the materials.

The work in question is:

* constructing a building designed as a dwelling or dwellings;
* constructing a building for use solely for relevant residential or relevant charitable purpose;
* a residential conversion.

You cannot use these rules to recover VAT on work you have done on a new house you have bought. See earlier in this chapter under *The decorations and other last-minute choices pitfall.*

If the project is a *residential conversion*, VAT on services carried out by a contractor is also recoverable — but not the services of an architect, surveyor, consultant or someone acting in a supervisory capacity. A *residential conversion* means converting a non-residential building, or a part of one, into a building designed as a dwelling or number of dwellings or intended for use solely for relevant residential purpose. Conversion for a relevant charitable purpose is not included. See earlier in this chapter under *What is a non-residential building?*

A DIY builder's claim can thus be made only for certain conversion projects — those where a developer doing the same work would be able to zero-rate an onward sale of the finished result and thus recover the input tax incurred. For instance, work to convert a house into flats does not qualify under *s 35* because, although work by a contractor would be eligible for the 5% rate, the onward sale would be exempt. It follows that a private individual working on such a project should consider whether the reduction to 5% on work involving expensive materials might make it worthwhile having it done by a contractor.

See earlier in this chapter under *Does a house converted to another use count as non-residential?* for a case in which a house, converted 60 years previously into a hotel, was held to be residential because of subsequent use as a house.

Building materials are defined by *Note (22)* to *Sch 8 Group 5*, as explained earlier in this chapter. The other Notes to *Group 5* also apply. Thus, the pitfall in *Note (18)* for projects, such as barn conversions, applies to DIY projects too. See earlier in this chapter under *The existing house/granny flat pitfall.*

The work must be lawful so the necessary planning permission must have been obtained. Only a single claim for repayment is allowed and it must be in the form and with the supporting evidence required by Notice 719 *VAT refunds for do it yourself builders and converters.*

Lady Blom-Cooper (LON/00/1342 No 17481; CA [2003] STC 669) was held not to be entitled to a repayment of the VAT incurred in converting a pub into a house.

The Court of Appeal disagreed with the view of the Tribunal and the Divisional Court that *Note (9)* to *Sch 8 Group 5* did not apply to *s 35*. Since the building already included living accommodation no additional dwelling was created. See earlier in this chapter under *The pub conversion problem* for more about this.

Sales and long leases of zero-rated buildings

Sch 8 Group 5, Item 1 zero-rates the grant of a major interest, ie a sale or a lease exceeding 21 years (20 years or more in Scotland):

- of a zero-rated building;

- for the first time, which might be several years after construction was completed;

- by the 'person constructing' it;

or

by its converter of a non-residential building converted into:

- a building designed as a dwelling or a number of dwellings;

- a building intended for use solely for a relevant residential purpose.

Note that there is no relief for a building which has been converted for a relevant charitable purpose.

See earlier in this chapter under *What is a non-residential building?* for the definition of this phrase and, in particular, concerning dwellings not occupied for 10 years. The sale of the latter, after renovation, became zero-rated from 1/8/01.

Meaning of 'person constructing'

Taken literally, the zero-rating for the sale of a building by the 'person constructing' would mean that, once it was completed, the zero-rating ceased. Presumably, the draftsman used the word 'constructing' instead of the phrase 'has constructed' so as to allow for the sale of a building not yet finished. The Courts have interpreted the phrase as covering the sale by the original constructor, no matter that this is years after completion.

In *Link Housing Association ([1992] STC 718)*, it was held that the sale by a housing association of dwellings to tenants was zero-rated even though a tenant had to occupy a property for 2 years in order to acquire the right to buy it.

The sale by the reconstructor of a 'reconstructed' listed building is zero-rated if it is a zero-rated building. Subsequent sales are exempt. See page 259 of this chapter.

Major interests in renovated dwellings

The revised zero rating for the sale of a renovated house now requires the latter to have been empty for 10 years. That means prior to the date on which the major interest in the finished property is granted, not the date on which work begins — so you can start work within the 10-year period.

The dwelling could be in a block of flats, some of which are occupied. It is the dwelling in question, which must have been empty for 10 years.

If the building is intended to be used for a relevant residential purpose, the developer will need a certificate of that intention.

Grants of major interests in reconstructed listed buildings

As with a new zero-rated building, a major interest in a reconstructed listed zero-rated one is zero-rated for the initial premium or rent and exempt thereafter. *Note (4) to Sch 8 Group 6* contains the following test of substantial reconstruction:

- at least 60% of the cost of the work must qualify for zero-rating; or
- the finished result must incorporate no more of the original before the reconstruction began than the external walls together with other external features of architectural or historic interest.

See the law for the precise wording.

The short lease pitfall

Do not grant a short lease of a new zero-rated building or of one which you have reconstructed. To recover the associated input tax, you need a major interest lease; ie one exceeding 21 years (20 years or more in Scotland).

The test of reconstruction noted above is not easy to meet, so the number of cases has been small.

Sales of land

The sale of land is exempt unless:

- it includes a new civil engineering work — which could be below the surface;
- the vendor opts to tax — see below concerning the option to tax for restrictions regarding dwellings.

Granting a major interest in a converted non-residential building

Group 5, Item 1(b) zero-rates a major interest in a non-residential building, which has been converted into:

- a building designed as a dwelling or number of dwellings; or
- a building intended for use solely for a relevant residential purpose.

The pitfall in this is that the zero-rating is for the sale of the finished dwelling or relevant residential building. With the exception noted earlier under *Conversion work for housing associations*, the conversion work itself is standard-rated. In order to recover this VAT, the site owner must either:

- create a zero-rated output by granting a major interest in the finished project to another legal entity; or

- use the DIY builders rules in *s 35* to recover input tax incurred on the project — but such a claim cannot be made by anyone using the building for a commercial purpose, such as renting out accommodation in it.

The DIY builders rules are in many cases a second best alternative because:

- only a single claim is possible and not until the project is completed;

- records must be kept as required by Customs in Notice 719;

- although VAT on conversion services can be recovered as well as that on materials, this still leaves professional services and overhead expenses for which no claim can be made, in contrast to the position where the project is handled as a business transaction and it is sold.

Thus, the planning point of whether to carry out the conversion as a business transaction should be considered before the project begins. Of course, stamp duty and other costs associated with a sale might wipe out the additional VAT recovery.

What is a non-residential building?

A *non-residential building*, or part thereof, means a building which:

- is neither designed nor adapted for use as a dwelling or dwellings nor for a relevant residential purpose; or

- if so designed or adapted, no part of it has been used for such a purpose in the last 10 years *(Sch 8 Group 5, Notes 7 and 7A)*.

Until 1 August 2001, the time limit for that use was 1 April 1973.

However, a *non-residential building* does not include a garage occupied together with a dwelling *(Group 5, Note (8))*. An agricultural barn is obviously a non-residential building. A public house may appear to be non-residential but it normally includes living accommodation for the landlord. Thus, when a former public house was split vertically to create two dwellings, the sale of the latter did not qualify for zero- rating *Calam Vale Ltd (LON/99/977* No *16869)*. See also earlier under *The pub concession problem* and *What is a dwelling?*

Note (9) to Group 5 says that the conversion of a non-residential part of a building, which already contains a residential part, does not qualify unless the conversion:

- creates at least one additional dwelling; or

- is to a building designed for a relevant residential purpose.

Apportionment for mixed use buildings

If a building only partly qualifies as zero-rated, there will have to be an apportionment of the price for its construction between the zero-rated and standard-rated elements *((Group 5, Note (10))).*

Examples

- office block including a penthouse or a caretaker's flat;
- shop with living accommodation;
- farm buildings, which include a farmhouse.

Sales of new commercial buildings and civil engineering works

The sale of a new building or civil engineering work is standard-rated because it is an exception to the exemption for interests in land in *Sch 9 Group 1:*

- up to 3 years from the date of completion *(Notes (2) and (4)),* no matter how many other sales there may have been; and
- unless it is a zero-rated building.

This is nothing to do with the option to tax.

Note that *sale* means a sale. Do not confuse the sale of the freehold with the assignment of a lease at a premium!

Once a building is over 3 years old, the sale is exempt, unless it is opted to tax. A building is completed when the architect issues a certificate of practical completion of the building or, if earlier, when it is first fully occupied.

A civil engineering work is complete when an engineer issues a certificate of completion or, if earlier, when it is first fully used *(Sch 9 Group 1, Notes (2), (4) and (5)).*

What is a 'civil engineering work'?

There is no definition of *civil engineering work* in the law. One might think that it would cover any structure which is not a building. However, in *GKN Birwelco (MAN/82/74 No 1430),* a Tribunal suggested that the construction of an oil refinery was not a work of civil engineering. It thought that a key factor was whether a civil engineer would be able to design a particular project and that something was not civil engineering merely because a civil engineer was amongst the designers working on the scheme. The point is potentially important because a new civil engineering work is automatically standard-rated for 3 years after completion.

In *En-tout-cas Ltd ([1973] VATTR 101),* the construction of a running track and of a sports ground were held to be civil engineering works. Because of the degree of levelling, grading and draining, the works were much more than landscaping. A similar conclusion was reached in *St Aubyn's School (Woodford Green) Trust Ltd (LON/82/260 No 1361),* which concerned the conversion of an orchard into a playing field.

In theory, anyone selling land on which such work had been done would have incurred substantial input tax and would therefore opt to tax the sale if they did not realise that it was standard-rated anyway. However, one should take nothing for granted in VAT! Suppose you own some building land on which substantial work is needed to clean up the site and prepare it, such as drainage and flood control works. If you do that work using your own employees and equipment, the input tax involved may be small. Suppose you then receive an offer for the land, which is too good to refuse. Given that much of the work is below the surface or involves earthworks, which have been re-seeded, will you realise that you are selling a site which includes a new civil engineering work? In *Scotia Homes Ltd (EDN/90/211 No 6044)*, house plots, which included civil engineering work, had been sold without charging any output tax. One cannot opt to tax a house plot to a private buyer but the option to tax is irrelevant where the civil engineering work is new, so some output tax was due. Thus, there is a pitfall in the rules on new civil engineering works, just as there are pitfalls everywhere else in VAT!

The option to tax or waiver of exemption

The option to tax — strictly speaking the waiver of exemption — converts an exempt sale or rent of property into a standard-rated output. The advantage of this is that related input tax is then recoverable. Given that this could include tax incurred on the purchase, construction or renovation of a building, large sums can be involved. The rules are in *Sch 10 paras 2–3*. Apart from buildings and bare land, the option also applies to the rental or sale of civil engineering works. Since large sums can be involved, check Notice 742A *Opting to tax land and buildings* for any guidance from Customs additional to or subsequent to my comments here.

You cannot opt to tax — or rather, if you do, the option is of no effect — for (*para 2(2)* and *(3)*):

- a building intended for use as dwelling;
- a building intended solely for relevant residential or charitable use as defined — except use by a charity as an office; see pages 3 and 4 of this chapter;
- a house plot sold to a private individual on which a dwelling is to be built for that person;
- land sold to a housing association or social landlord (in either case registered under the relevant legislation) for the construction of dwellings or of buildings for relevant residential use;
- a pitch for a permanent residential caravan; or
- a mooring for a residential houseboat — residence permitted throughout the year.

Who can opt to tax?

Anyone can opt in respect of any property — but of course the option has no effect until you have an interest in that property. Where the legal owner of a property is, say, a bare trustee but the beneficiary receives the income, it is the latter who is treated as making the supply and who should opt in respect of it (*Sch 10 Group 8*).

If a property is in joint ownership and the supply is therefore by the 2 owners together, they must jointly elect. They will be treated as a single taxable person and must register as a partnership, even if there is no other joint income.

When should one opt to tax?

There is no need to opt to tax until you have incurred input tax related to the property. If you are occupying the property for your business, your right to recover input tax will depend upon the nature of that business. Opting makes no difference *at that stage* if there is no rental income.

It does if you sublet a part of or the whole of the property because your right to recover then depends on the rental income being standard rated. Even then, this only becomes critical once significant input tax is incurred. Note, however, the pitfall of VAT already incurred on a building subject to the *Capital Items Scheme*. See Chapter 24 for what happens if the use of the building changes from taxable to exempt and why you may have to opt to tax in order to prevent that happening.

See also later in this chapter under *Take care with notifications to Customs* and *Buying and selling tenanted opted property* for further potential problems.

Check your lease

Section 89 allows VAT to be added if a rent is opted, unless the terms of the lease preclude that, so a landlord should check before acting.

The intention pitfall

If your purchaser claims that the option to tax is disapplied because of an intention as to use, ask for evidence of that intention. In *SEH Holdings Ltd (LON/98/1362 No 16771)*, a public house was resold instead of being converted by the purchaser. In confirming that the first sale was standard-rated, the Tribunal commented that, for the option to tax to be disapplied because of an intention to use a building as a dwelling, a vendor must be aware of the purchaser's intention which must be of use by that purchaser. The option was not disapplied where the purchaser was to sell on to another party, who would use the property.

On the other hand, you can opt to tax the sale of a non-residential building to a developer, who intends to convert it into dwellings or a relevant residential building, the sale of which will be zero rated under *Sch 8 Group 5, Item 1* — see earlier in this chapter under *Sales and long leases of zero rated buildings*. *Sch 10, para 2(2B)* permits the option to apply if you get the written agreement of the purchaser together with his statement that the land will be used solely for such zero rated supplies.

The apportionment trap

If an opted property includes a zero-rated building, usually a dwelling, the sale or rent must be apportioned as partly exempt. Examples include a shop with a flat above and an office block with a caretaker's flat.

The scope of the option

The option applies to (*para 3(3)*):

* the entire building including land within its curtilage;
* complexes consisting of a number of units grouped around a fully enclosed concourse or buildings linked internally or by a covered walkway.

An initial 3-month cooling off period is allowed during which you can withdraw the option, subject to the written consent of Customs, if (*para 3(5)*):

- you have neither charged VAT nor reclaimed input tax as a result of the election; and

- there has been no outside the scope disposal of the property as the transfer of a going concern.

After that, the option is irrevocable for 20 years. Do not therefore exercise the option lightly. It has long-term consequences.

What about a building standing in a large area of land?

The curtilage of the building and thus the area affected by the option depends on the circumstances. In Notice 742A *(March 2002) Opting to tax land and buildings,* Customs say the key is how far the services of the building can be utilised. They quote the example of a racecourse grandstand, which may provide electricity and shelter for stalls or other facilities within its peripheral area. The option would cover all the land using those benefits.

Is there a link or not?

An internal fire door between two properties, and which can only be opened in an emergency, does not count.

Covered walkways come in many forms. If you have a situation in which it is questionable whether two buildings are linked, possibly because the walkway is long and not fully enclosed, opt for both of them to be sure. On the other hand, if you do not want the other one to be covered by the option to tax, explain that you do not think it is and send a site plan and description of the walkway, perhaps with photographs, when you write to Customs to opt on the first one. They take a case-by-case view.

If the question has arisen subsequently following the rent or sale of one of the buildings, discuss the facts with Customs.

Subsequent additions to an opted site

Changes to a site after you have waived exemption can complicate matters. The following is what I understood Customs to say at a conference which I attended.

If, having opted to tax building A, you buy more land adjacent to it and build an extension B, the latter is automatically covered by the existing option.

If you then build a separate building, C, this is *not* covered. If you then link C to B, C is still not covered by the option.

Of course, Customs may in due course change their views or a tribunal decision may alter everyone's understanding of such situations.

It follows that:

- It would be sensible in many cases to attach a site plan to your notification to Customs.

- Each time further development occurs, consider whether a fresh notification is required or whether the existing one covers the new work.

Example

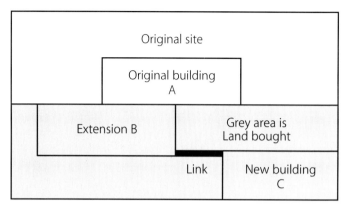

The pitfall in demolishing an opted building

The option terminates if a building is demolished. That means that you must waive exemption for a second time in respect of the building, which you are about to construct, if you intend to let it.

Take care with notifications to Customs

Customs will accept notifications from you in respect of:

- individual buildings;
- all your buildings — unwise; or
- all your buildings with specific named exceptions — also unwise.

You must tell Customs in writing (*Sch 10, para 3.6*) within 30 days for the option to be effective. In *Blythe Ltd Partnership (LON/98/868 No 16011)*, it was held that:

- an election to waive exemption and its notification are separate matters;
- a notification is of no effect if an election has not been made or if the person signing it has no authority to do so.

The case arose because the notification to Customs covered more properties than the partnership had intended. Fortunately for the partners, the Tribunal held that the individual, who signed the letter, had not had authority to do so and, most importantly, that it had never been the intention of the partners to opt in respect of the additional properties. Thus, whilst notification is normally evidence of the election, it can be important to make a formal note of the decision to elect and of the properties which that decision covers. Include a plan of the site indicating the extent of the option.

The 20 year pitfall

How will you ensure that your organisation is aware of which properties have been opted, given that the resulting need to charge VAT lasts at least 20 years? Suppose you opted to tax the rent charged to an associated business occupying part of a new factory. You would do that to protect the right to recover the input tax incurred on it. If that business moved out after a few years and the factory was then fully used by the owner, the people running the business perhaps 10 years later would know nothing about the letting and could easily sell the factory without charging VAT on it. So:

- When a opting a property, think what permanent record/warning you can create.
- Before selling or renting out a property, check whether it could have been opted long ago. Probably, that means asking Customs.

Buying and selling tenanted opted property

The date of notification is a potential pitfall when you buy or sell tenanted commercial property. It is critical if the transaction is to qualify as outside the scope of VAT under the *Transfer of a Going Concern* rules. See Chapter 37, *Buying or Selling a Business* about these.

A deposit creates a tax point, if it is held by the receiving solicitor as agent for the vendor rather than merely as stakeholder for both parties. You must post to Customs your notification of the option to tax at the latest on the same day as you pay the deposit. *Art 5(3) Special Provisions Order (SI 1995/1268)* makes the *relevant date* of the transfer the earliest tax point; ie that created by the deposit rather than when the balance is paid on completion.

In *Higher Education Statistics Agency Ltd ([2000] STC 332)*, a deposit had to be paid on the spot when the property was bought at auction. The subsequent notification was held to be too late.

Then, in *Chalegrove Properties Ltd (LON/99/851 No 17151)*, concerning a negotiated sale rather than an auction, Customs argued that the notification was late because, despite being posted first-class the day before the Friday on which the deposit was paid, it was not *given* to them no later than the *relevant date*, as required by *Art 5(2)*. Customs did not receive the letter until the following Tuesday.

The Tribunal saw it as unreal that letters of notification must be received before a deposit is paid on an agency rather than a stakeholder basis. To be safe, potential purchasers would have to confirm that receipt with Customs. If Customs were right, it also meant that transactions requiring a deposit were disadvantaged compared with those that did not. It held that notification was made in time if posted on the day on which the deposit was paid.

The rationale of the Tribunal's decision was as follows:

- *Section 98 says that any . . . notification . . . to be served on . . . any person for the purposes of this Act may be served . . . by serving it by post in a letter addressed to that person . . . ,*

- *Interpretation Act 1978, Section 7 says that service is deemed to have been effected by posting at a time at which the letter would be delivered ordinarily unless the contrary is proved.* The exception is *unless the contrary intention appears* in the relevant legislation.

- The Tribunal said that *receipt* by Customs of the notification was not required under the scheme of the *TOGC* code. A more balanced and workable interpretation was that *written notification* of the election was *given* when put in the post. In the circumstances of *Article 5(2)*, the Tribunal was satisfied that a *contrary intention appeared*.

Customs have accepted this decision and have revised their policy. However, that they should have taken such a nitpicking point in the first place emphasises the need for care.

If paying VAT on an opted property, get evidence of notification

If asked to pay VAT on the purchase price of the property or on a rent because it is opted, request a copy of the notification to Customs. Completion of the purchase of the property will involve paying a large sum of VAT, which it might be impossible subsequently to get back from the vendor, should it transpire that the latter had not notified Customs. Paying rent involves a longer-term relationship and the possibility of being able to withhold the VAT from subsequent payments. All the same, it is wise is to make sure that the option is effective.

In *Russell Properties (Europe) Ltd (EDN/95/330 No 14228)*, input tax on the purchase of a property was held to be irrecoverable because the vendor had failed to notify Customs of its option to tax.

This is potentially a very serious pitfall for purchasers. Suppose the vendor had moved abroad. How would you set about recovering the VAT?

The service charges trap

Exercise of the option entails standard-rating service charges, since these are rent under a different name. It would be easy to overlook this, especially if the charges are collected by an agent separately from the rent.

Anti-avoidance rule

An anti-avoidance rule disapplies your option if:

- you are selling or renting a property, which is subject to the Capital Items Scheme; and

- the use of the land will not be wholly or mainly for making taxable supplies; and

- that use will be by you, a person responsible for financing the development of the land or a person connected either with you or with such a person.

The rule is complicated as you will discover if you try to follow it through the subparagraphs added to *Sch 10 paras 2 and 3*. You can tell which these are because of their peculiar references!

However, you will not need to worry about this anti-avoidance rule in most ordinary commercial projects to develop a property for sale or letting. It is aimed at preventing partly exempt businesses, such as banks and insurance companies, from reducing the non-recoverable input tax, incurred when they need to refurbish existing offices or to move into new ones, by having an associated company incur the expenditure and rent the property to them. If the option to tax were effective in such a situation, it would enable the recovery of all the VAT on the capital expenditure and the payment of much smaller amounts on the annual rent.

An example of the complexity of this anti-avoidance rule is *Schedule 10, paras 3A(7)* and *(13)*. These rules say that land is exempt and that an option to tax is therefore disapplied if, despite granting a lease, you still occupy the land either alone or together with others and even if you occupy only part of it.

In *Brambletye School Trust Ltd (LON/2000/0456 No 17688)*, a school built a sports hall, which it let to a company it controlled. Although the rent of £28,000 a year was paid, the company had no employees and was managed by the school bursar.

There were some bookings from outside organisations but there were no outside members and the main use was by the school. The membership fees to pupils were charged as part of the school fees and the pupils used the facilities under supervision by the staff. The Tribunal held that the school therefore occupied the sports hall itself. 'Occupation' was a less formal concept than 'possession'. Even if the pupils occupied the hall as members of the club rather than as pupils of the school, the latter also occupied the hall at the same time through the presence of its staff.

If you think you might be affected by this rule, take professional advice.

Input tax incurred prior to opting to tax

If, prior to opting to tax a property, you have already made exempt supplies in respect of it — whether to a tenant or in using yourself for a business making exempt supplies — you must agree with Customs what input tax now becomes recoverable. An apportionment of the tax already incurred must be made — that related to the past exempt outputs remains unrecoverable. See the *Royal and Sun Alliance* case in Chapter 23, *Partial Exemption* re situations in which a property has remained unoccupied pending finding a tenant.

If VAT was incurred more than 6 months prior to registration you would not normally be able to recover it because of the time limit in the rules explained in Chapter 3, *Should I or Must I Register for VAT?* However, an extra statutory concession, referred to in *Para 7.6 of Vol V1–13, Chapter 2, Section 7* of Customs' internal guidance, accepts that that creates an anomaly compared with the position of a business already registered and says that each case will be considered on its merits.

Some questions to check your understanding. Review your answers with the text.

- What are the three kinds of property, the construction of which is zero-rated?
- An electrical subcontractor wins a contract to do the wiring for a new old people's home. The main contractor has told him the work is zero-rated. Is that correct?
- What kind of goods do not qualify as 'building materials'?
- What are the requirements for work on a listed house to be zero-rated?
- How many kinds of project eligible for the 5% reduced rate can you remember?
- You can opt to tax single buildings. However, there are two cases in which more than one building may be involved. What are they?
- There are six property situations in respect of which any option to tax has no effect, not counting those caught by the anti-avoidance rule. How many of the six can you remember?
- What is a 'non-residential building'?
- You are about to exchange contracts to sell a commercial property, which you built 2 years ago. The purchaser wants a clause in the contract that you shall not opt to tax the deal. What do you say to your solicitor?

26.   Recovery of Foreign VAT: the 8th and 13th Directives

This chapter describes the system which enables you to reclaim VAT, which you incur in another Member State of the EU, from the fiscal administration of that State. Similar rules apply to businesses established outside the EU. You may even be able to reclaim from countries outside the EU.

Law

The law is in *Part XX, VAT Regulations (SI 1995/2518)* for EU traders and *Part XXI* for non-EU traders. Notice 723 covers both sets of rules.

VAT incurred in other EU States

The *8th Directive* enables traders registered in an EU State to recover input tax incurred in another EU State provided that they are not liable to register there.

The rules apply primarily to services. Although you may succeed with a claim for minor expenditure on goods used at, say, a trade exhibition, you cannot use the *8th Directive* to reclaim on goods bought for resale. Normally, these would be zero-rated by the supplier on removal to the UK anyway under the rules explained in Chapter 19 on *Exports*. If they remain in the other State, you will have to register there and account for VAT when you dispose of them.

You claim from the fiscal administration of the country concerned:

- using a form, the format of which is standard throughout the EU. Some States accept the English version;
- but it must be filled in in their language and accompanied by:
- a certificate of status; and
- *original* invoices which must comply with the rules for tax invoices in the country concerned.

Claim form *VAT 65* can be obtained by downloading from Customs' website (see page viii). When on the homepage, click *Forms & publications* in the top line and then *Forms – VAT*. Alternatively, you can ring the NAS or write to the Londonderry address on the next page.

To obtain your certificate of status, contact the National Registration Service VAT 66 Section, Deansgate, 62–70 Tettenhall Road, Wolverhampton WV1 4TZ; fax: 01902 392202; e-mail: VAT66@hmce.gsi.gov.uk. Think carefully about the information it must show, such as a trading name, if this appears on the invoices on which you are claiming.

Note:

- Certificate of status, original, not a photocopy, must be submitted to each Member State; then valid for 12 months from the date of issue.
- If you use an agent, a letter of authority or a power of attorney may be needed.

- Invoices should be in the name of the business, not of individuals.
- Minimum claim is £16 for a calendar year.
- Time limit for a claim is 6 months after the end of the calendar year.
- Quarterly claims are possible for claims of at least £130.

Bad news on travel costs

Unfortunately, many other Member States, including France and Italy, do not allow recovery of input tax by their own traders on such travel costs as hotel rooms and meals. That being so, they will not repay you either. The position does vary from State to State so, if the VAT is significant, it is worth checking.

However, all repay on exhibition stand costs, though with varying standards of efficiency. For example, Italy has a poor reputation.

Claims by overseas traders under the EC 13th Directive

The *13th Directive* permits traders overseas to make claims from the VAT administrations of EU States. The rules are similar to those applicable to *8th Directive* claims but the claim year runs to 30 June.

Claim form *VAT 65A* can be downloaded from Customs' website; see re form *VAT 65* on the previous page. Alternatively, write to VAT Overseas Repayments, 8th/13th Directive, Custom House, POB 34, Londonderry BT48 7AE, Northern Ireland.

Beware the time limits

Watch the time limits for claims. These are often enforced.

Claims from non-EU countries

You may be able to claim from non-EU countries. Some non-EU States, such as Iceland, the Czech Republic, Liechtenstein and Estonia have a similar system. If you are incurring significant non-EU VAT, ask if you can make a claim. If your claim is refused, you can complain to Customs because they have power to withhold repayments under the *13th Directive* from traders in a country which does not reciprocate!

Some questions to check your understanding. Review your answers with the text.

- What is the difference between the *8th* and *13th VAT Directives*?
- What supporting documentation do you need for an *8th Directive* claim?

27.   Am I in Business?

The question 'Am I in business?' may seem unnecessary at first thought; the difference between a private individual and a business appears obvious. However, like so much in VAT, it is not as simple as that. Take a charity for the relief of distress like Oxfam; its charitable activity is obviously not a business. However, its retail shops create substantial taxable supplies and thus a liability to be registered for VAT. Many other charities are in business through their fund-raising activities. This chapter explains the consequences and illustrates the problem with stories from the large number of cases on the subject.

Examples of activities which are partly business

There are far more organisations whose activities are partly non-business than you might think. Examples are:

● relief of distress charities, which raise funds through trading;

● colleges and educational establishments, such as colleges and universities, which are engaged in the economic activity of education for fees but which have some students under 19, who do not pay;

● museums, which do not charge for entry to the main collections but which do for special exhibitions or which have shops;

● public bodies, like the House of Commons, whose main activity is non-business but which have income from sources such as restaurants and bars;

● churches, which charge for entry to parts of the building or which have shops.

Special rule for free entry to museums and galleries

Section 33A provides for a special refund to museums and galleries, which do not charge for entry. This is claimed separately from the normal VAT system. Only bodies specified by the Treasury are eligible. The *Refund of Tax to Museums and Galleries Order (SI 2001/2879)* lists a wide range of such bodies of national importance, most, if not all, of which, are publicly funded. The special refund is intended to encourage such institutions not to charge for entry.

A small museum owned by a charity could presumably apply to the Treasury to be added to the specified bodies but it would only be worth doing so if the VAT reclaimed would exceed the possible income from admission charges.

Free entry does not necessarily mean non-business

Input tax is not necessarily disallowed just because an activity includes doing something without charge. In *Imperial War Museum* (*LON/92/118 No 9097*), the Tribunal held that there was only a single business activity when admission charges were waived from 4.30–6pm each day and for school parties and certain visitors. It rejected Customs' argument that, although the business activity did not cease, the free admissions amounted to 'non supplies'.

Taxable income was generated, even when entry was free, from:

- sponsorship — the proposition to sponsors was based on *total* visitor numbers;

- takings in the restaurant and the shop.

The strength of an argument that free entry does not necessarily mean loss of input VAT varies from case to case. For instance, a cathedral or large church will normally solicit donations from visitors but may charge fees to enter a part of the building, such as the crypt and/or have a shop. Thus, as taxable income is generated, there is a right to recovery of a proportion of the input tax incurred in maintaining the building as a whole. How to calculate that proportion must be negotiated.

Charities

You do not avoid being in business simply because you are a charity. Charities benefit from numerous reliefs from VAT. Examples are the zero-ratings in *Sch 8, Groups 12 and 15*, and the exemptions in *Sch 9, Group 7, Item 9* and in *Groups 10, 12 and 13*. However, charities are subject to the same rules as everyone else. If they make taxable supplies in the course or furtherance of a business to a value exceeding the registration limit, they must register for VAT.

The consequences of being partly in business

Being VAT-registered because of a business activity does not mean that all the input tax which you incur can be recovered. You are only entitled to reclaim the tax which relates to a taxable activity *(s 24(5))*. Thus a charity can recover:

- all the VAT directly attributable to its taxable activities; and

- a proportion of that incurred on that part of its overheads, which is partly devoted to running the business side.

This is similar to the partial exemption calculations discussed in that chapter, although, in theory, the calculations are in two stages. That is to say:

- First you identify the VAT attributable to the business activities. All that related to the non-business ones does not qualify as input tax, let alone input tax which might be recoverable.

- Second, you then identify the business VAT, which is related to the taxable activities. In other words, if there are any exempt supplies made by the business, you carry out a partial exemption calculation.

In practice, the business/non-business and the taxable/exempt calculations are often done as a single combined stage because it is difficult to separate the VAT related to the non-business side of an organisation, which operates out of a single office and in which everyone is involved in both the business and the non-business activities. Of course, to do the calculation as a single stage, one needs to be able to value both activities on the same basis. Typically, this means using money values, those of the non-business side being represented by grants and donations, but each case depends upon its facts. However, this approach was rejected as inappropriate by the Divisional Court in *Whitechapel Art Gallery ([1986] STC 156)*.

Customs announced subsequently that they regarded this as applying only to these circumstances — a gallery many of whose exhibitions were free but which charged entry fees for some events. They said nothing about the basis negotiated with *Whitechapel* and they continue to use the method in other situations.

Planning to be in business

Most of the time, one is 'in business' for VAT purposes whether one likes it or not. However, sometimes one wants to be in business in order to recover input tax being incurred on a project.

Suppose you are a local group, which has undertaken a project to restore a feature of historic interest such as a derelict house or garden; the work will take many years and substantial VAT will be incurred on the cost. If you can obtain VAT registration on the grounds that you either open it to the public or intend to do so as soon as sufficient progress has been made, the VAT recovered will be substantial. Having to account for output tax on the entry charges and other income will be relatively unimportant, so this planning point could make an important contribution to the success of the project.

Demonstrating that there is a business

The above example is relatively straightforward. Assuming that your group has got itself organised, there will be a plan with some financial projections of costs and possible income. As is discussed later in this chapter, it is now well-established that one is entitled to register in advance of making any taxable supplies provided that input tax is being incurred for the purposes of a business.

It is not always clear that a business exists or, if it does, when it began. VAT is often incurred a long time, sometimes several years, before the taxable output, to which it is attributable, takes place. Property development projects are examples. In those cases, there is no doubt about there being a business since expenditure is being incurred in the hope of creating an asset, which can be sold at a profit. However, what about an engineer who spends several years working on a machine in his garage in his spare time, more as a hobby than with any expectation that a saleable product will result?

There is no simple answer. Each case depends upon its facts. In many instances, the VAT being incurred is relatively trivial anyway. However, an engineer, who can show a credible intention to develop a machine into a saleable product, is entitled to registration. Having obtained that registration, the engineer is entitled to retain all the VAT claimed, even if the project fails.

Remember, VAT is not taxable on profits or losses but on transactions. Even if all the transactions are expenses, there can still be a business. Naturally, Customs will look carefully at whether the expressed intention to develop a business is credible and at whether each expense incurred is properly attributable to that intention.

What about VAT incurred before I realised I had a business?

Customs have no hesitation in demanding VAT from people who unexpectedly develop hobbies into full-scale businesses. Examples include:

- a professor, who wrote a specialist book on a medical subject which sold so well that the royalties exceeded the registration limit;

- a vintage car enthusiast, who restored vehicles as a hobby, which he developed into a business only to find Customs refusing to allow him to offset the costs on the vehicles restored during the hobby period.

Of course, in such situations, the problem often is that there are no records of those costs, let alone VAT invoices.

The basis for claiming registration at the outset

Article 4(1) of the *6th VAT Directive* defines a 'taxable person' as *any person who independently carries out in any place any economic activity specified in paragraph 2, whatever the purpose or results of that activity.*

Paragraph 2, paraphrased, defines economic activities as all activities of producers, traders and persons supplying services including mining, agriculture and activities of the professions. It says that the exploitation of tangible or intangible property to obtain an income is included. In other words, both rents and royalties are caught.

The CJEC ruled in *Rompelman v Minister van Financien ([1985] 3 CMLR 202)* that one was entitled to VAT registration as soon as one started to incur VAT with the intention of creating taxable outputs. *Rompelman* was a Dutch case concerning the purchase of a flat with a view to making taxable supplies from it, presumably of holiday lettings.

Whilst it would no doubt be wrong to say that Customs ignored *Rompelman* altogether, they continued to demand a close relationship between the expenditure being incurred and the prospect of taxable supplies until they lost *Merseyside Cablevision ([1987] VATTR 134)*. This involved a project to develop cable TV. Before any work on the cable system could start, a licence had to be obtained and substantial costs were incurred in putting together the application for this. Customs said there could be no business until *Merseyside* had the licence, which provided the legal authority for making taxable outputs in due course.

There may have been other issues but, on the face of it, Customs never had a chance of winning this case. Whilst Customs' policy-makers get it right most of the time, they do make mistakes so, if they say you are not in business, don't assume that they are necessarily right!

The National Trust — a business/non-business situation

(*Note:* Though detailed, the following comments are not based on any client relationship with the National Trust.)

An organisation like the National Trust has income from entrance fees, whether paid at the gate or through membership subscriptions and from shops at its properties. You might think that this would mean that all the input tax incurred on a property open to the public is recoverable. However, there is probably room for argument about this at the largest properties.

For example, some are lived in by members of the family which gave the property to the Trust, and all or part of their living quarters are usually closed to the public. Costs related to this part of a property are not incurred for business purposes unless it can be argued that the family act as guardians. Any rent charged to them is an exempt supply against which input tax is disallowed.

In a big house, there are always areas not open for other reasons, such as that the access is unsuitable, they are of no interest or whatever. The question then arises whether these areas count as business because they are merely adjuncts to the main parts on display or whether they are not used for business. Often, it will be apparent that the areas not open are essential to the business consisting of those which are, not some separate activity. Alternatively, they may be used for the agricultural activities, which often take place on the surrounding estate. However, the point should not be taken for granted.

Then, there are the properties not open to the public or for which there are no entrance fees. There are various reasons for this such as

- the property is currently being restored;
- the property is too small or of insufficient interest to be worth opening regularly and is therefore let to a tenant; or
- the property is open space, such as seashore or downs to which it is not feasible to restrict access.

VAT on restoration costs is recoverable, assuming that it is intended to open the property in due course. Properties without regular public access may still be viewable by Trust members, who contact the tenant. Since the rent of a dwelling is exempt, this creates an interesting technical problem to decide which VAT is attributable to the exempt rent and which to maintaining the property for viewing by members. If you add to that the possibility that the tenancy provides for the tenant to spend money on doing up the property in the first place, so that the VAT is not incurred by the Trust, there has to be a planning point here! If the property is open space and charges are not made for access, Customs are likely to argue that it is not a part of the business activity.

If so, the case of *British Field Sports Society ([1998] STC 315)* may be some help. The Society received several million pounds from members as donations towards a campaign on behalf of field sports. The Court held that the Society could recover the VAT incurred on the costs paid for by the donations because the Society was carrying out activities on behalf of its members of the kind which they expected in return for their subscriptions. This was despite the donation income being much the larger sum. It suggests that the National Trust might be able to argue that property from which it does not derive an income is nevertheless held by it in the fulfilment of its general objectives for which its members pay subscriptions.

The definition of 'business'

There is no definition in the law of what is a business activity. *Section 94* does say that 'business' includes any 'trade, profession or vocation' and adds that 'deemed to be the carrying on of a business' are:

- club subscriptions;

- admission charges to premises.

Political, religious, patriotic, philosophical, philanthropic and civic bodies are in business on account of their subscriptions but the latter are exempt under *Sch 9 Group 9, Item 1(e)*. See Chapter 11 on *So What is Exempt?*

You can be in business without making a profit

There is no relief simply because you are loss-making or because you do not attempt to make a profit.

In *Morrison's Academy and Boarding Houses Association ([1978] STC 1)*, the Court of Session pointed out that the meaning of business does not require the objective to be to make profit. This case concerned the provision at cost of accommodation to pupils of the Academy. This was not covered by the exemption for education in *Group 6, Sch 9* because the Association was independent of the Academy. It was irrelevant that it was a charity and that any surplus income had to be applied towards scholarships at the school with which it was connected.

The Court pointed out that the supplies of accommodation were, with differences of detail, similar to those made commercially. The Association's activities were predominantly concerned with the making of taxable supplies to consumers for a consideration.

Asking for money does not of itself create a business

In *Lord Fisher ([1981] STC 238)*, the judge commented that the Court in *Morrison's* had not intended to lay down principles which, if satisfied, would in all cases show that an activity was a business. They were *indicia*, some more useful than others. Lord Fisher had collected from relations and friends contributions towards the cost of running a shoot. It was held that this was not the making of taxable supplies in the course of a business. 'Business' excluded any activity, which is no more than an activity for pleasure and social enjoyment.

Thus, there are no hard and fast rules as to what is or is not a business. One must look at all the facts and come to a view in the light of the overall picture.

To be a business, there must be some consideration

Before starting to incur VAT, stop to think what the output will be against which you will recover. There may be an important planning point to consider. In *Royal Exchange Theatre Trust ([1979] STC 728)*, a charity raised the money to build a theatre, which it then handed over to the company, which was to operate it. The Divisional Court held that the gift of the completed theatre was not a supply. A gift could be made in the course or furtherance of a business but 'business' was not to be construed so widely as to cover a case in which there was no money paid. Moreover the majority of the sums raised had been by donations from the public.

Thus, the problem was the absence of any taxable supplies by the trustees and, without such supplies, they could not register for VAT and recover their input tax.

That their activities had been carried on in a businesslike manner was not sufficient. Looking at those activities as a whole, there was no commercial element which could be regarded as a business.

The *Trustees of the British European Breeders Fund ([1985] VATTR 12 No 1808)* did not want to have to charge VAT on the contributions which the fund collected from the owners of participating stallions based in the UK. It distributed those contributions, plus money added under an agreement with the equivalent bodies in other countries, as prize money for sponsored races. On the basis of *Royal Exchange Theatre Trust*, the Tribunal held that *the activities of trustees, who receive money in circumstances in which they do not make taxable supplies in exchange and who then merely distribute such money in accordance with the relevant trusts in circumstances in which they do not receive any goods or services in return are not, in the absence of any other relevant factor, to be regarded as constituting a business.*

The Fund might have lost if it had itself published the lists of participating stallions. Entry in races sponsored by the Fund was restricted to their progeny and publication might have been held to amount to something done in return and thus consideration for the contributions. However the lists were published by the Thoroughbred Breeders Association, not by the trustees, and the latter had no contractual obligation to the owners of the participating stallions. The trustees therefore did nothing in return for the contributions paid to them.

However, consideration can be provided by a third party. See *Largs Golf Club ([1985] STC 226)* where loans to the trustees owning the course, which were made to finance its purchase, were held to be part of the consideration for the facilities of membership in addition to the subscriptions paid to the club.

Contributions towards costs may not be consideration

In the *Greater London Red Cross Blood Transfusion Service ([1983] VATTR 241)*, 'capitation fees' or 'transfusion fees' negotiated with the DHSS were held not to be taxable supplies made in the course or furtherance of a business. They were intended to be a contribution towards the administration expenses of finding the volunteers. The latter donated their blood and this was not a business activity. That the blood was donated did not of itself mean that the Service was itself in business, that illustrated the distinction between a voluntary service to the community and a business. The sole object of the Service was to provide a contact point between hospitals and those willing to provide blood and this was not a business activity.

An activity may be a business despite much donation income

In *Yoga for Health Foundation Ltd ([1984] STC 630)*, a registered charity was held to be carrying on a business even though up to 43% of its income had come from donations. The Tribunal accepted that there was no commercial element or profit motive in the Foundation's activities. Nevertheless they 'bore the indicia of a business'. *YFH* demonstrates how difficult it can be to show that a charitable activity is not a business.

The *RSPCA (LON/90/1111 No 6218)* was held to be in business when it made charges for treating animals at its clinics. The clinics were running at a substantial loss. By agreement with the British Veterinary Association, local vets provided their services in rotation. Treatment at the clinics was only for emergencies and where the owner was unable to pay normal veterinary fees. If an operation was done, a fee was agreed in advance and, in about 80% of cases, the whole fee was recovered, possibly in instalments. The Tribunal accepted that services in the clinics were akin to those in veterinary practices. There was a direct link between the payments made and the treatment provided. That much of the RSPCA's income came from legacies was relevant only to the dividing line between its business and non-business activities. Having held that the income at the 37 clinics was received in the course of a business at those clinics, the Tribunal sent the parties away to consider an appropriate apportionment.

Courses in religion can be a business activity

Similarly, in the *Holy Spirit Association for the Unification of World Christianity (LON/84/179 No 1777)*, courses of a religious nature at a residential centre were held to be taxable supplies made in the course or furtherance of a business. The Association earned only a small part of its income from the courses. Substantial deficits were met by donations and a subsidy from the Moon Foundation. The Association argued that religious teaching by a religious charity was not a business and that it had no overall business activity. The Tribunal held that the charges, even if only made to discourage those wanting a free weekend, were 'businesslike'. In *Church of Scientology of California ([1979] STC 297)*, the Divisional Court had held that, as a matter of law, there was no reason why a body, which promoted a religion or a religious philosophy, could not do so as a business. That the Association was subsidised did not prevent it carrying on a business.

In *Creflo Dollar Ministries (MAN/01/64 No 17705)* a religious convention, to which admission was free, was held to be partly a business activity because its purpose, apart from promoting the Christian faith, was to publicise the videos produced both at it and at earlier events, together with books and audio tapes, which were sold by the Appellant. The Tribunal held that the input tax incurred in putting on the convention was recoverable in the proportion that *CDM's* business income bore to its total income

Relief of distress at below cost is non-business

Customs say on page 12 of the VAT Notice 701/1/95 *Charities* that

- welfare services and related goods supplied by charities are non-business when made consistently below cost to distressed people for the relief of their distress;

- meals on wheels delivered by a charity as the agent of a local authority are part of the local authority's non-business activities; and

- 'below cost' means the cost of providing the welfare is subsidised by at least 15% from the charity's own funds; ie that the recipient of the welfare supply pays no more than 85% of the cost of making the supply.

Some questions to check your understanding. Review your answers with the text.

- What is the difference between VAT related to a non-business activity and that incurred on an exempt one?

- How many examples of businesses with a non-business side to them can you recall?

- What is the fundamental difference found by the Courts between charges made by a boarding house run by a charity for children attending a college and contributions collected from friends by the owner of a shoot?

- To establish that you have a business activity in order to reclaim the VAT incurred on it, what must you make sure that you achieve?

28.   Agency is Special

A contract of agency involves arranging for a supply of goods or services in return for a commission, rather than buying them and reselling at a profit margin. You knew that? Well then, why is it that so many people fail to recognise an agency situation when they see one, let alone work out its consequences and whether any action is needed to change them?

Although *s 47* contains some rules on agency, they only deal with certain situations. Agency crops up all over the place in VAT. Insurance and finance brokers earn commissions which are specialist subjects in their own right. See the comment on *Sch 9 Groups 2 and 5* in Chapter 11 on *So What is Exempt?* Then there are zero-ratings for several kinds of commission in *Sch 8 Group 7*, International Services. The *Place of Supply of Services Order* contains relief for various agency commissions in *art 14* and in *art 16* via *Sch 5 para 8*. See Chapter 22, *Exports and Imports of Services*.

Thus, agency is to a large extent part of other subjects rather than one in its own right. However, there are points which need to be understood. This chapter explains them and why sometimes one wants to be an agent and sometimes not.

Why agency is special

Agency is special because it involves a different kind of situation to the one normally met, one which can catch you out if you do not think carefully about it. People in business are often casual in their use of language. They use the word 'agent' without understanding its legal significance. Thus, 'motor agents' are no such thing. They buy and resell vehicles.

Understanding the difference between acting as an agent and as a principal is important. An agent sells on behalf of a principal. Thus, for a sale for £100 on which the commission is 10%, the output is the £10 commission, not the £100. The latter is an output of the principal. This of course makes a big difference to their respective VAT responsibilities.

So, if a contract is of agency there are two supplies, of the goods or services by the principal and of the agency services by the agent. The VAT treatment can be different. For example, a commission is not zero-rated merely because the goods are. Thus food and books are zero-rated, but a commission for selling them is standard-rated.

The undisclosed agent rules for goods

An 'undisclosed' agent is a term meaning an agent who acts in his own name, so that the supplier and the customer do not know each other's identity. A commercial reason for this might be that, if the parties did know, they could deal direct and cut out the agent.

If the transaction is in goods, an agent acting in his own name is regarded for VAT purposes as buying and reselling them. That means that the agent is responsible for collecting and accounting to Customs for the output tax on the full value of the sale. The position on the commission differs according to whether the supplier is another UK business or is outside the UK.

Non-UK suppliers of goods

If the supplier is in another EU State, the supply is dealt with under what Customs call the 'commissionaire' arrangements. Despite the contract being one of agency, the agent is treated for VAT purposes as buying and reselling as a principal. The agent must obtain an invoice from the supplier for the value of the goods net of commission. Thus, if an agent sells on 20% commission:

- the agent invoices in his own name to the UK customer for £100 plus VAT;
- the non-UK supplier invoices for the goods at £80.

For goods from an EU source, the agent accounts for acquisition VAT, which he offsets in the usual way as input tax. However, he still has the output tax on the sale to pay to Customs.

If the goods are imported, the agent will have import VAT to pay, which is reclaimed in the usual way, as explained in Chapter 20 on *Imports and Acquisitions of Goods*. The agent accounts for output tax when he collects this on the sale in due course.

Customs accept that costs incurred in the UK, such as warehousing and handling, can be seen as supplies to the agent, who can therefore recover VAT on them. *Business Brief 9/2000*, which announced the change of policy on commissionaire arrangements, does not say how the charge to the principal to recover such costs shall be treated. Presumably, it will be treated as outside the scope of VAT but the basis for this is unclear. If the supply is seen as being, for VAT purposes, to the agent, the refund from the principal can hardly be seen as repayment of a disbursement. Unfortunately, *VAT Information Sheet 3/00* does not deal either with this point or with how VAT on any retrospective volume rebate is to be dealt with.

These 'commissionaire' arrangements for goods brought into the UK avoid the UK agent having to charge VAT on commissions to non-UK principals, who might be reluctant to pay it, even though they could reclaim it under the 8th or13th VAT Directives. They were introduced from July 2000 because of the problem that, elsewhere in the EU, Roman law treats an agent acting in his own name as making the supply of goods. That meant that UK agents were at a competitive disadvantage in having to charge VAT on commissions to non-UK principals.

Why buy as agent?

To ensure that you need only charge VAT on your commission, make sure you inform the customer that you are selling as an agent in order to avoid the undisclosed agency or commissionaire rules in *s 47*. Notices in a shop and wording on any invoice you issue should say so — quoting the supplier's name where that is practicable.

An alternative to acting as an agent is to have a contract under which the goods are bought at whatever sale price is achieved, less the agreed commission. That works for perishable items, such as vegetables, fruit or flowers, where the price varies according to market demand and unsold goods have to be destroyed.

UK suppliers of goods

The normal position for supplies from UK suppliers is that the agent obtains a VAT invoice from the supplier for the same value as the sale. The input tax thus offsets the output tax. The agent's commission and VAT thereon is invoiced separately to the principal, whether this is the supplier or the customer. If the principal is the customer, the transaction can be shown on the same invoice as for the goods, in which case there are then two supplies and two sums of VAT on the document. If the principal is the supplier, you can, if you wish, use the commissionaire arrangements explained above.

Non-UK suppliers of services

Similarly, the commissionaire arrangements mean that UK undisclosed agents for supplies of services are treated as making the supplies. Where the place of supply for the service in question is the country of the supplier, this means that the onward supply is by the UK agent. If the service is covered by *Sch 5*, it will be subject to the reverse charge when imported by the agent. See Chapter 22, *Exports and Imports of Services*. In both cases, the onward supply by the agent is standard-rated to a UK principal unless, of course, it is exempt.

Planning points on agency

Sometimes you want to be an agent and sometimes you do not. Take second-hand goods, such as women's clothing. There is an active market in expensive dresses, suits and accessories, which are lightly worn. Typically, a shop will take these in, charging commission of 25% or so, on a basis such as this:

- initial price   £100
- if unsold after, say, 2 months, cut to   £50
- if unsold in a further 2 months, cut to   £25
- if unsold after, say, 6 months in shop, recycled or given away.

What is a VAT-efficient structure for such an arrangement? Since the private owner of the clothes and any purchaser are unregistered, the shop should minimise the output tax on a sale. It could do this by using the *Second-hand Scheme* under which it would only have to account for VAT on the profit margin. See that chapter for details. However, using the *Second-hand Scheme* involves keeping special records. It might well be simpler for the contractual arrangement to be one of agency selling on commission rather than buying and selling the clothes. The owner would not wish to buy the clothes before selling them anyway in order to avoid unsold items.

If the shop was selling clothes for babies and young children, and you used the same arrangement, the commission would be standard-rated. Yet the clothes are zero-rated! The VAT-efficient arrangement this time is for the shop to take the clothes in on terms that, on selling an item, it buys it for, say, 75% of the sale price.

Another case in which you might want to sell as an agent is new goods, such as craft items, produced by unregistered suppliers. If you handle the goods as an agent, you account for VAT only on your commission to the vendor. The sale of the goods themselves is outside the scope of VAT being made by the owner (who is unregistered), not by you. The point does not apply to works of art bought from the artist because a gallery is allowed to use the *Second-hand Scheme* for these.

An example of a pitfall in agency

One of the reasons agency causes problems is that its existence is not always obvious. For example, a music publisher had a contract with a newly formed rock group under which he:

- hired recording studios and incurred various similar costs for which he paid; and

- was to recoup these in due course by deduction from the group's royalties.

The publisher was thus incurring the costs as the agent of the group and therefore had no right to recover as input tax the VAT on them. The problem was that the input tax incurred on the costs was not input tax of the publisher, despite the fact that he had a legal responsibility to the various suppliers to pay for them. He was merely disbursing the money as the undisclosed agent of the rock group.

The contract ought to have provided for the publisher:

- to incur the various costs necessary to enable the group to make the recordings; and

- to make charges to the group, the amount of which would relate to stated expenses incurred in making the recordings, which charges would only become payable once there were royalties to meet them — when the rock group would either be liable to register or could do so voluntarily and recover the VAT on the charges.

That would have ensured that the publisher incurred the costs in the first place and subsequently made an onwards supply to recover the amount of them if the recordings were a success.

The law of agency has been the subject of numerous commercial law cases, let alone VAT ones. The relevant considerations as to what makes a contract of agency depend upon the circumstances and it would be counter-productive and potentially misleading to attempt to summarise them here.

Allergycare (Testing) Ltd (LON/99/1338 No 18026) is another example of misunderstanding of agency causing much financial damage. *Allergycare* charged a franchise fee to self-employed food allergy testers. It arranged with organisations such as health food shops, gymnasia, hotels, and pharmacies for the testers to carry out tests on their premises. The fee paid by the customer was split between the tester, the venue and *Allergycare*. The latter thought that it was supplying exempt medical tests to the public, the testers acting as its agents. The Tribunal found the tests were standard rated but, luckily for *Allergycare*, it agreed with Customs that the testers were not agents. VAT was therefore due on the sums received from the testers, not on the total charged to the customer. That was of course bad enough but, if *Allergycare* really had achieved an agency agreement, it would have been far worse.

Does an agent collect money on your behalf?

There is a pitfall in any situation in which someone else collects money due to you. The liability for any output tax is yours, not that of the agent. You therefore need to make sure that you obtain statements promptly, showing the output tax for which you are liable and any input tax you can reclaim on expenses disbursed on your behalf with, of course, the tax invoices related to the latter. Examples of possible situations are:

- Standard-rated rents collected, maintenance expenditure paid out on your behalf by a property agent.

- Takings collected by door-to-door salesmen.

- VAT on the sale of a commercial property, which is held by your solicitor.

In theory, these sums should have arrived in your bank account by the time that the VAT return is due at the end of the month following the end of the period to which it relates. However, that does not mean that they will have been accounted for as outputs of the period to which they relate, rather than of the one in which they are received. See Chapter 7, *The Time of Supply Rules* for more comment.

Some questions to check your understanding. Review your answers with the text.

- What is an undisclosed agent?

- How do the rules differ for a transaction carried out by an undisclosed agent as compared with one where the supplier invoices the customer direct?

- If you were selling second-hand children's clothing, would you wish to do so as an agent for the unregistered vendor?

29. Joint Ventures

'Joint venture' is a term used by people to describe a variety of situations. Few people understand the ramifications of these and each case has to be looked at in the light of the facts. Everyone, including Customs, finds this a difficult and complex subject in which each situation differs from the next. This chapter therefore only attempts to provide some general guidance.

People use the term 'joint venture' loosely and without really understanding what they mean. This can create the dangerous situation that legally incorrect 'facts' are given to advisers. That is a recipe for trouble!

People devise schemes for making money in combination with others on the basis that they will share in the profit resulting. To them, the arrangement is straightforward. The lawyers then get involved and agreements are drawn up, which become more and more complicated as negotiations proceed. I have often found with property deals for example that, by the relatively late stage at which I am asked for advice, the legal contracts are so complicated that it takes several hours of reading to discover what is supposed to be happening!

For what it is worth, I have usually found at least one weakness or non-sequitur in such agreements, which is nothing to do with VAT but which is apparent to someone reading the agreements from cold. Be warned! It is all too easy for lawyers to lose track of points of detail in the course of protracted negotiations during which they have to amend agreements. Keep it simple if possible and make sure you read the finished result before you sign it!

Examples of joint venture arrangements are:

- simple agreements to cooperate together, each side bearing its own costs;

- partnerships, albeit limited to a single project — though many agreements claim that they are not intended to create a partnership;

- a limited company in which each party has shares;

- an agreement under which a property entrepreneur takes possession of a site on terms which provide for a building to be constructed for the site owner, the remuneration to the entrepreneur depending upon success in meeting an agreed price and with a bonus or a penalty if the cost comes in either lower or higher than budget.

Sometimes, it is practicable for the VAT accounting to be through the existing VAT returns of each party. This is most likely to be possible when the project is to produce a product or service, which can readily be sold by one or both the parties. It is unlikely to be feasible where a single asset, such as a property or a ship is involved — unless it is owned by only one of the parties.

Planning points

Where a property is concerned, each party probably requires some security for the expenditure it incurs, especially if it is paying for renovation or construction costs. That usually means some form of joint ownership with the proceeds being paid into a joint venture bank account before being distributed. Since it is not practicable to split a property sale into two or more parts so as to account for them through separate VAT returns, it follows that the joint venture is likely to have to register as such.

If the parties each make sales and incur costs and simply combine the figures from these to arrive at a notional income and expenditure account for the venture, the resulting balance payable from one to the other could be a taxable supply or merely an outside the scope division of the profit or loss thereon, depending upon the precise facts. Thus, in *Thorstone Developments Ltd (LON/01/0007 No 17821)*, a 'share of profit' was held to be standard rated because there was no partnership. It was therefore a charge between the parties to a joint venture.

If a partner in a separately registered joint venture incurs costs related to it, they must be recharged with VAT to that joint venture. An example might be staff time. The division of the profit or loss resulting is then an outside the scope distribution to each of the joint venturers.

Since few people understand the VAT aspects of joint ventures, it follows that, as with agency, this is an aspect of commercial life, the VAT aspects of which need carefully checking in each case.

A question to check your understanding. Review your answer with the text.

- How many kinds of joint venture can you think of?

30.   The Second-hand Goods Scheme

The *Second-hand Goods Scheme*, often called the *Margin Scheme,* helps anyone who deals in goods bought from people not registered for VAT. It also covers second-hand cars on which no input tax was recovered when bought new.

The law

The *EC 7th VAT Directive* sets the rules for a scheme for second-hand goods throughout the European Union. In UK law, the *Special Provisions Order (SI 1995/1268)* contains the main principles. Notice 718 sets out detailed rules on, for instance, records and contains regulations made by Customs under powers given to them in the Order. The Notice thus itself has legal effect.

This chapter covers the main principles of the Scheme. For more details including comment specific to vehicles, horses and ponies, see the Notice.

Key points

The *Second-hand Goods Scheme* covers most second-hand goods, works of art, collector's items and antiques. The key points are:

- You pay tax on your profit margin, not on the selling price — though the latter remains the value of the supply. It is therefore sales, not the profit margin, which decides the liability to register.

- You must have bought the goods either from an unregistered person, usually a private individual, or from another dealer under the Scheme.

- For items costing more than £500, a stock book and purchase and sale invoices are needed.

- *Global Accounting* allows purchases of all items costing less than £500 to be lumped together and offset against the total sales of such items. VAT is only due on the difference between total sales and total purchases of them. If purchases exceed sales, no VAT is due and the excess is carried forward to add to purchases in the following period.

- For sales under *Global Accounting*, you must have purchase invoices, although full supplier details are not required. Sales invoices are not compulsory unless the sale is to another dealer.

- Goods, which you have created yourself, are not second-hand. That includes a horse or pony bred by you.

The Second-hand Goods Scheme is optional

You do not have to use the Scheme either generally or for individual transactions but you are likely to wish to do so, unless you are selling to a VAT-registered buyer, who is not a dealer.

Goods eligible for the Scheme

Whilst most second-hand items are eligible, not everything is. The rules are:

- The goods must be *moveable tangible property* so buildings are not eligible (*Special Provisions Order (SI 1995/1268), Art 2*).

- The item must be 'suitable for further use as it is or after repair'.

- You must not buy on a tax invoice — if you do you can offset the input tax against the output tax on the full price outside the Scheme.

- Whilst an item purchased from a vendor in another EU state under the Scheme is eligible, one bought from outside the EU or as an acquisition is not.

A trader in parts, such as components from scrapped cars, can use the Scheme subject to allocating a cost to any item costing more than £500.

The requirement that the goods be not bought on a tax invoice means that, within the UK, goods are not eligible until they have passed through the hands of someone not registered for VAT. Exceptions are:

- Second-hand cars on which the input tax was blocked.

- Works of art bought from the creator or the creator's heirs.

If an item is bought from a private individual or a dealer in another EU State, the former will not issue a tax invoice and the latter will probably use the Scheme. No acquisition VAT is then due and the goods are eligible. See later under *Buying from another EU State* for more on this.

VAT on repair and restoration costs

VAT on the cost of restoration or repair is recoverable outside the *Second-hand Goods Scheme*. That means that such costs cannot be added to the purchase price of the goods for Scheme purposes.

Global Accounting

Global Accounting calculates output tax liability on the excess, if any, of sales over purchases in each VAT period so:

- Output VAT is due on the total margin using the VAT fraction 7/47ths.

- Any losses on individual items are allowed against profits on others within the overall total of sales.

- The offset of total purchases against total sales means that, when large purchases are made, the strain on cashflow is mitigated by the reduction in the output VAT payable. Of course, you must understand this delaying of your output tax liability. Otherwise, in a corresponding period of high sales and low purchases, the VAT due will be a nasty surprise.

- Any excess of purchases over sales is carried forward to add to purchases in the next period.

The £500 limit

Global Accounting cannot be used for items which individually cost more than £500. If a number are bought as a lot, *Global Accounting* can still be used provided that, on the basis of a fair apportionment of the cost, no item exceeds £500. If one or more do, their cost values must be removed from the Global Accounting records and they must be sold under the ordinary *Second-hand Goods Scheme*.

Other goods not eligible

The following goods are also not eligible for *Global Accounting*:

* motor vehicles;

* aircraft;

* boats and outboard motors;

* caravans and motor caravans;

* motorcycles;

* horses and ponies.

This is because dealers in these goods have no difficulty in keeping records item by item and in using the normal *Second-hand Goods Scheme*. In any case, the majority of items cost more than £500 each.

Initial stocks when starting to use Global Accounting

When starting to use *Global Accounting*, existing stock on hand can be counted as purchases for the first period. This of course requires a stock valuation.

There is no set basis for valuing stock. If you do not have records of the purchase cost of items held, selling prices less estimated profit margins might be an acceptable basis. The requirement to 'identify separately any eligible stock on hand' suggests that Customs will require a detailed listing of stock quantities, even if an overall value is used.

It would be wise to discuss the facts of each case with Customs and to agree the valuation used.

Records for the Second-hand Goods Scheme

The records required for goods sold under the full Scheme are a stock book and purchase and sale invoices containing the information specified below. Purchase invoices from other dealers and all your sales invoices must include the declaration *Input tax has not been and will not be claimed by me in respect of the goods sold on this invoice*.

Those for *Global Accounting* transactions are more simple. A stock book is not required for goods sold under *Global Accounting*.

Purchase and sales invoices

Purchase invoices for *Global Accounting* are made out:

- if buying from a private vendor — by the dealer buying;

- if buying from another dealer — by the dealer selling.

Purchase invoices must show:

- the buying dealer's name and address;

- the seller's name and address;

- invoice number;

- date of transaction;

- description of goods stating their nature and number. 'Assorted goods' will not do;

- total price;

- endorsement as a *Global Accounting Invoice*.

Sales invoices for *Global Accounting* must show the selling dealer's name and address and similar details to those for purchases — though the buyer's name and address are only required if the buyer is another dealer, who needs a purchase invoice. On a sales invoice, you can avoid mentioning *Global Accounting* by making the declaration quoted above under *Records for the Second-hand Goods Scheme*.

Purchase records

Purchase records must show invoice numbers, date of purchase, description of the goods and total price. Even if Customs are satisfied with a note of the nature of the goods and the total number of items rather than a full description of them, such a purchase record is more detailed than many dealers would otherwise keep, especially when buying for cash.

Sales records

The records you need are:

- your normal cash sale records, such as till rolls; and

- a list of sales to other dealers for which you have issued invoices.

Any sales on credit must be accounted for at the time of sale, not when the cash is received.

How do I treat part-exchange goods?

If you take goods in part-exchange, the selling price for Scheme purposes must include the value of the part-exchanged goods. Suppose you sell a car for £2,500 and take one in part-exchange for which you allow £500. The selling price in your stock book must be £2,500. The purchase price of the part-exchange car in the stock book would be £500 regardless of its trade value, since this is the amount, which you have allowed to the customer.

For various cases on this subject, see *Trade in values offered by motor dealers* in Chapter 8, *The Value of Supply Rules — How Much You Must Pay*.

If you are buying from a private person or unregistered dealer, you can show the part-exchange items on your sales invoice provided you include the information needed for a purchase invoice

Losses due to breakages, theft etc

The *Global Accounting* purchases total must be reduced by the cost of losses due to breakage, theft etc. This is because the global margin subject to VAT would otherwise be reduced by the full cost of losses. Under the normal *Second-hand Goods Scheme*, VAT is only due on those goods sold but the margin earned on them is not reduced by the cost of losses.

The theory of this is understandable; how it is to be applied in practice is not, given the difficulty of identifying such losses. In practice, Customs may only be able to enforce it where evidence of individual losses exists, such as an insurance claim.

Stock adjustment on ceasing to use Global Accounting

If you cease to use *Global Accounting*, when, for instance, you deregister or sell your business, you must make a closing adjustment by adding your *Global Accounting* stock at cost to the value of your sales. You then deduct, as usual, your purchases during the period in arriving at the VAT due under your *Global Accounting* calculation. This collects from you VAT on the unsold stock, which has previously been allowed as a deduction from sales.

Goods sold to foreign customers

Second-hand goods taken out of the UK remain eligible for zero-rating under the rules applicable to all goods. In practice, sales to customers within the EU are likely to be dealt with under the Scheme.

Do not confuse an export outside the EU with a removal within the EU. Second-hand goods sold *under the Second-hand Goods Scheme* are taxed in the country where they are sold. There is no zero-rating merely because they are removed to another EU state but a VAT-registered buyer in that State does not incur acquisition VAT.

Selling to foreign customers under the normal rules

You can account under the ordinary rules for an export to a customer outside the EU but you must issue an invoice in the usual way. Although this will show the sale as zero-rated, proof of the physical export of the goods must be obtained. See Chapter 19, *Exports of Goods*.

If the customer takes the goods abroad, Notice 704 *VAT Retail Exports* applies. See in particular the comments re second-hand goods.

If you sell for export, you must so arrange your scheme records as to be able to separate the zero-rated margins from those which are standard-rated.

For sales within the EU, both proof of removal and the customer's VAT number are required. As the EU purchaser will then have to account for acquisition VAT and will not be able to sell the goods under the Margin Scheme in his own country, he is unlikely to wish to give a VAT number. Thus, in practice, you are likely to account for VAT on your profit margin on sales to dealers elsewhere in the EU rather than claim the zero-rating.

Adjusting Global Accounting purchases for foreign sales

If you zero-rate an export or a removal of goods included in *Global Accounting* stocks, you must reduce your purchases for *Global Accounting* purposes by the cost of the item zero-rated.

Buying from another EU State

Correspondingly, beware of this pitfall if you buy from a dealer elsewhere in the EU. Do not give your VAT number. If you do, you may be able to negotiate a lower price for the purchase to reflect the VAT saving to the vendor, but you then will have to account for UK acquisition VAT and charge output VAT on the full price.

If you buy from a registered trader in another EU State, who recovered input tax on its purchase, that trader must charge tax on its resale. He will zero rate it as a removal to the UK. Acquisition VAT is then payable by you and the item is not eligible for the *Second-hand Goods Scheme*.

VAT on imports from outside the EU

The importer of goods purchased from outside the EU must pay import VAT. These goods are not eligible for the Margin Scheme except for cars and works of art, antiques and collector's pieces.

A car bought under the Scheme from a dealer in another Member State, who has imported it, can be sold in the UK under the Scheme. It cannot if the car is bought from the other dealer zero rated as an acquisition — explained in Chapter 20, *Imports and Acquisitions of Goods*. Various tribunal cases have shown that this pitfall has caught numerous UK dealers — in particular when buying cars from Ireland, which were imported secondhand from Japan.

Works of art, antiques and collector's pieces are taxed on import at 5% but remain eligible for the *Second-hand Goods Scheme*.

Agents who sell second-hand goods in their own name

An agent, who acts in his own name in the sale of goods, is regarded as buying and selling those goods, as explained in Chapter 28, *Agency is Special*. The agent must account for output tax on the sale of the goods but can use the *Second-hand Goods Scheme*, subject to meeting its rules. The net effect is the same provided that the *Second-hand Goods Scheme* is used.

Acting for the buyer

If the agent acts for the buyer under the *Second-hand Goods Scheme*, the selling price of the goods for VAT purposes will be the buying price plus the commission. Thus the VAT due will be on that commission, but under the Scheme.

If the goods are ineligible for the Scheme because the seller charges VAT on them to the agent, VAT is due on the full selling price including the commission to the buyer. However, the input tax is recoverable, so the net VAT due from the agent is the same.

Acting for the seller

If the agent acts for the seller, the purchase and selling prices will be the same. If the *Second-hand Goods Scheme* applies, no output VAT is due under the Scheme. It is due on the commission via an ordinary tax invoice issued independently of the Scheme.

If the seller is VAT-registered and charges VAT on the goods to the agent, the input tax incurred on the purchase will equal the output tax charged to the buyer. Both entries must of course be included on the agent's VAT return. The agent separately invoices his commission plus VAT to the seller.

Need for VAT invoices in the correct name

Agents, who act in their own names for sales not under the *Second-hand Goods Scheme*, should be careful to obtain purchase invoices from sellers addressed to them, not to the buyers. Theoretically, this should be automatic since the seller will usually not know who the buyer is, but it would be wise not to take it for granted. Customs may not take the point if invoices are incorrectly addressed but this cannot be relied upon.

The Auctioneers' Scheme

The *Auctioneers' Scheme* is a method of accounting similar to the *Second-hand Goods Scheme*. It covers the same goods as the *Second-hand Goods Scheme*. Thus, if the vendor charges VAT on the goods, they are not eligible for the Scheme. However, the auctioneer is still treated as buying and reselling the goods and the normal rules for agents apply as explained earlier.

The auctioneer will normally wish to use it in order not to have to charge VAT on the full selling price to the buyer. The normal rules also apply if the auctioneer chooses not to use the Scheme.

An auctioneer might not wish to use the Scheme when selling to a dealer, who intends to export the goods. If the auctioneer sells on a tax invoice, the dealer will then recover the VAT on any buyer's premium, in the form of a profit margin included in the selling price, against the zero-rated export sale.

Under the *Auctioneers' Scheme*, the accounting is not the same as for sales by an agent despite similarities.

How the Auctioneers' Scheme works

The auctioneer is liable for output tax at 7/47ths of the margin between the purchase price and the selling price of the goods.

The purchase price is the hammer price less his commission.

If an exempt charge is made for insurance, this is also not a part of the margin calculations.

The selling price is the hammer price plus any buyer's premium and any other charges made to the buyer such as packing, transport and insurance unless these services are a separate supply in their own right.

Example

This example is based on a selling commission of 11.75% and a buyer's premium of 17.625%.

	£
Hammer price	1,000.00
Less commission 11.75%	117.50
Purchase price	£882.50
Selling price £1000 plus buyer's premium	1,176.25
Margin — selling price less purchase price	293.75
Output VAT × 7/47ths	£43.75

Invoices to vendors

The auctioneer issues an invoice showing:

- auctioneer's name and address;
- vendor's name and address;
- invoice number;
- date of sale;
- hammer price of goods (and, presumably, catalogue number if any, though Customs do not state so);
- commission due from vendor;
- net sum due to vendor;
- when the vendor is registered, a declaration signed by the auctioneer that 'input tax deduction has not been and will not be claimed in respect of the goods sold on this invoice'.

Invoices to buyers

The invoice issued to the buyer must show:

- the auctioneer's name, address and VAT number;
- buyer's name and address;

- invoice number;

- date of sale;

- catalogue number;

- hammer price;

- buyer's premium and any other charges which are part of the margin;

- amount due from buyer;

- the certificate 'input tax deduction has not been and will not be claimed by me in respect of the goods sold on this invoice'.

Reference to VAT on invoices

The auctioneer must not show the amount of VAT on either purchase or selling invoices. Customs accept references such as *VAT-inclusive commission at 11.75%* or *commission at 10% plus VAT at 17.5%*. However, if such a reference to VAT is made, they require the addition of a statement on the invoice that *this amount includes VAT which must not be shown separately or reclaimed as input tax.*

Zero-rated goods sold at auction

If the goods are zero-rated, such as books, so is the margin. VAT is only due on any charges made outside the Scheme.

Correct identification of goods is important

Whilst most of the goods sold by auction will be eligible for the *Second-hand Goods Scheme* and therefore for the *Auctioneers' Scheme*, not all will be. The following appear to be examples of where the auctioneer will have to collect VAT on the full selling price because the sale to him by the vendor will carry VAT on the purchase price.

- Industrial equipment, such as the contents of a factory.

- Farm sales — though some items might be non-business assets of the farmer.

- Retail stocks.

Auctioneers should be wary of handing over the proceeds including VAT of the sale of such goods without obtaining a tax invoice to support recovery of the input tax offsetting the output tax.

Example of a lot sold plus VAT

The arithmetic works thus:	£
Hammer price	1,000.00
VAT thereon at 17.5%	175.00
Total purchase price to auctioneer	£1,175.00
Hammer price	1,000.00
Buying premium @ 15%	150.00
	1,150.00
VAT thereon at 17.5%	201.25
Total selling price by auctioneer	£1,351.25

Thus, the auctioneer has output tax to account for of £201.25 against which he offsets the £175.00 input tax from the vendor.

As this is not a *Second-hand Goods Scheme* sale, the auctioneer invoices separately to the vendor his selling commission plus VAT, just as any other agent would.

Some questions to check your understanding. Review your answers with the text.

- What is the difference between a sale made under the *Second-hand Scheme* and an ordinary sale?

- What does *Global Accounting* involve?

- Can you recover VAT on repair costs for an item sold under the Scheme?

- If you buy goods from a dealer in another EU State, why should you normally not want to give your VAT number?

- How are auctioneers affected by the Scheme?

31.   The Retail Schemes

The *Retail Schemes* are needed because retailers sell mostly for cash or against credit cards. It would be much too cumbersome for them to issue tax invoices. Even though modern tills increasingly provide most of the detail needed, many small shops do not have such systems.

The Schemes are a means of estimating the amount of VAT due on retail sales. It is 'estimating' because, if you could calculate accurately what you owed, you would not need a Scheme! Users often do not realise this. They see the Schemes as a substitute for issuing tax invoices. In reality, the accuracy of a Scheme depends on the circumstances in which it is used and you need to think carefully about which is the best for you.

The Schemes use such methods as calculating the estimated selling prices of only a proportion of your purchases of goods for resale or using a ratio of goods bought at one rate as a proportion of total goods. Whilst this may have the merit of simplicity, it is all too easy for errors in the calculations or distorting factors to produce a result, which causes an overpayment compared with that produced by the most favourable available Scheme.

The law

The *VAT Regulations, Regs 66–75* say little. Notice 727 *Retail Schemes* and its various subsidiary notices and updates thereto contain all the detailed law. This has to be published in the form of a Notice in order that the rules on the records to be kept and the calculations to be made shall be enforceable in law.

Past disasters

Take care over your choice of Scheme. Numerous tribunal cases have concerned the wrong Scheme chosen and too much VAT paid in consequence. That reduces the profit margin and might well provoke a Revenue inquiry.

Time and again, in cases where traders and their accountants have at last woken up to the problem, Customs have refused to allow a retrospective change and the tribunals have supported that refusal.

So, before choosing which Scheme to use, take professional advice!

Do you have a mix of sales?

If you make both retail and wholesale sales, the retail scheme can only be used for the retail sales. VAT on the non-retail sales must be accounted for in the normal way.

Sales to other VAT-registered businesses must not normally be included in a *Retail Scheme*. However, *occasional* cash sales, such as a garage supplying petrol to businesses or a retail DIY store supplying building materials to builders, may be included within a *Retail Scheme*.

Bespoke schemes for sales above £100m

If your sales exceed £100m, you are not allowed to use the standard Schemes. You must agree a bespoke Scheme with Customs. It is usually based on a published Scheme and may be a combination of them. Notice 727/2 gives some outline guidance.

The figure was raised in April 2000 from £10m.

The basic schemes

There are 5 basic schemes as follows:

- *Point of Sale Scheme* — You identify the correct VAT liability of supplies at the time of sale, eg by using electronic tills.

- *Apportionment Scheme 1* — This is a relatively simple apportionment scheme, designed for smaller businesses with an annual VAT-exclusive turnover of less than £1m. Each VAT period, you work out the value of purchases for resale at different rates of VAT, and apply the proportions of those purchase values to sales.

  For example, if 82% of the value of purchases are standard-rated, it is assumed that 82% of takings are from standard-rated sales. Once a year, a similar calculation is made based on purchases for the full year, and any overpayment or underpayment is adjusted accordingly.

- *Apportionment Scheme 2* — Under this scheme, you calculate the expected selling prices (ESPs) of standard-rated and lower-rated goods received for retail sale. You then work out the ratio of these to the expected selling prices of all goods for retail sale, and apply this ratio to your takings.

  For example, if 82% of the ESPs of goods received for retail sale are standard-rated and 18% are zero-rated, then 82% of takings are treated as standard-rated and 18% as zero-rated.

- *Direct Calculation Scheme 1* — You can use this scheme if your annual VAT-exclusive turnover does not exceed £1m. It works by calculating expected selling prices of goods for retail sale at one or more rates of VAT, so that the proportion of takings on which VAT is due can be calculated.

  You calculate the ESPs for minority goods; ie those goods at the rate of VAT which forms the smallest proportion of retail supplies. So, if 82% of sales are standard-rated and 18% are zero-rated, you have to calculate the latter sales.

  ESPs of the zero-rated goods received, made or grown for retail sale are deducted from takings to arrive at a figure for standard-rated takings.

- *Direct Calculation Scheme 2* — This works in exactly the same way as Direct Calculation Scheme 1 but requires an annual stock-take adjustment.

Comparing the Schemes

Here are some comments to help you choose the right Scheme for your business.

Point of Sale Scheme

● This is the only available Scheme if all supplies are at the same rate;

● It does not involve stock-taking or working out expected selling prices;

● No 'annual adjustment' is required;

● If you sell at two or more rates, the Scheme is the simplest and the most accurate if you and your staff can consistently record sales by rate of VAT accurately. However, many shops have been caught out over that accuracy. It is suitable primarily for businesses with tills, which can recognise the VAT rates from product bar codes.

Apportionment Scheme 1

● It cannot be used for services, catering supplies, self-made or self-grown goods.

● There is a maximum turnover limit of £1m.

● It does not involve stock-taking or working out expected selling prices.

● An annual adjustment is required.

● The Scheme is relatively simple. However, if on average a higher mark-up is achieved for zero-rated goods than for standard-rated or reduced rate goods, more VAT could be payable under this Scheme than under an alternative.

Apportionment Scheme 2

● It cannot be used for services or catering supplies, but can be used for self-made or self-grown goods.

● Stock-taking is required at the start of using the Scheme, but not thereafter.

● Expected selling prices must be worked out.

● No annual adjustment is required but a rolling calculation is used.

● The Scheme can be complex to operate but, if worked properly, it will provide a more accurate valuation of supplies over a period of time.

Direct Calculation Scheme 1

● Services can only be included if they are liable at a different rate from the minority goods.

● It cannot be used for catering supplies but can be used for self-made or self-grown goods.

● There is a maximum turnover limit of £1m.

● Expected selling prices must be worked out. The Scheme can produce inaccuracies if these are not calculated accurately. In addition, where expected selling prices are set for standard-rated goods and the stock of these goods has a slow turnover, the Scheme may not be appropriate, as VAT is paid in the period in which the goods are received and not necessarily when they are sold.

- Stock-taking is not required.

- No 'annual adjustment' is required.

- The Scheme is relatively simple where goods are sold at 2 rates of VAT, and most of the supplies are at the same rate. However, it can be complex where goods are sold at 3 rates of VAT.

Direct Calculation Scheme 2

- Services can only be included if they are liable at a different rate from the minority goods.

- It cannot be used for catering supplies but can be used for self-made or self-grown goods.

- Expected selling prices must be worked out. The Scheme can produce inaccuracies if these are not calculated accurately. In addition, where expected selling prices are set for standard-rated goods and the stock of these goods has a slow turnover, the Scheme may not be appropriate, as VAT is paid in the period in which the goods are received and not necessarily when they are sold.

- Stock-taking is required at the start of using the Scheme, and annually thereafter.

- An annual adjustment is required.

Do I need permission from Customs?

You do not have to ask Customs before starting a particular Scheme. Customs have power to tell you to stop using it in the following circumstances:

- if its use does not produce a fair and reasonable valuation during any period;

- if it is necessary to do so for the protection of the revenue;

- if you could reasonably be expected to account for VAT in the normal way.

Another disaster story

Alan and Pamela Renshall (MAN/98/1092 No 16273) had a general store selling mainly food but also confectionery and fancy goods. Their first 6 returns went in on time showing small sums due to Customs. Then came 6 repayment returns. Repeated repayment claims for a retailer are self-evidently incorrect!

A one-off claim is possible due to exceptional input tax on, say, re-fitting the premises but not 6 in a row. It is unusual for a retailer to convert goods bought at standard rate, into zero-rated sales. Normally, zero-rated sales mean no input tax. The relatively small VAT on such costs as telephone, stationery and the audit fee is unlikely to exceed the margin between output tax and input tax on standard-rated sales unless VAT is payable on the rent as well and the standard-rated sales are a small proportion of the total.

The assessment for the 6 periods was £17,187. Mr Renshall said that, when doing each VAT return, he looked back to see what he had done last time. Having inexplicably used the wrong column, he simply went on doing so.

Suppose this had been your business or your client. Would you or your staff have noticed what was wrong? Theoretically, the gross profit margins had inexplicably gone up, thus of course creating an incorrect direct tax liability, though the extent of this might have been masked by losses due to other problems. Would you have noticed the change from payments to repayments? Do you even look at the VAT returns, let alone do the check on the underlying calculations, which would have immediately revealed the mistake?

Some questions to check your understanding. Review your answers with the text.

*   Why are the *Retail Schemes* the only means of estimating a retailer's VAT liability?

*   What is the main problem with the *Point of Sale Scheme*?

*   What are the other four Schemes on offer?

*   When do you have to agree a Scheme with Customs?

32. The Annual Accounting Scheme

The purpose of the *Annual Accounting Scheme* is to help small businesses by allowing them to submit only one return annually. In the meantime, they pay fixed sums based on the previous year's liability.

Professional accountants tend not to like the Scheme much because they think that the discipline of preparing a quarterly VAT return helps clients to keep their records up-to-date.

The law

The law is in Part VII of the *VAT Regulations (SI 1995/2518)*. Notice 732 (April 2002) *Annual accounting* refers.

Key points of the Scheme

The key points of the Scheme have been amended and, for periods starting on or after 25 April 2002, are as follows:

- You must have been VAT registered for a year unless your taxable turnover in the coming year is expected to be below £150k; in that case you may join the Scheme when you register for VAT.

- To join, your taxable turnover limit must not exceed £600k pa. You must cease using the Scheme if your taxable turnover exceeded £750k in the previous accounting year of the Scheme.

- You make 9 monthly payments of 10% of the total you paid in the previous year or, if newly registered, are expecting to pay in the next 12 months. Alternatively, you can choose to pay 25% quarterly.

- Payments start on the last working day of the fourth month of your Scheme accounting year. They must be by standing order, direct debit or other electronic means, not by cheque.

- You submit your annual VAT return, together with any balance due to Customs, two months from the end of the Scheme accounting year; ie you get an extra month over the time limit applicable to a normal return.

- You are not allowed to start the Scheme if you owe a significant debt to Customs but they will not necessarily refuse the use of it if you owe a small sum.

Notice 732 *Annual Accounting* sets out the full details.

Users of the *Annual Accounting Scheme* can also use the *Flat Rate Scheme for Small Businesses*. See Chapter 34.

33. Cash Accounting

The *Cash Accounting Scheme* is a valuable concession for small businesses. If your turnover does not exceed £600,000 a year, you can use the Scheme without reference to Customs. You issue tax invoices as normal but only account for VAT when and to the extent that payment is received. Thus, you get a cash flow advantage, which can be considerable, depending on how long your customers take to pay their bills, plus automatic bad debt relief.

This advantage is offset by the fact that you cannot recover input tax until you pay your bills, so the Scheme is most useful to a business selling services rather than goods and which therefore has relatively low taxable inputs.

Retailers selling for cash do not use the Scheme because they already have the money so there is no point.

The law

The law is in *Part VIII* of the *VAT Regulations (SI 1995/2518)*. Notice 731 (March 2002) *Cash accounting* refers.

Advantages and disadvantages of the Scheme

The advantages are:

- Output tax is not due until you receive payment of your sales invoices. If your customers pay promptly, the advantage will be limited to the tax on invoices issued in the last few weeks of each VAT quarter for which payment is not received until into the following one. Even so, the gain may be material.

- No VAT on bad debts because, if no payment is received, no output tax is due. There is an exception to this if you have to leave the Scheme — see later.

The disadvantages are:

- No input tax recovery until you pay suppliers' invoices.

- Your accounting system must record your output tax when you receive it from your customers and your input tax when you pay it to your suppliers. Your computer system must allow this.

- A business just starting up, which has substantial initial expenditure on equipment, stocks, etc so that input tax exceeds the output tax, should delay starting to use the Scheme. That way, it recovers the initial input tax on the basis of input invoices as opposed to payments.

Note that the normal rules apply concerning recovery of VAT incurred prior to registration. See Chapter 3, *Should I or Must I Register for VAT?* under *VAT which you can recover upon registration*.

Key rules

You can use the Scheme if you have reasonable grounds for believing that your taxable sales in the next 12 months will not exceed £600,000 provided that:

- You are up to date with your returns; or

- You have agreed a basis for settling any outstanding amount in instalments; and

- You have not in the previous year been convicted of a VAT offence, compounded proceedings in respect of one or been assessed to a penalty for conduct involving dishonesty.

Zero-rated supplies count towards the limit but exempt ones do not.

You can start using the Scheme without informing Customs.

You start at the beginning of a VAT period. The Scheme does not cover:

- Lease or hire-purchase agreements.

- Credit sale or conditional sale agreements.

- Supplies invoiced where full payment is not due within 6 months.

- Supplies invoiced in advance of delivering the goods or performing the services.

You must withdraw at once if your taxable sales, including any sales of assets (as confirmed in *Evans (t/a Coney Leasing) (LON/98/217 No 17510))* in the previous four VAT quarters have exceeded £750,000: ie, if your sales in the quarter to 31 May and the previous three VAT quarters were £750,100, you must leave the Scheme as at 1 June. If a sales increase is exceptional and you can show Customs that your sales in the next 12 months will be below £600,000, not £750,000, they may allow you to stay in the Scheme.

On leaving the Scheme, VAT is due on all supplies on which it has not already been accounted for.

Tax points under the Scheme for sales and purchases

The date on which you become liable for VAT under the Scheme on a sale is that on which you receive payment in cash or by cheque or, if the cheque is postdated, the date of the cheque.

You must account for credit card and debit card vouchers on the date on which they are signed by the customer, not when you are paid by the card provider.

The tax point on which you can recover input tax under the Scheme is the date on which you pay in cash or post a cheque to the supplier — but if the cheque is postdated, it is the date of the cheque, not that of posting.

If you pay by credit card or debit card, the tax point is the date of the payment voucher.

Imports of goods are not covered by the Scheme so you recover any import VAT under the normal rules. See Chapter 20, *Imports and Acquisitions of Goods*.

VAT return statistics

The figures of outputs and inputs for your VAT return are the payments you have made and received, not the normal invoice basis.

A transitional pitfall

On starting the Scheme, your records must differentiate between:

- Payments received against invoices — VAT already accounted for under the normal system.

- Those for invoices dealt with under the Scheme. Otherwise, you will pay the VAT twice.

Special records required

The normal requirements for records, including lists of sales and purchase invoices, still apply.

You still issue tax invoices at the normal tax point. Your customers will usually require these before they will pay you and they need them as evidence to justify the recovery of input tax, whether or not they are themselves users of the Scheme. Similarly, you still need tax invoices showing the VAT which you are reclaiming.

In addition, you must keep a cash book summarising payments received and made, with a separate column for VAT, or some other record from which payments in and out can readily be checked to your records of sales and purchases.

You must also obtain dated receipts for any payments in cash to your suppliers. The usual 6-year period applies for all records, which must be complete and up to date and must cross-refer. Thus, it must be possible to check each sales invoice with the cash received later and each purchase invoice with the payment for it, using, for instance, bank statements, cheque stubs, returned cheques and paying-in slips. These comments from Notice 731 may be impractical if taken literally. For instance, many businesses do not have their cheques returned to them.

In practice, your paying-in book may be an adequate detailed record provided that it identifies the customers by name and sales invoice number.

Beware of calculating the output VAT by applying the VAT fraction to the total banked. Even if all your normal sales are standard-rated, an invoice could include an amount not subject to VAT because it is either zero-rated or is a disbursement outside the scope.

Beware also of net payments

If payments from your customers are received net of deductions, such as commission due by you to a third party, you must account for output tax on the full sum, not the net amount received, so an adjustment will be needed in your records.

If the person to whom you pay the commission is registered, the VAT charged by him to you will be recoverable as input tax.

What about part payments or barter transactions?

If the part payment is of an invoice, which includes both standard-rated and zero-rated or exempt supplies, it must be apportioned between the supplies. Customs say that this must be 'fair and reasonable'. This will normally mean that the standard-rated part of the payment is calculated in the ratio that the standard-rated supplies bear to the total of the invoice.

If you pay or are paid either entirely or partly in kind, ie you barter goods or services for other goods or services, output tax is payable and input tax recoverable on the normal values of the transactions, not upon any net sum received or paid.

The figures for your VAT return

Not only your output and input tax figures for your VAT return are derived from payments; so are the respective values of supplies. Notice 731 says nothing of how these are to be calculated from the tax accounted for and zero-rated or exempt amounts added.

Your liability if you leave the CAS

If you leave the CAS of your own choice or because your sales exceed the Scheme limit, *Reg 61* provides that you must account for the VAT included in all your outstanding invoices to customers. You can claim an immediate offset for any debts over 6 months old under the rules for bad debt relief, as described in that chapter, provided that Customs are not compelling you to leave the Scheme.

You can offset all the input tax on invoices from suppliers, which you have not yet paid — though, not on any over 6 months old once that rule is in force. See Chapter 16 on *Bad Debt Relief*.

Transfers of a business or part of a business as a going concern

If you sell all or a part of your business as a going concern, the transaction is outside the scope of VAT under *Article 5* of the *Special Provisions Order (SI 1995/1268)*. See Chapter 37, *Buying or Selling a Business*.

VAT Regulations (1995/2518), Reg 6(3) allows for the purchaser to retain your VAT registration number. This is intended for such circumstances as when a partnership becomes a limited company. If used, this rule means the transferee accounts for tax on supplies made and received prior to the date of transfer, just as you would have done and takes over any liability for past errors.

Unless *Reg 6(3)* is used, you have to account for output tax when you sell your business.

Some questions to check your understanding. Review your answers with the text.

- What are the advantages of the *Cash Accounting Scheme*?
- What are the disadvantages of it?
- Do you have to tell Customs when you start using the Scheme?
- When must you leave the Scheme?

34.   The Flat Rate Scheme for Small Businesses

Do not confuse the *Flat Rate Scheme for Small Businesses*, which is applicable to any small business, with that for farmers only — described in the next chapter.

The law

The law is in *s 26B* and *Part VIIA* of the *VAT Regulations (SI 1995/2518)*. Notice 733 (April 2003) *Flat rate scheme for small businesses* explains the rules and contains certain statements concerning records, which have the force of law. *The Small Business Scheme* came in for periods ending on or after 25 April 2002.

An outline of the Scheme

- You calculate the VAT due on your *Scheme Turnover* using a Flat Rate % instead of the standard rate. That % depends on the trade sector into which your business fits.

- Your *Scheme Turnover* is gross of VAT, not net. Moreover, it includes any zero rated and exempt sales, not just your standard rated and reduced rated ones.

- The sum calculated with the Flat Rate % is what you owe Customs. You cannot reclaim input VAT on costs, except for capital expenditure exceeding £2k including VAT. See later under *Capital assets*.

Will I pay less VAT under the Scheme?

You *could* pay less VAT using the Scheme — it does work for some businesses. However, the two examples I prepared for this chapter suggest that it is more likely to cost extra. Comments I have heard from professional accountants confirm that only a minority of clients benefit from the Scheme! Key points include:

- Which trade sector applies — sometimes, as I explain later, two sectors could and it is possible to justify using the one with the lower Flat Rate. You have to decide on the right one from a list shown later in this chapter.

- How close your overall profit margin and your positive rated expenses are to the average used by Customs when deciding on the Flat Rate % for that trade sector. As businesses with similar descriptions often sell different mixes of goods or services and their profit margins vary accordingly, the Flat Rate % decided on by Customs can only be for what is supposedly a typical business of that description. Many will differ.

- I suggest you do not adopt the Scheme unless you are sure that you will pay less under it. You should compare the VAT you would have paid under the Scheme during the last year or, better still, 2 years with that you did pay, or would have paid, under the normal rules.

Does the Scheme simplify VAT accounting for small businesses?

I believe the Scheme's claim to simplify VAT accounting has no basis!

- The only significant simplification in your VAT accounting under the Scheme is that you do not need to record your input tax — but, unless you do, you cannot confirm the saving under the Scheme. Moreover, purchase invoices must still be listed and analysed in order to produce accounts for the Inland Revenue. Customs' claim that a small business may save up to £1k pa in bookkeeping costs is, in most cases, fantasy!

- A business, which sells to other VAT registered businesses, must still issue VAT invoices — showing VAT at standard rate, not the Flat Rate. Even private customers may expect to get VAT invoices if prices quoted to them are plus VAT.

- Moreover, if all dealings are with private customers for cash without sales invoices, it is easy under the normal system to apply the VAT fraction to the total sales for the quarter to calculate the output tax. A retailer selling at 2 or more rates of VAT might find the Flat Rate calculation marginally simpler than a retail scheme but the Flat Rate is more of an output tax guestimate.

The dangers of the Scheme

The Scheme will get some people in trouble because they have not understood the key rules. I have seen professional advisers getting the calculation wrong! I have also found Customs themselves making mistakes in publicity for the Scheme — such as saying that you calculate the VAT due by applying the Flat Rate to your *taxable* sales. If you do not immediately pick up that error, re-read what I have said so far!

The Scheme is not simple. Writing this chapter originally took me several days because of the need for careful study of both the law and Notice 733. In its third version the Notice remains, in my view, poorly written and with various ambiguities.

The importance of reading Notice 733

I am trying here to provide clear guidance on the possible advantages and disadvantages of the Scheme. I have ignored various points in Notice 733, which seem irrelevant to most small businesses. Thus, if you decide to use the Scheme, check the Notice for any further relevant detail.

I have deliberately written the following explanations as if addressed to a potential user although, of course, a reader of this book is more likely to be a professional adviser. Any professional fees in advising such a small business are likely to be low and it will help you to provide the right advice if you can merely copy the appropriate parts of what I say — which you can do provided that you acknowledge the source as being this book.

The turnover limits

You can use the Scheme if:

- Your expected *taxable* turnover in the next 12 months will not exceed £150k (£100k up to 9/4/03) net of VAT; and

- Your expected *total* turnover, including exempt sales, will not exceed £187.5k (£125k up to 9/4/03) net of VAT.

The turnover for the Scheme limit

The £150k figure is taxable supplies so it includes those at standard rate, reduced rate and zero rate, including the sale values of any dealings in second-hand goods or investment gold. The £187.5k figure includes exempt supplies but not any anticipated sales of capital assets held at the date you join the Scheme.

Customs say in paragraph 3.3 of Notice 733 (April 2003) that you must also include *income which is technically 'nonbusiness' income such as income arising from charitable or educational activities.* What that means is a mystery to me! An ordinary business could not have any charitable income. That from providing education for profit is usually standard rated.

Keep a record of your calculations of your expected turnover. If it exceeds the limits, you must be able to show Customs that your estimate had a reasonable basis.

The turnover to which you apply the Flat Rate

Do not confuse the two turnover tests for Scheme limit purposes with the *Scheme Turnover* to which you apply the Flat Rate. Your *Scheme Turnover* to which you apply the Flat Rate is:

- Your sales values including VAT — gross sales invoices or total retail takings.

- *Plus* any zero rated and exempt sales. That includes sales of goods to business customers in other EU States. See later in this chapter under *Beware of exempt turnover*.

- *Plus* any sales of capital assets, such as equipment, the purchase of which was dealt with under the Scheme. For more details, see later in this chapter under *Capital assets*.

Para 6.2 of Notice 733 (April 2003) says that you do not include non-business income or *any supplies outside the scope of VAT*. Presumably, that means any *services* on which you do not charge VAT to a customer outside the UK — in contrast to zero rated sales of *goods* to foreign customers.

Acquisitions and imports of goods

Beware the pitfall of buying goods zero rated from a supplier in another EU State. Don't forget to account for the acquisition VAT in box 2 of your return as normal. Ie, you must pay the VAT, in addition to the Flat Rate VAT, to Customs because you have not paid it to the supplier. Just as with UK purchases, you cannot then recover the import VAT.

In contrast, VAT on imported goods has to be paid at the time the goods enter the UK so the position is the same as with ordinary input tax.

Exports and imports of services

Para 11.3 of Notice 733 (April 2003) says that no VAT is due on imported services, which are normally subject to the reverse charge. The latter is explained in Chapter 22, *Exports and Imports of Services*. Notice 733 says nothing about exports of services, which are outside the scope of VAT. Presumably, they are covered by the reference in para 6.2 to the exclusion of supplies outside the scope of VAT from the turnover, to which the Flat Rate is applied.

Sales to or purchases from other countries

You include in your Scheme turnover any sales to customers outside the UK, whether in or outside the EU.

You have to account, as usual, for acquisition VAT in box 2 of your VAT return on any purchases of goods from suppliers in other Member States. This is then not recoverable in box 4 under the Scheme, just as any other input tax is not. That puts you in the same position whether you buy from a UK supplier or one in another Member State.

Imports of goods from outside the EU will be subject to import VAT, which will not be recoverable.

However, the reverse charge on services, whether bought elsewhere in the EU or outside it, does not apply — presumably because, for a small business, it would not normally be practicable to avoid non-recoverable input tax by buying a service outside the UK.

Restrictions on use of the Scheme

You can use the Scheme in conjunction with the *Annual Accounting Scheme* — described in Chapter 32.

But you *cannot* use the Scheme if:

- You use the *Second-hand Goods Scheme*, the *Auctioneers Scheme* or the *Tour Operators Scheme* — described in Chapters 30 and 36.

- You have to operate the *Capital Items Scheme*. See Chapter 24.

- Your business is *associated with another person*. That means another business in a situation in which one business is under the dominant influence of the other or they are closely bound to one another by financial, economic and organisational links. Customs say that the test here is of commercial reality rather than the legal form. If you are associated with another business, they will still consider an application from you to be allowed to use the Scheme. In para 12.7 of Notice 733 (April 2003), they say that a husband and wife may be seen as not associated. They quote the example that he pays a market rent for the upper floor of her antique shop to use as his office as an architect. Obviously, their concern is to prevent people artificially splitting a business into two or more parts and then using the Scheme for one or more of them.

- Your business is a company which is *eligible* for registration in a VAT group, whether or not it has been or which is registered separately as a division of a company or, in either case, has been during the previous 24 months.

Or, in the previous 12 months,

- You have ceased using the *Flat Rate Scheme*.

- You have been convicted of any offence in connection with VAT or have made any payment to compound proceedings in respect of VAT under *CEMA 1979, s 152*.

- You have been assessed to a penalty under *s 60* for alleged conduct involving dishonesty.

An example of how the Scheme works

Suppose you are a management consultant, an accountant or bookkeeper, an architect or a lawyer. Those descriptions cover many people, who start to work for themselves — often from home. The flat rate percentage applicable to them is 13.5%. Your figures might look like this.

		Output tax @ 17.5%	Flat Rate 13.5% on *VAT inclusive* turnover £94k
Turnover	£80,000		
		£14,000	£12,690
Costs not subject to VAT such as secretarial help, insurance postage, rail and taxi fares and depreciation: say	£20,000		
Vattable costs such as stationery, telephone, computer software, advertising, some travel costs, heat and light and sundries: say	£20,000	Input tax £3,500	
		Payable to Customs	
Net profit	£40,000	£10,500	£12,690
Result of using Scheme Payable to Customs		£12,690	
Deduct net VAT retained; ie £14,000 VAT collected from customers (turnover in accounts being net of VAT) less VAT on expenses paid to suppliers £3,500		£10,500	
Net result of Scheme:	Deducts from net profit	(£ 2,190)	

Another example — a business selling goods

The lowest flat rate is 5% for a retailer of food, confectionery, tobacco, newspapers or children's clothing. There will not be many such retailers eligible to use the Scheme because, even if the profit margin is as high as 20% on sales of £100k net of VAT, that only leaves £20k out of which to pay the overheads, let alone provide a profit. The figures might look like this.

Turnover	£100,000	Output tax (assuming 25% sales zero rated) @ 17.5%	Flat Rate 5% on *VAT inclusive* turnover
		£13,125	£113,125k
		Input tax on 75%	
Cost of goods sold	£80,000	£10,500	
Non Vatable expenses: say	£7,000		
		Input tax	
Vatable expenses: say	£7,000	£1,225	
		Payable to Customs	
Net profit	£6,000	£1,400	£5,656
Result of using Scheme VAT payable to Customs	£5,656		
Deduct VAT retained; ie £13,125 less VAT paid to suppliers £11,725	1,400		
Net result of scheme:	Deducts from net profit (£4,256)		

The sensitivity of the above figures

Obviously, the precise position will vary from business to business but the figures in both examples demonstrate that the sum payable under the Scheme could easily be more than under the normal system. One can check how sensitive to changes those in the first example concerning services are by adding £20k plus VAT to the sales. That would create output tax of £3.5k and flat rate tax on £23.5k of £3,172.50. If the standard rated expenses remained the same, the overpayment under the Scheme would be reduced by about £330.

Alternatively, on the turnover of £80k, standard rated expenses would need to be about £12.5k less, thus reducing the input tax by £2,188, for the VAT payable to be the same under the normal system as under the Scheme.

If the Flat Rate % applicable to your trade sector is more favourable than in the above example, the closer your turnover gets to the limit of £100k, the bigger any potential saving is likely to be, assuming that, for a business supplying services, the standard rated costs tend to rise more slowly.

On the other hand, it will often be a mistake for such a business to adopt the Scheme in the first year or so during which the overheads are relatively high in relation to sales and there is start-up expenditure, such as on equipment. Note that the loss of VAT on equipment etc is reduced by the rule, explained later, which allows you to recover separately VAT on capital expenditure exceeding £2k including VAT.

The disaster for the business selling goods is only partly due to 25% of them being zero rated under the normal system but subject to the flat rate under the Scheme. Increasing the standard rated sales to 100% still leaves a net additional cost under the Scheme of £2,275.

These examples are of course only valid to the extent that the figures compare with those of your business. Nevertheless, they suggest that, before adopting the Scheme, you should first review the likely result using figures based on your VAT returns for the last year or, in the case of a new business, your budgeted ones.

Beware of exempt and zero or reduced rate turnover

The total turnover limit allows for some exempt sales on top of the taxable sales limit. The most likely examples of exempt ancillary income are bank interest, lottery commissions or property rents since exempt insurance or finance commissions are primarily received by brokers.

If you have any exempt sales, the Scheme will probably mean paying more VAT because the Flat Rate % applies to your total turnover. The extra VAT under the Scheme is money, which you will not be collecting on your exempt income. You do avoid having to do any partial exemption calculation, no input tax being recoverable under the Scheme anyway — but then, under the normal system, you may be recovering the input tax related to your exempt income if it does not exceed the de minimis limit for Partial Exemption. See Chapter 23.

Also, beware if a proportion of your sales are taxable either at zero rate or the reduced rate. This will cut your output tax, even if you normally pay Customs, so that applying the Flat Rate % to your total sales may create a larger sum due.

Choosing your Flat Rate %

To decide the Flat Rate % you must use, you choose the trade sector in the table below, which most closely reflects your business. If you make supplies in more than one sector, you choose the one in which your sales are largest.

I wondered whether to create an alphabetical list of the kinds of business covered by the different sectors. I decided not to because I thought there would be a danger of someone finding alphabetically a heading which appeared suitable without realising that there was another either closer or equally applicable and with a lower percentage! For instance, a farm secretary probably does more bookkeeping than secretarial work. The rate for bookkeeping is 13.5%; that for secretarial services is 11.5%.

So, before you choose, read the entire table of sectors, marking all the headings which have any relationship to your business. Then, consider whether you can justify the one with the lowest Flat Rate % as that most closely reflecting your business or the one in which you sell the most.

I also worry that the categories are far from clear. Suppose you are an individual working as a 'consultant'. What are the differences between:

- management consultancy;

- accountancy and bookkeeping;

- lawyers and legal services;

- computer and IT consultancy or data processing;

- investigation or security;

- all other activity not elsewhere specified; and

- business services not elsewhere listed?

Each of these categories might arguably cover some forms of consultancy; yet the rates vary from 11% to 14.5%.

For instance, is it obvious where a tax consultant like myself fits in? Such work is not 'management consultancy' in the usual sense. It can involve tax 'investigations' and 'legal services' in handling tribunal appeals. The consultant may well be a qualified accountant or lawyer so the 'accountancy' or 'lawyer' category could apply. Probably, it is a 'business service' at 12.5 %. However, there is no definition of that and some people, especially those not calling themselves consultants, will wish to qualify as an 'unspecified activity' at 11%. Trouble and tribunal cases are, in my view, a racing certainty!

Review of the trade sector

You only need to review the balance of your ongoing business between sectors at each anniversary of joining the Scheme. You use the Flat Rate of the sector in which you expect to make the largest sales in the following year.

If you *stop* making sales in a sector or *start doing* so in a new one during the year, the % applicable from *then on* is that of the sector which you expect to make the largest sales.

FLAT RATE %	TRADE SECTOR TABLE
5.0%	Retail of food, confectionary, tobacco, newspapers or children's clothing
6.0%	Postal and Courier Services
	Public House
6.5%	Agriculture not elsewhere listed
7.0%	Membership organisation
	Retail of goods not elsewhere listed
	Wholesale of food or agricultural products
8.0%	Retail of pharmaceuticals, medical goods, cosmetics or toiletries
	Sport or recreation
	Retail of vehicles or fuel
	Wholesale not elsewhere listed

FLAT RATE %   TRADE SECTOR TABLE

FLAT RATE %	TRADE SECTOR TABLE
8.5%	Manufacture of food
	Library, archive, museum or other cultural activity
	Printing
	Vehicle repair
9.0%	Packaging
	General building or construction services. *Note: See the 14.5% rate for the 10% materials rule.*
	Social work
	Agricultural services
9.5%	Rental of machinery, equipment, personal or household goods
	Manufacture of textiles or clothing
10.0%	Forestry or fishing
	Other manufacture not elsewhere listed
	Mining or quarrying
	Personal and household goods repair services
	Photography
	Publishing
	Transport, including freight, removals and taxis
	Travel agency
10.5%	Hotels or accommodation
11.0%	Advertising
	Animal husbandry
	Manufacture of fabricated metal products
	Investigation or security
	All other activity not elsewhere listed
	Veterinary medicine
	Waste and scrap dealing
11.5%	Estate agency or property management
	Secretarial services
12.0%	Entertainment excluding television, video and film production
	Journalism *from 1/5/03*
	Financial services
	Laundry services
12.5%	Business services not elsewhere listed

FLAT RATE %	TRADE SECTOR TABLE
13.0%	Restaurants, takeaways or catering services
	Hairdressing or, *from 1/5/03*, other beauty treatment services
	Real Estate activity not elsewhere listed
13.5%	Computer repair services
	Management consultancy
	Accountancy and book-keeping
	Architects
	Lawyers and legal services
14.5%	Computer and IT consultancy or data processing
	Labour-only or construction services *Note: 'Labour-only' means building or construction services where the value of materials supplied is less than 10% of relevant turnover from such services. If it is over 10%, you may use the 9% rate.*

Pitfalls for builders

The 10% materials requirement in order to use the 9% Flat Rate rather than the 14.5% one creates a pitfall for anyone who often does not supply materials.

Equally, a builder could suffer severely under the Scheme if contracts obtained turned out to be for zero rated new dwellings or alterations to listed ones or for reduced rate conversion work rather than standard rated projects.

The pitfall in changes to the Flat Rate trade sectors

The Flat Rate trade sector table in Reg 55K(4) was amended from 1/5/03. The changes are noted in the table above. On this occasion, they were relatively minor but there was virtually no publicity for them. That created a pitfall, which may well become far worse on a future occasion.

Anyone using the Scheme must apply a change in the table from its start date, which may well mean splitting the calculations for the VAT return in which the change occurs. Someone using the *Annual Accounting Scheme* as well might have two or more changes during the 12-month period.

Given that many small users of the Scheme are supposed to be minimising their bookkeeping costs and will not normally use a professional adviser to prepare their VAT returns, I do not see how Customs suppose that users will discover relevant changes in time to apply them correctly.

Time of supply under the Flat Rate Scheme

There are three possible methods of arriving at your Scheme turnover.

The *Basic Turnover Method* under the Scheme follows the normal rules. That is to say, if you issue tax invoices, they create tax points and are the basis of your Scheme turnover. However, if you issue requests for payment under the rule for continuous services, described in Chapter 7, *The Time of Supply Rules — When You Must Pay*, the tax point will be when you receive payment.

Although you are not allowed to use the *Cash Accounting Scheme*, you can use what Customs call the *Cash Based Turnover Method* of calculating the VAT due in each period. You apply the Flat Rate % to the cash received rather than the invoices issued. This does not alter the tax point itself although that only matters if, for instance, there is a change in the VAT rate applicable to your sales.

If you are already using the *Cash Accounting Scheme*, you can change to this one without having to calculate the tax still owed at the time of change. You simply account under the *Flat Rate Scheme* for VAT on payments received subsequently. The same applies if you leave the *Flat Rate Scheme* and go back to that for *Cash Accounting*.

If you cease to use the *Cash Based Turnover Method* of calculating your turnover, you have to include in your Scheme turnover, for the period in which you revert to the invoice basis, the sales made whilst using the Scheme for which you have not yet been paid.

Under the *Retailer's Turnover Method*, you apply the Flat Rate % to your retail takings as calculated under the usual rules for retailers. For instance, you have to include credit card sales as they are made by creating the voucher rather than when you receive the money from the card issuers.

Stocks and other assets held at the date of registration

If, on registering for VAT, you immediately start using the Scheme, you can recover VAT on stocks and assets at the date of registration under the usual rules. See Chapter 3, *Should I or Must I Register for VAT?*

A business already registered has of course already reclaimed VAT incurred on the stock and assets held. If there is a substantial stock of goods for resale, there may be a marginal gain under the Scheme. The Flat Rate % is reduced to take account of input tax, which will not be recoverable on future purchases but which has already been recovered on the stock. However, a business, with sales under £100k, would not usually have enough stock for this to be a significant advantage unless the Flat Rate % happens to be favourable too.

The turnover limit once in the Scheme

Once in the Scheme, you have to check your turnover on each anniversary of joining it. If your turnover has exceeded £225k for all supplies except capital assets, you cease to be eligible to use the Scheme unless you can persuade Customs that there are reasonable grounds for believing that your turnover in the next 12 months will not exceed £187.5k for all supplies — including zero rated and exempt ones.

You also cease to be eligible if there are reasonable grounds for thinking that your turnover will exceed £225k in the next 30 days alone. Notice 733 does not say so but this is, of course, an anti-avoidance rule. Anyone signing a contract likely to create such a situation would be aware of the sales implications.

If you become ineligible because of a rise in turnover, you leave the Scheme at the end of the quarter following the anniversary of joining, at which you checked the total.

If you become ineligible for any other reason, you must cease to use it at once.

In both cases, you must tell Customs in writing.

Stock adjustment on leaving the Scheme

If, on leaving the Scheme but remaining VAT registered, your standard rated stock exceeds the value when you joined the Scheme, you calculate the increase, work out the standard rate VAT on it and claim this on the next VAT return.

Capital assets

VAT on capital equipment bought when using the Scheme is treated like other input tax and ignored unless the VAT inclusive value is £2k or more. In the latter case, you can recover the VAT on your VAT return as usual if the goods are not:

- For resale or for inclusion in goods for sale — but then they would not be capital goods anyway!

- For hiring, leasing or letting — presumably because the input tax is then equivalent to VAT on goods bought for resale.

- Covered by the *Capital Items Scheme* — unlikely for a small business but see Chapter 24.

A complication of the Scheme concerns assets on which you recover VAT either at the date of registration or under the Scheme because the VAT inclusive cost exceeded £2k. If you sell such an asset whilst using the Scheme, you have to charge tax in the normal way and at the standard rate, not at the Flat Rate %.

If, at the date at which you leave the Scheme, you still hold capital equipment on which you recovered VAT under the Scheme, you have to account for output tax, presumably on the value at that date, although Notice 733 does not say so. You can offset a corresponding sum as input tax, assuming that you go on using the equipment to make taxable supplies.

Applications to use the Scheme

There is a simple application form in Notice 733, which can also be found on Customs' website. You send it to the office, which handles registrations for your area. Keep a copy of it — you may need to check, for instance, the Flat Rate % which you stated as applicable to your business.

You cannot start to use the Scheme until you have been notified by Customs of the date from which you may do so.

If you wish to use the *Annual Accounting Scheme* as well, use the joint application form in Notice 732 *VAT: Annual Accounting*.

Bad debt relief under the Scheme

The bad debt relief rules, as described in Chapter 16, apply in the normal way if you calculate your Scheme turnover based on invoices under the *Basic Turnover Method* and the invoice remains unpaid after six months.

If you use the *Cash Based Turnover Method*, you get a special additional relief if you have written off the debt. Customs also say you must not have accounted for the VAT on it, which, of course, you will not have done under this method. Presumably, they mean that you must not have accounted for VAT under the normal rules prior to joining the Scheme.

You deduct, from the VAT at the normal rate, the sum you would have paid under the Scheme if your customer had paid up. The balance is a special allowance, which you can reclaim as input tax on your next VAT return. Thus, on an invoice of £1,000, the VAT is £175. If your Flat Rate % is 10%, that is £117.50 on the total of £1,175. You can reclaim the difference of £57.50.

Appeals against decisions by Customs

You can appeal to the VAT Tribunal if Customs refuse to authorise use of the Scheme, demand you cease using it or disagree as to the trade sector and thus the Flat Rate %, which applies to your business — or against an assessment resulting from such a decision.

Unfortunately, the Tribunal can only allow the appeal if it considers that Customs could not reasonably have been satisfied that there were grounds for their decision *(section 84 (4ZA))*. This will make such arguments difficult to win.

Some questions to check your understanding. Review your answers with the text.

- How do you calculate what you owe to Customs under the *Flat Rate Scheme for Small Businesses*?

- Do you include exempt turnover in the total to which you apply the Flat Rate?

- How do you choose the Flat Rate applicable to your business?

- How do you invoice under the Scheme for sales to other VAT registered businesses?

- Which other Scheme can you use at the same time as the Flat Rate one?

- What is the turnover limit above which you have to leave the Scheme?

35. The Flat Rate Farmers Scheme

The objective of the *Flat Rate Farmers Scheme* is to provide a means for small agricultural businesses to escape the responsibilities of having to submit a VAT return whilst at the same time reducing the input tax, lost as a result of not being registered. This chapter explains how the Scheme achieves this. The Scheme is not confined to farmers. As can be seen from the list of activities below, various kinds of small enterprise can use it.

However, do not confuse it with the *Flat Rate Scheme for Small Businesses* described in Chapter 34.

The Scheme is an alternative to VAT registration. A trader, who qualifies, has the choice of staying VAT-registered or deregistering and using the flat rate scheme. A trader not registered because his turnover is below the registration limit can also use the Scheme.

A Scheme user charges a flat rate addition of 4% to his sales to *VAT registered customers only*. He has no VAT return to complete and he keeps this sum as compensation for being unable to recover any input tax in the normal way. The registered customer can recover the flat rate addition as input tax.

Section 54 and *Part XXIV* of the *VAT Regulations (SI 1995/2518)* contain the rules, which are explained in Notice 700/46 *Agricultural flat rate scheme*.

Qualifying activities

Agricultural production activities

- General agriculture including viticulture.

- Growing fruit, including olives and vegetables, flowers and ornamental plants, both in the open and under glass. Production of mushrooms, spices, seeds and propagating materials, nursery stock.

Stock farming together with cultivation

- General stock farming, poultry farming, rabbit farming, beekeeping, silk worm farming, snail farming.

Forestry

Fisheries

- Fresh water fishing, fish farming, breeding of mussels, oysters, other molluscs and crustaceans, frog farming.

Processing

- Where a farmer processes, using means normally employed in an agricultural, forestry or fisheries undertaking, products deriving essentially from his agricultural production, this is regarded as agricultural production.

Agricultural services

- Field work, reaping and mowing, threshing, baling, collecting, harvesting, sowing and planting.

- Packing and preparation for market, for example, drying, cleaning, grinding, disinfecting and ensilage of agricultural products.

- Storage of agricultural products, technical assistance.

- Stock minding, rearing and fattening.

- Hiring out for agricultural purposes, of equipment normally used in agricultural, forestry or fisheries undertakings.

- Technical assistance.

- Destruction of weeds and pests, dusting and spraying of crops and land.

- Operation of irrigation and drainage equipment.

- Lopping, tree felling and other forestry services.

Non-qualifying activities

- Dealing in animals.

- Training animals, such as horses, dogs or racing pigeons — although breeding horses, pigeons or sheepdogs do qualify.

- Breeding pets such as cats, dogs other than sheepdogs, budgerigars or butterflies.

- Activities once removed from farming, such as processing farm produce. Examples are dairy cooperatives producing dairy products and sawmills.

Apart from those non-qualifying activities, individual sales, which are of goods or services not listed above, do not qualify, even if the customer is a farmer. Examples are:

- Sales of machinery.

- Sales of milk quota.

- Repair and maintenance of farm buildings.

- Bed and breakfast or holiday accommodation.

- Charges to visit the farm.

- Livery for horses and riding lessons.

If the value of your non-qualifying taxable sales exceeds the registration limit, you cannot use the *Flat Rate Farmers Scheme* and must register under the normal system for all your sales. A possible solution is to put the non-qualifying activities into a separate business, such as a partnership or a limited company. If you do that, be careful not to recover input tax related to the Scheme activities through the VAT registration.

No output tax due on deregistration

If you deregister in order to use the Scheme, you do not have to account for output tax on stocks and assets on hand, even where input tax on them has been recovered.

The flat rate addition applies to zero-rated agricultural produce

A Scheme user will charge the flat rate addition to VAT registered customers on his zero-rated agricultural produce. It is not a VAT rate, just a compensating amount to reflect irrecoverable input tax. The VAT liability of your outputs is irrelevant to whether the flat rate addition is added.

You do not *have* to add the flat rate but, since the VAT registered customer can reclaim it as input tax and you do not have to pay it to Customs, you will want to do so.

Flat rate invoices

You issue flat rate invoices for all supplies to which the flat rate addition applies. Self billing by customers is possible with permission from Customs.

An invoice must show:

- Invoice number.

- Your Flat Rate certificate number.

- Your name and address and that of your VAT registered customer.

- The date and description of goods or services.

- The price before adding the Flat Rate.

- The rate and amount of the Flat Rate addition, described as *Flat Rate Addition* or *FRA*.

Records required

You keep your normal business records. Nothing special is required for the Scheme.

Auctioning agricultural produce

If the auctioneer acts as an agent, he does not take title to the goods so the sale does not attract VAT. You can charge the flat rate addition to a purchaser of the goods, who is registered.

If the auctioneer acts as a principal, you charge the addition to the auctioneer.

Sales and purchases within the EU

If you sell to a customer in another Member State under the *Flat Rate Farmers Scheme*, you only charge the flat rate addition if that customer is registered in his country. He can then recover the addition presumably, although Notice 700/46 (January 2002) does not say so, under the *8th Directive*. See Chapter 26, *Recovery of Foreign VAT*.

Similarly, you only have to pay a flat rate addition to a farmer in another Member State, under the equivalent scheme in that State, if you are VAT registered in the UK. You then reclaim it under the *8th Directive*.

Sales outside the EU

If you sell under the Scheme to a customer outside the EU, who buys for the purpose of a business, you can also charge the Flat Rate. That customer will then reclaim under the *13th Directive*, which is also explained in Chapter 26, *Recovery of Foreign VAT*.

The £3,000 limit

Customs can refuse your application to join the Scheme if the Flat Rate kept by you is over £3k more than the input tax, which you lose.

Leaving and rejoining the Scheme voluntarily

To leave voluntarily, you must have used the Scheme for at least a year. You can then rejoin at any time unless you have registered for VAT. In the latter case, at least three years must pass — or one year if the VAT due on your assets on hand is less than £1k.

Some questions to check your understanding. Review your answers with the text.

- What sorts of business are eligible for the Scheme?
- What kinds of business are not eligible?
- Is there a turnover limit for the Scheme?
- How much is the flat rate addition and what does the farmer do with it?

36.   The Tour Operators Scheme

The *Tour Operators Scheme* is mainly intended to deal with the problem of package holidays sold in one country by a tour operator and taken in another.

Without the Scheme, a tour operator who provided package holidays in other EU Member States would have to account for VAT in each country where his customers received the services. The Scheme is a simplification measure under *Article 26* of the *EC 6th VAT Directive*. It allows tour operators to account for VAT entirely within their home country.

How it works

You cannot recover VAT which you incur either in the UK or in any other EU member state on services which you buy in for the purpose of providing your package holidays. Having been disallowed the input tax on the costs directly related to your package holidays, you only pay output tax on your gross profit (or 'margin'). Thus:

- the Member States where the services are enjoyed get the tax on the hotel accommodation, meals etc;

- UK Customs get the tax on your gross profit margin.

The law

The UK law is in *s 53* and in the *Value Added Tax (Tour Operators) Order 1987 (SI 1987 No 1806)*. Under the Scheme:

- VAT cannot be reclaimed on *Second-hand Goods Scheme* supplies bought in for resale;

- VAT is only accounted for on the difference between the VAT-inclusive purchase price and the selling price (the 'margin');

- there are special rules for determining the place, liability and time of *Second-hand Goods Scheme* supplies;

- VAT invoices cannot be issued for *Second-hand Goods Scheme* supplies;

- there are special rules for calculating the VAT due on the margin; and

- the value of turnover for VAT registration purposes is the margin.

Invoices to business customers

If you sell travel to business customers, you can issue tax invoices to them outside the scheme if you ask permission from Customs.

Holidays outside the EU

If you sell holidays outside the EU, you must still use the Scheme but your profit margin on them is zero-rated.

Scope of the Scheme

The Scheme does not just apply to anyone calling themselves a tour operator. Anyone who buys in, and resells, travel facilities for the direct benefit of a traveller, regardless of whether the facilities are used for holiday or business purposes is likely to be covered.

There is no statutory definition of when a taxable person is acting as a tour operator for the purposes of the scheme. The CJEC has held that the *Second-hand Goods Scheme* can apply to a trader who is not formally classified as a travel agent or tour operator. See *Madgett and Baldwin ([1998] STC 1189)*.

VAT on in-house costs

The disallowance of VAT under the Scheme is only on bought in costs which are re-sold. Hotel accommodation and air travel are obvious examples. If you provide services from your own resources, such as a hotel, which you own, you do recover the VAT on these costs. This then produces the complication that your profit margins have to be split between bought in costs and in-house ones.

VAT on overheads

You also recover VAT on all overheads, such as office expenses.

The *Tour Operators Scheme* is a part of VAT which most people avoid if possible! This means that, if you are involved, you will need to do your homework carefully. There have been various important cases over the years, which you may need to study. For more detailed coverage of the subject, see *Tolley's Practical VAT Service*.

Some questions to check your understanding. Review your answers with the text.

- What is the purpose of the *Tour Operators Scheme*?
- What is the difference between a bought-in and an in-house cost?
- Can you issue a tax invoice to a business customer?
- What difference does it make if the holiday is outside the EU?

37.   Buying or Selling a Business

Buying or selling a business involves VAT just like any other business transaction. Yet, amidst all the stress and excitement, it is all too easy for it to be overlooked. This chapter deals with a number of the potential pitfalls.

Are you selling the company or its business?

If your business is owned by a limited company, you have a choice:

* you can sell the share capital of the company; or

* the company can sell its business, leaving you still owning the shares.

A sale of the shares is an exempt transaction in securities, unless the buyer belongs outside the EU. See Chapters 11 on *Exemption*, 22 on *Exports and Imports of Services* and 23 on *Partial Exemption* for further comment on the various rules and implications. There is one important comment to make here concerning the problem of buying the share capital of the company, which is a member of someone else's VAT group.

Insolvent VAT groups — the joint and several pitfall

A company, which is grouped with others under *s 43* is 'jointly and severally' liable for any tax due from the representative member of the group (*s 43(1)(c)*).

* Therefore it is liable for all the tax due from the rest of the group.

* Liability is preferential in the 6 months prior to the insolvency.

If you buy a company out of a VAT group which is insolvent, it may be several years before the balance of tax not paid by the rest of the members is determined and Customs claim from you. See Chapter 4, *VAT Groups* under *Group liability pitfall* for more comment.

Preferably, do not buy the share capital, just the assets. If that means forfeiting substantial tax losses, and security adequate to cover the possible VAT liability cannot be obtained from the liquidator, try asking Customs what terms they might accept for restricting it.

It is difficult to see how they could be helpful in most cases, so it might be best to abort the deal.

In principle, VAT is chargeable on assets sold

If you sell assets, VAT is chargeable on them in principle. It makes no difference that they are a bundle of assets making up a business. VAT is even due on goodwill because it represents the right to carry on the business in that location and under that name etc.

However, a set of rules known as the *Transfer of a Going Concern (TOGC)* rules take the sale of a business outside the scope of VAT if certain conditions are met. These rules simplify the sales of many businesses because it is not necessary, for VAT purposes, to put values on individual assets and the purchaser's cash flow situation is eased because the price does not include VAT. The rules are also there to protect Customs. Without them:

- VAT charged would become part of the vendor's assets and at risk of being used to pay creditors or, in an insolvency situation, subject to the claims of other preferential creditors before it was payable to Customs on the next VAT return; or

- a vendor selling a business for a substantial sum could collect the VAT and retire abroad without paying it to Customs.

The transfer of a business as a going concern

If the assets transferred constitute:

- an entire business transferred as a going concern; or

- a part of the business capable of separate operation; and

- the purchaser uses the assets in the same kind of business; and

- the purchaser registers for VAT, if not already registered,

the transaction is outside the scope of VAT. No VAT must be charged on any of the assets (*Special Provisions Order (SI 1995/1268, Art 5)*).

Strictly, the last requirement is that the purchaser '… immediately becomes as a result of the transfer, a taxable person …', which means becomes liable to register (*s 3*). However, it is safest to regard the rule as meaning that the vendor should obtain proof that the purchaser has applied to register immediately. Not only does this minimise the risk of any possible inquiries by Customs; it deals with the pitfall of a very small business with sales below the registration limit, the purchaser of which would not therefore automatically become a taxable person and who would have to register voluntarily in order to do so.

Although simple in concept, these rules have tripped up many clients and their advisors. The subtleties of what is or is not a business, as opposed to a collection of assets, have been explored in numerous tribunal cases.

Common pitfalls

No tax is charged on the main assets of the business. This is correct, but one common mistake is that when the stock is counted at completion, the vendor and purchaser often deal direct without professionals on hand. The vendor sometimes wrongly adds VAT to the stock valuation, saying the purchaser can recover this. Subsequently, Customs disallow the VAT as input tax because the vendor has failed to account for it to them. Customs would not disallow the input tax if they had had the output tax — but they haven't! It is then irrelevant whether the 'VAT' went to pay creditors or whether the vendor simply pulled a fast one. Since the tax was not chargeable in the first place, there is no defence against the assessment.

Worse still, VAT is sometimes charged on the entire assets because the vendor and/or his professional advisors assume it ought to be and do not check the rules. The purchaser and advisors do not challenge this, and again the vendor fails to account for the tax, possibly because he is insolvent; same story, just a bigger mess!

You do not need many assets for there to be a business

In *R Cuthbert (EDN/99/611 No 6518)*, there was a *TOGC* because contracts were taken over and the trading name retained even though there was little stock, no other assets and no employees.

Similarly, in *Associates Fleet Services Ltd (MAN/00/419 No 17255)*, the purchase of a batch of vehicle leasing contracts was held to be a *TOGC* despite there being no transfer of goodwill, trading name, other assets, premises or staff. The purchaser did not need these in order to carry on the business transferred. The vendor's financial position was so weak that the absence of a restriction of competition clause in the contract did not matter to the purchaser.

Usually, a short period of closure is irrelevant

Normally, a short period of closure between changes of ownership does not mean the transaction is not a *TOGC* because it is the same kind of business being re-opened and in the same location. That was held to be so in *H Tahmassebi (t/a Sale Pepe) (MAN/94/197 No 13177)* in which an Indian restaurant was closed on the day prior to the transfer and then re-opened after a complete refurbishment as a pasta house. The Tribunal accepted that the new business was as different to the old one as chalk to cheese. However, the point was what had been transferred to the purchaser, not what he had subsequently done with it. He had bought the rights to the existing restaurant including a substantial payment for goodwill and a key condition was that the alcohol licence was transferred to him. He could have operated the existing restaurant without a break. That he had instructed the vendors to close it the day before the transfer did not affect this.

In contrast, in *Sawadee Restaurant (EDN/98/43 No 15933)*, there was no transfer of a going concern when a Japanese restaurant closed down, the staff were dismissed and stock returned to suppliers and a partnership of three terminated and, seven weeks later, a new partnership, including one of the previous partners who held the lease, opened a Thai restaurant. The only assets re-used were a few chairs and the lease but the real difference was that the previous business was not transferred. It had ceased.

Are the assets to be used in the same kind of business?

Do not take it for granted that the assets you are selling will be used in the same kind of business. Of course, this will usually be the case.

In *Paula Holland (MAN/98/1031 No 15996)* the transfer of a pub from management by the owner to a tenancy was held to be a *TOGC*. Although the owner was now renting the premises, the business of carrying on a pub was continued under the same name and with the same staff in the same location. In various other cases concerning public houses, there has been held to be a *TOGC* even though the existing business was almost non-existent, the premises being in poor condition and trade very low.

In *RN Banbury (t/a Creative Impressions) (LON/96/1720 No 15047)* the sale of an embroidery machine by a limited company to its director was held to be a *TOGC* even though the work was then for wholesale customers, not retail and not on goods for sale in a shop. Those were points merely relevant to the manner of carrying on the business, not to the kind of business.

However, in *Delta Newsagents Ltd (MAN/86/69 No 1220)* a franchisee bought the goodwill and fixtures and fittings of a retail shop and the franchise agreement was terminated. The franchisee was already running the business so, although some assets were sold, no business was; or rather the franchise business ceased in respect of the shop. Therefore, there was no *TOGC*.

The pitfall in records required on transfer

Section 49 requires the vendor of a business as a *TOGC* to transfer the records to the purchaser. With small businesses, this may well not happen unless the parties realise the problem. In the case of more substantial businesses, records will normally be part of what is passed on because the purchaser needs them to be able to carry on. Examples of where specific records are needed are:

- Retail and second-hand schemes because they are part of the basis for the VAT return.

- Property subject to the *Capital Items Scheme* either because scheme calculations already have to be made or because information about the cost might be needed on a future change of use.

- Partial exemption calculations if the basis of these is a method agreed with Customs.

In *East Anglia Motor Services Ltd (LON/99/64 No 16398)*, the purchaser of a garage and service station bought shortly afterwards the vendor's stock of second-hand cars under a separate contract. The vendor had intended to retain the cars but changed his mind. The transaction was held to be part of the *TOGC*. This was a disaster for the purchaser because he had not acquired the records of the vendor and he therefore had no details of the purchase prices of the cars. Consequently, he had no defence against an assessment from Customs based on the assumption that his profit margin was 50% of the sale prices.

The pass the parcel pitfall

There is a serious pitfall when a business is transferred only to be passed on again immediately. Examples are:

- A professional partnership breaks up. Two of the partners take part of the business as a going concern and immediately join another partnership.

- Part of the business of a company is sold as a going concern to another company, which immediately passes it to a new subsidiary.

- A property, let to tenants and counting as a business, is resold immediately.

In none of these cases does either stage of the transaction qualify as a *TOGC* because the business in the middle does not trade. It therefore does not use the assets in the same kind of business.

Kwik Save Group plc (MAN/93/11 No 12749) showed this point to be a real problem. Various food stores were bought by *Kwik Save* from *Gateway Corporation* and other vendors. Some were immediately transferred to a subsidiary, *Tates Ltd*. Although the £395,000 VAT assessed on the invoices from *Gateway* to *Tates* for these stores was recovered by *Tates*, there was a £32,000 interest cost for this error.

The problem if the assets include property

If the assets include property which is:

- a 'new' building or civil engineering work;

- land, a building or a civil engineering work in respect of which the option to tax has been exercised;

the sale of the business as a going concern would enable the purchaser of the business to avoid VAT. Customs accept that a single building let as an investment property can constitute a business for this purpose so, if there were no legislation to prevent this, the avoidance possibilities would be significant. To prevent such avoidance, *Art 5(2)* takes the value of such property outside the Order and thus makes it standard-rated unless:

- the purchaser of the business opts to tax the property from the date of the transfer; and, by the date of the transfer;

- gives Customs such written notification of the election, as may be required by *Sch 10 para 3(6)*.

Therein lies a pitfall! In *Churchview Ltd (MAN/01/0762 No 17919)*, the sale of industrial units let to tenants did not qualify as a *TOGC* because the purchasers did not opt to tax, despite a warranty in the contract that they had done so.

The purchase of a business by partially exempt VAT group

If a partially exempt VAT group buys a business as a *TOGC*, *s 44* requires it to account for output tax on the value of the assets, other than items covered by the *Capital Items Scheme*, bought by the vendor during the previous 3 years and on which the vendor recovered VAT. Corresponding input tax can only be recovered by the group to the extent allowed by the partial exemption rules. This prevents such a group from acquiring assets free of VAT in the course of a *TOGC*, after they have been bought by an associate company, used for a taxable business and input tax recovered on them.

The pitfall if the landlord and tenant are in the same VAT group

A single tenanted building can count as a business for *TOGC* purposes. However, that is not so if it is sold to a company in the same VAT group as the tenant. This is because Customs interpret the grouping roles as meaning that, as there is no supply within the VAT group, the business ceases to exist.

Similarly, if the landlord sells the property to a third party outside the VAT group, thus creating supplies, the position is not that of an ongoing business being transferred.

In Notice 700/9 (March 2002) *Transfer of a business as a going concern*, Customs do accept that there is a *TOGC* if there are other tenants outside the VAT group.

The pitfall in Art 5(2) Special Provisions Order

Firstly, the above rules create a pitfall for all concerned because of the need for the vendor to ensure that the purchaser opts to tax in respect of any property affected by the rule and the need for the purchaser to understand that something done, probably through solicitors, in the course of the purchase of the property has long-term consequences. For more on the option to tax, see Chapter 25 on *Property*.

Secondly, there is a particular pitfall if you buy a property at auction. Under the present rules, a tax point is created when you pay a deposit immediately after the auction to the vendor's solicitors. This is because such a deposit is held by the solicitors as the agent of the vendor, not as stakeholders; ie, the deposit is not returnable because you are committed to the purchase on the terms set out in the auction documents.

In *Higher Education Statistics Agency Ltd (LON/98/296 No 15917:* [*2000*] *STC 332)*, confirmed in the Divisional Court, the purchase of a rented property at auction was held not to be a *TOGC* because the purchaser only opted to tax after the auction date and therefore after it had paid a 10% deposit. Thus, if you contemplate buying a property at auction, you must notify Customs of your election to waive exemption before you are the owner of it!

Do not take over the vendor's VAT number

VAT Regulations (SI 1995/2518), Reg 6 allows the purchaser of a business to take over the vendor's VAT Number. This creates a pitfall because, in doing so, you take on all the VAT liabilities of the existing registration and could be caught out by an assessment for mistakes made by the vendor. The procedure is therefore only suitable when the two parties are closely connected.

However, in *Pets Place (UK) Ltd (LON/95/2986 No 14642)* the purchaser was held not to be liable for an assessment disallowing input tax to the vendor. *Pets Place* had taken over the VAT number and signed a VAT 68 but the latter referred only to paying VAT on supplies made by the vendor, ie to output tax, not to input tax.

Some questions to check your understanding. Review your answers with the text.

- What is the potential pitfall in buying a company out of a VAT group?
- What are the requirements for the sale of a business to qualify as *TOGC*?
- What is the 'pass the parcel' pitfall?
- What is the risk in taking over a vendor's VAT number?
- If you buy at auction a taxable investment property, which is already let, what must you consider doing beforehand?

38.   Assessments and VAT Penalties

You never know when you may be faced with an assessment based on assertions by Customs that you have made mistakes in your VAT returns and you need some idea of how to deal with such a situation.

Hopefully, you will never need to study most of the penalty rules in any detail but it is as well to be aware of their existence, if only because you might have to point them out to colleagues or clients, who you find doing something which you believe to be incorrect. See later in this chapter under *The cost of getting it wrong*.

Customs' power to assess

Section 73 gives Customs power to assess if they think that you have declared too little output tax or reclaimed too much input tax on your VAT returns. Such an assessment is not in itself any suggestion of dishonesty, merely that you have made a technical mistake. If the value of the mistake exceeds the de minimis limit, Customs can assess a penalty as well. Interest is also payable.

Time limits and the three-year cap

An assessment must be made within (*s 73(6)*):

- 2 years of the end of the VAT period in question; or

- 1 year after evidence of facts, sufficient in the opinion of Customs to justify the assessment, comes to their knowledge.

In practice, it is often the 1 year limit on which Customs rely because the long gaps between their visits to smaller businesses tend to mean that they are outside the 2 year one.

However, when Customs assess within a year of discovering the problem, *s 77* imposes a 3-year time limit for the returns for which they can assess. Thus, they must assess within 3 years of the end of the VAT period in which the underpayment occurred — except in a case of dishonesty or late registration in which case the time limit is 20 years, or 3 years after your death.

A penalty must be assessed within 2 years of finally deciding how much tax is owed.

Having made an assessment, Customs can reduce it or issue a supplementary one but, outside the 2-year period, they cannot withdraw it and substitute another one on the same basis unless they have new facts.

Customs can make alternative assessments

In *University Court of the University of Glasgow (EDN/01/28/76/91/12 No 17372: CA [2003] STC 495)* it was held that alternative assessments based on different legal analyses of a situation can be made — just as for Direct Tax.

Form and notification of an assessment

The law does not state the form in which an assessment should be made or how it should be notified to you. Usually, Customs use standard paperwork produced by their computer system. However, various decisions, such as *Piero's Restaurant and Pizzeria (LON/2001/927 No 17711)*, have established that an assessment can be in the form of a letter, provided that it clearly expresses a decision to assess and that it or accompanying schedules give details of the amounts for each VAT period.

In *Courts plc (LON/00/048 No 17915)*, a *protective assessment* was held to be valid, the amounts and periods having been notified in a letter, even though it had not been processed and the debt was not recorded in the traders' account in Customs' books.

Although the law merely requires an assessment to be *made* within the time limit, not *notified* as well, this has created problems in the past when there has been a delay between the making of the assessment and the notification to the trader. Customs have now decided, as a matter of policy, that they must also notify within the time limit.

An assessment must be for the correct period

Customs' power to assess under *s 73* relates to a return which a trader is required to make. In *M Weston (MAN/01/0914 No 18190)*, an assessment was held to be invalid because it was for a final 5-month period for which Customs had not issued any direction requiring a return. They had ignored the normal return for the first 3 months, which the Tribunal held to be valid even though it was on a photocopy of a previous return with the details altered. Thus, it is sometimes possible to win an appeal on the basis of a technicality. Always look carefully at such details of an assessment as the date of issue and the period covered.

Appeals

You appeal to a VAT Tribunal. If you write to Customs asking them to think again, that is a request for a review. There are important differences.

Think twice before asking for a review

Asking Customs to review an assessment is often a waste of time. In my experience, reviewing officers sometimes do not even recognise a mistake when the assessment has no basis in law and when that has been pointed out to them. Moreover, gathering all facts and presenting the defence case properly usually takes enough time for costs to begin to mount. If you do not appeal immediately to the Tribunal, you risk running up costs which cannot then be claimed because the time was spent before the appeal was lodged.

Although time spent prior to making the appeal in establishing the facts and preparing the grounds of appeal can be included in an eventual costs claim if the appeal was lodged promptly, time spent negotiating with Customs before appealing is not claimable.

VAT under-declaration cases often start with claims by Customs which are either overstated or are unsound for one reason or another. To establish this and negotiate a reasonable settlement, or even withdrawal of the assessment, often takes much work and many months. You cannot claim the cost of such discussions with Customs prior to lodging the appeal.

Usually, an officer, who has issued or is threatening an assessment based on allegations of undeclared takings, has already made up his or her mind that the returns are inaccurate. Although the degree of obduracy varies, it is often only the fact, not just the threat, of a tribunal appeal combined with detailed argument, schedules of figures etc, which induces a more reasonable approach and/or a willingness to settle.

Sometimes, it does pay to negotiate on the basis of a review by Customs rather than a formal appeal. However, in my experience, this is only where the client is in the wrong and there is little prospect of a successful defence in law but a reasonable officer might, with luck, be persuaded to agree a lower figure. Such cases are more likely to concern technical points of law than under-declaration or dishonesty cases.

This is not to suggest that all Customs officers get the law wrong. Some are very good indeed. However, advisers tend to see the less satisfactory cases for obvious reasons and the above remarks are based on long experience.

Of course, having lodged an appeal, you should still write a detailed letter in response to the assessment or the decision, setting out why you think it is wrong. Once an appeal is lodged, Customs appoint a different officer to review the position. If there has been a mistake, this may be accepted by the reviewing officer. If the assessment or decision is then withdrawn, you can claim costs. See the end of Chapter 39, *Taking an Appeal to the Tribunal* for more comment on costs claims.

Time limit for an appeal

You are supposed to appeal to the Tribunal within 30 days of the decision or assessment in question. However, the Tribunals routinely extend this time limit. If you are out of time, lodge the appeal quoting whatever excuse you may have. Customs will probably not object unless you are years rather than months late or they think that the appeal is frivolous.

Best judgement

An assessment for *output* VAT must be to the *best judgement* of Customs (*s 73(1)*).

One for *input* tax is made under *s 73(2)* for which there is no such requirement. It must merely be bona fide and not based on a mere whim.

Frequently, Customs' officers jump too readily to conclusions when assessing for output tax on alleged under-declarations. Often, they do not marshal the evidence properly. If this is the case and especially if that evidence, such as observations of the premises, test meals etc, covers only a short period, it may be possible to defeat the assessment in its entirety on the grounds that it was not made to the best judgment of the Commissioners. Possible reasons include such mistakes as an unsound basis for the assessment, numerous errors in the calculations or a failure to take into account some important factor or information.

In *Mohamed Hafiz Rahman (t/a Khayam Restaurant) (MAN/96/133 No 14918; [1998] STC 826; No 17135; [2002] STC 73; [2002] EWCA Civ 1881; [2003] STC 150),* the judge in the first Divisional Court hearing commented:

The Tribunal should not treat an assessment as invalid merely because it disagrees as to how the judgement should have been exercised. A much stronger finding is required; for example, that the assessment has been reached 'Dishonestly or vindictively or capriciously'; or is a 'spurious estimate or guess in which all elements of judgement are missing'; or is 'wholly unreasonable'.

After a re-hearing by a different tribunal, the case was appealed again to the Divisional Court and on to the Court of Appeal. The latter commented that, in the usual situation in which the Tribunal can see why Customs made the assessment, it should concentrate on deciding the correct amount of tax due. If that is close to the sum assessed, it may be a sterile exercise to consider whether Customs exercised best judgement. If it is not close, the assessment may not have been to best judgement. However, even then, a tribunal could substitute its view of the correct tax due, it being the underlying purpose of the law to collect that sum.

Thus, when it is clear that a VAT return was wrong, it is now unlikely that the Tribunal overturns an assessment on the technical grounds that it was not to best judgement, if it is able to decide the correct sum due.

The cost of getting it wrong

If you get it wrong, you may have to pay:

- Interest at a rate high enough to hurt and which is not allowable for corporation tax; and

- A penalty of 15%.

Those sanctions are for *innocent* errors. Interest is automatic but you may be able to reduce the penalty if you have a reasonable excuse — difficult in the case of a substantial business employing qualified accountants and advisers — or you can show reasons why it should be mitigated.

You *may* also escape a penalty if you voluntarily disclose it to Customs.

The following pages discuss the detailed rules, including those on the *Default Surcharge* for late returns.

Interest is due on your mistakes

Interest is due under *s 74* on errors made, no matter what their value. Interest is based on the average of the base lending rates of the 6 largest clearing banks *plus* $2^1/2$% (*Air Passenger Duty and Other Indirect Taxes Order (SI 1998/1461)*). At the time of writing, it is 6.5%. As this is not allowable for corporation tax, it is sensible to pay up once you or Customs discover errors exceeding £2,000, so as to stop interest running — even if the assessment has not yet been issued.

Customs do not have to assess for interest — the officer can 'inhibit' it. However, if it is assessed, there is no appeal against the liability. You can appeal against the basis of calculation but not against whether you ought to pay interest.

Customs have said that they will not normally assess for interest if the error is merely one of timing, such as accounting for output tax late or recovering input tax early, which was corrected on the next return.

If you have made a voluntary disclosure of VAT overpaid, which offsets part of an assessment, check whether the interest calculation has taken account of this. Customs' computer system may have failed to do so.

For comment on your right to interest if you overpay Customs, see Chapter 18, *VAT Housekeeping for Finance Directors* under *The interest problem*.

The misdeclaration penalty: s 63

If you make a mistake, the value of which exceeds the de minimis limits, you are liable for the misdeclaration penalty of 15%. Your innocence is irrelevant. Dishonesty carries a 100% penalty under *s 60*.

Section 63 applies even if the error is merely a timing one, such as recovery or payment in the wrong return and regardless of whether the tax is recoverable from the customer.

De minimis limits

If the net value of errors in a period is less than the following limits, you escape:

Both penalty and interest

* £2,000 — you can correct on your ordinary return and no interest is charged.

Penalty only

* 30% of the *gross amount of tax (GAT)* meaning the total of your output tax plus your input tax;
* but you are caught if the net value of the error(s) exceeds £1m.

Thus, from £2,000–£1m an error escapes if it is below 30% of *GAT*. That is a generous limit for many businesses. However, it becomes much less generous if your outputs are either zero-rated or exempt so that you only have input tax on which to calculate it.

Overstating a repayment claim is caught as well as understating a sum due. However any offsetting errors in favour of Customs are taken into account to reduce the sum of *tax lost*, which is measured against the above limits and on which any penalty is calculated.

Possible defences

You will have a defence:

* If you can show a *reasonable excuse* for your conduct. Lack of money is not a reasonable excuse (*s 71*).
* If you voluntarily disclosed the error at a time when you had no reason to think Customs were investigating your VAT affairs (*s 63(10)* or *s 64(5)*).

Reasonable excuses for innocent mistakes

Reliance on another person to perform any task is not an excuse (*s 71*). *Task* has been held by the High Court in *D & DA Harris ([1989] STC 907)* to cover advising.

Typical reasonable excuses are:

* Sickness, departure of key staff or computer faults but only until you could have been expected to cope by taking action to recruit, obtain backup etc; or in circumstances where the problem caused extra stress, which could not have been anticipated and which lead to the error.

- Complexity of the legal point involved.

- That, in the light of the information available to you and of your understanding of the situation, your actions were reasonable, judged by the standards of the ordinary businessman.

Mitigation

Section 70 allows mitigation by either Customs or the Tribunal of a penalty as far as zero but excludes lack of funds, no loss of tax and good faith as factors.

When you can voluntarily disclose

In practice, Customs accept voluntary disclosure up to the time when the officer starts investigating the matter in question. Often disclosure is accepted during a control visit — though not if it is felt that it was only made because of the visit.

Once the officer has asked about a matter, he or she will not normally accept a disclosure as voluntary. If you spot a problem in an aspect of your affairs, which is being looked at by Customs at that moment, record the error and your intention to disclose in a memorandum to the Board and/or the auditors, so as to preclude any suggestion of dishonesty. Wait until the visit is acknowledged by the officer to be terminated before disclosing.

The period of grace

Customs will not normally demand a penalty when they find an error on a return during a visit prior to the date on which the return is due for the following period. This lets off those cases where, had the officer not come in just after the return was sent, the trader might have found the error when preparing the next return.

Compensating errors

Nor will an error normally be penalised if it is 'corrected' by a compensating one in the following period. However, Customs will do so if the error is a repetitive one — otherwise, they could never catch such mistakes.

Disclosing errors

Errors cannot be corrected on your VAT return *unless* the net value of errors you find in a period is under £2,000 (*VAT Regulations (SI 1995/2518), Reg 34(3)*). Correcting on the current return means that you escape interest as well as any penalty.

Errors totalling above £2,000 must be disclosed separately. Customs provide form 652 but a letter will suffice provided that you give details of the periods involved. You pay interest but no penalty, provided disclosure counts as voluntary.

In order to keep track of the value of errors on previous returns, period by period, you need to be able to identify the journal entries correcting them or, where the tax is on purchase or sales invoices recorded late, to identify those invoices.

Instant disclosure is not essential. If you normally disclose at the end of each period, it will still be regarded as voluntary even if a visit has meanwhile uncovered the problem. However, you should make a journal note of the correction as you find each error as proof of an intention to disclose.

The persistent misdeclaration penalty: s 64

If you make a *material inaccuracy*:

- Customs can serve a *penalty liability notice (PLN)* on you before the end of your fourth subsequent VAT period.
- The next material inaccuracy during the following 8 periods, starting with that in which the *PLN* was issued, escapes; but
- A second one earns a penalty of 15% of the error.

A material inaccuracy is one which exceeds:

- 30% of *GAT*; or
- £500,000.

The default surcharge for late returns: s 59

If you are late with your return and/or payment, Customs can issue a *surcharge liability notice (SLN)* to you. This lasts for 12 months from the date of the default. See Chapter 5, *The VAT Return* re the due date.

Once an *SLN* has been served on you, the surcharges are:

- for the next default in the next 12 months; 2% of the unpaid tax (minimum £30).
- for a second default in the next 12 months; 5% (minimum £30).
- from then on; by 5% a time, to a maximum of 15% (minimum £30).

If a surcharge at the 2% or 5% rate is under £400, Customs do not assess it but:

- a *Surcharge Liability Extension Notice* is issued extending the surcharge period; and
- the surcharge rate for the next default goes up.

What if a business disaster makes the figures late?

Ask Customs for permission to estimate the missing information for the period for which you have been unable to process the figures. Customs can allow that for either input or output tax either in an emergency or regularly if, in the exceptional circumstances of your business, you cannot have the figures ready on time.

You must ask permission. Don't wait until you are late: ask as soon as you realise that sickness, a computer breakdown or whatever risks making you late.

Excuses for late payment

You have a defence to missing the time limit on any of the occasions for which a default is 'material to the surcharge' if:

- the return or tax was despatched *at such a time and in such a manner that it was reasonable to expect* that Customs would get it on time; or
- you have a reasonable excuse for that not having been done.

Lack of money is not such an excuse. Late delivery by someone who prepares your return for you is unlikely to be an excuse either. As the Minister commented in Parliament, that would be too easy. It would put a premium upon the services of dilatory advisors!

See also earlier re excuses for innocent errors concerning sickness etc.

Failure to register on time: s 67

The penalty for failure to register on time is a percentage of the net tax due from the correct date of registration to that on which you tell Customs or on which they become *fully aware of* your liability to register. The percentages are:

- 5% up to 9 months late;

- 10% up to 18 months late;

- 15% thereafter.

The percentage is a flat rate for the whole period, not a stepped one.

Dishonesty cases

Customs have powers under *s 60* to assess a penalty of up to 100% of the tax evaded for conduct involving dishonesty.

They have power under *s 61* to assess part or all of that penalty on an individual director if they think that the behaviour of the company was due to the dishonesty of that individual.

Alternatively, *s 72* provides a financial penalty of up to 3 times the amount of the VAT or 7 years in prison if Customs choose to prosecute.

Only the most serious VAT frauds result in criminal prosecutions. For these, a solicitor is required to handle the legal aspects of the prosecution even if you provide the technical input on VAT.

However, most cases are dealt with under *s 60*. The 100% penalty is mitigable under *s 70* if the trader helps establish the amount of the dishonesty. In practice, the maximum likely mitigation for full co-operation is a reduction to 50%.

Whilst you may need a solicitor's help with a *s 60* case, especially if it goes to a hearing, much of the groundwork is likely to be of an accounting nature.

Get the facts agreed

As soon as you are aware of an investigation by Customs, establish the facts as best you can with the client: ie

- Does the client admit any inaccuracy in the returns?

- If so, roughly how much, for how long etc?

- Get any admission confirmed in writing with authority to disclose to Customs. You may or may not already have the right to disclose under the terms of your engagement letter and/or, to the Revenue, by virtue of acting as your client's agent in relation to his direct tax affairs. In any case, you should tell the Revenue of the investigation by Customs if only because Customs probably will and because you must try to resolve the problem with both sets of tax authorities at the same time.

Own up at once

If any inaccuracy is admitted to, it should be disclosed as soon as possible to both Customs and the Revenue. If work still has to be done to clarify the extent of the problem, indicate its general nature and promise fuller information once available.

If the cause is an enquiry by one tax authority, say so to the other. Do not pretend that the admission is unprompted.

Conclusion

This chapter provides only a brief review of the various penalties. In my experience, each situation is different and, sometimes, it is only after a most careful review of the facts against the law that one can find the weakness in Customs' case.

VAT law is complicated, as are the penalty rules which deal with infringements of it. Customs officers under pressure of work tend to issue assessments plus penalties and wait to see what defence the trader can produce. They do make mistakes and it is often possible for a VAT specialist to find something wrong with an assessment for tax and/or the penalty based on it.

Unfortunately, the amount of money at stake for a small trader often does not justify spending the necessary time to do this. Luckily, the ability to obtain costs from Customs in the event of success does make it possible in some cases for advisers to take on small cases. Nevertheless, I believe that many assessments for tax and some for penalties are collected in cases in which the assessment is unsound. Of course, in some of these, the trader does owe some money and, it not being a fair world, there is an element of rough justice in the system!

So, if you believe that Customs are wrong, do not be afraid to appeal.

Some questions to check your understanding. Review your answers with the text.

- What is the rate of the Misdeclaration Penalty?

- What is the rate of penalty for conduct involving dishonesty?

- What are the de minimis limits above which an error makes you liable for a Misdeclaration Penalty?

- Once Customs have found an error, what are the two grounds on which you may be able to get the penalty removed or reduced — apart, of course, from showing that the assessment was wrong?

- What are the differences in the rules under which you can become liable for a Persistent Misdeclaration Penalty as opposed to a Misdeclaration one?

- How does one become liable for a Default Surcharge?

39. Taking an Appeal to the Tribunal

This chapter discusses appealing to a VAT Tribunal against an assessment for tax and the penalties which Customs can impose for innocent errors and in a variety of other situations. As explained in the previous chapter, *Assessments and VAT Penalties*, an appeal is to a VAT Tribunal, not to Customs. That chapter also explained why it is often better to lodge a formal appeal to the Tribunal rather than merely request Customs to review the matter.

Taking a case to a VAT Tribunal is a subject in itself and there is only space here for a few brief comments. You will find more detailed coverage in *Hamilton on VAT and Duties Appeals*.

A trader can represent him or herself. Many do and some win their cases. However, many more make a mess of presenting the case because they have no idea how to do it. Unfortunately, that is also true of many professional accountants and some solicitors when they take cases on behalf of clients. So this chapter is intended to ensure that you do understand the basics of handling an appeal.

Human Rights

The *Human Rights Act 1998 (HRA)* provides various rights to the citizen. Most are not strictly relevant to VAT but they include the right to a fair trial.

HRA, Article 6(3) gives everyone charged with a *criminal* offence the following minimum rights:

(a) to be informed promptly, in a language which he understands and in detail, of the nature and cause of the accusation against him;

(b) to have adequate time and facilities for the preparation of his defence;

(c) to defend himself in person or through legal assistance of his own choosing or, if he has not sufficient means to pay for legal assistance, to be given it free when the interests of justice so require;

(d) to examine or have examined witnesses against him and to obtain the attendance and examination of witnesses on his behalf under the same conditions as witnesses against him;

(e) to have the free assistance of an interpreter if he cannot understand or speak the language used in court.

On occasions, officers can be either careless or over-zealous in the way they deal with assessments and in their handling of relationships with traders. However, it is questionable whether the *HRA* will affect civil penalties other than the one of up to 100% under *s 60* for conduct involving dishonesty. In *GK Han & D Yau ([2001] STC 1188)* the Court of Appeal confirmed the view of a Tribunal that *s 60* penalties are similar to ones imposed under criminal prosecution, even though *s 60* is part of the civil code in *VATA 1994*. That does not mean that the *HRA* can be quoted in relation to the rest of the civil penalties, although, of course, Customs have always had a duty to behave fairly and reasonably. This was then confirmed in *Ferrazzini v Italy, (Application No 44759/98)([2001] STC 1314)*. The European Court Of Human Rights (Note: Not the CJEC) held (6 out of 18 judges dissenting) that tax disputes fell outside the scope of civil rights and obligations regardless of the financial cost to the taxpayer. *Article 6(1)* was therefore not applicable.

In *N Ali & S Begum (t/a Shapla Tandoori Restaurant) and five other appellants (LON/95/355 No 17681)*, the Tribunal sided with the minority in *Ferrazzini* and held that the other civil penalties, such as that for misdirection in *s 63*, late registration in *s 67* and the default surcharge in *s 59* , together with the power in *Sch 11, para 4(2)* to demand security, were *civil* in nature and within the scope of *HRA Article 6.1*. However, it then held that they were not *criminal* in nature but were regulatory, being designed to penalise a failure to meet the standard of compliance demanded by the VAT system. Reversing this burden of proof would not assist a trader when the misdirection penalty, for example, was arithmetical exercise.

In my view, human rights as an appeal point may well be valuable in individual cases but usually as part of a good defence, which shows that Customs have got it wrong in other ways too. It will be rare to win just because Customs have not followed the procedures as fairly as they might have, given that we already have rules concerning time limits etc and a requirement that Customs assess to 'best judgement'. Indeed, in *Nene Packaging Ltd: KM Curtis Watkins: P Collins: A Ponte Sousa and MA Ponte Sousa: A M Rahman: D R M Spankie and B Spankie: (LON/00/355 No 17365)*, the *Tribunals Rules (SI 1986/590)*, which require from Customs a statement of case and list of documents and give the trader the right to ask for additional material held by them, were said to be adequate protection. Issues, such as pre-trial disclosure, should be viewed in the light of the overall fairness of the proceedings.

Of course, the *HRA* emphasises the need for care by Customs in ensuring that the trader has a fair hearing at every stage of their investigations, never mind before the Tribunals. For example, an interpreter may be needed if the trader does not speak good English.

Ajay Chandubhai Kumar Patel (LON/99/1144 No 17248) illustrates what seems likely to be the main problem in many cases. The decision contains the following points based on the right to a fair trial:

- Any admissions by the Appellant must have been properly obtained.

- An Appellant is presumed innocent until proved guilty. One cannot imply under s *60(7)* any burden of proof on an Appellant in respect of the amount of the sum evaded.

- An Appellant is entitled to be informed in detail of the allegations against him. Customs' statement of case must be in proper detail and their list of documents complete. Presumably, a tribunal would allow subsequent additions if notified to the Appellant in good time.

- An Appellant is entitled to examine Customs' witnesses. Matters, which ought to be established by a witness, should not be introduced in another way — such as by a copy of a visit report.

- An Appellant has a right to silence and, once criminal proceedings, including (per *Han & Yau*) civil penalties for conduct involving dishonesty, are contemplated, the trader must be cautioned before further questions are put, even by letter. The Tribunal noted the view expressed in *JL Murrell (LON/99/121 No 16878)* that the inducement to speak in Notice 730, in order to obtain a reduction in the penalty for cooperation, was the opposite of telling the trader of his right of silence.

- The requirement in *rule 7(1)(b), Tribunals Rules (SI 1986/590)*, as amended, to serve a defence setting out the matters or facts on which an Appellant relies can only be reconciled with the right to silence if the Appellant need not state any matters or facts, which do not advance his case.

The Tribunal found that Customs had failed to adhere to several of these points. For example, their bundle of documents included a visit report typed and not signed and without the officer's original notes. The officer had left the Department and was not called as a witness. This conflicted with the right to the Appellant to examine the witness. The Tribunal disregarded the visit report, except in so far as facts in it were admitted by the Appellant. A witness statement taken from an accountant, who had prepared the Appellant's VAT returns during most of the period covered by the assessment, was brief and inadequate — and conflicted with the evidence given at the hearing by that accountant.

The interview with the Appellant had not included any caution and Notice 730 had been given to him. A joint typed note, produced by the two officers the next day, was misdescribed as a 'transcript' in Customs' list of documents. It was in fact a reconstruction of an interview of which no proper note was taken and it included considerable material not in the notes and left out material which was in them. The Tribunal disregarded this evidence too.

Despite these flaws in Customs' case and what the Tribunal called their *casual approach to inquiries into serious matters*, it upheld most of the penalty because Mr Patel could not explain the difference between the sales declared on his VAT returns and those in the annual accounts. Thus, however clumsily Customs may handle an investigation and despite the burden of proof of dishonesty being on Customs, a trader must still be able to explain seeming discrepancies. If there is an apparent case to answer, it must still be answered before the Tribunal even if earlier interviews etc can be disregarded.

Some people have suggested that advisors should take great care to argue any possible point under the *HRA* because otherwise they run the risk of being sued for negligence. I suspect that, in practice, it will be found that any significant point would be raised by a good adviser anyway. Moreover, the objective is usually to settle a dispute with a tax authority quickly and at the lowest practicable cost. I question whether that responsibility will be met in the majority of cases by dragging out proceedings in raising technical issues, such as demanding formal interviews with interpreters etc and thus raising costs, rather than dealing with the matter more informally. Of course, one must be alert to the possibility of Customs putting pressure on the trader to admit something is wrong just to settle the matter but that has always been a problem. In those cases, which involve an admission of some under disclosure and the possibility of settling for relatively small sums of money, I suspect that it may even be counter-productive to worry too much about the *HRA*.

Of course, in a case of alleged dishonesty, one should always mention its existence to the client, in case the latter feels aggrieved at some aspect of his or her treatment. However, I think that it is only in the large cases that it will be found to have any real significance.

Basic procedure

The Tribunal Centre will acknowledge your appeal and forward a copy to Customs, who then have 30 days within which to submit a *Statement of Case* in response, which justifies the original assessment or decision. Customs hardly ever meet that time limit because of their workload. Usually, they will submit several requests for an extension of time.

If the case is urgent, contact the Solicitor's Department a few weeks after you have received the acknowledgement from the Tribunal and ask to speak to whoever is handling the appeal. This may be, at that stage, merely one of the administrative staff, rather than a solicitor. By explaining the need for urgency, you may be able to get the matter looked at by a lawyer and dealt with as a priority. Even then, it is unlikely that a hearing can take place within 6 months; 12 months is more typical and a written decision by the Tribunal can then take anything from 2 weeks upwards, frequently 2 months and sometimes longer.

When Customs submit their *Statement of Case*, the Tribunal Centre will forward it to you. A little later, they will ask you for dates over the next few months during which you are not available, which of various possible locations you would prefer for the hearing, how many days you think it will take and how many witnesses you will wish to call.

Careful consideration of the likely duration of the hearing is important. Whilst it is possible to get through a case in a single day, this becomes less likely if you or Customs have a witness and unlikely if there are two or more because of the time taken up in the giving of evidence and cross-examination on it by the other side. If in doubt, discuss the point with the solicitor representing Customs — whose name you may find at the end of the *Statement of Case*. It is better to ask for two or three days if you are not sure that the matter can be dealt with in a single one. Although this may delay the hearing, it is much better to complete it in one than to find that there is not enough time and it has to be postponed to a further hearing 2 or 3 months later. Not only does that tend to increase costs because of the need to go through the file again; everyone involved forgets the issues, evidence given etc. and has to refresh their memories.

Preparation, preparation, preparation!

A case is often won on the basis of evidence carefully prepared. Good preparation requires careful assessment well in advance of:

- facts upon which the case depends;
- evidence of those facts;
- relevant documentation, such as copies of contracts;
- possible witnesses.

One can still occasionally read reports of cases presented by Counsel where a failure to identify the key facts and/or to bring evidence of those facts has undermined the trader's case. On one occasion, I was talking to a client on a different matter when the fact of the appeal and the imminent date of the hearing were mentioned. The conference with Counsel had been arranged a bare two weeks before the hearing! The client decided to come to see me after I had expressed surprise. I identified the evidence, which I thought that Counsel would ask for. They were therefore able to present it to Counsel at the conference and it was on these documents that the case was largely won! Now Counsel would probably have identified the same evidence as required but what a scramble it would have been to produce it!

Prepare a skeleton argument

A *skeleton argument* is a set of notes prepared in advance, which you hand in at the start of the hearing. As with your bundle of documents, which is commented on later, you will need at least three copies — for the Tribunal Chairman, for Customs' representative and for yourself. Check with the Tribunal Centre before-hand whether there will be one or two lay members sitting with the Chairman because they will want copies as well. So will your client, if you are a representa-tive.

In your skeleton, set out the key facts on which you are bringing documentary evidence, cross referring to the document in your bundle. Then set out the law upon which you rely. Doing this in advance will help you to organise the presentation of your case and may speed things up by reducing the number of notes which the Tribunal members have to take.

Do not write your presentation word for word. That will tend to make it more difficult for you to add extra points, as you think of them at the last minute. Moreover, it is boring for the Tribunal members to have to listen someone reading a prepared text which is already in front of them. You want to be able to help them stay awake by varying your pace, introducing the odd aside etc! You cannot readily do that if you are reading rather than speaking to a list of prepared headings and key points.

List of documents

In theory, a list of documents must be provided to the other side within thirty days of the Tribunal Centre acknowledging the appeal. Both sides often ignore this time limit, the problem being to identify all the documentation in question until much nearer the hearing. However, you must make sure that you supply copies of docu-mentary evidence, such as contracts, brochures and the like, to Customs before the hearing. Otherwise they are entitled to ask for an adjournment with you paying the costs of the extra time.

Make sure that you also study Customs' list and obtain copies of anything which you do not have. If Customs' case depends upon the observations of the business, discussions during visits or whatever, make sure you have copies of all the calculations and notes made by the officers.

Evidence

Letters from friends, suppliers, customers or competitors supporting you are usually useless as evidence because Customs cannot cross-examine the writers. The Tribunal is unlikely to take any notice of them whatsoever unless you have shown them to Customs beforehand and have persuaded them to accept the statements they make without the writers attending to give evidence.

Documents, such as contracts or customer brochures, will usually be accepted by Customs without formal proof.

Witness statements

A formal witness statement can be lodged with the Tribunal but Customs usually object to it because they wish to cross-examine the witness. However, a written statement of evidence by a witness — in legal jargon, a *proof of evidence* — is well worth preparing in advance. Not only does this help to clarify precisely what evidence the witness can give; Customs will probably not object to it being produced at the hearing, provided that the witness is there to be cross-examined on the statement.

Often, the Tribunal Chairman agrees to read the statement, following which you can ask supplementary questions and Customs can cross-examine the witness. This speeds up proceedings because you do not have to extract the evidence by question and answer and the Chairman does not have to write everything down.

Agreed bundle

Often, both sides produce a bundle of documents, many of which duplicate each other. Try to agree a bundle with Customs before the hearing. Bundles should commence with the assessment or decision in dispute and immediate supporting papers followed by the correspondence etc in date order, earliest date first.

All pages of a bundle should be numbered sequentially 1,2,3, etc even if, within the bundle, individual documents already have their own page numbers. This is because, in the middle of a hearing, it wastes time if everybody cannot find their way quickly to the page to which you are referring the Tribunal.

Procedure at hearing

A tribunal hearing is relatively informal but evidence is given on oath.

- Normally, you, the Appellant, must present your case against the assessment or decision and call your witnesses.

- Customs then reply and call their witnesses.

- You have a right of reply.

In dishonesty cases, Customs start first because they have to prove the dishonesty.

Presenting your case

Do not assume the Chairman understands the case. He or she will have looked at the papers beforehand but, possibly, not until just prior to hearing. Depending on how much detail is with notice of appeal etc, he or she may know little of the case. In any event, do not assume the Chairman understands the nature of your business. Take care to clarify the background of business practices etc as well as the nature of the law in dispute.

Having explained the nature of the dispute, you set out the facts either by reference to documents or by calling witnesses. You then demonstrate how the law relates to those facts.

One of the reasons for preparing a statement by your witness beforehand and asking if the Tribunal will either read it or allow the witness to do so is that you cannot 'lead' your witness. That is to say, your questions must not suggest the answer which you want. It can therefore sometimes be quite difficult to extract information from your witness under oath in the witness box, which the witness gave you readily when you took your 'proofs of evidence' beforehand!

You do not need to worry about leading Customs' witnesses. In cross-examining them, you can suggest what you like!

Remain calm and courteous

Just occasionally, a trader representing him or herself in the Tribunal gets upset and accuses Customs of malpractice of one kind or another. It is unusual for officers to misbehave. They get the wrong ideas and demand VAT, which is not due but that is not misbehaviour. If you do feel that an officer has done something wrong, say so quietly, understating rather than overstating the point. If you have a valid complaint, the Tribunal will take due notice without you having to complain vociferously about it!

Costs

In most cases, the decision is not given on the day and it can be many weeks before it is issued.

Do not forget to ask for costs in the event of your success. Customs usually do not ask for their costs unless the case is a major one involving Counsel on both sides, they consider the appeal to be vexatious or frivolous or if it is a dishonesty case.

Once you have succeeded, do not withdraw your appeal until you have settled the costs claim with Customs. If you do withdraw — as the local VAT office may well ask you to do — you give up your right to ask the Tribunal for a settlement on costs. Write to the Tribunal stating that the matter has been settled except on the question of costs and that you expect to be able to settle these and then to withdraw the appeal in due course.

Costs, for which you can claim, are primarily the time of a professional adviser, expert witness or interpreter. A sole trader or partner cannot claim for his own time, although he can for travel and subsistence expenses associated with the appeal, together with those of any witnesses. A limited company may succeed with a claim for the time of an in-house lawyer.

If you are a professional adviser, it is vital that you record your time in detail as the case develops. That means in lodging the appeal, consulting with your client, building up the evidence, asking witnesses about the evidence they will give and so on. It is not sufficient merely to keep the usual professional time records, which tend to contain very little detail.

I start a computer record of my time when I lodge each appeal and update it as the matter proceeds. This means that, if I win the case or the assessment or decision is withdrawn by Customs, I can promptly submit a costs claim in detail. Not only does that keep the task of putting the claim together off the heap of other things to do as a task less urgent than other client problems; it is the only way to provide the detail, which enables Customs to consider the claim properly. As a result, I usually obtain satisfactory settlements in costs claims. In contrast, if all Customs get is an outline of the time spent with little detail about the work done, they are bound to reduce the offer they will make!

If you do not like the offer of costs from Customs, you can continue the appeal before the Tribunal on that point alone. In major cases, the costs may be referred to a Taxing Master of the High Court in which case you will probably have to use a costs draughtsman. However, it is always worth asking Customs for an offer in the hope of settling the matter informally.

The above is only a brief collection of points about making an appeal. If you think you have a good case, it is well worth having a go yourself if you cannot afford professional fees. However, it might well pay to take advice beforehand on how to present it from someone experienced in the Tribunals.

Some questions to check your understanding. Review your answers with the text.

- How many of the preparatory steps, which were suggested when appealing to a VAT Tribunal, can you remember?

- Why should one normally lodge a formal appeal to the Tribunal rather than a request for a review with Customs?

Table of Cases

L

M

Decisions of the European Court of Justice are listed below numerically.
These decisions are also included in the preceding alphabetical list.

Index

Your Feedback is Valuable

I have tried to help you, the reader, with a book that explains VAT clearly. I greatly value your feedback. Have you any comments?

What do you think of the book?

- Writing style
- Technical coverage
- Layout and presentation

What do you most like about the book?

Is there anything you dislike about it?

Is there any part of the book you had difficulty in understanding?

Please note any errors or misprints you have spotted.

Please send your replies to me either by email at asjohnprice@btopenworld.com or by post, to Lisa Zoltowska, LexisNexis UK, Halsbury House, 35 Chancery Lane, London WC2A 1EL.

A St John Price FCA

Tolley's Value Added Tax *2003*

By **Robert Wareham** BSC (Econ), FCA and **Alan Dolton** MA (Oxon)

Tolley's Value Added Tax 2003 *(Second Edition Only)* is the most authoritative reference work on VAT available, providing in-depth coverage of UK and EC legislation, Customs and Excise material and relevant case law.

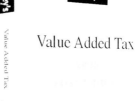

The 2003 edition includes:

- An updated section regarding VAT

- A refined version of treatment of bad debts and repayment of input tax

- Revised chapters on land and buildings

- Revised chapters on supplies to the disabled and charities

Tolley's Value Added Tax is essential to those who seek up to date information regarding VAT.

Tolley's Value Added Tax 2003 is published in two editions providing you with a bi-annual authority on VAT. These two complete volumes are published in April and September, allowing the practitioner to keep up to date with rapid rates of change.

Both:
Price: £105.00
Product code: VAT3
ISBN: 0 7545 2136 2
Publication date: April 2003

Second Edition:
Price: £75.00
Product code: VAT203
ISBN: 0 7545 2137 0
Publication date: April 2003

How To Order

To order, please contact LexisNexis UK
Customer Service Dept: Lexis Nexis UK,
FREEPOST SEA 4177, Croydon, Surrey CR9 5WZ
Telephone: 020 8662 2000   Fax: 020 8662 2012

 LexisNexis™ UK
35 Chancery Lane, London WC2A 1EL
A division of Reed Elsevier (UK) Ltd
Registered office 25 Victoria Street London SW1H 0EX
Registered in England number 2746621
VAT Registered No. GB 730 8595 2

Prices may be subject to change

Tolley's VAT Cases 2003

By Alan Dolton MA (Oxon) and Robert Wareham BSc (Econ), FCA

Tolley's VAT Cases 2003 contains concise summaries of more than 3,500 essential Court and VAT Tribunal decisions relevant to current legislation, dating from 1973 to 1 January 2003, making this one of the most comprehensive listings available.

New to this edition:

- Includes summaries of more than 250 important court and tribunal decisions reached in 2002

- Introductory survey discussing the leading decisions reached in 2002

- The chapter on 'Supply' has been revised with a new section on the 'Halifax' principle, including summaries of the cases of Blackqueen Ltd and University of Huddersfield

- The chapter on 'Motor Cars' has been substantially revised to include the important and conflicting recent decisions in Upton and Skellett

- New chapters on Capital Goods Scheme and Reduced-rate Supplies

- Concise summaries of more than 3,500 essential court and VAT Tribunal decisions, from 1973 to 1 January 2003, relevant to current legislation.

- An introductory survey discussing the leading decisions reached in 2002

Price:	£99.00
Product code:	VC03
ISBN:	0 7545 2133 8
Publication date:	April 2003

How To Order

To order, please contact LexisNexis UK
Customer Service Dept: Lexis Nexis UK,
FREEPOST SEA 4177, Croydon, Surrey CR9 5WZ
Telephone: 020 8662 2000   Fax: 020 8662 2012

35 Chancery Lane, London WC2A 1EL
A division of Reed Elsevier (UK) Ltd
Registered office 25 Victoria Street London SW1H 0EX
Registered in England number 2746621
VAT Registered No. GB 730 8595 2